Opera in the Media Age

OPERA IN THE MEDIA AGE

Essays on Art, Technology and Popular Culture

Edited by Paul Fryer

McFarland & Company, Inc., Publishers
Jefferson, North Carolina

ALSO BY PAUL FRYER AND FROM MCFARLAND
The Opera Singer and the Silent Film (2005)

BY PAUL FRYER AND OLGA USOVA
*Lina Cavalieri: The Life of Opera's Greatest Beauty,
1874–1944* (2004)

EDITED BY PAUL FRYER
*Women in the Arts in the Belle Epoque:
Essays on Influential Artists, Writers and Performers* (2012)

LIBRARY OF CONGRESS CATALOGUING-IN-PUBLICATION DATA

Opera in the media age : essays on art, technology and popular culture / edited by Paul Fryer.
    p.   cm.
Includes bibliographical references and index.

ISBN 978-0-7864-7329-8 (softcover : acid free paper) ∞
ISBN 978-1-4766-1620-9 (ebook)

1. Opera. 2. Mass media and music. 3. Music and technology. 4. Music—Social aspects—History. I. Fryer, Paul, 1955– editor of compilation.
ML3858.O54 2014
792.502—dc23   2014013477

BRITISH LIBRARY CATALOGUING DATA ARE AVAILABLE

© 2014 Paul Fryer. All rights reserved

No part of this book may be reproduced or transmitted in any form or by any means, electronic or mechanical, including photocopying or recording, or by any information storage and retrieval system, without permission in writing from the publisher.

On the cover: Tod Machover's modern opera *Death and the Powers* © Jonathan Williams

Printed in the United States of America

*McFarland & Company, Inc., Publishers
  Box 611, Jefferson, North Carolina 28640
  www.mcfarlandpub.com*

To those who ask the questions...

Table of Contents

Introduction   1

The Business of Opera: Opera, Advertising and the Return to Popular Culture
   Paul Fryer   7

Making Culture Popular: Opera and the Media Industries
   Sam O'Connell   32

Opera Criticism: State of the Art and Beyond
   Daniel Meyer-Dinkgräfe   43

Gods and Heroes or Monsters of the Media?
   Trevor Siemens   65

Opera and the Audio Recording Industry
   Robert Cannon   89

Opera Singers as Pop Stars: Opera Within the Popular Music Industry
   Christopher Newell and *George Newell*   116

Cross-Cuts and Arias: The Language of Film and Its Impact on Opera
   Kevin Stephens   149

Opera on Optical Video Disc, or the Latest (and Final?) Avatar of the Gesamtkunstwerk
   Pierre Bellemare   173

Wunderkammer: Light as a Scenographic and Dramaturgical Tool in Opera
   Hansjörg Schmidt   198

Opera, Art and Industrial Production: Lighting at the Royal
Opera House, London
  Nick Hunt   212

After *The Twilight of the Gods*: Opera Experiments, New Media
and the Opera of the Future
  Michael Earley   229

About the Contributors   249

Index   251

Introduction

The genesis of this collection of essays, which explore the relationship between opera and aspects of the media of the later twentieth and early twenty-first centuries, lies in a casual comment made to me by a student after I had given an introductory lecture on opera as a feature of contemporary culture. Half-jokingly the student commented on the way in which even opera, which he considered to be a decidedly "high art" form, had now, through wider popularization become fair game for the advertising industry. Ignoring the fact that the barrel organ players of Victorian England would regularly grind out tunes from the latest opera success on the street corners of London from the mid–nineteenth century onwards, the point was made that it was now possible for a member of the casual television audience to get to know quite a large number of opera "tunes" simply by watching the commercials aired in the breaks between one television program and the next.

In many ways this is not in the least surprising. The classical repertoire contains just as many good tunes as its popular counterpart. Why should it not be mined in the same way? After all, this was a repertoire which already enjoyed a wider popular recognition. Many opera and classical themes already enjoyed wider familiarity from being adapted for the pop or easy listening market: Bach, brilliantly reconceived by the jazz pianist and composer Jacques Loussier, Tchaikovsky, Rachmaninov, Debussy, and, perhaps the most banal (or inventive depending on your viewpoint) example of all, Eduardo di Capua's "O Sole Mio" (1898), used on British television to advertise a popular ice cream, with Giovanni Capurro's Neapolitan lyrics substituted by the more product-friendly phrase "Just one Cornetto, give it to me."[1] The British newspaper *The Daily Mail* recently described this as "the catchiest advertising jingle of all time," achieving 45 percent of a popular vote.[2]

Familiarity itself proved not always to be the deciding factor in this success story. When the Fiat car company utilized the well-known aria "Largo al Factotum" as a soundtrack for the promotion of its new Strada model in 1979 (one of the longest-running and most memorable television advertising campaigns ever mounted by the automobile industry), the success of the campaign relied largely on the popularity and familiarity of Rossini's original tune. However, some of the most interesting and successful campaigns which followed charted much less familiar territory.

In 1993, Nike, surely one of the world's most recognizable contemporary brands, commissioned three commercials from their advertising agency, Wieden and Kennedy, in the form of thirty-second mini-operas, designed to promote the Air Max brand primarily to the European market: the first of these, "Barkley of Seville," which featured basketball star player Charles Barkley, offered a parody of baroque opera written by U.S. composer Randall Davidson, sung in Italian with English subtitles. It was followed by "The Magic Shoe" (with music borrowed from Tchaikovsky), which featured pole-vaulter Sergei Bubka, and "Don Quincy" (borrowing heavily from Bizet) with the then world 400 meter record holder, Quincy Watts.[3] Barkley's short film, first aired in 1993, subsequently gained cult status with a number of opera and sports fans alike.

Linking the mainstream and highly commercial international sports goods markets with opera may seem unlikely enough, but this was not by any means the most unusual example to emerge. In 1989, British Airways commissioned a new television advertising campaign from the agency Saatchi and Saatchi, which launched a new slogan, "The World's Favourite Airline." They were set the task of finding suitable music, and came up with "The Flower Duet" ("Sous le dôme épais") from the largely forgotten nineteenth century French opera *Lakme* by Léo Delibes.[4]

The popularity of the stylish new commercial was matched only by that of the music. British Airways' customer service lines were bombarded with enquiries about the identity of the music, most of which they later stated, coming from people who had no idea that the tune had operatic origins. Other than the popular "Bell Song," a much favored encore aria popularized by singers such as Lily Pons, much of Delibes' score had been virtually forgotten until its adoption by the advertising industry. The opera had previously been known largely to modern audiences through a complete stereo recording made for London/Decca by the late Joan Sutherland and released in 1968. Now, however, a plethora of recordings flooded the market, made by both classical and cross-over artists, including Lesley Garratt and Katherine Jenkins. The aria, which has been described as Delibes' "hit single," has also featured in the soundtrack of several popular movies, including Tony Scott's *The Hunger* (1993) and in 1998, EMI released a new complete recording of the opera, featuring the popular French soprano Natalie Dessay.

The Sound Agency, a company which specializes in the use of music and sound in achieving effective branding for companies and products, gives the British Airways use of "The Flower Duet" as a prime example of the impact of music in establishing brand recognition. Their website states that "research shows that advertising sound is very powerful, and we know that brands are enhanced by consistency."[5] In 2007, British Airways withdrew all of their television advertising, largely as a response to the downturn in international air travel. However, when they returned to the TV advertising arena with a new campaign in September 2009, this time designed by agency Bartle Bogle Hegarty, they once again utilized arrangements of Delibes' now universally popular tune, which had become indissolubly linked with the BA brand in the public imagination.

Examples of opera used in advertising are far too numerous to list individually in this introduction: In the United States, Kentucky Fried Chicken made good use of the Prelude to Bizet's *Carmen*, and Aquafresh utilized Ponchielli's "Dance of the Hours" from *La Giaconda*. Television audiences in Europe have enjoyed or endured Offenbach to promote Audi cars, Dvořák for bathroom cleaner, and Verdi for frozen pizza.

The interest extends of course from the operas themselves to those who perform them. From the earliest examples of the names and images of opera stars utilized to sell even the most mundane of products advertising has shown a consistent interest in the operatic star as a marketing tool. Jenny Lind, renowned as the Swedish Nightingale, and a phenomenally popular performer, introduced the notion of merchandising by licensing her image to appear on matchboxes, pocket handkerchiefs, soap and perfume, and even promoted a Jenny Lind candle-snuffer in the shape of her body topped with the head of a nightingale. Contemporary consumers have been exposed to the sophisticated images and personas of Renée Fleming and Placido Domingo advertising Rolex watches, and Katherine Jenkins promoting Mont Blanc pens, in up-market magazine ads. Today, U.K. television audiences may wince when the comedic figure of the "Go Compare" tenor, played by the real-life opera singer Wynne Evans, perpetuating every possible operatic cliché, encourages us to purchase our insurance via a price comparison website, however, the image of Enrico Caruso promoting dress shirts and evening attire lies in our not so distant past. Artists such as Mary Garden, Geraldine Farrar and Lina Cavalieri endorsed and promoted a range of goods from gramophones and gramophone records to soap, face-cream and perfume—and even the tobacco industry thrived by association with opera performers as recently as the 1950s. The Camel brand ran an entire series of full-page color press advertisements featuring stars from the New York Metropolitan Opera, including Dorothy Kirsten, Risë Stevens, Patrice Munsel, Eleanor Steber, Richard Crooks and Ezio Pinza, each endorsing their product. Earlier generations had witnessed exactly the same form of brand association with Enrico Caruso (American Tobacco Co., 1915), Clarence Whitehill (Lucky Strike, 1927), Lawrence Tibbett (Old Gold, 1930), and Elizabeth Rethberg (Lucky Strike, 1937).

Advertising, however, provides us with only one example to support the fact that since the very beginning of the media age,[6] opera has enjoyed and occasionally tolerated a fascinating symbiotic relationship with the media. Some of the earliest major contributors to the audio recording, moving picture and radio broadcasting industries, opera stars also played a significant role in the development of the "star structure" that has always been a central pillar of the entertainment industries, especially the Hollywood movie industry which they helped to create.

Throughout the twentieth and into the twenty-first centuries, the media have enabled opera (earlier considered a "popular" art form) to move from its later position as "high art" and "elitist" back to a form of accessible, popular culture—via the movies, audio and video recordings, television and radio broadcasts, and press and television advertising. And also through opera's use of contemporary media technology in both live and recorded performances.

As our attitude towards opera has shifted, so too has opera itself in the way in which it is written, performed, staged and marketed. The *Three Tenors* phenomenon, which began with a gala concert in Rome to mark the FIFA World Cup final in 1990, and continued for more than a decade, was simply part of a much wider shift in attitude, largely enabled by opera's engagement with the available media.

Contemporary media developments have also had a significant effect on how audiences witness opera in "live" performance. Starting in the 2006/7 season, the Metropolitan Opera New York, in an effort to generate additional sources of income and to build new audiences, began to broadcast live performances by satellite to movie theatres, in High Definition. So successful has this proved that the company recently announced that they had sold more than ten million tickets to these screenings worldwide, thereby vastly increasing the number of people able to see each production.

The company has stated that their aim is to "reach existing audiences and to introduce new audiences to opera through new technology." In this, they are not alone. In the summer of 2013, the Royal Opera House Covent Garden, sponsored by BP, broadcast live performances to big screens in 27 locations across the United Kingdom. This collection of essays will demonstrate that such developments are part of an ongoing progression that has been taking place for more than a century—that the recording of operatic arias on gramophone records, the filming of opera extracts on silent or synchronized sound film, the broadcast of radio signals live from the stages of opera houses—have exploited the newest technology of the time, have widened access to a global audience, and have changed the way in which we experience opera.

The writers who have contributed to this collection have freely interpreted the notion of contemporary "media." Therefore, as well as exploring opera as a contemporary art form, we examine the relationship between opera and advertising, opera and popular culture and opera and the audio recording industry. We have included two essays which explore opera's relationship to aspects of performance technology in the form of lighting and, in Nick Hunt's description, "industrial production." We further explore the role of contemporary opera as a feature of twenty-first century culture, the role played by the contemporary critic, opera's relationship with the popular music industry, and the influence on and of opera in the burgeoning video disc market and the movie industry.

Marshall McLuhan's assertion that the modern media should be recognized as an art form in itself and therefore placed in the hands of artists who would understand how best to use it[7] clearly recognized a link which both new and established (historical) art forms and artists could exploit just as effectively—as well as being exploited by. Of all existing art forms, it is perhaps opera, which unifies music, text, drama, scenography and technology in its realization, and which has proved equally as successful and influential in so many different aspects of the modern media, which still continues to provide us with the some of the greatest challenges, triumphs and occasional disasters of the media age.

Notes

1. Cornetto was a popular ice cream cone, sold by the Walls Company in the United Kingdom, now owned by Unilever. The tune was adapted for a highly successful television advertising campaign starting in 1983 and running for ten years. The campaign was revived in 2006.
2. "Just One Cornetto ... Hum It to Me: Britain's Catchiest Advertising Tunes Revealed," *The Daily Mail*, 13 June 2012.
3. Matthew Grim, "Nike Spends a Hard Day's Night at the Euro Opera," *Adweek*, 1 February 1993.
4. Delibes' work had premiered at the Opera Comique in Paris in 1883, set in British colonial India. The duet, sung by Lakme and her servant Malika, is in the first act of the opera.
5. "Brandsound Revealed," The Sound Agency, www.thesoundagency.com. Accessed on 28 May 2013.
6. Establishing a suitable date for this is difficult, but for the purposes of this collection we will settle upon 1895: being the year in which gramophone recoding and moving pictures both achieved commercial viability.
7. Marshall McLuhan, *Counterblast* (Toronto, 1954; re-published by Gingko, 2011).

Bibliography

"Brandsound Revealed." *The Sound Agency*, www.thesoundagency.com. Accessed 28 May 2013.

Grim, Matthew. "Nike Spends a Hard Day's Night at the Euro Opera." *Adweek*, 1 February 1993.
Ind, Nicholas. *Great Advertising Campaigns*. London: Kogan Page, 1993.
"Just One Cornetto ... Hum it to Me: Britain's Catchiest Advertising Tunes Revealed." *The Daily Mail*, London, 13 June 2012.
Martorella, Rosanne. *The Sociology of Opera*. New York: Praeger, 1982.
McLuhan, Marshall. *Counterblast*. Berkeley: Gingko, 2011. First published 1954.
O'Reilly, Daragh, and Finola Kerrigan. *Marketing the Arts: A Fresh Approach*. London: Routledge, 2010.

The Business of Opera: Opera, Advertising and the Return to Popular Culture

Paul Fryer

During the first decade of the twenty-first century it appeared that the popularity of opera was, once again, on the decline. In many places this was marked by a significant reduction in funding, closure of several opera companies while others introduced major cost-saving measures, popular works and revivals dominated the repertoire of most large-scale companies. While the average age of opera attendees reached the mid–50s and the youth market, dominated by the download and social media culture, appeared to show no interest whatsoever in the art-form, Mark Moorman, then the New York City Opera's Manager of Institutional Gifts, was quoted as saying, "We are like a museum preserving ancient music for ancient people."[1] At the time, NYCO's ticket sales had dropped to an average of 60 percent capacity, in spite of a major popularization program under the slogan "Opera for Everyone," reducing ticket prices and offering half-price tickets for students.

In October 2013, the New York City Opera announced that it has been forced to close. The company, founded in 1943, had made it public knowledge that there was a $7 million deficit. George Steel, artistic director, was quoted in *The New York Times*: "New York City Opera did not achieve the goal of its emergency appeal, and the board and management will begin the necessary financial and operational steps to wind down the company."[2] The company's final performance, given at the Brooklyn Academy of Music, was *Anna Nicole*, by Mark-Anthony Turnage, an example of the valuable work that the company has done to promote and popularize contemporary opera. The American baritone Sherrill Milnes who had started his career with NYCO in the early 1960s acknowledged this, telling *The Wall Street Journal*, "It's a huge blow, not just for the American composer, but for modern composers worldwide."[3]

Alex Ross, writing in *The New Yorker*, stated that, "the quality of operatic programming and production in New York has lately plummeted, to the point where the city may no longer qualify as a pace-setting opera capital. The Met still puts on big, starry shows, with hundreds of gifted people laboring behind the scenes to bring them to life. But one staging after another has failed to catch fire, and the most ambitious undertaking of the Gelb era, Robert Lepage's production of Wagner's "Ring," is a very damp squib."[4] After noting that any real artistic development in opera is being made in London, certain European houses or by regional American companies, Ross concludes that "although the economic crisis has taken its toll, the problem is less a lack of money than a lack of intellectual vitality" (Ross, *Diminuendo*). It might reasonably be argued of course, that in the case of opera, the most expensive of all live art-forms, you cannot have one without the other.

We have been here before, of course. The principal players may have new identities, but the game remains largely the same: can opera survive in contemporary popular culture?

The 1980s and '90s witnessed a remarkable rise in the popularity of opera, in which an art-form, widely and traditionally perceived as elitist was seen to transform into an entertainment available to be enjoyed by everyone. But this development raised a number of important questions: was it really possible for an art form such as opera to achieve such a wide-spread, catholic popularity or was this simply the result of a highly effective marketing campaign, the effects of which would fade over the succeeding decades? Was this development consumer-led or market-led, and what effect would popularization have upon opera as a quality product? Did this popularization result in the creation and nurturing of a whole new generation of sophisticated opera-goers or rather in the reduction of a complex art-form to a series of easily digested lowest common denominators, and if this was the case, could serious opera production ever recover from the damage that might be inflicted by a pop opera culture?

The period in question certainly showed that opera could become a major business concern, and make substantial profits, but did this mean that opera would be able to pay for itself in the future? Or, conversely, would we face the prospect of being left only with box-office certainties, endlessly revived, opera spectaculars and rock-star style concerts amplified to fill huge auditoria, high on volume, but low on content? A higher level of promotion which borrowed liberally from the popular end of the music industry might lead to mass audiences, but instead of encouraging the development of a living art-form, the trend of economic influence, driven by enhanced marketing, could just as easily lead us into a future in which serious and challenging works, which could not be made to pay for themselves, would only be found in audio or video recordings, made for a restricted specialist market. Therefore, the process that would gradually eliminate aspects of elitism in opera, could just as easily result in the imposition of a new form of reverse cultural elitism, which might prove to be far more damaging than the socially imposed restrictions of the past.

Amongst these questions however, there is no doubt that the media—in this case in the form of commercial audio and video recording, television and radio broadcasting—and advertising were to be the principal contributors.

In the spring of 1986, when the current economic downturn seemed like a very remote prospect for many people, John Whitley reported in *The Sunday Times* (London) on what he categorized as "The new craze for opera... a revolutionary bid to revive a popular art form."[5] In fact Whitley was a little late in heralding this since the revolution which was to transform opera into a "boom industry" had already occurred, becoming, as Luke Rittner, then secretary general of the Arts Council in the United Kingdom, said, "very much more a part of people's daily lives than we would have dreamed of, ten or fifteen years ago."[6]

As the journalist Gilbert Adair noted: "Alongside such art forms as comic books, rock promos, TV commercials and Arnold Schwarzenegger movies ... incredibly dumb affairs during which the soprano, baritone and tenor sing a jolly little trio before stabbing each other to death"[7] suddenly acquired popular and commercial appeal to rival any marketing agency's wildest dreams.

In 1755, the Venetian scholar, philosopher and critic Francesco Algarotti described opera as having "fallen from heaven upon the earth, and being divorced from an intercourse with gods, to have humbly resigned itself to that of mortals."[8] In terms at once both more prosaic and more appropriate to our own decade, this heavenly art-form now took on the decidedly earthly attributes of a profitable business enterprise, ripe for exploitation and fuelled by a trend of popularity.

And as the 1980s progressed the trend spread across Europe, resulting in elaborate plans to build new opera houses in Paris (Opera Bastille, 1989), Amsterdam (De Nederlandse Opera, 1986) and Essen (Aalto Musiktheater, 1988), at a cost then estimated to be around £217 million. Farther afield, in Manaus, Brazil, the legendary Teatro Amazonas, which had first opened in 1896, but had been closed for over 80 years, now re-opened after a three-year restoration at a cost of $8 million.

The wider European tradition of opera performances might be expected to easily support such extravagant investment, but what about the United Kingdom, where, as John Whitley bluntly stated, "opera is normally equated with snobs, foreigners and stout prima donnas" (Whitley, *The New Craze for Opera*). Britain's conversion however seemed secure, with performances on the increase, and more companies than ever before being formed to meet the growing demand.

At the height of the trend, Policy Studies Institute reports revealed that between 1984 and 1989, the number of performances given by the major subsidized opera companies in the United Kingdom rose from 706 to 747; the number of seats sold rose from 985,745 to 1,174,417, and the average attendance from 78 percent to 85 percent. By 1989, English National Opera attendances had reached an average capacity of 87 percent, and the Royal Opera House, 90 percent.[9] A supplementary survey published in 1990 revealed even more encouraging statistics; Glyndebourne Touring Opera played to 97 percent capacity audiences, Opera North in Leeds reached 87 percent and Scottish Opera on tour, 92 percent.

But quantity seemed to have very little effect on either quality or, more crucially variety. It might have been hoped that such an increase in revenue might lead to a comparable investment in new or more challenging repertoire. There is virtually no evidence however that this took place. A popularity chart provided by Welsh National Opera to supplement the 1990 survey shows that the three most popular operas were, predictably perhaps, *La Traviata*, *La Bohème* and *Le Nozze di Figaro*. Tom Sutcliffe, then opera critic of *The Guardian* (London), reached the regretful conclusion that "there is no evidence that difficult or challenging work is reaching a wider audience ... without a genuine extension of public interest based on a real exploration of the market."[10]

The '80s boom was not to last. By the spring of 1993, when the United Kingdom government issued fresh assurances that recession was coming to an end, the arts pages in the U.K. press had already begun to toll the death knell for this great operatic renaissance. The distinguished British tenor, Robert Tear, expressed the belief that the only way in which this operatic rebirth could be sustained, was for opera companies to provide a complete diet of *La Bohème* and *La Traviata*—a kind of operatic Top 20—perpetuating a culture based upon easily digestible highlights. Hardly a recipe for sustaining artistic growth. The notion that the correct way to fuel the opera boom of the late '80s so as to project it through to the millennium was to provide the public with either more of the same, or thinly disguised reworkings of that repertoire proved fruitless. Alex Ross's response to the current offer of the Metropolitan Opera referred to earlier, suggests that little has changed in the last 20 years.

In the nineteenth century, opera was the great popular art form. In the early years of the twentieth century, Enrico Caruso became the very first recording artist to sell one million discs with a rendering of the aria "Vesti la giubba" from Leoncavallo's *Pagliacci*, recorded in 1902, only 20 years after the opera had first been produced, and the tune itself was very well-known. Opera was solidly linked to popular culture. Operatic music, played in a wide variety of settings and arrangements, was one major source of the popular music of the time. But writing in 1992, Geoffrey Wheatcroft drew an important parallel: "good or bad, pop music is living music. But the huge explosion in opera audiences is an audience for a dead, or at least dying genre.... There have been remarkable achievements in opera in the last fifty years, but numbers from Peter Maxwell Davies's operas are never going to be whistled by taxi drivers; nor, I suspect, did our lads in the Gulf sing Harrison Birtwhistle's greatest hits to keep their spirits up."[11]

But, to return to a question posed in the opening paragraph of this essay, was the burgeoning popularity of opera in the decade between the 1980s and '90s consumer-led or market-led? If the latter, then how had this come about. What part had media and marketing played in the great enterprise, and, assuming that opera's future may be as uncertain as it's past, what can we learn from this?

Opera's incursion into the popular media of the twentieth century is most easily noted by its use in cinema. Long before Jean-Jacques Beineix re-awakened interest in a half-forgotten opera by Catalani by his use of the aria "Ebben? Ne andro lontano" from *La Wally*, in his 1981 film *Diva*, "serious" music had been widely used as incidental music in films. There are many examples; *Brief Encounter* (David Lean, 1945), *Citizen Kane* (Orson Welles, 1941), *The Lost Weekend* (Billy Wilder, 1945), et al. Along with a rash of operatic films, including work by Ingmar Bergman, Joseph Losey, Franco Zeffirelli, Luigi Comencini and Francesco Rosi, which served to keep opera in the public's eye, in one of the most easily accessible media formats.

One particularly acute example specifically links opera with money and the media. Oliver Stone's 1987 film, *Wall Street*, is a powerful indictment of materialism in 1980s America, personified in the amoral monetarism of New York City stock dealers. A young broker played by Charlie Sheen, motivated by greed and misplaced admiration for Michael Douglas's high-flying financial master-mind, is inveigled into illegal share-dealing, for which eventually he pays the price. We see Sheen's character gain financial advantage and social status as he is drawn further into the crooked dealings of his hero. He acquires a beautiful woman, a designer penthouse, and, to complete this material perfection, a sudden love of opera. As the camera pans around his new apartment for the first time, the music that we hear playing on an expensive audio system is Verdi's aria "Di Quella Pira" from *Rigoletto*. Whereas is an earlier era, Sheen's character might have taken to listening to the Modern Jazz Quartet, a Bach cello sonata or a Mahler symphony, in the material mid-'80s the most easily assimilated musical under-scoring of his new-found wealth and status (and perhaps his attitude as well), is opera.

Stone correctly assumed that audiences would equate opera with a certain style and quality of life, something that was worthy, desirable, and above all, expensive. In this respect he was not alone. If we examine the ways in which opera was being used in advertising at this time we can readily see the new power and influence that it had gained. Here translated into financial power (as a selling tool) and marketing influence (as a means of brand categorization and recognition). If we subscribe to the "four Ps" approach to marketing—product, price, promotion and place—all being necessary to create the right "marketing mix,"[12] the value of opera as a marketing tool becomes even clearer. Establishing opera as a "quality" product creates a consumer demand; establishing opera as a high-priced (i.e., high value) product, promoted widely in recording, broadcasting and film, and increasingly made available in a wider range of places, creates a highly desirable marketing tool, when focused correctly upon the right market. Advertisers would discover, sometimes to their surprise that opera could be used to sell a very wide range of products, anything from beer, pizza and ice cream to Rolex watches and luxury cars.

After all, classical music had already become firmly established as a marketing tool. How many consumers over more than a decade, happily whistled or hummed a theme popularly known as "Going home," perhaps never realizing that it was in fact the slow movement of Dvořák's 9th symphony. Composed in 1893, while the composer was working in America, a popular song based upon the slow movement and given the title, "Goin' Home" was arranged by William Arms Fisher, a pupil of Dvořák's at the National Conservatory of Music, who also wrote the lyrics. The use of the tune in a series of television commercials for Hovis bread in the United Kingdom, linked the tune forever with that product.

An earlier generation of TV viewers in the United Kingdom had been entertained by the lyrics to an advertising jingle which claimed that "everyone's a fruit and nut case," but might not have been aware that the tune which accompanied it was taken from Tchaikovsky's ballet *The Nutcracker*. This popular commercial for Cadbury's Fruit and Nut chocolate, first appeared in 1975. Tchaikovsky's music proved popular in television advertising, most likely because the works were highly tuneful, memorable and familiar—even if the audience could not immediately identify their original source. Later examples would include The Overture 1812 (used to promote Kleenex tissues in 1990, and Iceland Frozen Foods in 2001), and the Chinese Dance from *The Nutcracker* (used by Terry's to advertise confectionary in 1999, and by Gerber Foods to promote a brand of grape juice in 2006).

The very simple objective of the advertising agencies was to find a good tune that was easily memorable and which the audience would immediately identify with the product. However, in these earlier examples very little effort was made to associate the idea of quality music with quality products. This was about to change however with the introduction of opera into television commercials. Speaking about the power of music as a marketing tool, leading marketing consultant Tim Hunt, one of the pioneers of this kind of advertising campaign, said in 1993: "Music is a strong motivator ... the right music can be highly evocative."[13]

In the late 1970, the agency Collett Dickenson Pearce handled the U.K. marketing for the leading Italian car manufacturer, Fiat. Fiat U.K. were looking to develop a campaign to promote their new Strada model. The television campaign, which was launched in June 1979, became the first major campaign in the United Kingdom to exploit the power of operatic music to sell a product, by deliberately linking the up-market image of opera to the stylish, quality image of the product.

This three-minute commercial was the first ever to occupy a complete commercial break on U.K. television, and is still one of the most expensive commercials ever made. Directed by Hugh Hudson and written by Paul Weiland, the film possessed the kind of production values then only seen in Hollywood movies. The impact of the Fiat Strada commercial, which emphasized the high-technology aspects of the car by using the slogan "built by robots," was so widespread that it is still distinctly remembered today both in the advertising trade and by the general public, even though it has not been shown for more than thirty years. The commercial was a gold award winner at the 1980 British Television Advertising Awards.

Tim Hunt placed the significance of the commercial clearly in perspective: "Most major companies produce one TV ad that sticks firmly in the public consciousness, for Fiat, this was the one" (Hunt, 1993).

The tremendous success of the Strada commercial was due in no small part to the choice of a familiar Rossini aria as a soundtrack: "Largo al Factotum," Figaro's much-loved aria from *Il Barbiere di Siviglia*. This music was chosen for two principal reasons. First, operatic music was perceived to have an immediate association with Italy, and Fiat was keen to exploit its Italian pedigree, emphasizing "positive virtues of Italian culture, flair and brio, warmth, charm, humour ... positive associations" (Hunt, 1993) These "positive associations" also influenced the second reason. Opera was seen as "possessing an up-market, stereotypical image ... emphasising style, and style was commonly associated with Italian design" (Hunt, 1993).

It might seem strange that so many positive images of material twentieth-century commercial virtues could be conjured from an extract from a comic opera, based upon a play by Beaumarchais, which had first been heard in Rome in 1816. Yet, such was the power of positive association vested in opera by the advertising agency, and their belief proved to be completely justified.

The success of the Strada campaign was still fresh in the memory when, in 1989, during a period of peak popularity for opera in the United Kingdom, Fiat returned to the opera format to promote a new car, the Tipo. This commercial was set as a stylized eighteenth century Baroque opera, using completely bogus, mock-operatic music, specially composed, with equally cod lyrics appropriate to the product. The timing of the launch of this campaign could not have been better judged, although the advertising agency were quick to emphasize that it had been planned a year in advance: "The campaign was devised before the interest in Pavarotti came to a head with the Hyde Park concert ... though it appeared to be just part of the resultant vogue for opera in advertising, in fact, it wasn't" (Hunt, 1993).

The concert that Hunt refers to took place in London's Hyde Park in August 1993. A crowd of 100,000 people stood in the rain to hear the tenor, accompanied by the Philharmonia Orchestra and Chorus, sing some of his most popular repertoire in a free concert. VIP guests, who had paid up to £400 each for their tickets, including Prince Charles and the late Princess Diana, added celebrity appeal to the event. Billed as the biggest outdoor music event since the Rolling Stones' concert there in 1969, the concert marked Pavarotti's thirtieth anniversary on the opera stage. The BBC Home website claims that the concert cost £900,000 to stage.[14] One young man interviewed, who had camped out overnight to ensure that he had a good position for watching the event, was very clear on his reason for attending: "I discovered opera during the World Cup when one of Pavarotti's songs ('Nessun Dorma') was used as the tune" (BBC Home website).

The presentation of opera, even when reduced to the most popular extracts, in easily accessible formats, was already contributing to the growing interest which the advertising industry were able to exploit with great success.

The main significance behind the very stylish Fiat Tipo campaign was that, unlike the earlier Strada campaign, no genuine opera music was used. So confident had the advertisers become that opera was acceptable and accessible to everyone, that they no longer needed to utilize a popular operatic tune which would already be familiar to the majority of the audience, even if they were entirely unfamiliar with the work from which it came. What we were now witnessing was the concept of opera itself being used to clearly convey the message—opera is classy, so is this car.

In the following year Fiat moved away from the concept of opera in a new campaign to promote the Uno model. Instead of opera, jazz music was used. This car was specifically marketed to appeal to a female consumer and it was felt that jazz would hold a wider appeal, perhaps challenging the commonly held view that women generally influence attendance at opera performances. Strangely enough, this conflicts sharply with the results of a survey carried out in the same year for the magazine *Opera Now*. It emerged that out of "the various categories that comprise those who declared an interest in opera,"[15] 60 percent were women, although women overall declared a higher interest in jazz than in opera.

The Uno campaign was a great success, particularly amongst its target group, indicating that statistics can be open to a range of different interpretations, and that in advertising, as in many other areas, a well-judged risk can often pay off, as it had done with the original Strada campaign a decade earlier.

Fiat was not alone in recognizing the value of opera's contribution to advertising. From the viewpoint of popularization, a campaign that began slightly later had an even more surprising impact. If Jean-Jacques Beineix's film *Diva* (1981) deserves credit for rescuing an opera by Catalani from obscurity, British Airways is due even greater recognition for bringing about a yet more startling revivification of the opera *Lakme*, by the nineteenth century French composer Leo Delibes, probably best known for his ballet scores for *Sylvia* and *Coppelia*.[16]

Rarely produced for nearly 25 years until it was revived at the 1970 Wexford Opera Festival in Ireland, and with few major productions since, this colorful, oriental tale set in British colonial India, rocketed to almost instant fame through its use in a major series of commercials for British Airways. The extract used, popularly known as "The Flower Duet" (its original title is "Sous le dôme épais") scored for two sopranos and appearing in the first act of the opera, was first used in 1989 and is still featured in British Airways marketing today.

The agency commissioned to create the campaign, Saatchi and Saatchi (now M&C Saatchi), were given no specific brief to use operatic music. Their task, described by Carrie Hindmarsh, now CEO of M&C Saatchi, was only to find "a good tune with the right feel for the campaign."[17] An operatic duet was finally chosen to "communicate quality and distinction ... give a feeling that was uplifting and relaxing ... presenting established values" (Hindmarsh, 1993). The positive, desirable image of opera was again seen as a clear and easily communicable indicator of a quality product. Now however, the brief had widened, and the image of opera defining quality was being used not simply to promote a specific product, but rather to promote an idea, a corporate image for British Airways as a whole. Although this began as a regular advertising campaign, and a number of different arrangements of the duet were subsequently used including one by Malcolm McLaren, the original version created for the first television commercial, was eventually restricted for "master-brand advertising, of the corporate B.A. image" (Hindmarsh, 1993).

From the very start of the campaign, there was a constant and increasing public interest in the music. Both British Airways and Saatchi and Saatchi received multiple telephone enquiries about it on a daily basis: "from the general public, not from established opera-lovers ... mostly interested in obtaining a copy of the original music ... and many people were surprised when they heard it was an opera aria" (Hindmarsh, 1993).

The British Airways commercials spread the name of Delibes far wider than he could ever imagined would be possible, and added more fuel to the popularization of opera via the most commonplace of everyday media, the commercial break.

One of the later and perhaps more unexpected successes of the decade in question involved one of the world's most prominent sports shoes manufacturers, Nike, and the campaign for the European launch of their Air Max range. This campaign launched a new premium range product which would retail in U.K. stores for £89 (approximately $130) a pair. The aim of the campaign therefore was to convey an "upmarket, classy image,"[18] terms which, at this time seemed to become almost synonymous with the entire notion of opera in advertising.

Nike, an American company, were keen to emphasize their European links, and were seeking a way to connect a quintessentially American sport, basketball, with an image that would be instantly recognized as typically European. They chose opera as a cultural icon in the belief that, "audiences could now relate easily to the idea of opera and are even prepared to see humour in it, without being alienated by the very idea of opera" (Trainer, 1993). Three versions of the commercial were made. The first used the format of a mock opera in which the central character is played by the black baseball player, Charles Barkley. Titled "Barkley of Seville" (a not especially complex pun on Rossini) emphasis was placed on the humorous aspects of the juxtaposition, since the target group was very clearly "the youth market, 15 to 20 year olds ... the ads needed to have wide appeal, and to contain enough humour to catch a younger imagination" (Trainer, 1993).

The commercial worked on the basis of taking a context from one cultural extreme and placing within it a product from an entirely different cultural extreme. Few concepts would seem further apart that Baroque opera and training shoes. The entire concept could only succeed however, if the target audience, the 15-to-20-year-old market which Trainer identified, those who would want to wear the shoes, or whose parents would purchase them, could recognize that which was being parodied and were able to share the joke. Advertising that, for whatever reason rises above the comprehension of its target audience is very unlikely to prove successful. It is therefore reasonable to draw the conclusion that in the case of this campaign—and others mentioned previously in this essay—advertising agencies and their clients, often representing very high levels of investment, could now clearly view opera as an easily assimilated, readily communicable concept which could be made to address a mass market with relative ease.

The music historian Henry Raynor, writing of the magnificent excesses of Baroque opera, observed, "There were productions of a startling sumptuosity and a dizzy refusal to consider expense ... intended to manifest the grandeur of the authority who sponsored it, therefore it had to be grand. The cost was not counted, because the symbolic value of opera was reckoned to be worth whatever exorbitant sums were spent on it."[19] In many ways the advertising agencies of the 1980s recognized this "symbolic value" and realized that it was communicable to a wide audience who would also recognize opera as a symbol of both monetary and artistic value and accept the concept that, as such, opera was a product that was worth being associated with.

It is not accidental of course that the rise in the popular profile of opera brought about in part by advertising coincided with another highly lucrative phenomenon: the broadcasting, recording and marketing of the large-scale, arena style opera concert, epitomized at this time by the arrival of the Three Tenors. This trend began with the now legendary concert broadcast live from the baths at Caracalla in Rome, on the eve of the World Cup final in 1990. Such a celebratory event featuring the world's three most prominent and popular male opera singers, Placido Domingo, Luciano Pavarotti and Jose Carreras, was a sure-fire success, even before the actual concert. Such was the celebrity of the singers and the hype of the event itself.

Even though this success was repeated in further outings for this particularly celebrated trio, in Los Angeles in 1994, in Paris in 1998 and in Yokohama in 2002, such success could not always be repeated. The opening concert of the Barcelona Summer Olympic Games in 1992 was only one of many far less successful imitations at this time: a group of Spain's greatest opera singers, led by Domingo and Carreras, miming ineptly to a pre-recorded vocal track, in a particularly poorly staged event. Not since the distinguished American soprano Jessye Norman was trucked down the Champs Élysées, singing "La Marseillaise" as part of the commemorative event to mark the bi-centenary of the French Revolution in 1989, have the eyebrows of so many serious opera-lovers been raised in simultaneous disbelief.

Such events of course are not targeted to that particular niche market. They generate enormous profits for the producers and artists alike, simply because they enjoy tremendous popular appeal, and they are marketed to a mass audience. The income from the sale of broadcasting rights is minimal compared with the recording and merchandising possibilities. Returning to the Three Tenors, PolyGram's commercial audio and video recordings of the original 1990 event became one of the biggest-selling recordings ever released. Reviewing the famous "free" concert that Pavarotti gave in London's Hyde

Park in 1991 marking his thirty years on the opera stage, the critic, Nicholas de Jongh could not help but observe "vans, stalls and caravans offering food and merchandise—tee shirts, key rings, sweatshirts."[20] The "free" one-hour performance earned Pavarotti more than £1 million in recording rights alone.

In terms of popularization, as marketing tools for the promotion of opera as a popular art form, it is impossible to overestimate the impact of these events on the wider market, and their potential for generating huge additional profits. By the start of the 1990s, opera stars had been fashioned into highly saleable commodities, inhabiting the same arenas as their rock counterparts and drawing the same responses from the marketing men. A spokesman for PolyGram described Pavarotti as "one of the most important pop artists of 1990 and '91."[21] A perfectly reasonable description for a singer whose recording of "Nessun Dorma," more popularly known as the theme song of the 1990 World Cup, became the first piece of classical music to reach the number two position in the British popular singles chart, and remained there for five weeks.

However, regardless of the convincing argument for opera as an advertising tool, enabled by the short case-studies included above, the following observation also remains true: Marketing can sell an individual work—it can certainly popularize a concept and encourage its wider acceptance, but can it lead to a sustainable and continuing growth after that marketing campaign has concluded?

One very appropriate example of this—although non-operatic—is provided by the fate of the Polish composer Henryk Gorecki's Third Symphony. This work, subtitled *The Symphony of Sorrowful Songs*, not only proved a worldwide bestseller but also became the subject of a documentary film directed by Tony Palmer and shown in the United Kingdom as part of the arts series *The South Bank Show*.[22] The worldwide popularity of this piece had hardly been reflected by some of the less than enthusiastic comments made by some critics: Alexander Waugh described it as "a load of gloomy piffle,"[23] while Michael Kennedy wrote: "why this really rather dreary symphony has sent all those people into the record shops baffles me."[24]

By June 1993 however, the recording of the work, featuring the American soprano Dawn Upshaw with the London Sinfonietta, conducted by David Zinman, released by Elektra/Nonesuch Records, had sold over 300,000 copies, had reached the number one position in the classical recording charts in both the United States and the United Kingdom, and had also become the first piece by a living classical composer to enter the British popular album chart. Such success for a piece of serious contemporary classical music was previously unthought-of, and it provides a valuable comparison with the growth in the popularity of opera at this time.

Michael Stewart, writing in *The Gramophone,* expressed great personal pleasure in witnessing this example of serious music reaching a wider popular audience. But he also sounded a well-considered cautionary note, entirely appropriate to the estimation of the sustained popularity of opera: "How far this new found audience is prepared to delve ... remains to be seen. Astute marketing has clearly played an important part.... I would be the first to admit that classical music can benefit from techniques such as this, especially if it encourages people to adopt a more adventurous attitude in their musical tastes."[25]

In common with the question raised in the pop-opera debate: Marketing can sell an individual work—that is clear. It can popularize a concept and encourage its wider acceptance in the popular market, but can it lead to sustainable, continuing growth, once the immediacy of the marketing campaign has ended? What has been the lasting legacy of the pop-opera revolution of the '80s and '90s? Does the casual radio listener tuned into Classic FM, or one of the many other popular classical music stations that are available either on the radio or via the internet, ever really make the leap from Mahler's Adagietto, popularized so effectively by the film of *Death in Venice*, to complete performances of his Fifth Symphony, or from Wagner's Ride of the Valkyres, with the benefit of endless exposure in the popular cultural forums of TV and film or cartoons, to a lasting devotion to the *Ring*?

Marketing may result in a previously obscure Polish composer receiving a gold disc for sales of the CD of his Third Symphony, but what about his Fourth, Fifth or Sixth?

This is a question to which we shall return at the conclusion of this essay. But there is one further aspect of the opera and marketing debate that needs some exploration, namely the revitalization of the cult of the opera singer, which also made a significant contribution to the rise in the popular interest in opera, and in many cases was directly attributable to marketing.

The popularity cult of the opera star returned with a vengeance in the '80s and '90s, recalling the days when the media reveled in the stories of Maria Callas, publicly vying with Jackie Kennedy for the attentions of Aristotle Onassis. Opera singers readily joined the ranks of the popular media stars, returning to a status that they had enjoyed in the era of Caruso, Farrar, Garden and Cavalieri. In the words of one popular opera performer of the time, "People want to read what Pavarotti thinks about pasta, or Kiri feels about playing golf."[26]

Public appearances and recordings began to be marketed with the same hype and vigor as those of rock stars. Seemingly endless profiles, interviews and features were published, not only in specialist magazines and journals, but in every branch of the popular press, reflecting the huge rise in popular interest. It seemed that readers of popular papers in the United Kingdom, such as *The Sun* and *The Daily Mirror*, were genuinely interested in the problems that Pavarotti experienced with his knees. An interest not confined to the tabloid market: his aliments were treated to a quarter-page article in *The Sunday Times* (London) under the distinctly tabloid-style headline "The Great Airship of Opera May Be on His Last Legs."[27] British opera singer Lesley Garrett saw that as the logical result of opera stars losing some of their historical mystique, "appearing to be more like everyone else ... easy to relate to as real people" (Lesley Garrett, 1993).

There is no doubt that the popular medium of advertising, particularly on television, contributed to this in a major sense, and as these stars became more visible, recognizable and familiar to that wider audience, so their private lives also became fair game for the Fourth Estate. Sections of the European press had been happy to exploit the often very public rows between Maria Callas, her co-stars and her employers at La Scala, the Metropolitan Opera and Covent Garden throughout the late 1950s and early 1960s and observers might have thought that they had slipped into a time warp as they read reports such as "Battle of the big men" in *The Mail on Sunday*,[28] which detailed a largely spurious and highly speculative rivalry between Placido Domingo and Luciano Pavarotti.

The marketing and media hype of this time was not the exclusive preserve of major international stars. More local singers had also been treated to a similar elevation in the public consciousness. The British soprano Lesley Garrett, at this time a leading artist with the English National Opera and a lively and voluble supporter of opera as a popular medium, also received increased press attention. The subject of numerous interviews and articles, Garrett had a refreshingly honest response to those who would question the validity of the commercialization of opera: "As long as it is exciting it doesn't matter.... I want opera to be exciting, to be relevant to everyday life" (Garrett, 1993). In her case, this included combining a leading role in Handel's opera *Ariodante*, with highly lucrative recording sessions for television commercials.

This was perhaps a new breed of opera star, but in many ways returning to the ethos of earlier days. Prepared to promote opera in every conceivable way and happy to be part of a commercial and marketable business: "as long as it's done as well as it can possibly be done, I don't have any time for this precious, up the bum attitude ... it may be art, but it's still got to be sold, so we have to use whatever methods that we can to sell it. That's how we can ensure that opera will exist in the future" (Garrett, 1993).

Garrett's own career certainly benefitted from this kind of marketing hype. Her record company promoted her CDs with a slinky, sexy, Madonna of the opera stage image, and the cover photographs on two of her early solo recordings, *Diva* and *Prima Donna*, project an image of almost erotic abandonment. In an interview at the time, Michael Owen questioned Garrett on what he described as "lingeringly languorous promotional material of the Garrett body, usually draped in chiffon, which could be described as high art or merely flaunting."[29] The singer's response was both direct and honest: "I like to be adventurist and my feeling is, yes, go for it. These things either turn out tacky or high class. I hope I'll always be found in the latter" (Owen, 1993).

Whether this was a genuine response to the challenge of promoting opera with contemporary marketing methods, as Garrett would have had us believe, or simply yet another example of marketing exploitation, it is hard at this distance to ascertain. Garrett's first album enjoyed sixteen months in the British classical music chart, and eight months in the American Billboard classical chart. Although the aesthetic value of this remains hard to assess, the commercial value is obvious. Britain's "glamour queen of modern opera" (Owen, 1993) may promote the persona of an ordinary Yorkshire lass, but like many of her contemporaries, her success was as equally dependent on the continued interest of media and marketing executives as upon the support of audiences. Perhaps the media could not make an operatic career, but it could certainly support, sustain and promote or significantly damage one.

Amidst the glamour of international performances, high-profile television and film exposure and high-expenditure advertising, radio might appear relatively insignificant, but a study carried out by the Policy Studies Institute at this time confirmed a major increase in radio listening in the United Kingdom, with a greater market share going to independent, commercial radio stations, which relied, in a very large part upon advertising revenue. Although the British Broadcasting Corporation (BBC) had held an almost complete monopoly on radio broadcasting in the United Kingdom for 70 years, this situation was radically altered by the launch of Classic FM in September 1992. Although the station held no specific brief for opera, it did (and still does) broadcast a significant amount of popular opera extracts.

Much emphasis had been placed on establishing that Classic FM and BBC Radio Three (the BBC's classical music and arts station, formerly known as the Third Programme, and launched in 1967) were complimentary to each other rather than in direct competition. In the early months, Classic FM certainly appeared to be content to cater for the less specialist sector of the market. Both stations, however, ran carefully targeted advertising campaigns in order to clearly establish their audience share, and create a clear identity for potential listeners. Classic FM, using the slogan "A Different Kind of Soul Music," targeted print publications such as *Gramophone* magazine, while Radio Three's campaign included a series of adverts for its monthly program *Opera News* in English National Opera program booklets. Radio Three continued its policy of broadcasting regular live and complete opera performances, while Classic FM opted for a "top twenty" tunes approach. Classic FM also established a more recognizably popular style of broadcasting by using jingles regularly throughout the broadcasting day, and employing celebrity presenters who were encouraged to adopt a far more casual style, reminiscent of popular music stations.

Although branded as a "popular" broadcaster, Classic FM did make a considerable commitment to widening the understanding of its audience, by including programs such as *Introduction to the Opera* and *The Classic Opera Guide*, both of which were designed for the inexperienced listener and presented opera in an entertaining, accessible format.

The impact of this new station can also be assessed on the range and nature of the advertising that it attracted in the first years: this included major arts organizations such as English National Opera, and, perhaps ironically, the BBC themselves, who ran a campaign on Classic FM to promote the 1993 Promenade Concerts season.

It is worth noting that in May 2013, Classic FM was awarded the Sony Radio Academy Award in the United Kingdom as Brand of the Year. Further to this, the station's *More Music Breakfast Show* received a silver award for Best Promotional/Advertising Campaign. The Radio Academy is a professional broadcasting organization representing both commercial and funded broadcasters. Established more than 30 years ago, the Sony Awards cover five main areas—programs, individuals, marketing initiatives, production and station/brand. The judges' commendation for Classic FM noted the centrally important feature of marketing and brand recognition to the contemporary broadcasting industry: "Their longevity, attention to detail and understanding of their audience on all media platforms ensures its place as the inaugural winner of this award…. Classic FM is not just a great radio station, it is also a superb brand."[30]

Other retail markets also reflected what the critic Tom Sutcliffe described as "this new high level of interest in music in the 1980s."[31] A rush of print publications appeared at the time, catering for the new boom industry of opera, and classical music in general, all of which not only promoted the art form as a product, but also relied on advertising of the art form, and related products, in order to survive. *Gramophone*, the world's longest-established monthly magazine devoted to audio recordings of primarily classical music, published a sister magazine, *Classic CD*, concentrating on the lower priced sectors of the market, in a style deliberately designed to be more casual in tone and appeal to a new, non-specialist readership. BBC Publications followed suit shortly afterwards with the launch of *BBC Music* magazine, a monthly title covering, in an easily digestible style, the full range of music available in broadcast, recorded and live performance throughout the United Kingdom.

In the wake of a number of previous monthly part-works, dedicated to the classical main-stream, each issue usually devoted to a particular composer and complete with a recording of a representative and usually popular work, *Discovering Opera* was launched. Each issue included a recording of highlights from a major operatic work, and even though the publication was obviously aimed at the newcomer, the standard of writing was sufficiently scholarly to be worthy of the attention of the more experienced opera-lover. The Italian publisher Fabbri also launched a new title called *Opera*, presented in a similar format, but designed for an entirely different market. Fabbri was fully aware of the historical status of opera as a popular art form in Italy, and its place in popular Italian culture. Each issue of *Opera* included a complete performance, but what distinguished this publication was the nature of these performances. No random back-catalogue material here. Each was a vintage recording, some dating from as long ago as the mid–1930s, and including some relatively rare and off-air tapings. With this publication, classic opera performances now became available from roadside news-vendors.

One very glossy magazine to appear at this time was designed, in the words of its editor, to specifically appeal to a radically changing audience.[32] *Opera Now*, which first appeared in April 1989, moved away from the relatively conservative format and style of existing rivals such as *Gramophone*, and in its layout design, content and advertising indicated that it targeted the *Vogue/Country Life* life-style and fashion sector of the market. This was a major un-exploited gap in the publishing market, and *Opera Now* moved very quickly to fill it.

Once again, opera was seen as a generator of major business, as it had already proved in advertising, recording, marketing and the media. *Opera Now* succeeded in exploiting that business potential, by judging the market with unerring accuracy. In its first few years, the magazine subsisted on a healthy mix of gossip and more serious content, but unlike its more scholarly and long-established rival, *Opera*, it very obviously targeted not only the popular market, but the more affluent section of that market. Although the magazine adopted a popular stance, it was hardly egalitarian in its composition, as a glossy format publication which clearly signaled to the prospective reader that opera was a glamorous pursuit. This is clearly supported by the nature of the advertising, which appeared from the earliest issues: This included companies such as Christies, Mercedes Benz, General Motors, Yamaha, Jaeger and Le Coultre watches. Kiri Te Kanawa endorsed Rolex watches, sharing space with Jameson Irish Whiskey and Naim audio equipment.

Any casual observer leafing through the pages of *Opera Now* at that time would be left with the impression that opera was inflation-proof. This, however was not the case. Within eight months of the launch of the magazine, the editor's tone had tempered: "Not in a long time have the arts been so beleaguered by under-funding."[33] He went on to question the very nature of funding and, more particularly of sponsorship. *Opera Now* had clearly been one of the major benefactors of the pop-opera revolution, but it was becoming clear that what should have been the principal recipient, the actual art of live opera, was now itself under considerable threat. Many writers concluded that opera was hardly likely to be able to pay for itself. Opera was "high art" and as such it was desirable. It should be available to all, its benefits far outweighing the costs. This was a quality concept, based upon cultural desirability, exploited by one of the most extensive and effective marketing campaigns that any branch of the arts had ever experienced. Although enterprises such as *Opera Now* were clearly part of the campaign, their future was entirely dependent upon its success. It is arguable that the greatest benefits that emerged from the popularization of opera in the '80s and '90s, turned out to be the financial benefits that ancillary businesses such as publishing and advertising accrued from the accompanying spin-offs and that little had been invested in the future growth or sustainability of opera.

When Robert Tear expressed his opinion that art forms such as opera can never really achieve true popularity, he overlooked the combined power of the press, television, radio, video, compact discs, cinema and advertising. For the marketing men, responsible for sustaining high-profile public interest, opera could not have been more popular and, at least as a marketing tool, audiences enabled that popularity to flourish in a much wider arena than ever before. Business had certainly benefitted from the image and concept of opera, but there is little evidence of a two-way traffic of benefits. What then has opera as a business, characterized through advertising, contributed to the future of opera as an art-form? Returning to the sentiments expressed in the opening paragraphs of this essay, one might be tempted to say, very little. Looking back, as we have just done, it might well appear that opera has simply been exploited by commercial enterprise, exemplified by the advertising industry, during periods of peak popularity and then simply dropped when that popularity began to wane. We may not quite have come full-circle, but a brief examination of the opera-advertising relationship today however, might suggest that very little has changed, other than the scope and technology available to support the media.

The 1990s presented a series of dangerous, and in some cases, fatal or near-fatal cutbacks in arts funding. This was reflected in the levels of sponsorship available and then in the revenue from advertising that opera and opera-related industries had enjoyed throughout that decade. The global economic recession of the 2010s has provided a similar narrative. Writing in 2010, Peter Aspden, while noting the major contribution made to major arts organizations in the early 2000s by commercial sponsors noted that: "Many U.S. institutions have gone under following the onset of the recession, while European arts centres have been unable to act quickly or flexibly as a result of their dependence on government funds. But Colin Tweedy, chief executive of Arts & Business, a charity that acts as a mediator between the two sectors, says private and public money are inexorably linked, emphasising that any cuts to the public purse will have a detrimental knock-on effect on private investment in the U.K."[34]

An article published in *The Guardian* at approximately the same time explored the global view of cuts to arts budgets: "the list of U.S. cultural casualties is large and -growing: opera houses in Baltimore and Connecticut, a musicals theatre in San Jose, an art museum in Las Vegas, a dance company in New York ... by some estimates, one in 10 of the country's 100,000 arts organisations are in such financial straits they have been forced to make swingeing cuts or consider closing."[35] With reference to the situation in Ireland, one of the European Union countries to be worst affected by the financial downturn, the article stated that, "€9m (£7.9m) was taken from the arts budget. Opera Ireland, Opera Theatre Company and the Wexford Opera festival will have their funds cut by up to 7 percent. Around 300 artistic companies will have their grants cut this year. Only 10 will see an increase" (Pilkington, Davies and McDonald, 2010).

Surely we might expect that in such a fragile economy, marketing would be one of the very first casualties. Some observers however, suggested a different approach. John Quelch and Katherine Jocz, writing in the *Harvard Business Review* proposed the following strategy: "Although it's wise to contain costs, failing to support brands or examine core customers' changing needs can jeopardize performance over the long term. Companies that put customer needs under the microscope, take a scalpel rather than a cleaver to the marketing budget, and nimbly adjust strategies, tactics, and product offerings in response to shifting demand are more likely than others to flourish both during and after a recession."[36]

So, having established that opera has always been viewed as a representative element of the higher end of the advertising market, have those who use opera to promote their products changed their allegiances? The evidence would suggest that, perhaps against the odds they have not. Three brief examples offer us a view of the current position.

Firstly, the marketing power of the opera celebrity: Andrea Bocelli, described on his own website as "the world's most beloved tenor,"[37] provides us with the ideal example. Bocelli was born in Tuscany in 1958 and lost his sight as the result of a sporting accident at the age of 12. He originally studied law at university, but then began singing in clubs and cafés, eventually coming to prominence after winning a prize at the Sanremo Music Festival in 1994. He recently celebrated his twentieth anniversary as a performer, and has sold more than 80 million CDs worldwide. His website offers the following statement: "At last, a legend for the new millennium. A legend in the Homeric sense of a myth, the 'word that speaks,' flowered through singing, just like Caruso, Gigli, Del Monaco, Corelli.... A legend of Andrea Bocelli's stature cannot be built through design: not even the most astute marketing would be able to come up with such a result" (Andrea Bocelli website, 2013).

Although the majority of serious opera lovers would dispute the claim that he might be compared to Caruso or Gigli, and his work often receives very mixed critical responses, he is a hugely popular singer of what has been described earlier in this essay as the "pop-opera" genre. It is possibly true that "even the most astute marketing" would not be able to create the Bocelli phenomenon, but marketing certainly plays a major part in sustaining Bocelli's career, ensuring that the product—CD, concert appearance, TV special—clearly reaches the target audience.

His recording company, Universal, aggressively promotes his many CD albums and DVD recordings, the latest of which, *Passione*, features popular material, including duets with Jennifer Lopez and Nelly Furtado, and a digitally enabled performance of "La Vie en Rose" with the late Edith Piaf. Although he has not become widely involved in advertising or endorsing products, his voice has been heard on a TV commercial for pasta. In a scenario that is in some ways similar to the popularity of the late Mario Lanza, Bocelli occupies a middle-ground partway between recordings and performances of complete operas—*Werther, Carmen, Roméo et Juliette, Il Trovatore*—and albums of popular arias, ballads or cross-over repertoire. Winner of a Golden Globe, nominated for an Academy Award and selected by *People* magazine as one of their 100 Most Beautiful People, Bocelli now enjoys a career above the potential damage of negative criticism in which he has become his own most effective marketing tool.

Although Bocelli is an example of the marketing of the artist, rather than the artist as marketing tool, other major operatic performers have continued to engage in TV advertising of a whole range of products, continuing to exploit the star quality of the opera singer and the up-market image of the art form. One of the most surprising recent examples featured the Siberian-born baritone Dmitri Hvorostovsky, advertising the popular chocolate brand Ferrero Rocher, a commercial in which he also sings a short extract from "The Toreodor's Song" from Bizet's *Carmen*. Hvorostovsky is, in every sense a serious artist; winner of the prestigious Cardiff Singer of the World Competition in 1989, he has subsequently performed leading roles at many of the world's greatest opera houses including Covent Garden, The Met, the Vienna State Opera and La Scala Milan. In appearing in a TV commercial for a very popular product, Hvorostovsy is simply joining the ranks of his many colleagues from

Caruso to Renée Fleming, who have promoted both the product and their own popular image in this way.

Secondly, opera in popular advertising: As we have already seen, the "idea" of opera, or the parody of either operatic performance or opera singers has been used very effectively in a number of very successful campaigns. The current television campaign for the insurance comparison website Go Compare in the United Kingdom was launched in 2009. Featuring a genuine opera singer, the Welsh tenor Wynne Evans, as the fictional character Gio Compario, the commercial uses a re-arranged version of George M. Cohan's patriotic 1917 song "Over There," with newly written lyrics encouraging the consumer to compare different insurance service quotes by using the company's website. Voted as the "most irritating advert of 2009,"[38] an achievement repeated in the following year,[39] the campaign has, none the less embedded itself within the public consciousness, and made the company's name familiar to the vast majority of television viewers. From simply being the figure of fun, conforming to every possible operatic stereotype, and singing the insistent "theme tune," the character has now become a spokesperson for the brand, and has been given dialogue in the most recent versions.[40]

Even though the character that Evans portrays is highly recognizable and very closely associated with the product he promotes, involvement in advertising does not appear to have damaged his serious musical career. He has sung leading roles with Welsh National Opera, English National Opera, at Covent Garden and with Opera de Lyon. He has also appeared at The Proms and in recital at Wigmore Hall, and has a recording contract with Warner Classics. His first solo CD, *A Song in my Heart*, reached the number one position in the U.K. classical album charts.[41] Here we are presented with the perfect example of advertising promoting the advertiser as effectively as the product that is being advertised, and at the same time reminding the popular audience that opera and opera singers are quite prepared to join in with the joke. Once again, advertising proves that opera can be fun.

Finally, the opera media responding to contemporary technology: In order to benefit from a higher media profile, whether in advertising or indeed in any other forum, opera has been required to embrace technology. Although aspects of this are addressed in other essays in this book, it may be helpful to make a brief reference to one, particularly apposite example. In June 2013, when the Royal Opera House Covent Garden began to promote its "free" screenings of live performances direct from the stage of the theatre to large outdoor screens across the United Kingdom, other areas of the opera media were moving rapidly to keep abreast of what contemporary technology can offer them. Following the lead of other publications such as *Gramophone*, the editor of *Opera Now* made the following announcement: "Speaking of thinking outside the box, I'm delighted to introduce our new digital edition of *Opera Now*, available with dynamic content which links you to clips of performances and interviews—so next time one of our critics takes issue with a wobbly contralto or an out-of-tune tenor, you don't have to take their word for it. You'll be able to see and hear it for yourself."[42]

At a time in which opera, in common with many other serious art forms, faces significant financial difficulties, it may well be that the familiarization and demystification that can be achieved by opera and opera singers appearing in advertising and other branches of the popular media, may make a significant contribution to bolstering the profile of the art form for an audience who would not consider a trip to The Met or Covent Garden as a high cultural priority, thereby combatting the image of "ancient music for ancient people" (Covington, 2013) that may seriously threaten its future.

Opera, via the medium of advertising amongst many other aspects of the modern media, has established a secure place in contemporary popular culture, and often entertains and informs us in a way that is entirely divorced from the composer's or librettist's original intent. As an exploitable concept, opera continues to convey the message of quality, but now, due to the inventiveness of the advertising industry, it also contributes to a comedic element that supports brand recognition (often by placing the operatic music in a completely unexpected context), and provides us with some of our most memorable experiences during those commercial breaks. Here are just a few examples from current and recent television campaigns:

- The Kohler synchronized shower head system: "Fini ... Me lassa" a duet for Act III of Bellini's *I Puritani*.
- Extra chewing gum: not a genuine opera, but set in an opera house during the performance of a Rossini-esqe piece, drawing a parallel between the soprano's extended high note and the long lasting flavor of the pomegranate flavor gum.
- Pepsi: A modern take on Bizet's *Carmen*, featuring the popular singer Beyoncé Knowles, with suitably updated lyrics, perhaps owing more to *Carmen Jones* than it does to the operatic original.
- Ghirardelli, chocolate products: uses the same duet from Delibes' opera *Lakme* that proved so successful for British Airways.
- Budweiser, Bud Light: set in the auditorium of an opera house, the soprano's sustained note causes the illicit bottles of Bud light smuggled in by two reluctant husbands, to shatter.
- Carlton Draught beer: An Australian commercial, uses "Nessun Dorma," from Puccini's *Turandot*, with lyrics rewritten to "Men look better in slow motion."

- Dove Men, skin care products: The overture from Rossini's *William Tell*, with comedic lyrics added.
- Jean Paul Gaultier "Le Male" and "Classique" brands: "Casta Diva," from Bellini's *Norma*.
- Heineken beer: "Libiamo ne' lieti calici," popularly known as The Drinking Song, from the first act of Verdi's *La traviata*.[43]

Notes

1. Linnea Covington, "Until the Fat Lady Sings: Can Opera Survive the 21st Century," *The Brooklyn Rail*, online, accessed 29 May 2013.

2. Michael Cooper, "New York City Opera Announces It Will Close," *The New York Times*, available at http://artsbeat.blogs.nytimes.com/2013/10/01/new-york-city-opera-announces-it-will-close/?_r=0, accessed 2 October 2013.

3. Jennifer Maloney, "New York City Opera Closes Its Doors," *The Wall Street Journal*, http://online.wsj.com/news/articles/SB10001424052702304373104579109623037365300, accessed 2 October 2013.

4. Alex Ross, "Diminuendo: A Downturn for Opera in New York City," *The New Yorker*, 12 March 2012.

5. John Whitley, "The New Craze for Opera," *The Sunday Times*, London, 9 February 1986.

6. Luke Rittner, interviewed by Sir Roy Strong, "Ministering to the Arts, 2—The New Patrons," BBC Radio, 1992, transcription supplied by BBC Publications.

7. Gilbert Adair, "Why Art Has Gone to Pop," *The Sunday Times*, London, 28 March 1993.

8. Francesco Algarotti, *Saggio Sopra l'opera in musica*, Livorno, 1764: quoted in *Opera Now*, October 1989.

9. *Arts Council of Great Britain, Opera Survey*, 1989, published in *Cultural Trends No. 16* (Policy Studies Institute).

10. Tom Sutcliffe, in conversation with the author, 26 April 1993.

11. Geoffrey Wheatcroft, "Is Popera at Its peak?" *The Daily Telegraph*, London, 26 March 1992.

12. The four Ps was an approach originally proposed by Jerome McCarthy in 1960. The notion of the marketing mix was defined by Neil H. Borden of the Harvard Business School and outlined in a paper in *The Journal of Advertising Research* in 1984.

13. Tim Hunt, in conversation with the author, 20 April 1993.

14. "1991: Pavarotti Sings in the British Rain," BBC Home, http://news.bbc.co.uk/onthisday/hi/dates/stories/july/30/newsid_2491000/2491731.stm, accessed 30 May 2013.

15. British Market Research Bureau survey, quoted in "Who Are the Opera Lovers?" *Opera Now*, November 1990.

16. Leo Delibes was born in Saint-Germain-du-Val in 1836. *Lakmé* was premiered in Paris in 1883. Although performed more than 500 times at the Opera Comique over the next three decades, it failed to keep a place in the international repertoire.

17. Carrie Hindmarsh, in conversation with the author, 27 April 1993.

18. Stephen Trainer, in conversation with the author, 20 April 1993.

19. Henry Raynor, *A Social History of Music*, quoted by Rosanne Martorella, *The Sociology of Opera* (New York: Praeger, 1982), p. 19.

20. Nicholas de Jongh, "Pavarotti Triumphs in the Rain," in *The Guardian*, London, 31 July 1991.
21. Terri Robson, quoted by Alexander Waugh, "Top Tenors Outsell the Pop Chart Superstars," in *The Mail on Sunday*, London, 29 March 1992.
22. Made in 1992, Palmer's film had such impact that it was broadcast on commercial television in the United Kingdom without any commercial breaks. An almost unknown occurrence.
23. Alexander Waugh, *The Evening Standard*, London, 8 April 1993.
24. Michael Kennedy, *The Sunday Telegraph*, London, 11 April 1993.
25. Michael Stewart, *The Gramophone*, Vol. 70, No. 839, April 1993.
26. Lesley Garrett, in conversation with the author, 3 June 1993.
27. Headline to an article by Peter Millar, *The Sunday Times*, London, 21 March 1993.
28. Headline to an article by Alexander Waugh, *The Mail on Sunday*, London, 21 March 1993.
29. Michael Owen, "Lesley's Last Laugh," *The Evening Standard*, 23 April 1993.
30. "Classic FM Scoop Brand of the Year at Sony Radio Academy Awards," *Classic FM*, http://www.classicfm.com/music-news/latest-news/classic-fm-brand-year-sony-awards/, accessed 27 June 2013.
31. Tom Sutcliffe, in conversation with the author, 26 April 1993.
32. In the editorial to the first edition, Mel Cooper wrote: "Opera audiences are changing radically. Their numbers have grown phenomenally over the past decade.... We are launching *Opera Now* to entertain and inform this growing audience" (editorial, *Opera Now*, April 1989).
33. Mel Cooper, editorial, *Opera Now*, December 1989.
34. Peter Aspden, "Sponsorship: Effect of Recession Is Playing on Stages and in Galleries," FT.com, http://www.ft.com/cms/s/0/93ca64aa–66c8–11df-aeb1-00144feab49a.html#axzz2VWqzIAyt, accessed 4 June 2013.
35. Ed Pilkington, Lizzy Davies and Henry McDonald, "Hard Times: How the Recession Is Affecting Arts Funding Around the Globe," *The Guardian*, http://www.guardian.co.uk/culture/2010/feb/19/arts-funding-global-recession, accessed 1 June 2013.
36. John Quelch and Katherine Jocz, "How to Market in a Downturn," *Harvard Business Review*, http://hbr.org/2009/04/how-to-market-in-a-downturn/ar/1, accessed 1 June 2013.
37. Andrea Bocelli website, http://www.andreabocelli.com/en/#!/career, accessed 7 June 2013.
38. "Go Compare Advert Voted the Most Irritating of 2009," *The Telegraph*, 17 January 2010, http://www.telegraph.co.uk/news/newstopics/howaboutthat/7010129/Go-Compare-advert-voted-most-irritating-of-2009.html, accessed 10 June 2013.
39. "The Most Irritating Adverts of 2010," *The Telegraph*, 12 January 2011, http://www.telegraph.co.uk/culture/tvandradio/8252335/Most-irritating-adverts-of-2010-money-saving-websites.html, accessed 10 June 2013.
40. This, and earlier versions of the commercial can be seen at http://www.gocompare.com/tv-advert/?Media=A008772&PST=1&gclid=CNPw_aGx2bcCFXLLtAodsTwAQA, accessed 10 June 2013.
41. "Beyond Compare: TV Ad Singer Tops Classical Charts," *The Times*, http://www.thetimes.co.uk/tto/arts/music/classical/article2963752.ece, accessed 10 June 2013.
42. Ashutosh Khandekar, *Opera Now* editorial, http://www.rhinegold.co.uk/magazines/opera_now/editorial/opera_now_editorial.asp?css=1, accessed 7 June 2013.
43. These and other examples can be viewed at websites including http://www.

huffingtonpost.com/justin-moss/opera-in-tv-commercials_b_1669470.html#slide=1232 973, accessed 1 June 2013.

Bibliography

Abercrombie, Nicholas, et al. *Contemporary British Society*. London: Polity, 2000.
The Arts Council, England. http://www.artscouncil.org.uk/.
Arts Council of Great Britain, Opera Survey. In *Cultural Trends No. 16* (Policy Studies Institute), 1989.
Arts Marketing Association. *JAM*, the arts marketing journal. http://www.a-m-a.co.uk/.
Carboni, Marius. *Marketing Strategies in the UK Classical Music Business*. London: Lambert, 2011.
Cultural Trends. http://www.tandfonline.com/toc/ccut20/current#.UnKf4hBKTFA.
Dyer, Gillian. *Advertising as Communication*. London: Routledge, 1982.
King, Mike. *Music Marketing*. London: Berklee, 2009.
Kolb, Anita. *Marketing Cultural Organisations*. London, Oak Tree, 1999.
Ind, Nicholas. *Great Advertising Campaigns*. London: Kogan Page, 1993.
Martorella, Rosanne. *The Sociology of Opera*. New York: Praeger, 1982.
The Media History Digital Library. http://mediahistoryproject.org/.
The National Arts Marketing Project. http://artsmarketing.org/.
Opera Now. http://www.rhinegold.co.uk/magazines/opera_now/.
O'Reilly, Daragh, and Finola Kerrigan. *Marketing the Arts: A Fresh Approach*. London: Routledge, 2010.
Policy Studies Journal. http://onlinelibrary.wiley.com/journal/10.1111/%28ISSN%291541-0072.
Pricken, Mario. *Creative Advertising*. London: Thames and Hudson, 2008.
Snowman, Daniel. *The Gilded Stage: A Social History of Opera*. London: Atlantic, 2010.
Walmsley, Ben. ed. *Key Issues in the Arts and Entertainment Industry*. London: Goodfellow, 2011.
Wharton, Chris. *Advertising as Culture*, London: Intellect, 2013.

Making Culture Popular: Opera and the Media Industries

Sam O'Connell

In *Theatre Survey*'s special issue on operatic performance, Leo Cabranes-Grant writes, "Opera works at its best when the engaged eye submits to the enchantments of the engaged ear, when spectators abandon themselves to their role as audiences, when the visible enhances the invisible."[1] In this articulation of opera's best work, Cabranes-Grant elides the fluid relationship between performance (music, lyrics, *mise en scène*, and performers) and audience. Opera, he suggests, works best when its audience works with it or towards it to create an appropriate sensory-based reception of the live performance. The visual submits to the aural, the active audience becomes passive, and some invisible imaginary seems to emerge. This formulation of opera's best work begs the question of how opera works when other "live" media get involved.

Operas performed in such cultural institutions as the Metropolitan Opera in New York City have a long history with broadcast media, a history that is, importantly, both commercially and culturally invested. Launched with a near century-old radio-broadcast series that has expanded into their highly visible and profitable *Live in HD* series, the Met, for example, has engaged with broadcast media to both ensure their financial viability and cultural relevance in an increasingly mediated entertainment world. Building on the Met's history of interactions with broadcast media, this essay examines the ways in which broadcast media and the media industries affect operatic performances and challenge formulations like those of Cabranes-Grant on what opera is and how opera works. Additionally, this essay draws on the tension between the "high culture" history of opera and the "mass" or "popular culture" of broadcast media for a consideration of audience and mass audience experience and expectations in a mediated age. In the end, I hope to demonstrate the ways in which broadcast media and the media industries have altered both the audience and the audience experience of operatic performances.

The Metropolitan Opera and the Media

Sitting in the auditorium for a matinee performance of Englebert Humperdinck's *Hansel and Gretel* as part of the Metropolitan Opera's 2008 season, I was immediately struck by how many children there were in the opera house. As the pit orchestra could be heard tuning up, children could be seen everywhere in the auditorium: they were in the family circle, the dress circle, the grand tier, and the balcony. Some children even had the good fortune to have front-row seats in the Met's Orchestra section. From where I was sitting, these children were visible in every section of the house. Sure, Humperdinck's opera is based on a children's story by the Brothers Grimm, but it is a particularly dark story—even according to the Grimms' standards—and having this many children in attendance seemed unusual. What made the number of children in the audience at the Met even more surprising, though, than the dark subject matter and the fact that it was a Saturday afternoon at the opera, is that there were no children sitting near me. Rather, I was in an audience seated next to row after row of senior citizens in stadium seats who were enjoying the afternoon's pre-show entertainment. As we attended our afternoon performance at *The Met: Live in HD*, we watched all of the other audience members enter the auditorium, Renée Fleming's pre-show tour of the performance's backstage action, and the pit orchestra tuning up. We were given access to many aspects of the performance event, even if we actually happened to be sitting in a Fort Lauderdale movie theatre and not actually present in the dress circle. While the children at the Met and their families continued to fill the opera house before the show started, we, the cinema audience, watched them as part of the live broadcast transmission of the afternoon's show eating our popcorn. While the audience at the opera house was waiting for *Hansel and Gretel* to begin, our event had already begun.

In his *New York Times* review of the same performance of *Hansel and Gretel*, Anthony Tommasini calls into question whether or not those audiences who have been to the cinema would appreciate seeing the performances at the Met itself without being disappointed by their distance from the "live" experience of the auditorium itself. Upon praising the "sophisticated camera work" and the "scenes of backstage activity, even during the performance," Tommasini asks: "After experiencing *Hansel and Gretel* so intimately..., will seeing the same production from the Family Circle at the Met just make everything seem too flat and far away?"[2] While the very thought of a lesser aesthetic experience occurring at the Met than in a movie theatre may seem blasphemous to the Met's regular subscribers, Tommasini's question highlights an important issue that emerges when we examine *The Met: Live in HD* as a hybrid event in an attempt to locate the multiple audiences created in the age of digital performance. What Tommasini demonstrates is the fact that though the Met's audience and the cinema's audience are to some extent attending the same performances, they are having different aesthetic and cultural experiences.

By providing a brief context of the transmissions' place within the Met's tradition of outreach programs to its multiple audiences, I argue that the distinctions that emerge out of these different experiences, whether they are distinctions of space, class, or aesthetic quality, can ultimately help us unsettle the distinctions between live and liveness with which *The Met: Live in HD* directly encounters through its execution across multiple audience spaces. The location for beginning to analyze these distinctions exists at the nexus point that marks the moment of transition between spatial absence and spatial co-presence through which the theatrical performance and its cinematic transmission merge: the screen. For, it is ultimately through the employment of the cinema screen as an integral part of the series' existence that the notions of presence and absence that have long perpetuated a disciplinary binary between theatre and film, between live and "liveness," begin to shift away from the outmoded division and opposition between different media and towards a twenty-first century understanding that accounts for the cooperation and connection that can productively exist between disciplines.

The Met: Live in HD began to take shape when Peter Gelb took over for Joseph Volpe as the General Manager for the Metropolitan Opera after Volpe retired at the end of the 2005-06 season. As general manager, Gelb poured the Met's resources into developing a series of new outreach initiatives to broaden the Met's audience and increase its visibility. Importantly, many of these new initiatives involved creating access to the Met's performances through newly available media technologies. Prior to Gelb's taking the helm, the Met's primary attempt to reach out to a broader audience was through radio. However, under Volpe's direction, the Met had encountered trouble securing the future of its now 80-year-old tradition of broadcasting live performances via radio, which is "the longest running classical musical series in American broadcast history."[3] Having failed to maintain the viability of this radio series, Volpe lost the company's corporate sponsorship and was forced to set up a "Save the Broadcasts Campaign" in order to "secure the broadcasts' long-term future."[4] For the Met under Volpe's management, the radio broadcasts were the means through which the company envisioned itself as "a cultural ambassador to the world" since the international broadcasts "have brought opera into millions of ... homes and have enriched the lives of generations of our citizens and have contributed to the development and appreciation of opera throughout the [world]."[5] With the Save the Broadcasts Campaign, Volpe identified the Met's challenge in the future as needing "to continue to build [the] Broadcast Fund to guarantee the future of these treasured broadcasts."[6]

Knowing about Volpe's determination to maintain the radio broadcasts as the primary form of public outreach, it is interesting to note that in his taking over as general manager Gelb has been almost entirely uninterested in the radio broadcasts as a means of delivering the Met's operas to a global audience while also trying to keep opera connected to other mainstream forms of entertainment. Instead, Gelb has focused his attention on developing and instituting new methods of outreach that attract, importantly, a broader audience in terms of demographics than the radio broadcasts, particularly a younger one. While he has continued the tradition of the radio broadcasts, Gelb's new initiatives started with streaming operas live on the internet, which he saw as "the most immediate experience [the Met] can provide to opera lovers all over the world and a new way to introduce opera to the uninitiated."[7] Within a few months, though, Gelb had topped the immediacy of the experience provided by live streaming and the increased accessibility it enabled by creating the new program *The Met: Live in HD*, which Gelb and the Met have envisioned as a "groundbreaking series of live, high-definition performance transmissions to movie theatres around the world."[8] Through the development of this series, Gelb has actively courted a global audience in order to maintain the viability of the Met's brand as "a cultural ambassador to the world" as well as its financial stability in the face of competing forms of entertainment by joining the culture capital of opera as high art performed live with the superior distribution platform of high-definition technologies offered by both the twenty-first century cinema experience and the increasing trend towards hearing and viewing opera through HD home entertainment media.

As it has been conceived, *The Met: Live in HD* has been designed to merge the immediacy of live performance with the technological capabilities of reaching a global audience provided by the cinema, all while maintaining the allure and appeal of attending a live performance at the Met itself. In fact, the marriage of live performance and cinematic technique through high-definition digital technologies has arguably not only enhanced the experience of live performances for cinema audiences but also increased the allure of the Met and its cultural capital for those audiences attending a performance at the opera house itself. According to the Met, the series "captures the onstage action from striking angles and heightens attention to the narrative elements of both performance and production" by "using robotic cameras and state-of-the-art technology."[9] For Gelb, this initiative "[makes] the spectacle of live grand opera more broadly available," which is "part of the Met's new efforts to propel opera back into the mainstream."[10] In addition to using digital technology to transmit the events and "to capture the intensity and drama of the performances,"[11] the Met is attempting to provide an unparalleled depth of experience for live movie audiences through "behind-the-scenes features, live interviews with cast and crew, insightful short documentaries, and bird's-eye views of the productions."[12] Though Gelb acknowledges that "nothing is comparable to being at the Met for a live performance,"[13] it is possible that, through the live extras presented during the transmissions, the audiences who are attending the performances at their local movie theatres are actually getting more during their experience of the performance event while paying less than those who actually attend the Met itself.[14] Additionally, Gelb's claim that nothing compares to attending the Met itself for a live performance directly engages with the theoretical question Susan Sontag poses when she asks, "whether there is an unbridgeable division, even opposition, between the two arts" of theatre and film.[15] Through its use of new technologies of transmission, its existence as two types of performance text (theatrical and cinematic), and its creation of two spaces with two separate live audiences (the opera house and the movie theatre), *The Met: Live in HD* provides an ideal case study whereby we can begin to locate the multiple audiences present at hybrid events.

Now, as it begins to enter its eighth season of live transmissions and based in large part on its success with attracting larger and larger audiences that are increasingly global, *The Met: Live in HD* has begun to gather a fair amount of critical attention. There seems to be a sense of confusion among critics, though, as there is, as of yet, no consensus on exactly what this form of live opera transmission should be called, how it should be considered, who exactly its target audience is (or even who its target audiences are), and, presumably, how to market it. What is noteworthy about the critical response to these transmissions is that the performances are being hailed equally for their ability to capture, and even enhance, the live feel of the theatrical experience of attending the opera in person as they are for their adept utilization of cinematic techniques—close-ups, zooms, and wide shots, for example—to help structure the narrative and emotional content of the operas themselves, techniques that work to educate a non-traditional opera audience in to how to watch and understand the performance.

Writing for *The Toronto Star*, William Littler asks, "Who would have guessed that movie theatres across the continent could be packed by people willing to pay $17.95 (for advance purchase), $19.95 (for same-day purchase), or $14.95 (for children) for the privilege of watching a live performance of an opera far away in New York?"[16] Answering his own rhetorical question, Littler continues, "The reason people are gladly buying tickets at such prices is that they are not just watching a movie, they are participating vicariously in a live event" and that "even in a darkened movie theatre, [*The Met: Live in HD*] offers something of a 'you are there' experience difficult to imagine at home" (Littler, 2007). Importantly, the fact that you are not there—if we define "there" as being in the opera house in New York City and "not there" as being in any cinema around the world—no longer seems to matter to most critics or audiences. According to Francis Clines of *The New York Times*, the simulcasts "prove you don't have to be there in person to savor the thrill" of The Met's opera performances.[17] For Clines, you might actually benefit from not being there. He writes, "Fine cinematic technique—close-ups of radiant lovers, tracking shots...; backstage glimpses of scenery changes and the cast's sweaty exubsonerance—arguably makes the experience richer than through opera glasses atop the Met's Family Circle" (Clines, 2008). This suggestion of a heightened richness of experience in the cinematic versions of the operas that seems to be more the result of the cinematic techniques employed in the transmissions than the theatrical performances of the opera singers themselves highlights the importance of understanding these live events as they exist for the different audiences attending the event on both sides of the cinema screen.

In *The Language of New Media*, Lev Manovich writes, "the visual culture of the modern period, from painting to cinema, is characterized by an intriguing phenomenon—the existence of another virtual space, another three-dimensional world enclosed by a frame and situated inside a normal space. The frame separates two absolutely different spaces that somehow coexist. This phenomenon is what defines the screen in the most general sense."[18] There are two important features of this characterization of the screen that I want to examine more closely in discussing the distinctions between theatre audiences and cinema audiences and their manifestations as vital participants in *The Met: Live in HD* as both a live performance event and an aesthetic experience. The first is Manovich's delineation of one virtual, three-dimensional space situated inside a normal space. The second is his argument that the frame of the screen separates two absolutely different spaces that somehow coexist. By looking at the ways in which these two features apply to the function of the screen in connecting audiences to performances and enabling the global success of *The Met: Live in HD*, we can see how the Met's series of transmissions provides us with a contemporary example that allows us to newly examine the multiple, shared audiences of a hybrid event, which Philip Auslander defines as an event in which "live elements can be combined with recorded and otherwise technologically mediated."[19]

Drawing upon Manovich's definition, the first point I want to focus on is how the cinema screen in *The Met: Live in HD* is unique in that the intriguing phenomenon of a virtual space situated in another space is made all the more intriguing by it not involving a virtual space at all. Whereas traditional cinema does involve a virtual world—one that does not actually exist as depicted in a finished film despite its probable materiality during filming—to which Manovich refers, *The Met: Live in HD* is not working with a virtual, imaginary space. Rather, the space within the screen is very much a real space.

It is the space comprising the stage, the auditorium, and the backstage passages of the Metropolitan Opera House, and it is occupied by both the performers and the audience that are "there" at the Met. In addition to being a real space, the cinematic space of the opera house and its performance coexist simultaneously with the three-dimensional, normal space of the movie theatre and its cinema audience. Both spaces on either side of the screen are social spaces occupied by audiences who have gathered together to experience the performance event of the same opera. Importantly, each audience participates in that event, each experiences it as live, and each understands it as a performance.

In his definition of the theatrical event, William Sauter writes that the event "takes place at a certain place, at a certain time, and in a certain context. The theatrical event also presupposes two partners: those who make a presentation and those who perceive it."[20] For Sauter, there needs to be the mutual involvement between the partners and "the immediate presence of both performer and spectator [is] one of the basic experiences of the theatre" (Sauter, 172). In *The Met: Live in HD*, though, the cinema screen complicates this definition and blurs the line between presence and absence. The audience in the opera house and the audience in the movie theatre are both participating in the same performance event, and, as Gelb and the Met are fully aware and reliant on the presence of the cinema audience for the performances' commercial success, as well as the after-market success of DVD and Blu-ray sales, both sets of spectators are "vitally implicated" in the "dynamic process of communication" that makes up the theatrical event in Gay McAuley's definition.[21] Thus, through the screen and the way in which it connects cinema to opera house, the film in this case is not representative of absence as Sauter might have us believe. Instead, the relationship between performer and spectator is a matter of distance. Those in the opera house may be closer to the performance than those in the movie theatres scattered around the world, but all audiences are present to the production during the moment of its theatrical staging. While this is an important feature that distinguishes *The Met: Live in HD* from traditional film and cinema incarnations, it is not to say that all audiences are having the same experience.

To demonstrate what I mean by this, I turn now to Manovich's second feature of the screen: the frame of the screen keeps the spaces on either side absolutely separate. What this means is that while the audiences are involved in the communication process, which can be generally defined as "the transmission of a signal from a source to a destination,"[22] that makes up the theatrical event of the operatic performance, they are present to the performance event but not necessarily to each other. As Marvin Carlson has demonstrated, theatre is a socio-cultural event "whose meanings and interpretations are not to be sought exclusively in the text being performed but in the experience of the audience assembled to share in creation of the total event."[23] Within the events of *The Met: Live in HD*'s series of live performances, then, the audiences at the Met are participating in a strikingly different socio-cultural event than those attending the opera at their local movie theatres. Part of the distinction is, of course, economic given that one audience has paid several hundred dollars for their tickets while the other has paid on average only twenty dollars. Another distinction, though, particularly as it relates to the spaces separated by the screen is the ways in which the spaces of the two different types of auditorium shape the experience of their audiences respectively.

According to Carlson, the Met's audiences make meaning of their experience through their relationship to "the entire theatre, its audience arrangement, its other public spaces, its physical appearance, even its location in the city" (Carlson, 2). For the audience actually seated "there" within the 3,800-seat house of the Met, the experience of the performance is focused on the spaces of the Met and the theatrical production of the opera on stage. But, for the audiences in movie theatres around the globe, there exists a doubling in their experience of space. Not only do they have the signifying systems of the movie theatre but also they have the signifiers of the Met, including its audience seated within the opera house. Thus, while the two audiences coexist with one another, separated though they are by the screen, the signal being transmitted to them shapes their experiences differently. For the opera house, the signal transmitted is the staged production and the space of the Met. For the movie theatre, the signal transmitted via broadcast is the stage production, the space of the Met, and the Met's audience and backstage activities all of which become part of the show. Thus, for example, while the intermission at the Met is just an intermission; for the cinema audiences, the intermission becomes part of the show in much the same way the children in the audience became part of the pre-show entertainment during the matinee performance of *Hansel and Gretel*. Moreover, for the audience seated in the movie theatre, as pointed out by Littler, there is the pleasure of attending not just a movie and but also a live performance event. The experience of the event for cinema audiences becomes both cinematic and theatrical and is understood as such.

With this dual understanding of *The Met: Live in HD* being both cinematic and theatrical in its performance, then, I want to close with the suggestion that we as scholars and critics might benefit from moving past ontological concerns over liveness as oppositional to the live as it relates to the utilization of digital media in hybrid events. In *Theatre Semiotics: Signs of Life*, Marvin Carlson writes, "Theatrical experience thus occupies a strange, even uncanny position midway between arts of absence, such as the novel or cinema, and the experience of presence we have in everyday life."[24] Within this description of the theatrical experience, Carlson sets up a continuum of experience that travels between the two poles of presence and absence. If presence is defined by that which we experience materially and absence defined by those experiences which are in large part imaginary in our engagement with them, then Carlson positions, rightly so, the theatrical experience somewhere between them. There is the materiality of the stage and its performers but there is also the absence of the dramatic fiction. What *The Met: Live in HD* demonstrates, though, is that we might benefit from revisiting what we consider to be absent. Ultimately, through its use of live performance and its combination of presence and distance, which is notably not synonymous with absence, the experience of the broadcast transmissions also occupy an equally uncanny space as the theatrical experience on the continuum between presence and absence. In fact, *The Met: Live in HD*, allows us to move further from a discussion of live or liveness and closer to an understanding of hybrid events as simply live, despite the potential lack of spatially co-present audiences. Through the new digital HD technologies used as part of *The Met: Live in HD*, hybrid events increasingly create multiple audiences who understand each other as mutually informing partners vitally implicated in the creation and experience of the same event. Ultimately, *The Met: Live in HD* demonstrates the need for performance scholars to reinvestigate the connections between theatre and digital media as complementary aesthetic practices, particularly since audiences are increasingly unconcerned with whether they are "there" or not.

Notes

1. Leo Cabranes-Grant, "From the Special Editor," *Theatre Journal* 51:2 (November 2010), 187–190: 187.
2. Anthony Tommasini, "You Go to the Movie Theater, and an Opera Breaks Out," *The New York Times*, January 3, 2008.
3. "75th Anniversary Season of Live Metropolitan Opera Broadcasts Begins December 17 with 'Rigoletto,'" the Metropolitan Opera, http://www.metoperafamily.org/metopera/news/press/detail.aspx?id=2789 (accessed August 20, 2008).
4. "Met Presents First World Premier Broadcast Since 2000: Tobias Picker's 'An American Tragedy,'" http://www.metoperafamily.org/metopera/news/press/detail.aspx?id=2781 (accessed August 20, 2008).
5. "75th Anniversary Season of Live Metropolitan Opera Broadcasts."
6. "Toll Brothers Becomes New Corporate Sponsor for the Metropolitan Opera Radio Broadcasts," the Metropolitan Opera, http://www.metoperafamily.org/metopera/news/press/detail.aspx?id=2793 (accessed August 20, 2008).
7. "Met Opera and RealNetworks Partner to Reach a Worldwide Audience with Free Live Internet Streams," the Metropolitan Opera, http://www.metoperafamily.org/metopera/press/news/detail.aspx?id=2727 (accessed August 20, 2008).
8. "2008–2009 Live in HD!" the Metropolitan Opera, http://www.metoperafamily.org/metopera/broadcast/hd_events_next.aspx (accessed August 20, 2008).
9. "The Metropolitan Opera Announces Expansion of Live, High-Definition Trans-

missions to Eleven in 2008–09," the Metropolitan Opera, http://www.metoperafamily/org/metopera/news/press/detail.aspx?id=3810 (accessed August 20, 2008).

10. "Metropolitan Opera: Live in HD Makes Its Debut," the Metropolitan Opera, http://www.Metoperafamily.org/metopera/news/press/detail.aspx?id=2709 (accessed August 20, 2008).

11. "The Metropolitan Opera and the New York City Department of Education Bring Live Opera Transmissions to Public School Students and Teachers in Five Boroughs," the Metropolitan Opera, http://www.metoperafamily.org/metopera/news/press/detail.aspx?id=3171 (accessed August 20, 2008).

12. "The Metropolitan Opera Announces Expansion."

13. "Metropolitan Opera: Live in HD Makes Its Debut."

14. In arguing that the cinema audience gets "more" in their experience for their dollar, I am suggesting that they are getting a cinematic equivalent of a backstage pass. Their cinema seat enables them to a total experience. In the writing of this essay, I want to thank Paul Fryer for pointing out that this total experience might be equivalent to bonus material on DVDs and BluRays, which Fryer notes are often not viewed by the purchaser at all but allows the audience to think they are getting something extra for nothing.

15. Susan Sontag, "Theatre and Film," in *Theater and Film: A Comparative Anthology* (New Haven: Yale University Press, 2005), 134.

16. William Littler, "Opera at Movie Houses a Huge Hit; But Nothing Matches Thrill of Being at the Met," *The Toronto Star*, April 7, 2007.

17. Francis X. Clines, "A Day at the Opera, a Snack for the Soul," *The New York Times*, April 14, 2008.

18. Lev Manovich, *The Language of New Media* (Cambridge, MA: MIT Press, 2001), 95.

19. Philip Auslander, ""Live and technologically Mediated Performance," in *Cambridge Companion to Performance Studies*, ed. Tracy C. Davis, 107–119. (Cambridge, UK: Cambridge University Press, 2008), 109.

20. William Sauter, *The Theatrical Event: Dynamics of Performance and Perception* (Iowa City: University of Iowa Press, 2000), 30.

21. Gay McAuley, *Space in Performance: Making Meaning in the Theatre* (Ann Arbor: University of Michigan Press, 1999), 7.

22. Keir Elam, *The Semiotics of Theatre and Drama* (London: Metheun, 1980), 35.

23. Marvin Carlson, *Places of Performance: The Semiotics of Theatre Architecture* (Ithaca, NY: Cornell University Press, 1989), 2.

24. Marvin Carlson, *Theatre Semiotics: Signs of Life* (Bloomington: Indiana University Press, 1990), 96.

Bibliography

Auslander, Philip. "Live and Technologically Mediated Performance." In *Cambridge Companion to Performance Studies*, edited by Tracy C. Davis. Cambridge, UK: Cambridge University Press, 2008.

Cabranes-Grant, Leo. "From the Special Editor." *Theatre Journal* 51:2 (November 2010): 187–190.

Carlson, Marvin. *Places of Performance: The Semiotics of Theatre Architecture*. Ithaca, NY: Cornell University Press, 1989.

_____. *Theatre Semiotics: Signs of Life*. Bloomington: Indiana University Press, 1990.

Clines, Francis X. "A Day at the Opera, a Snack for the Soul," *The New York Times*, April 14, 2008.
Elam, Keir. *The Semiotics of Theatre and Drama*. London: Metheun, 1980.
Littler, William. "Opera at Movie Houses a Huge Hit; But Nothing Matches Thrill of Being at the Met." *The Toronto Star*, April 7, 2007.
Manovich, Lev. *The Language of New Media*. Cambridge, MA: MIT Press, 2001.
McAuley, Gay. *Space in Performance: Making Meaning in the Theatre*. Ann Arbor: University of Michigan Press, 1999.
The Metropolitan Opera. "Met Opera and RealNetworks Partner to Reach a Worldwide Audience with Free Live Internet Streams," The Metropolitan Opera, http://www.metoperafamily.org/metopera/press/news/detail.aspx?id=2727.
_____. "Met Presents First World Premier Broadcast Since 2000: Tobias Picker's 'An American Tragedy.'" http://www.metoperafamily.org/metopera/news/press/detail.aspx?id=2781.
_____. "Metropolitan Opera: Live in HD Makes Its Debut." The Metropolitan Opera, http://www.Metoperafamily.org/metopera/news/press/detail.aspx?id=2709.
_____. "The Metropolitan Opera and the New York City Department of Education Bring Live Opera Transmissions to Public School Students and Teachers in Five Boroughs." The Metropolitan Opera, http://www.metoperafamily.org/metopera/news/press/detail.aspx?id=3171.
_____. "The Metropolitan Opera Announces Expansion of Live, High-Definition Transmissions to Eleven in 2008–09." The Metropolitan Opera, http://www.metoperafamily/org/metopera/news/press/detail.aspx?id=3810.
_____. "75th Anniversary Season of Live Metropolitan Opera Broadcasts Begins December 17 with 'Rigoletto.'" The Metropolitan Opera, http://www.metoperafamily.org/metopera/news/press /detail.aspx?id=2789.
_____. "Toll Brothers Becomes New Corporate Sponsor for the Metropolitan Opera Radio Broadcasts." The Metropolitan Opera, http://www.metoperafamily.org/metopera/news/press/detail.aspx?id=2793.
_____. "2008–2009 Live in HD!" The Metropolitan Opera, http://www.metoperafamily.org/metopera/broadcast/hd_events_next.aspx.
Sauter, William. *The Theatrical Event: Dynamics of Performance and Perception*. Iowa City: University of Iowa Press, 2000.
Sontag, Susan. "Theatre and Film." In *Theater and Film: A Comparative Anthology*. New Haven: Yale University Press, 2005.
Tommasini, Anthony. "You Go to the Movie Theater, and an Opera Breaks Out," *The New York Times*, January 3, 2008.

Opera Criticism: State of the Art and Beyond

Daniel Meyer-Dinkgräfe

Formats of Criticism

Opera criticism is published across a range of media and formats. There are the reviews in the daily or weekly newspapers, both in print and online, reviews in specialist opera magazines, reviews in academic journals and blogs by individuals on the internet. In 2011, David Gillard retired from his role as opera critic of the popular British newspaper *The Daily Mail* after forty years in office. Online, his reviews come with snappy headlines, such as "A Tawdry Travesty of a Carmen from the Tarantino of Opera"[1] on a production of *Carmen*, or "Lady of the Lake Makes a Big Splash"[2] on a production of *Rusalka*. Below the heading follows a verdict, such as "A load of bull" (Gillard, 2012), or "One enchanted evening" (Gillard, 2011) on those productions of *Carmen* and *Rusalka*, respectively. Then there is a star-rating from one to five (one for *Carmen*, four for *Rusalka* in the above examples). The reviews that follow the pithy heading, poignant verdict and star rating are concise, to the point, assured, at times witty, and leave the reader in no doubt about Gillard's position. He provides some information about the essence, not details, of the plot, and about what he perceives to be strengths and weaknesses of the production and the achievements of singers, orchestra and conductor, in usually no more than one sentence each. Thus, on the production of *Rusalka*, he wrote: "Glyndebourne has imported two National Theatre stalwarts to ensure this production looks as good as it sounds. Director Melly Still (*Coram Boy*) and her designer Rae Smith (*War Horse*) bring Dvořák's spooky world to vibrant, quirky life" (Gillard, 2011). He then summed up the musical aspect of *Carmen* with the comments that "Bizet's score gets a decent playing under conductor Ryan Wigglesworth, but the singing is average, with the biggest cheer rightly reserved for Elizabeth Llewellyn's Micaela" (Gillard, 2012).

The scope of the reviews by Rupert Christiansen, who has been writing for *The Daily Telegraph* in the United Kingdom since 1996, is broader, in line with the extra space available for reviews, and with the assumed readership expectations. Online, the heading is a matter of fact information of genre: review, opera title and performing company, in case of touring productions the venue of the performance. This is followed by a sentence providing some essential excerpt from the review in the "says Rupert Christiansen" format, such as "Only a first rate production can release the full power of Massenet's *Werther*; luckily, Scottish Opera's new production is just that, says Rupert Christiansen."[3] As Gillard, Christiansen does not hold back his own views, but in addition to their statement, Christiansen addresses them from a critical distance. For example, here are his opening remarks in a review of *Medea* at the English National Opera:

> A small miracle has occurred at the London Coliseum. I was frankly dreading ENO's new production of Charpentier's *Medea*. French baroque opera is something I have never understood, let alone enjoyed, and after the last one I endured—Rameau's *Castor and Pollux*, also at ENO—I found myself in an embarrassing minority: all the top brass proclaimed it marvellous, while I slunk off bored silly.
> So here we go again. A deep breath, a stiffening slug of alcohol, and—well, it really wasn't as bad as all that. In fact, I largely enjoyed it.[4]

He then proceeds to elaborate on why he liked the production in contrast to prior expectations. Comments on the singers tend to be of similar length to those on production, which, as I argue later, is rare. For example, Christiansen comments on the tenor singing Werther:

> Jonathan Boyd is a young American tenor, with a light, sweet and heady voice that can't quite scale the climaxes or the broad phrases of Pourquoi me réveiller? But he looks the part, enunciates the text in excellent French, and seems to inhabit the music with genuine feeling [Christiansen, 2013a].

Gillard has around 270 words available for his online reviews in *The Daily Mail* (Gillard, 2012), Christiansen up to 400 (Christiansen, 2013b) in *The Telegraph*. Manuel Brug in the German national newspaper *Die Welt* has between 700 to 1,250 words available,[5] Bünning in German national newspaper *Frankfurter Allgemeine Zeitung* around 1,000 words.[6] This broader space allows their reviews to develop more depth, to compare with other productions, and to bring in the history of the opera.

The national newspapers in the United Kingdom will cover predominantly work in London, mainly from the Royal Opera House Covent Garden and the English National Opera, with less space available for some, not all, productions elsewhere in the United Kingdom. The national daily newspapers in Germany cover productions in the major opera houses across Germany, such as those in Munich, Berlin, Hamburg and Frankfurt, or those close to their location, while regional and local newspapers will cover productions in their areas. With more than half the number of all opera houses in the world to be found in Germany, there is a considerable demand on reviewing.

The German magazine *Opernwelt*, which appears monthly both in print and online with some eighty pages per issue in a slightly larger than A4/letter formats, runs around four major articles per issue, ranging from extensive discussions of one production, to comparisons of two relevant productions. Thus the January 2013 issue, for example, compares productions of *Pelléas et Mélisande* in Essen and Frankfurt, discusses the production by Jossi Wieler and Sergio Morabito in Stuttgart of Edison Denisov's *L'Écume des jours*, reviews a Handel-project by Christoph Marthaler in Zurich, and compares two approaches to Mozart by contemporary directors renowned for their *Regietheater* approach: Hans Neuenfels and *La finta giardiniera* and Barrie Kosky, *Die Zauberflöte*. The magazine features a major interview in each issue—for example one with Wolfgang Sawallisch in the January 2013 issue—provides a section of reviews of CDs and DVDs, a section of reviews of productions from across the country, indeed from across the world (fifteen in the January 2013 issue), a range of information services, such as brief news about singers, companies and productions, forthcoming events, and performance schedules of those opera houses across the world that choose to provide their information to the magazine. Altogether, at least three quarters of the material in the magazine is thus some form of review.

In the United Kingdom, the magazine *Opera*, published monthly with around 144 pages per issue in A5/half of letter size formats, has around fifty pages worth of reviews from across the world, and twenty pages of reviews from across Britain, in addition to ten pages of reviews of books, CDs and DVDs and Blu-ray (for the January 2013 issue). There are some major features on opera, such as profiles of artists and interviews, and service sections with information about performance schedules and industry news. *Opera Now*, also published monthly, in A4/letter format, sells at a similar retail price as *Opera*, but in comparison with both *Opernwelt* and *Opera*, it carries much less text and many more adverts for productions across the world.

Opera blogs are typically the work of individuals who go to the opera a lot and want to share their experience with others, inviting their readers to comment on their blogs. Examples are *oper aktuell*[7] by Kaspar Sannemann, who writes in German predominantly about opera in Switzerland and Germany, *wellsung*, with contributions from alex and jonathan,[8] and *Intermezzo*.[9] Some bloggers do not reveal their personal identity.

Comments on the Composer, Score and Libretto

For well-established opera of the canon, critics do not mention the composer at all, taking the knowledge of their readers for granted. For reviews of less well-known composers, or operas, and world premieres, critics provide context and description. Badelt, for example, provides the context for a (rare) production of Marschner's *Der Vampyr* with reference to Weber's *Freischütz* and Wagner's *Der Fliegende Holländer* concerning the plot elements of a damned man who has to carry out a horrible deed before a deadline, of a father who barters his daughter away, and the hero who has to see how his beloved falls for the villain.[10] Badelt provides information about the date of origin, 1828, and the place, Leipzig, and places the libretto in the context of gothic horror, more specifically the circle around Lord Byron. The critic provides further context by quoting Richard Wagner's pejorative comments on Marschner's opera, "gelehrt-impotente, deutsch versohlte und verlederte italienische Musik" (Badelt, 2013, 40) [academic-impotent Italian music that has been given a German sole and German leather], but points out that Wagner nevertheless learnt much from Marschner's *Der Vampyr* and developed it further for his own opera *Der Fliegende Holländer*. In these few words, Badelt creates a framework in which to consider Marschner's opera, with an accomplished achievement of putting the libretto to music, and a work of art that Wagner criticized perhaps more from envy, but used to develop his own (implicitly superior) work. The critic proceeds by referring to further common assumptions of *Der Vampyr* as the missing link between Weber and Wagner, adding that this evaluation does not do the music justice—an assessment that is in line with the evaluation that Wagner had much to learn from Marschner. About the music, Badelt writes:

> Die Partitur peitscht die Handlung in langen Bögen voran, die Streichertremoli der Gruselszenen kontrastieren mit den lieblichen Bläsermelodien des Liebespaares und derben, ausgelassenen Volkstümlichkeiten, wie sie Wagner später der norwegischen Besatzung von Dalands Schiff zuschreibt [Badelt, 2013, 40].
>
> [The score whips the narrative forward in long arcs, the string tremolos of the creepy scenes contrast with the sweet melodies of the couple and with rough, boisterous popularities in the ways that Wagner later attributes to the Norwegian crew of Daland's ship.]

Writing about a production of the opera *Le Bal* by Argentinian composer Oscar Strasnoy (b. 1970), Markus Thiel provides similar context. He tells his readers that the opera was premiered in 2010 at the State Opera in Hamburg, one of the leading opera houses in Germany: this gives weight to the revival under review, in 2012, of the opera by one of the leading German training institutions, Bayerische Theaterakademie. The critic provides further context with reference to the librettist's name, Matthew Jocelyn, and the source for the plot, a novella by Irène Némirovsky. Thiel describes the music as a bouquet, ranging from folk song via Charleston, the sound of sewing machines, small open loops, sheet lightning from sound in neon light all the way to quotes from Mahler.[11]

Kopernikus by Claude Vivier, composed in 1978/79, was presented by the Young Opera Company in Freiburg, Germany, in 2012. Georg Rudiger describes Vivier's music as "vertraut und fremd, beruhigend und verstörend"[12] [familiar and unfamiliar, comforting and unsettling]. He describes the composer's experiences with music on a long journey through East Asia as influential for the rhythms and instruments of his opera, and gives this example:

> Der geschärfte Ton von Trompete, Posaune, Oboe und Violine wird von den drei Klarinetten gebunden. Röhrenglocken, Tam Tam und ein balinesischer Gong schaffen eine spirituelle Atmosphäre" [Rudiger, 2013, 39].
>
> [The sharpened tone of trumpet, trombone, oboe and violin is bound by the three clarinets. Tubular bells, Tam Tam and a Balinese gong create a spiritual atmosphere.]

In her review of David T. Little's opera *Dog Days*, which premiered at Montclair State University in New Jersey in 2012, Heidi Waleson provides the context with brief reference to the plot—a post–World-War III scenario in which the main character, a thirteen-year-old girl, befriends a man disguised as a dog—her family initially tolerate his presence, but "when hunger wins out, they kill and eat him."[13] She describes the music as follows: "Composer David T. Little deftly incorporates music theatre as well as traditional operatic writing, and the score has an underlying rhythmic pulse that reflects his background as a rock drummer" (Waleson, 2013, 59). Waleson writes about the music of other recent opera premieres in North America with comments on the "banally tonal piano accompaniment," on the "exercise in musical obviousness, including some hackneyed 'Middle Eastern' melismas," and on the piece being "by turns wry and heartfelt, shifting in tone from the comic, swing-accompanied courtship, the jazz-inflected birth scene," and refers to a character's (!) vocal techniques and Lieder-inspired arias, to "rock'n'roll rebellion and romantic yearning" (Waleson, 2013, 59).

Comments on the Production

The debate regarding the role of the director in the context of an opera production has focused on the alleged binary opposite of *Werktreue* and *Regieoper* (applied to opera from the term coined in conjunction with theatre as *Regietheater*). *Werktreue* can be understood as the director's commitment to do as much justice as possible to the perceived intentions of the composer and librettist in the process of translating the libretto from page to stage in conjunction with the conductor who is in charge of the score. The director becomes the servant of the art form, in the service of the librettist, as much as the conductor is in the service of the composer. Related terms are *traditional*, *conventional* and *orthodox*. *Regieoper*, in contrast, places emphasis on the ideas that the director develops inspired by, and in relation to the combination of libretto and score. The director is no longer anyone's servant and develops an idea, often referred to as a concept, for the production and puts that idea or concept into practice over the rehearsal period. The historical development in opera is one from *Werktreue* to *Regieoper*, in parallel to the development within theatre: initially, the role of the director was to ensure singers or actors knew when to enter and exit the stage, leaving the activity of actors in theatre predominantly to improvisation, and not expecting from singers more than predominantly stationary delivery as close as possible to the ramp.

The opposition between the two comes into play if we consider results of the *Werktreue* approach as old-fashioned, lifeless, boring, and "fundamentalist in nature even if necessary for the discussion of opera and theatre"[14] and *Regieoper* as dynamic, associated with ideas, provocation and confrontation (Balme, 43). The opposition can be found equally between the view of *Regieoper* as the apparent disregard for the original work, with traditionalists unable to see directorial decisions as resulting from, or as intrinsic to the work, but as superimposed arbitrarily on the work and thus artificial, an expression of decadence. In contrast to that view of *Regieoper*, *Werktreue* represents the view that the director's role is to express for the audience the composer and librettist's perceived intentions without any conceptual superimposition of their own. As Heather MacDonald put it, productions following the *Werktreue* approach "allow the beauty of some of the most powerful music ever written to shine forth." MacDonald, writing in 2007, associates many European, in particular German, directors with *Regieoper* and sets up the Metropolitan Opera House in New York as a bastion of the *Werktreue* approach.[15]

According to Klonovsky, *Regieoper* is characterized by an egalitarian view of history and people, epitomized by the word "downwards": nothing is great, nothing is beautiful, nothing has turned out well, in particular no human being. The only acceptable perspective on important people is that of the valet (who does not understand or accept anything beyond his sphere), and great deeds are the results of addictions, vanity and inhibitions. The lowest common denominator is that all people have sex, and that needs to be presented on stage as a result. The existence of high culture is considered by leftist intellectuals, among whom Klonovsky counts representatives of *Regieoper*, as suspect and scandalous.[16]

Rather than remaining general, some critics provide details as to where libretto and score do not match directors' choices: MacDonald, for example, writes about the 2011 Salzburg Festival production of Mozart's *Le nozze di Figaro* by Claus Guth:

> Lost, too, is the humor. The recognition scene, in which Figaro and Marcellina improbably discover their mother-son relationship, embodied Guth's cluelessness about comic tradition. The repeated "Sua madre's!" and "Tuo padre's!" of the startled participants should be a moment of ebullient silliness, as indicated by the music's mounting pitches, unbroken major harmonies, and accelerating tempo; instead, the characters stood around woodenly, looking uncomfortable, alienated, and glum. Figaro nervously cleaned his glasses rather than joyfully embrace his long-lost mother. The delightful fillip dissing the Count which ends the episode fell hollowly among this unhappy new family. Not surprisingly, the scene elicited not a chuckle from the audience on the night I saw it, nor was it apparently meant to—contrary to the patent intentions of Mozart and Da Ponte.[17]

Regieoper finds many voices in its defense, which tend to be as sophisticated as those defending violence on screen or extreme body art among performance installations. A closer look at alleged analysis in favor, or even in defense of *Regieoper* tends to reveal much detailed description of offending productions, which is equally present in texts against *Regieoper*, in addition to phrases that reveal hermetically sealed jargon: Steier's comment on Bieito's 2003 production of Mozart's *Die Entführung aus dem Serail* is a suitable example.

> Setting the piece in a glittery, violent, vaguely eastern European whorehouse, peppered with guns, drugs, and all varieties of bodily fluid and physical assault, Bieito cut through any sentimental/contextual membrane protecting the opera from the stomach-churning brutality of such modern phenomena as human trafficking and snuff-films. In addition to the unswervingly committed cast, the Komische Oper hired 15 professional adult entertainers to fill out the sordid aesthetic texture of Bieito's vision.[18]

What precisely is a membrane of any further description (here: "sentimental/contextual") in relation to an opera? What does the specific descriptor "sentimental / contextual" mean, precisely? What is the relationship between this particular opera and modern phenomena such as "human trafficking and snuff films," precisely? What is the purpose of the employment of "professional adult entertainers," precisely? In each case, the argument lacks precision and does not hold up to scrutiny.

In the remainder of this section, I discuss a specific production of Wagner's *Tristan und Isolde*, and critical response to it, which was explicitly in the *Werktreue* tradition. There is a Richard Wagner Association in Minden, Germany, a town of 83,000 inhabitants on the river Weser in North-Rhine Westphalia. There is also a municipal theatre in the town, built in 1908 and refurbished in 2012. The theatre does not have its own company; it is a receiving house only. In 2002, Jutta Hering-Winckler, a solicitor in Minden and chair of the Richard Wagner Association, arranged a professional production of *Der Fliegende Holländer* to be produced in Minden and performed at the municipal theatre. In 2005, a production of *Tannhäuser* followed, in 2009 came *Lohengrin*, and *Tristan und Isolde* in 2012. The music for all four productions was provided by the *Nordwestdeutsche Philharmonie*, conducted by Frank Beermann. The production had been publicized, in the local newspaper, with special reference to Matthias von Stegmann as the director as a guarantor of the *Werktreue* approach. Von Stegmann had worked for many years as an assistant director at the Bayreuth Festival, including work with Wolfgang Wagner on numerous productions. He had assisted Wagner also for the 1997 production of *Lohengrin* at the New National Theatre in Tokyo, where he returned to direct his own productions of *Der Fliegende Holländer* (2009) and *Lohengrin* (2012). Von Stegmann has been known, in Germany, as an actor in dubbing; he has written German dubbing scripts, and directed dubbing; in particular, he has been in charge of the German dubbing of *The Simpsons* (translation and direction) for a number of years now.

In one of the numerous articles in the local newspaper, *Mindener Tageblatt*, prior to the opening night on 8 September 2012, von Stegmann pointed out that he does not always consider the intellectualizing of certain contents as healthy. For *Tristan und Isolde*, the spectator must take part in the life and the suffering.[19] The set for the production supports this directorial approach, designed by Frank Phillip Schlößmann, who created the set design for the 2006 production of Wagner's *Ring* cycle for the Bayreuth Festival. The orchestra pit in the Minden municipal theatre is too small to accommodate an 80 musician Wagner orchestra. Thus the pit was covered and the opera's action took place on top of it. In this constellation of the theatre space, the singers were literally within reach of spectators in the front row. Von Stegmann considered this proximity as a danger, but also an exciting challenge to develop the level of authenticity needed for spectators so close to the singers to believe their emotions fully and at every moment (Koch, 2012a). Some of von Stegmann's explanations to the singers at the first rehearsal were documented in the *Mindener Tageblatt*: "I want pure emotion up there. That will be demanding. At every second you need to know what you are doing and why you are doing it." With regard to the proximity of stage and spectators, he pointed out that "large gesture of opera will not work," and advised the singers to "think in filmic terms: the end result should look like Chekhov or Strindberg." Von Stegmann emphasized again that he does not want to hide behind a concept that he superimposes on the opera from the outside. He told his singers that they would all get to their emotional limits in working with this opera, but assured them that he was on their side.[20]

The orchestra was further back on the stage, and separated from the stage space allocated to the action by a gauze. The orchestra was thus in full view of the audience. The stage floor was built as a slope, rising towards the back of the stage. The front part, up unto the gauze, was made from wooden floor boards painted in a light lilac color. At the very back of the stage, behind the orchestra, was a screen on to which different shades and colors of light were projected, in line with the music and the plot. Overall, the set created the image of a ship, with the screen shaped as the bow, and the auditorium as the stern, with the stage up to the gauze as the main back part of the ship and the conductor as the helmsman. Within this image of a stylized ship, the breath of the audience could be considered almost as the wind in the ship's sails.

When the audience entered the auditorium, the stage was open to view fully, lit by the lights in the auditorium. The orchestra musicians were at their desks behind the gauze, which was lit blue. When the house lights went down, the lights on stage came on, Isolde took her place in one of the boats, Brangäne sat near another boat, and Kurwenal was in the background. The conductor arrived, the overture started. Isolde was reading a book, not quite able to concentrate, a number of books were piled on the floor next to the boat she was in, she flipped the pages, read here and there, nervous, agitated, possibly bored. Real life took place in front of our eyes: music, set, changing light, singers, singing, libretto, facial expressions, gestures and glances, all became one, illustrating in surprising detail what is likely the genuine meaning of *Gesamtkunstwerk*, total work of art.

Repeated viewing could possibly allow spectators to pick up on, and remember, all of the minute detail of what happened on stage. Most striking moments included the way Tristan and Isolde behaved when they had drunk the love potion instead of the death drink. Both became love-struck teenagers, in very different, but clearly masculine and feminine ways, respectively, very moving and only slightly comical, so as not to distract from the serious nature of the situation as highly problematic within the opera's overall plot. Neither could help the power of the potion, neither was able to "think straight" any more, all they knew was the attraction to each other, which is love in both a spiritual sense, as eros, and a physical sense as sexuality. The production managed to make this holistic level of their experience clear, for example when Tristan and Isolde moved closer to each other as if to kiss, only for Isolde to break away from the kiss when their lips were almost touching, to place her face on Tristan's chest in a loving embrace.

Kurwenal was very surprised at what he observed, helpless, confused, and the realization of what she had caused hit Brangäne quite visibly. Both had to use the maximum physical strength they had available to literally tear Tristan and Isolde apart so as to keep up appearances when King Marke arrived. When Marke discovered Tristan and Isolde at the end of Act II, the color of Isolde's dress matched that of Marke's coat and suit. While Marke lamented Tristan's betrayal, sitting on the sea trunk, Isolde came over to him and sat next to him, sad at his suffering, sad that it was caused by her, but at the same time not showing any signs of feeling guilty: she was under the influence of the love potion, and was thus not responsible for Marke's misery, and neither was Tristan. There was no conflict here for her, or for Tristan.

At the beginning of Act III, we saw Tristan resting in a derelict boat; Kurwenal was busy washing out bloodied bandages from Tristan's wounds. There were many of them, and they were quite bloody, and Kurwenal tried his best with them, without achieving much. It was an image for the moving care that Kurwenal took of Tristan, but it showed also the helplessness of the rather rough man in carrying out this work that he probably never thought he would be doing: his movements were awkward, clumsy, quite inefficient, without any idea of hygiene, as one would expect from a man like him, but the fact that he still tried, and tried so obviously hard to do something almost against his very nature was genuinely moving. Contrary to the ending of the opera as suggested in the libretto, according to which Isolde sinks, in Brangäne's arms, on top of Tristan's corpse, in the Minden production Isolde left the stage in very bright white light.

It is revealing to analyze the way critics wrote about this production. Some noticed and conveyed a brief impression of the detail of the characters' actions and motivations. Critics described some of the nuances of the production with regard to the singers, generally pointing to their intensity and authenticity,[21] and describing Andreas Schager's Tristan as a boisterous, passionate firebrand and dare-devil, whose ego does not have space for self-doubt (Helming, 2012), and noting the tear that Dara Hobbs sheds as Isolde during her *Liebestod* at the end of the opera.[22] Other details noted by the critics included the splinter from Morold's sword that Isolde wore as a memento on a necklace, with Tristan entering with the rest of the sword.[23] In a long review in *Der Neue Merker*, Pfabigan commented very favorably on the director's highly sophisticated attention to detail that renders every breath, every glance, every step and every phrase into a spectator's very personal experience.[24]

Critics also noted the imaginative, detailed use of light throughout the production, such as velvety blue for the love scene in Act II, complete with starry sky that changes its light constellation in line with music and libretto. The skeleton of a boat that hung high from the ceiling over the orchestra in Act III, was lit red during Tristan's long monologue of suffering (Groenewold, 2012). Groenewold referred to the production as a concentrated psychodrama, in which the effort to choreograph movements, gestures and glances as naturally and precisely as possible is evident, so as not to allow pathos to seep in. She attests a fine sense of stage dynamics, and awareness of the power of calmness to von Stegmann (Groenewold, 2012). In her review in the national newspaper *Frankfurter Allgemeine Zeitung*, Eleonore Büning concluded that it has been a long time since audiences were able to see emotion on stage and not only in the music (Büning, 2012). Brockmann combined observation of detail with more general writing, emphasizing what the director did not do rather than what he did, or what the effect may have been of what he did: von Stegmann told the story *without* inappropriate additions, interpretations, or references to Wagner's biography (Brockmann, 2012). Helming described the production in general terms as "directorial chamber theatre" and adds that it "abstains from updating and re-interpretations characteristic of *Regietheater*" (Helming, 2012). Similarly, Manuel Brug in the national newspaper *Die Welt* called von Stegmann's production simple but moving, with nothing negative distracting from the music (Brug, 2012).

Thus, the reviews of the Minden *Tristan und Isolde* praise the production; some critics described some instances of detail, others combined general comments with indications that the high quality of the production was achieved because of various things the director could have done but did not do, fortunately. Altogether, however, it is fair to say that directors of the *Regieoper* category can expect to get many more words for their concept and its details, even if that does not entail praise. Such an imbalance of direct critical attention to the director's work raises the question to what extent sparse comments on a director's high level of praiseworthy, but (?!) uncontroversial achievement, in comparison to more detailed and precise comments on controversial *Regieoper* directors, do in fact tempt or seduce particularly younger directors to abandon any attempt at *Werktreue* in favor of *Regieoper*.

Von Stegmann emphasized in interviews that several aspects of his production were based on gut feeling and intuition rather than intellectually conceived in terms of a concept. The violet color of the wooden floor boards is an example, as is Isolde's exit at the end of the opera. In the latter von Stegmann was inspired by the music, which does not suggest sadness any longer, but calm departure and closure: she is liberated, it is almost a kind of apotheosis, a dissolving. It may be that she dies, or that she moves into a different dimension,

Comments on the Orchestra and the Conductor

When it comes to the assessment of the achievements of orchestra and conductor, space typically given to that assessment is much shorter than for the production, which cannot achieve much depth. Here are some examples of this: "Patrick Fournillier conducted with energy and vitality, drawing some beautiful sounds from the orchestra."[25] "The Slowenian conductor Marko Leontja gave a sharply focused, balanced reading of this richly descriptive, colourful score that deserves to be heard more widely."[26] "Will Humburg proved once again that he is an explosively dramatic conductor, but he also granted the melodious highlights some intensity."[27] A few more words are given to more famous conductors, for example: "Daniel Barenboim, La Scala music director, shaped the preludes [of *Lohengrin*] as if they were velvet—shimmering and lustrous. The mellifluous strings in the orchestra were colourful but not oversaturated, and created an otherworldly vibe."[28]

More detailed, critical portraits of conductors can yield more meaningful information and both descriptive and evaluative vocabulary. In summer 2012, three critics writing for *Der Neue Merker* spent three hours with conductor Peter Schneider (b. 1939) in Bayreuth, where he has been the longest-serving conductor at the Wagner Festival to date (twenty seasons up to 2012). In what is part interview, part essay, they develop as close a portrait of his abilities as a conductor as possible. First of all, they consider him a conductor who is always and exclusively in the service of the composer, captures the composer's feelings and relates them to the audience. His intuition for the architecture and proportions of the music comes into play in this process, as does his hard work on the scores he conducts, allowing him to come to his conducting fresh, and frequently with new insights often confirmed by reference to the composer's letters. Beyond intuition and work, with a hot heart and a cool head, energies flow between him and his orchestra, and between the orchestra under his baton and the audience. It may be difficult to describe the energies themselves in more depth, but it is possible, the critics argue on the basis of having followed Schneider's work for years, to gauge the impact of those energies:

> Wenn sich etwa im Orchester während eines "Figaro"-Dirigates mehr und mehr fröhliche Leichtigkeit ausbreitet, die Musiker mit einem Lächeln auf den Lippen spielen, ein drive, ein Sog entsteht—solche Kommunikation, solch gegenseitiges Erspüren haben die Interviewenden immer wieder erlebt, wenn Peter Schneider am Pult steht.[29]
>
> [If, for example, more and more cheerful lightness spreads within the orchestra during a conducting engagement of *Figaro* and the musicians play with a smile on their lips and a drive and pull are created—again and again the interviewers have experienced such communication, such mutual sensing, when Peter Schneider is on the rostrum.]

In the production of Wagner's *Siegfried* in Vienna, John Treleaven as Siegfried and Linda Watson as Brünhilde had rehearsed the opera's finale in such a way that they were meant to roll around on the ground. However, Watson and Treleaven could not help but stand on the top of the rock that was part of the set, hand in hand, and joyously celebrate their "Leuchtende Liebe, lachender Tod," because of the way Schneider conducted the music. When he conducts, *Der Rosenkavalier* by Strauss turns into

> [zu einer einzigen, beschwingten Traumsequenz wird, als werde im Geiste ständig von Verliebten Walzer getanzt. Das Orchester trifft unter seiner Leitung sofort den richtigen „Tonfall" und führt Publikum und Sänger geradewegs hinein in die musikalische Seligkeit (vor allem im Terzett) und alle lassen sich tragen von diesen berückenden Klängen und ihrem Kraftstrom der Gefühle] [Voigt et al. 2012].

a single, lilting dream sequence, as if, in thought, lovers were dancing the waltz constantly. Under his direction, the orchestra immediately hits the right "tone" and leads the audience and singers straight into the musical bliss (especially in the trio) and all can be carried by these enchanting sounds and its forceful current of emotions.

Comments on the Singers

Singing is a major component of opera: together with the music created by the orchestra under the leadership of their conductor, and the production created by director and designer(s), it constitutes practice—the creative interpretation of the texts of score and libretto. As with the theatre and its actors, opera singers are in fact the artists whom audiences will be most immediately aware of in any operatic performance, because it is the singers that are in front of them on the stage throughout the performance. However, most critical reviews of opera might suggest otherwise: typically, two thirds of the review of a well-known opera from the canon will be taken up with comments on the production, the director's concept, and the related design, with one third dedicated to the singers and the conductor with his/her orchestra.

When it comes to describing the singer's achievements, and even their shortcomings, critical vocabulary can be limited in scope and imagination, vague, repetitive, and clichéd. Here is a selection of the more imaginative range of language found in reviews of recent and current Wagner tenors: Stig Anderson's singing has been described as effortless and lissome.[30] Two categories emerge from this account. On the one hand, while singing naturally requires an effort on the part of the singer, such effort shows with some singers, and does not show with others—the ability of singing that comes across as effortless is the ideal. The other category is the kind of sound the singer produces, here specifically its width. Some sounds come across as full, or ample, with "beefy" or "throaty" on the negative end of the spectrum, implying a certain unwieldy quality of the voice that lacks elegance, while others are slim, lissome or elegant.

In the Italian repertory, Jose Cura might be considered on the beefy side, while Alfredo Kraus's voice is definitely one of the most elegant in recorded history. The repertoire, of course is a factor in this but only to some extent. While Cura sings the part of Verdi's Otello, for which a heavier voice like his is required, Kraus never sang that part because his voice was not suited to it. However, in further comparison, Domingo's rendering of Otello never attracted the characterization of "beefy."

Further categories emerge in the critical assessment of Johan Botha, who gave Siegmund a bright glaze, singing him almost like Lohengrin[31]; he sings with vocal shading, nuances and elegant phrasing, and effortlessly.[32] "He sings with lyrical expression, excellent diction, and much tonal beauty—and his voice is quite smooth. ... He sings ... with melting tones."[33] Critics thus employ the category of effort, and add the category of comparing the singing of one role (Siegmund) with that of another role (Lohengrin). This approach implies assumptions about roles, canonized ideas of how a certain role should be sung (in this case, the specific expectations regarding the ways Lohengrin should be sung, or is commonly sung). In comparison, the role of Siegmund, which, this comment suggests, has often been sung in a way quite different from Lohengrin, so that a singer who does sing Siegmund in a Lohengrin fashion attracts (potentially favorable) attention. Further categories that can be isolated in comments about Botha are diction and phrasing, the ways in which the singer pronounces the words of the libretto. The descriptions above also add to the sub-categories of the kind of sound a singer produces: in addition to width, there are intensity of light emanating from a voice: "bright," the question of whether the voice produces uniform tone or "vocal shading," the quality of the voice in terms of whether it sounds rough or smooth ("quite smooth" for Botha), taken from the sense of touch, and "melting" as an example of the sub-category of relating the sound of the voice to qualities and characteristics of inanimate or even animate objects.

Another example of this particular sub-category is a critic's assertion that Richard Decker performed "rather woodenly" as Parsifal.[34] His Tannhäuser was praised as full of flexibility, richness of color and nuances, and a balance of lyric and dramatic sound.[35] Here, we can see the addition of the sub-category of color, and reference to the "Fach," that is the system of classifying the voices of operatic singers, with lyric and dramatic relevant in the context of a Wagner tenor. Burkhard Fritz sings with a voice that he guides, or controls, well, leading to a floating sound. He commands a mature, metallic vigor, "sounding as fresh and untroubled at the end of the evening as he did at the beginning."[36] Voice control emerges here as a further category. An adjective to add to the list of those in the sub-category of comparison with animate and inanimate objects is "metallic." A singer's ability to sustain his singing at an even level of achievement across the course of a long performance constitutes the category of energy and persistence. This characteristic is closely related to effort.

Robert Gambill gained both praise and criticism as Siegmund: he sings his "introspective passages with remarkable sweetness and sensitivity; as soon as he applies pressure, however, his not-so-heroic tenor trembles mightily."[37] As Tristan, critics commented on a "solid, shiny assumption, facing all the difficulties ... with genuine accomplishment,"[38] describing his voice as "youthful and baritonal."[39] As Tannhäuser, Gambill "delivers a thrilling performance. It cannot be said that the peaks are scaled without effort, but the account of the music is scrupulous down to the grace notes in the hymn to Venus, the articulation of the text incisive rather than rhetorical."[40] "Sweetness" is a further example of a term related to the sense of taste; "shiny" fits into the visual sense, light sub-category of kinds of sound. "Baritonal" adds a sub-category, closely linked to Fach, of the range of the voice. Other comments on Gambill address some of the categories defined above, such as effort, articulation, Fach, energy and persistence.

To Louis Gentile, critics have attested "A warm voice with baritone quality and ringing high notes." As for others, critics also note his "unmeasurable reserves for the third act" (here, for the part of Tristan in *Tristan und Isolde*). They comment on his "beautiful timbre, based in baritone color and full empathy, warm lyric, and clear diction."[41] Reference to the warmth of his voice suggests the new category of temperature within the context of the sense of touch; The description of the high notes as "ringing" is a rare instance of a sound being fathomed in terms of the sense that is in charge of perceiving sounds, hearing. "Baritonal" fits into the category of range of voice, "immeasurable reserves" into that of energy and persistence; diction is there, too. Ben Heppner has been praised for blend of bel canto smoothness and emotional subtlety.[42] This account brings us back to the sense of touch with "smoothness," technical terminology in "bel canto" akin to references to Fach and vocal range, and a new category can be isolated: the emotional dimension of singing, here captured as "emotional subtlety."

Jonas Kaufmann has a "lovely tenor voice, graced by a virile, burnished-baritonal timbre that took one by surprise when he skilfully flipped into a breathtakingly delicate, floated top."[43] Other varieties of comment include "Dark yet shining sound,"[44] "baritonally based tenor that can rise into gold-tipped high notes with a visceral thrust,"[45] and "his vocal palette ranging from lyric to dramatic, his top notes thrilling, his youthful enthusiasm ever-present, his communicative talent spellbinding,"[46] and "His singing was supple and resonant, his tone velvety on the edges but steely at its core."[47] Adjectives used in these impressions of Kaufmann's voice add to the list of existing categories: "burnished," "dark" and "shining" are part of the visual light category, there is the reference to the singer's range of voice, "gold" is part of the visual category of color, and "virile" and "visceral" suggest energy. "Resonant" is another rare contribution to describing a sound through a term specifically related to the sense of hearing; "velvety" comes under the sense of touch, and "steely" is a further example of the category of characteristics of animate/inanimate objects. An interesting spatial dimension of the voice is identified with reference to different characteristics at the voice's edges and its core.

Translated from German reviews, Scott MacAllister's tenor is praised for being "stay-the-course"[48] bright, slim, full of radiant energy, silvery trumpet sounds, cantilevered streaming voice.[49] "Stay-the course" refers to energy and persistence, "bright" is in the visual sense light category, "slim" in the visual sense width category, "silvery" in the visual sense color category, while "trumpet sounds" is a further example of a comparison from the auditory sense itself.

Simon O'Neill's debut as Othello drew this extended description:

> the voice, though absolutely not Italian-sounding, has a clean, clear, clarion ring to it—think maybe King, or Wunderlich—that struck me as plain thrilling. The opening "Esultate" was as rock-solidly focused, powerfully projected as I've ever heard, not the usual honking bronze (if you're lucky) but somehow more like silvery-blue tempered steel; and yet the plaintive tone required by the love duet, including an exquisitely floated, plumb-in-tune "Venere splende" at the very end was effortlessly, most beautifully forthcoming.[50]

In addition to the category of comparison with other roles, on the basis of references here to King or Wunderlich we can add the category of comparison with other singers. "Clarion ring" is appropriately from the context of sound, as is "honking." "Rock-solid" falls into the category of comparison with inanimate objects; "bronze" alludes to visual sense color, as does "silvery-blue," combined with a further inanimate object, "steel," and reference to effort.

Critics commend Lance Ryan's steely voice[51] (reference here to the inanimate object), with a secure and fanfarish upper radiance.[52] Security may be related to control, or represents a separate category. "Fanfarish" adds an adjective to the sound context. Peter Seiffert's singing has been described as open-throated, clearly projected and accurate,[53] "smooth, attractive but sometimes reedy-sounding."[54] "Open-throated" is an example of a separate category, relating to the singer's body. "Accurate" and "clearly projected" relate to control and security, together forming a category of singing technique. Klaus Florian Vogt's voice has been described as weightlessly high, bright, solid, gleaming, effortless, powerful, sweeping, and even, with beautifully heartfelt piano passages, which nevertheless reach all remote corners of the opera house; critics also commended his clear diction, which allows audiences to hear and understand every word.[55]

We have discovered a range of suitable categories in which to place descriptions of singing in opera. Critics can relate the singing they write about to singing that they consider well-known to their readers or listeners, in comparison with other roles or other singers. Technique comprises diction and phrasing, as well as accuracy of hitting the right notes, control of the singing, and that implies control of breathing, security and projection. Energy and persistence are related to this. With all of these, the singer has to make an effort, but the better the singer, the less of that effort will be obvious to the audience. Singers will be judged by the way they are able to convey the character's emotions not only in their acting on stage, but through their voices. Sometimes critics will relate singer's physical qualities to their singing. The kinds of sound the singer emits find a wide range of depictions, with comparisons or metaphors related to the music theory, to the senses, and to animate or inanimate objects. In the context of music theory, the sounds of voices are related to the Fach (such as lyric or dramatic), to the voice range (for example, a tenor who sounds baritonal), or epoch or style in the history of music (such as *bel canto*). In the context of inanimate objects, singing can be described as wooden, melting, or metallic. In the context of the senses, the visual sense dominates with terms from color, light and width (golden, silver; dark, bright, shiny; lissome, slim). The sense of touch appears in the context of singing described as smooth or rough, or velvety, or the metaphorical use of temperature, such as warmth. The sense of taste comes in through references to flavor, such as "sweet." The sense of hearing is represented by terms such as "resonant" and "ringing," or references to "clarion," or musical instruments such as trumpet, and fanfare.

In this essay I have considered opera criticism of live performance from a range of perspectives: the format or medium in which reviews are published, and the ways in which critics tend to comment on the composer, score and libretto (predominantly for new work). In terms of production, the essay focused on *Regieoper* versus *Werktreue*. I noted that most space of most reviews is dedicated to a discussion of the production, with much less space given to the orchestra, the conductor and in fact, and perhaps surprisingly, the singers, who are, after all, those whom the spectators (including the critics) see and hear on stage throughout a performance. Close analysis of the vocabulary used to describe and evaluate singers' achievements does reveal, however, the considerable range of categories of vocabulary available for that description and evaluation. The availability of, and ease of access to, recordings of the singers' voices through CD and DVD, TV and HD cinema broadcasts offers reviewers a considerable pool not only for comparison of live and recorded material, but also for the purpose of expanding and honing their own abilities of hearing in relation to the singers' voices, and their ability to describe critically the experience of what they have heard.

Notes

1. Gillard, David. 2012. A tawdry travesty of a Carmen from the Tarantino of Opera. *Mail online*, November 22. http://www.dailymail.co.uk/tvshowbiz/reviews/article-2237130/Carmen-London-Coliseum-review-A-tawdry-travesty-Calixto-Bieito.html (accessed March 29, 2013).
2. Gillard, David. 2011. Lady of the lake makes a big splash. *Mail Online*, July 29. http://www.dailymail.co.uk/tvshowbiz/reviews/article-2019929/Rusalka-review-Lady-lake-makes-big-splash.html (accessed March 29, 2013).
3. Christiansen, Rupert. 2013a. Werther, Scottish Opera, Theatre Royal, Glasgow, review. *Telegraph*, February 22. http://www.telegraph.co.uk/culture/music/opera/9888327/Werther-Scottish-Opera-Theatre-Royal-Glasgow-review.html (accessed March 29, 2013).
4. Christiansen, Rupert. 2013b. Medea, ENO, London Coliseum, review. *Telegraph*, February 17. http://www.telegraph.co.uk/culture/music/opera/9876030/Medea-ENO-London-Coliseum-review.html (accessed March 29, 2013).
5. Brug, Manuel. 2012. Liebestod im Lippischen. *Die Welt*, September 12. http://www.welt.de/kultur/musik/article109156791/Liebestod-im-Lippischen.html (accessed March 29, 2013).
6. Büning, Eleonore. 2012. Hier weht Bayreuths Fahne auf dem Dach. *Frankfurter Allgemeine Zeitung*, September 11. http://www.faz.net/aktuell/feuilleton/buehne-und-konzert/richard-wagner-in-minden-hier-weht-bayreuths-fahne-auf-dem-dach-11885449.html (accessed March 29, 2013).
7. *Oper aktuell* http://www.oper-aktuell.info/ (accessed March 29, 2013).
8. *wellsung*, http://wellsung.blogspot.co.uk/ (accessed March 29, 2013).
9. *Intermezzo* http://intermezzo.typepad.com/intermezzo/ (accessed March 29, 2013).
10. Badelt, Udo. 2013. Schön schaurig. *Opernwelt*. January. 40.
11. Thiel, Arkus. 2013. Ausser Sich. *Opernwelt*. January. 43.
12. Rudiger, Georg. 2013. Ihre Familie. *Opernwelt*. January. 39.
13. Weleson, Heidi. 2013. World Premieres in North America. *Opera Now*. February. 58.
14. Balme, Christopher. 2008. Werktreue. Aufstieg und Niedergang eines fundamentalistischen Begriffs. In *Regietheater! Wie sich über Inszenierungen streiten läßt*, ed. Ortrud Gutjahr, 43–52. Würzburg: Königshausen, 43.
15. MacDonald, Heather. 2007. The Abduction of Opera. *City Journal*, Summer. http://www.city-journal.org/html/17_3_urbanities-regietheater.html (accessed March 29, 2013).
16. Klonovsly, Michael. N.d. Herunter, Herunter. http://www.michael-klonovsky.de/content/view/104/42/ (accessed March 29, 2013).
17. MacDonald, Heather. 2011. Regietheater Takes Another Scalp. *City Journal*, August 24. http://www.city-journal.org/2011/bc0824hm.html (accessed March 29, 2013).
18. Steier, Lydia. 2004. Shock and awe in the German capitol. Online draft. July 24. http://www.striporama.com/steier_kids/Eine_Schande.htm (accessed March 29, 2013).
19. Koch, Ursula. 2012a. Zuschauer sollen mitleben und mitleiden. *Mindener Tageblatt*, April 21. http://www.mt-online.de/lokales/kultur/6621513_Tristan_und_Isolde_-_Zuschauer_sollen_mitleben_und_mitleiden.html (accessed March 29, 2013).
20. Koch, Ursula. 2012b. Erste Tuchfühlung mit der Mindener Bühne. *Mindener Tageblatt*, August 4. http://www.mt-online.de/lokales/kultur/6930162_Proben_zu_der_Eigenproduktion_Tristan_und_Isolde_starten.html (accessed March 29, 2013).
21. Helming, Christian. 2012. Premiere für "Tristan und Isolde": Kammerspiel und

Sinnenrausch. *Mindener Tageblatt*, September 10. http://www.mt-online.de/start/video/lokale_videos/7031059_Premiere_fuer_Tristan_und_Isolde_Kammerspiel_und_Sinnenrausch.html (accessed March 29, 2013).

22. Groenewold, Anke. 2012. Ekstatische Reise: Ein Erlebnis: Richard Wagners "Tristan und Isolde" in Stadttheater Minden. *Neue Westfälische Zeitung*, September 10. http://www.nw-news.de/owl/kultur/7022790_Ekstatische_Reise.html (accessed March 29, 2013).

23. Brockmann, Sigi. 2012. Minden: Tristan und Isolde—Premiere. *Der neue Merker*. http://www.der-neue-merker.eu/minden-tristan-und-isolde-premiere (accessed March 29, 2013).

24. Pfabigan, Sieglinde. 2012. Minden: Tristan und Isolde. *Der Neue Merker*. October. http://www.der-neue-merker.eu/minden-tristan-und-isolde (accessed March 29, 2013).

25. Lynn, Karyl Charna. 2013a. Manon Lescaut Puccini. *Opera Now*. February. 65.

26. Lynn, Karyl Charna. 2013b. Der Ferne Klang Schreker. *Opera Now*. February. 64.

27. Zimmermann, Christoph. 2013. Cologne. *Opera* 64 (1): 51.

28. Smith, Courtney. 2013. Lohengrin Wagner. *Opera Now*. February. 56.

29. Voigt, Kerstin, Sieglinde Pfabigan, Johann Schwarz. 2012. Peter Schneider: Dem Werk dienend, die eigene Person hintan stellend. *Der Neue Merker*. August. http://www.der-neue-merker.eu/peter-schneider-dem-werk-dienend-die-eigene-person-hintan-stellend (accessed March 29, 2013).

30. Pluta, Ekkehard. 2008. Schön erzählt. *Opernwelt*, September/October: 66.

31. Mösch, Stephan. 2008. Der innere Puls. *Opernwelt*, January: 48.

32. Persché, Gerhard. 2006. Traum vom Messias. *Opernwelt*, February: 48.

33. Moses, Kurt. 2005. Johan Botha. *American Opera Guide*, November/December: 274.

34. Hastings, Stephen. 2005. Venice. *Opera News*, June: 65.

35. Voigt, Kerstin. 2009. Tannhäuser. *Der neue Merker*. 26 November.

36. Bünning, Eleonore. 2005. Brust, Bauch, Helm, Speer. *Frankfurter Allgemeine Zeitung*, March 21. http://m.faz.net/aktuell/feuilleton/buehne-und-konzert/oper-brust-bauch-helm-speer-1211199.html (accessed March 29, 2013).

37. Bernheimer, Martin. 2007. Wagner: Die Walküre. *Opera News* 71 (7).

38. Hall, George. 2003. Glyndebourne. *Opera News* 68 (4).

39. Braun, William R. Video. 2008. *Opera News* 73 (1).

40. Gurewitsch, Matthew. 2009. Opera. *Opera News* 74 (6).

41. Gentile, Louis, Website. http://www.louisgentile.com (accessed March 29, 2013).

42. Freeman, John W. 2006 Ben Heppner. *Opera News* 71 (3).

43. Ketterson, Mark Thomas. 2008. Manon. *Opera News* 73 (6).

44. Shengold, David. 2008. International Export. *Opera News* 72 (11).

45. Mudge, Stephen J. 2007. Paris. *Opera news* 72 (3).

46. Leipsic, Jeffrey A. 2009. Munich. *Opera News* 74 (5).

47. Delacoma, Wynn. 2006. Sound Bites: Jonas Kaufmann. *Opera News* 70 (8).

48. Brug, Manuel. 2010. "Wagner's Tannhäuser ist jetzt bei der Heilsarmee." *Welt online* 10.3. Online at http://www.welt.de/kultur/article6715405/Wagners-Tannhaeuser-ist-jetzt-bei-der-Heilsarmee.html. Accessed 25.8.2010 (accessed March 29, 2013).

49. MacAllister, Scott, website http://www.scottmacallister.com/ (accessed March 29, 2013).

50. Jay-Taylor, Stephen. 2009. *Opera Britannica*, December 5.

51. Rothkegel, Thomas. 2007. Fest der Stimmen. *Opernwelt*. February: 45.

52. Kraft, Manfred. 2007. *Orpheus*. March/April.

53. Cohn, Fred. 2005. Tannhäuser. *Opera News* 69 (8).

54. Moses, Kurt. 1995. *American Record Guide* 58 (1): 244.
55. Zibulski, Axel. 2011. Schwerelos. *Allgemeine Zeitung*, July 29, http://www.allgemeine-zeitung.de/nachrichten/kultur/10995683.htm (accessed March 29, 2013); Döring, Ralph. 2011. Grandioser "Lohengrin" "Ein Wunder! Ein Wunder!" *Neue Osnabrücker Zeitung*, July 28. http://www.noz.de/deutschland-und-welt/kultur/56025209/grandioser-lohengrin-ein-wunder-ein-wunder (accessed March 29, 2013); Schreiber, Wolfgang. 2011. Wagner-Energien: Neuenfels und Nelsons begeistern in Bayreuth mit dem "Lohengrin." *Süddeutsche Zeitung*, July 29. http://www.sueddeutsche.de/Y5338W/126052/Wagner-Energie.html (accessed March 29, 2013); Anon. 2011. Sternstunde der Oper: `Vom Feinsten: der "Lohengrin" reißt die Besucher der Bayreuther Festspiele zu Beifallsstürmen hin. *Welt Online*, July 29. http://www.welt.de/print/welt_kompakt/kultur/article13514088/Sternstunde-der-Oper.html (accessed March 29, 2013).

Bibliography

Anon. 2011. Sternstunde der Oper: `Vom Feinsten: der "Lohengrin" reißt die Besucher der Bayreuther Festspiele zu Beifallsstürmen hin. *Welt Online*, July 29. http://www.welt.de/print/welt_kompakt/kultur/article13514088/Sternstunde-der-Oper.html (accessed March 29, 2013).
Badelt, Udo. 2013. Schön schaurig. *Opernwelt*. January. 40.
Balme, Christopher. 2008. Werktreue. Aufstieg und Niedergang eines fundamentalistischen Begriffs. In *Regietheater! Wie sich über Inszenierungen streiten läßt*, ed. Ortrud Gutjahr, 43–52. Würzburg: Königshausen, 43.
Bernheimer, Martin. 2007. Wagner: *Die Walküre*. *Opera News* 71 (7).
Braun, William R. Video. 2008. *Opera News* 73 (1).
Brockmann, Sigi. 2012. Minden: Tristan und Isolde—Premiere. *Der neue Merker*. http://www.der-neue-merker.eu/minden-tristan-und-isolde-premiere (accessed March 29, 2013).
Brug, Manuel. 2010. "Wagner's Tannhäuser ist jetzt bei der Heilsarmee." *Welt online*, March 10. Online at http://www.welt.de/kultur/article6715405/Wagners-Tannhaeuser-ist-jetzt-bei-der-Heilsarmee.html (accessed March 29, 2013).
_____. 2012. Liebestod im Lippischen. *Die Welt*, September 12. http://www.welt.de/kultur/musik/article109156791/Liebestod-im-Lippischen.html (accessed March 29, 2013).
Büning, Eleonore. 2012. Hier weht Bayreuths Fahne auf dem Dach. *Frankfurter Allgemeine Zeitung*, September 11. http://www.faz.net/aktuell/feuilleton/buehne-und-konzert/richard-wagner-in-minden-hier-weht-bayreuths-fahne-auf-dem-dach-11885449.html (accessed March 29, 2013).
Bünning [Büning], Eleonore. 2005. Brust, Bauch, Helm, Speer. *Frankfurter Allgemeine Zeitung*, March 21. http://m.faz.net/aktuell/feuilleton/buehne-und-konzert/oper-brust-bauch-helm-speer-1211199.html (accessed March 29, 2013).
Christiansen, Rupert. 2013a. Werther, Scottish Opera, Theatre Royal, Glasgow, review. *Telegraph*, February 22. http://www.telegraph.co.uk/culture/music/opera/9888327/Werther-Scottish-Opera-Theatre-Royal-Glasgow-review.html (accessed March 29, 2013).
_____. 2013b. Medea, ENO, London Coliseum, review. *Telegraph*, February 17. http://www.telegraph.co.uk/culture/music/opera/9876030/Medea-ENO-London-Coliseum-review.html (accessed March 29, 2013).

Cohn, Fred. 2005. Tannhäuser. *Opera News* 69 (8).
Delacoma, Wynn. 2006. Sound Bites: Jonas Kaufmann. *Opera News* 70 (8).
Döring, Ralph. 2011. Grandioser "Lohengrin" "Ein Wunder! Ein Wunder!" *Neue Osnabrücker Zeitung*, July 28. http://www.noz.de/deutschland-und-welt/kultur/56025209/grandioser-lohengrin-ein-wunder-ein-wunder (accessed March 29, 2013).
Freeman, John W. 2006 Ben Heppner. *Opera News* 71 (3).
Gentile, Louis, Website. http://www.louisgentile.com (accessed March 29, 2013).
Gillard, David. 2011. Lady of the lake makes a big splash. *Mail Online*, July 29. http://www.dailymail.co.uk/tvshowbiz/reviews/article-2019929/Rusalka-review-Lady-lake-makes-big-splash.html (accessed March 29, 2013).
_____. 2012. A tawdry travesty of a Carmen from the Tarantino of Opera. *Mail online*, November 22. http://www.dailymail.co.uk/tvshowbiz/reviews/article-2237130/Carmen-London-Coliseum-review-A-tawdry-travesty-Calixto-Bieito.html (accessed March 29, 2013).
Groenewold, Anke. 2012. Ekstatische Reise: Ein Erlebnis: Richard Wagners "Tristan und Isolde" in Stadttheater Minden. *Neue Westfälische Zeitung*, September 10. http://www.nw-news.de/owl/kultur/7022790_Ekstatische_Reise.html (accessed March 29, 2013).
Gurewitsch, Matthew. 2009. Opera. *Opera News* 74 (6).
Hall, George. 2003. Glyndebourne. *Opera News* 68 (4).
Hastings, Stephen. 2005. Venice. *Opera News* 69 (7).
Helming, Christian. 2012. Premiere für "Tristan und Isolde": Kammerspiel und Sinnenrausch. *Mindener Tageblatt*, September 10. http://www.mt-online.de/start/video/lokale_videos/7031059_Premiere_fuer_Tristan_und_Isolde_Kammerspiel_und_Sinnenrausch.html (accessed March 29, 2013).
Intermezzo http://intermezzo.typepad.com/intermezzo/ (accessed March 29, 2013).
Jay-Taylor, Stephen. 2009. *Opera Britannica*, December 5.
Ketterson, Mark Thomas. 2008. Manon. *Opera News* 73 (6).
Klonovsly, Michael. N.d. Herunter, Herunter. http://www.michael-lonovsky.de/content/view/104/42/ (accessed March 29, 2013).
Koch, Ursula. 2012a. Zuschauer sollen mitleben und mitleiden. *Mindener Tageblatt*, April 21. http://www.mt-online.de/lokales/kultur/6621513_Tristan_und_Isolde_-_Zuschauer_sollen_mitleben_und_mitleiden.html (accessed March 29, 2013).
_____. 2012b. Erste Tuchfühlung mit der Mindener Bühne. *Mindener Tageblatt*, August 4. http://www.mt-online.de/lokales/kultur/6930162_Proben_zu_der_Eigenproduktion_Tristan_und_Isolde_starten.html (accessed March 29, 2013).
Kraft, Manfred. 2007. *Orpheus*. March/April.
Leipsic, Jeffrey A. 2009. Munich. *Opera News* 74 (5).
Lynn, Karyl Charna. 2013a. Manon Lescaut Puccini. *Opera Now*. February. 65.
_____. 2013b. Der Ferne Klang Schreker. *Opera Now*. February. 64.
MacAllister, Scott. Website http://www.scottmacallister.com/ (accessed March 29, 2013).
MacDonald, Heather. 2007. The Abduction of Opera. *City Journal*, Summer. http://www.city-journal.org/html/17_3_urbanities-regietheater.html (accessed March 29, 2013).
_____. 2011. Regietheater Takes Another Scalp. *City Journal*, August 24. http://www.city-journal.org/2011/bc0824hm.html (accessed March 29, 2013).
Mösch, Stephan. 2008. Der innere Puls. *Opernwelt*, January: 48.
Moses, Kurt. 1995. *American Record Guide* 58 (1): 244.
_____. 2005. Johan Botha. *American Opera Guide*, November/December: 274.
Mudge, Stephen J. 2007. Paris. *Opera news* 72 (3).
Oper aktuell http://www.oper-aktuell.info/ (accessed March 29, 2013).

Persché, Gerhard. 2006. Traum vom Messias. *Opernwelt*, February: 48.
Pfabigan, Sieglinde. 2012. Minden: Tristan und Isolde. *Der Neue Merker*. October. http://www.der-neue-merker.eu/minden-tristan-und-isolde (accessed March 29, 2013).
Pluta, Ekkehard. 2008. Schön erzählt. *Opernwelt*, September / October: 66.
Rothkegel, Thomas. 2007. Fest der Stimmen. *Opernwelt*. February: 45.
Rudiger, Georg. 2013. Ihre Familie. *Opernwelt*. January. 39.
Schreiber, Wolfgang. 2011. Wagner-Energien: Neuenfels und Nelsons begeistern in Bayreuth mit dem "Lohengrin." *Süddeutsche Zeitung*, July 29. http://www.sueddeutsche.de/Y5338W/126052/Wagner-Energie.html (accessed March 29, 2013)
Shengold, David. 2008. International Export. *Opera News* 72 (11).
Smith, Courtney. 2013. Lohengrin Wagner. *Opera Now*. February. 56.
Steier, Lydia. 2004. Shock and awe in the German capitol. Online draft. July 24. http://www.striporama.com/steier_kids/Eine_Schande.htm (accessed March 29, 2013).
Thiel, Markus. 2013. Ausser Sich. *Opernwelt*. January. 43.
Voigt, Kerstin. 2009. Tannhäuser. *Der neue Merker*. 26 November.
Voigt, Kerstin, Sieglinde Pfabigan, Johann Schwarz. 2012. Peter Schneider: Dem Werk dienend, die eigene Person hintan stellend. *Der Neue Merker*. August. http://www.der-neue-merker.eu/peter-schneider-dem-werk-dienend-die-eigene-person-hintanstellend (accessed March 29, 2013).
Waleson, Heidi. 2013. World Premieres in North America. *Opera Now*. February. 58.
Wellsung. http://wellsung.blogspot.co.uk/ (accessed March 29, 2013).
Zibulski, Axel. 2011. Schwerelos. *Allgemeine Zeitung*, July 29, http://www.allgemeine-zeitung.de/nachrichten/kultur/10995683.htm (accessed March 29, 2013)
Zimmermann, Christoph. 2013. Cologne. *Opera* 64 (1): 51.

Gods and Heroes
or Monsters of the Media?

Trevor Siemens

In a book that focuses on opera's place in a contemporary media culture, this essay provides a survey of the place of media culture in contemporary opera. Beginning with myth as a basic paradigm for operatic storytelling, this essay explores the relationship between myth and media in the narratives of operas composed over the past thirty years. To place these works in context, examples of operas that herald a changing approach to subject matter are drawn from earlier in the twentieth century; works that bridge the gap between the elevated characters, Gods and Heroes of myth, and a stage populated with the "ordinary" of contemporary life, works that mark a shift from magic to technology.

Whatever the subject matter, there is an important question to be answered when setting out to compose opera. For a composer in search of the sublime, wanting to avoid the ridiculous, the choice of subject and story was and is crucial in determining success. And the question that lies at the heart of this decision, the answer to which will make a piece work as music theatre: what makes the story sing?

For the Florentine Camerata, that select gathering of Renaissance intellectuals, artists and musicians who acted as opera's midwives, the answer flowed directly out of the very principles that informed the development of the first operas. In a desire to re-create an ancient and lost theatre out of the theories of Aristotle, the descriptions of Plato and the works of Euripides, these thinkers and composers naturally turned to the extant plays and literature of ancient Greece and Rome for their subject matter. The stories of Gods and Heroes provided an obvious, tangible and direct link to the past. More importantly for the development of the form however, was a cast of super-human characters in extraordinary circumstances that provided a rationale for the use of an elevated manner of communication; creating a drama in song instead of speech.

The earliest examples, Peri's *Euridice* and Monteverdi's *Orfeo*, put music at the heart of the drama, in stories that portray music's ultimate power, a power that triumphs over death.

The power of music to give voice to noble sentiment and to invoke pathos through stories of Gods and Heroes is a paradigm that works through much of the history of opera. Though this model can be most obviously traced in works from Baroque *opera seria* to Wagner, in the most general terms it also holds true in genres where composers have turned to more contemporary subject matter. Even in the comic operas of the eighteenth and nineteenth centuries the elevated status of the characters and the exceptional circumstances in which they find themselves places the drama at a remove from the mundane.

While composers and librettists have continued to place the gods and heroes of myth and literature on the operatic stage, there has been a move to engage more directly with contemporary life over the last century. Although the most obvious examples would be the *Zeitopern* created during the interwar years of the Weimar Republic, the concept of "opera of our time" has been pushed much further in our own generation. Beginning with John Adams' *Nixon in China* (1987), which was based on reports of the American President's landmark visit of 1972, the burgeoning media culture has fed stories and characters into opera. And not just the larger-than-life figures of international statesmen, but a spectrum including the 2003 story of Manchester teenagers caught up in an attempted murder in Nico Muhly's *Two Boys* (2011) and the rise and fall of a reality television star in Mark-Anthony Turnage's *Anna Nicole* (2011). The subject matter of these recent operas brings us to question whether celebrity has replaced the hero or has the media informed a new understanding of Gods and Heroes?

Early Models

Before turning our attention to operas composed in the past thirty years, it is worth exploring a few select works from the first half of the twentieth century; works that signal changes in composers' approach to operatic subject matter. To consider contemporary opera in the context of mass media and global communication, a context that holds the promise (if not the reality) of a more egalitarian social order, then it is worth starting with an opera that first placed the working classes center stage.

LOUISE

Gustave Charperntier's *Louise* (1900) is a kitchen-sink drama that focuses on the strained relationship between the eponymous shop-girl seamstress and her small-minded parents who try to thwart her relationship with the young bohemian, Julian. The story and libretto are Charpentier's own, although the narrative model may be found in a combination of familiar fairy-tales. At its core *Louise* is a mix between *Rapunzel* and *Beauty and the Beast*. It is the tale of a girl kept in isolation by a domineering parental figure, trapped in her parents' apartment, escorted to and from work by her mother and unable to explore the joys of Paris. Escaping this situation and having fallen in love with, if not a beast, then a member of the bohemian underclass, she is persuaded into a brief return to her parents' home to see her ailing father where an attempt is made to entrap her in her former state, deprived of life and love.

The narrative frame is classic fairy-tale, but with a cast devoid of witches and princes Charpentier uses it to directly address the political and social issues of his time. He places particular focus on the division of labor and the antagonism that lies between the weary, working poor and the free-spirited bohemians, as well as the challenge to the moral order presented by free-love. As a political gesture, it is clear that the composer meant *Louise* to challenge opera's bourgeois *status quo* and to democratize the form. As Steven Huebner points out, Charpentier argued "that only when characters from lower social classes carried as much "heroism and divinity" as figures from mythology could the lyric stage be a force for democracy."[1] During an interview given while still working on the opera, the composer spoke of his characters thus:

> they are workers. I have settled upon a milieu that I know well, and I make my workers sing as if they were dressed in armor [*sic*] or the usual doublet. It is not only kings and queens who have elevated sentiments; as far as I know, they do not have a monopoly on these. So why always put them on the stage? Why always champions, knights, and warriors of all kinds? [Quoted in Huebner, 144].

The elevated sentiment that lies at the heart of the drama and gives the characters voice is love.

Julian is a young man in love, and it is the serenade that he sings to Louise under her window at work that precipitates the crucial action of the drama—her running away with him at the end of the second act. But it isn't just Louise that Julian is in love with, it is Paris itself. And perhaps this is the true music at the heart of the opera—the music of Paris. As Julian sings in Act II, scene 4:

> Ah! chanson de Paris, où vibre et palpite mon âme!
> Naïf et vieux refrain du faubourg qui s'éveille,
> aube sonore qui réjouit mon oreille!
> Cris de Paris ... voix de la rue:
> Êtes-vous le chant de victoire de notre amour triomphant?
>
> [Oh song of Paris, wherein my soul trembles and beats.... The ancient and innocent refrain of the city as it wakes, the sound of

dawn that gladdens my ear, Cries of Paris ... the voice of the street,
Are you the victory song of our love triumphant?]²

This scene is set against Charpentier's re-creation of the sounds of the street; a chorus built of the contrapuntal cries and songs of the street vendors and cleaners, starting their day and selling their wares. Paris' significance is reinforced at the close of the opera when Louise's parents lose her for the second and final time. After calling out after his departed daughter, it is not "Julian" that the father cries, fist raised in the air, but "Paris," the city that has seduced her away.

JONNY SPIELT AUF

The trend towards *Neue Sachlichkeit* or the New Objectivity amongst the German intellectual and artistic community in the 1920s resulted in a body of music theatre known as *Zeitopern*. This was neither a movement nor a school, there is no associated manifesto or authoritative definition for the term; instead composers' focus turned away from the highly charged emotional content of Expressionism and toward an external, objective reality. The works reflect an active engagement with contemporary ideas of progress, advances in technology, communication and transport, as well as looking to find a musical connection with the everyday life of a broader audience. For many, the sensibility of *Neue Sachlichkeit* was embodied in the American way of life; for composers this could be integrated musically by embracing the popular genre of jazz.

The fascination with jazz, and the juxtaposition of a tired Europe with an energetic and progressive America sits at the center of Krenek's 1927 hit *Jonny Spielt Auf*, represented by the title character, a black jazz-band leader. As with Charpentier, Krenek created his own story and libretto for *Jonny*. Instead of following the pattern of a fairy tale, *Jonny* is a comedy; a story of lovers meeting, followed by a state of general confusion and mixed messages, with order being restored in a moment of absurd resolution at the close of the opera.

In *Jonny* the characters are neither drawn from the most elevated nor the lowest ends of the social spectrum, but neither are they ordinary for they are almost all musicians. Representing the Old World is Max, the northern European composer whose stagnation is embodied in his muse, a mountain glacier.³ Max's partner is an opera singer, Anita. Their foils symbolizing the "new world" are Jonny and his partner Yvonne, a maid and the only non-musician. One final character lies between these pairs of lovers, the charismatic (and southern European) violin virtuoso, Daniello. Over the course of the opera there is much swapping and stealing—of music and morals and partners. Jonny, with his looser moral code and his looser music, challenges the staid European establishment of Max and even Daniello. The defining action of the drama comes with Jonny's theft of Daniello's violin, an object that represents the best of the Old World, and leads the rest of the cast into pursuit as he attempts to take it back to the New World. Jonny summarizes the situation: "Mir gehört alles, was gut ist in der Welt. Die alte Welt hat es erzeugt, sie weiß damit nichts mehr zu tun. Da kommt die neue Welt" (I own everything that is good in the World. The Old World has produced it; they don't know what to do with it any more. Here comes the new world!).[4] The opera ends with Jonny and Yvonne on their way to America, followed by Max and Anita in search of new opportunity and rejecting the European establishment. Without a partner and with his violin transferred to Jonny, Daniello is dispatched under an oncoming train.

There is really no question as to why these characters sing: in a story peopled with musicians, whether it be *Orpheus* or *Jonny*, then music naturally permeates the story. As with Julian's serenade in *Louise*, there are instances of diegetic or "phenomenal"[5] music in *Jonny Spielt Auf*, including Max and Anita rehearsing a duet, and the off-stage jazz bands in the hotels. But the idea of voice plays two further roles of very different character in this work. In scene seven, Max, believing that he has lost Anita to Daniello, goes to commune with the Glacier. This is Max's descent to Hades to consult with the infinite—and Krenek gives the Glacier a voice—a chorus supported by sustained metallic percussion, a voice that sends Max back to the world. But before Max can act on the unwelcome command of the Glacier, he is summoned by the disembodied voice of his lover. Music that he has composed, sung by Anita, and played over the loudspeaker of a nearby hotel summons Max back to the world.

The fascination with the latest means of sound production and transmission and its incorporation at a critical moment of the story is an important feature that arises out of *Zeitopern*. In addition to sound technology, Krenek incorporates much contemporary "machine life" into *Jonny*, with working telephones, onstage train arrivals and a car "chase" all integral to the story. Where once composers used stage machinery to create the magic of other worlds onstage, Krenek and his contemporaries incorporated stage magic to bring the machinery and technology of everyday life into the theatre.

LA VOIX HUMAINE

Where the previous operas exemplify the democratization of culture of the media age and the placing of the drama into a contemporary technological context, the final example places communication technology at the core of the drama. Francis Poulenc's *tragédie lyrique*, *La Voix Humaine* (1959) is based on Jean Cocteau's play of the same name from 1930. This quasi-monodrama is set within the disheveled bedroom of a young woman, and opens with her prostrate on the floor in front of the bed; the action is precipitated by the ringing of the telephone. Over the course of a single act the opera follows the woman's side of a telephone conversation with the lover who has abandoned her after a five-year relationship. The woman passes through various states of agitation and desperation, as it is revealed that the man she still loves is on the eve of marriage to another woman. The opera closes with the suggestion that the woman will not make it through the night, as she winds the telephone cord around her neck.

Although this opera is written for a single performer onstage, the drama does not function as a monodrama like Schoenberg's *Erwartung*; essentially an extended soliloquy. In *La Voix* the telephone comes to signify the second character and provides a vital but transitory link to humanity and the world outside. It matters little that the telephone was not cutting-edge technology at the time, what is important in this context is the mediation of human communication, relationship and interaction through technology. Cocteau sums ups the situation perfectly in the woman's words: "Un regard pouvait changer tout. Mais avec cet appareil, ce qui est fini est fini" (Just a look could change everything. But with this telephone between us, what's done is done).[6]

It is also, perhaps, the telephone that gives this play voice as an opera. The woman's vocal lines rarely rise above a recitative; the closest Poulenc comes to providing an aria is an arioso-like section when the woman tells of her attempted suicide the previous evening to the accompaniment of a waltz. The dramatic scenario provides little opportunity for "phenomenal" music, only a few strains of jazz coming down the telephone line to make the woman aware that the man is not at home. The music instead functions in place of the unheard half of the conversation, although Poulenc never resorts to "composing" out responses. In the composer's own words "The entire work should be bathed in the greatest orchestral sensuality."[7]

In Our Time

In considering the approach of contemporary composers to both myth and media in operatic drama, an ideal starting point is a pair of works from the mid-eighties, John Adams' *Nixon in China* (1987) and Harrison Birtwistle's *The Mask of Orpheus* (1986). Although there is no definitive demarcation of musical eras in the mid-eighties, one can see the current compositional landscape as part of a continuum that arises from that time. Over the last three decades there has been a shift from the rigors of the high modernism of the

Cold War period, whether the Integral Serialism associated with Darmstadt or the Indeterminacy associated with certain American composers (both perceived as being antithetical to opera), to a more plural and encompassing aesthetic. This shift has allowed for individual composers to embrace elements such as tonality from earlier music, as well as popular and non-western forms in combination with modernist principles. This period also coincides with the boom in mass global media, marked by the rise of personal computing, the availability of 24-hour news, the ubiquity of the Internet and Web and instant global communications.

THE MASK OF ORPHEUS

The Mask of Orpheus stands as a monumental return to the very roots of opera and a testament to Birtwistle's fascination with myth. Birtwistle does not use myth and a cast of gods and heroes to justify his theatre; instead, he seeks to explore the universal nature of myths through ritualization in music. Orpheus' story, in the hands of earlier composers was often presented in a humanized version that focused on the relationship between Orpheus and Euridice and the triumph of music over death; going so far as to give the drama a happy ending. Birtwistle steps back from the personal, and places Orpheus' tragedy in the context of Apollo's gift of music, from bestowing to the eventual silencing.

Peter Zinovieff, an inventor and early pioneer of sound synthesis collaborated with Birtwistle to produce the very detailed and formalized libretto for *The Mask of Orpheus*. The drama is written for three characters, Orpheus, Euridice, and Aristeaus, each of whom is embodied in three ways on stage: the Man/Woman as singer, the Hero/Heroine as mime, and the Myth as puppet accompanied by offstage singer. The use of three physical aspects for each character allows Birtwistle to present different angles and differing versions of the legend, either simultaneously or serially. Despite the non-linearity inherent in multiple perspectives and the occasionally fragmented nature of the text, the overarching dramatic structure clearly follows the chronology of Orpheus' story. The opera opens with the electronic music that signifies Apollo's teaching of Orpheus and the giving of music. Orpheus' stuttering vocal utterances are then superimposed and eventually build to recount the memory of his journey with Jason as one of the Argonauts. The first act proceeds to the story of the couple's wedding, Euridice's death and subsequent funeral; the second follows Orpheus' progress across seventeen arches of an aqueduct, during which his descent to Hades and the unsuccessful retrieval of Euridice are enacted. In the third and final act, the three deaths of Orpheus are presented over the course of nine episodes, and the Myth of Orpheus decays.

With triadic characterization, and a libretto that employs a formalized language in a procession of ritualized scenes, there is no room in this lyric tragedy for the kind of "noble sentiment" that gives rise to song, and yet music lies at the heart of the myth. The musical core of the opera can be found in Apollo's gift of a harp to Orpheus and by extension to all humanity; Birtwistle transforms this gift into the electronic music that frames the opera and envelopes the audience in sound. Working with the composer Barry Anderson, who realized Birtwistle's intentions at the IRCAM studios in Paris, the fabric of the web of electronic music was created out of four sampled harp sounds. The voice of Apollo also becomes part of the fabric of the music; the god's disembodied voice was created through a voice synthesis program developed at IRCAM, his language completely comprised of the syllables from the spoken names of Orpheus and Euridice.

Nixon in China

On most levels Johns Adams' *Nixon in China*, which premiered just a year after *Orpheus*, is diametrically opposed to the Birtwistle work. Where Birtwistle's musical language flows out of a post-war European modernist tradition, Adams' is closely related to the minimalist music of composers like Glass and Reich, with its repetition, a return to a tonally based harmonic structure and driving rhythmic energy, as well as the American orchestral tradition of Copland and Ives. Where Birtwistle turned to ancient myths to present enduring themes, the story for *Nixon* was drawn from media reports of relatively recent historical events, while all the characters were still living.

Adams' opera presents the state visit of U.S. president Richard Nixon to China in 1972, an important event in American and global political life; an effort to build bridges and develop new relationships during the Cold War. Although the opera has a more narrative style than Birtwistle's there is less of a dramatic arc than that contained in the Orpheus story. The structure of *Nixon* is a series of tableaux that over three acts move from the external, public personae of the main characters, Richard and Pat Nixon, Mao and Chiang Ch'ing and the Chinese premier, Chou En-lai, to reveal more intimate, personal perspectives of the humans underneath.

The first act focuses on presenting the public images; celebrating the arrival of the President and first lady, the first meeting between Nixon and Mao and a state banquet. These are all part of a deliberately staged and self-conscious media event, as Nixon's speech in the third scene makes clear:

> A vote of thanks to one and all
> Whose efforts made this possible.

> No one who heard could but admire
> Your eloquent remarks, Premier,
> And millions more hear what we say
> Through satellite technology
> Than ever heard a public speech
> Before. No one is out of touch.
> Telecommunication has
> Broadcast your message into space.[8]

In the second act "China" presents itself to its foreign guests; the opera highlighting the disparity between the two cultures and the inability to create a sense of understanding between them. This central section of the opera is dominated by the female characters; the first scene centers around Mrs. Nixon, an innocent abroad, unable to comprehend the subtleties around her. The second revolves around Chiang Ch'ing, the wife of Chairman Mao, staging one of her revolutionary ballets, and presenting her as a powerful force behind the cultural revolution: "I cut my teeth upon the land / And when I walked my feet were bound / On revolution" (Adams, 616–617). The final act is a more intimate affair, originally conceived as a social dance, wherein the characters have their public personae stripped away and they reveal their memories, hopes and faded dreams to their partners and themselves.

Unlike *Orpheus*, there is no intrinsic music in this story, no compulsion for the characters to sing. This may derive from the fact that the project was not composer led but was conceived by the director, Peter Sellars. The musical idea behind the opera appears to have sprung from Sellars' plan to stage one of Madame Mao's revolutionary ballets[9] in America, a plan that he claims to have abandoned on moral grounds. From the remnants of the abandoned ballet developed an opera based on the presidential visit in which another of Madame Mao's ballets, *The Red Detachment of Women,* was a central feature. Instead of turning to an established opera composer or a Chinese composer, Sellars chose Adams to provide the music for *Nixon* after meeting him at a summer music festival where he heard *Shaker Loops* performed. One assumes that Sellars appreciated the potential of Adams' minimalist style, the highly repetitive and static nature of the music, to create a sense of formalism and ritual. And Sellars can hardly have been unaware of Robert Wilson and Philip Glass' trilogy of minimalist music theatre portraits, the final one, *Akhnaten* premiering before compositional work began on *Nixon*.

This process of ritualization through music is where parallels with *The Mask of Orpheus* can start to be drawn. There is little traditional operatic characterization in Adams' work, at either the level of individual characters or in the setting. This is a story of the meeting of two cultures but there is only one music. Adams makes very little concession to the musical elements of the story;

moments of "phenomenal" music, such as the American-style dance in the third act are briefly woven into the musical fabric, but there are no noticeable Chinese features assimilated. In an interview with Andrew Porter, Adams admits that he was "nervous about too much research when it comes to the creative act,"[10] and so kept his distance from the actual ballet music for *The Red Detachment of Women*. By not focusing on the particular, and allowing the music to create ritual through repetition and the juxtaposition of energy and stasis, the characters of the opera are universalized, giving them god-like stature as incarnations of Young America and Old China.

At another level, neither opera is prescriptive. Birtwistle allows the audience to find its own resonances within the multiple layers of myth, while Adams and his librettist Alice Goodman pass no moral judgement on their characters; there is no good side and bad side, only China and America. This universality separates *Nixon* from its *Zeitopern* predecessors, operas that were not created to last but made fleeting by their very location in a specific moment.

In the context of these models, the rest of this essay will consider operas composed since the mid-eighties, grouped to highlight particular aspects of contemporary media culture and myth. The first group of operas combine myth and recent news items in the world of air travel, while the second examine relationships mediated through technology. The third collection focuses on the power of television; the final pair turns attention back to classical myth, and its interpretation in a modern context.

Heavens Above

The dream of flying is one that has loomed large in the human psyche for millennia, from Icarus to the Wright brothers. A mythic subject matter by any account. Three recent operas that draw on air travel as their departure point, however, have narratives grounded not in myth but in a reality reported in news media.

Flight (1998), by the British composer Jonathan Dove, with a libretto by April de Angelis, was inspired by the story of an Iranian refugee, Mehran Karimi Nasseri, who had been living in the departure lounge at Charles de Gaulle airport since 1988. Instead of creating a purely biographical opera based on Nasseri's story, Dove and de Angelis "were struck by its almost mythic quality: a man trapped between two worlds, living in a kind of limbo. It made [them] think about what an extraordinary place an airport is, how full of stories, hopes and dreams."[11] Out of the refugee's predicament they fashioned a drama with all the qualities of a Shakespearian comedy.

The opera covers twenty-four hours in an airport departures' lounge, where three couples and a woman looking for love are stranded by an electrical storm. In this closed world two figures stand apart from the travelers. The Controller, who oversees everything, is a figure like Prospero or Oberon, but not being powerful enough to have summoned the storm her role is slightly more passive; she acts as Chorus, commenting on the action. The refugee, who, like Puck or Ariel has little freedom or autonomy, endeavors to spread love and peace amongst the passengers, although he gets it wrong on occasion. Dove confers the refugee's status as an outsider, separate and other, with a hint of magic, as Britten does, by casting him as a countertenor. Each couple's story is introduced as they come in contact with the refugee; the married couple trying to rekindle romance by way of a holiday in the sun, a diplomat and his heavily pregnant wife on their way to Minsk, and a rather randy Steward and Stewardess. With the storm come the elements of comedy; muddles and mistakes, too much alcohol, misunderstandings and mixed partners. The new day brings the end of the storm and a restoration of order, with happy endings for all. This includes the refugee, who is given the opportunity to tell his own story and is then redeemed by an Immigration Officer; given his freedom within the confines of the closed world.

Here lies the paradox. There is nothing intrinsic in the story or the characters that cries out for song, and yet *Flight* is probably the most traditionally operatic work under consideration here. Perhaps this lack of impetus toward song is less of an issue for a comedy of this kind; not dissimilar in spirit to Mozart's comedies. A parallel with eighteenth century opera can go further, as de Angelis' libretto has been crafted to create a numbers opera, with notable arias, numerous duets, trios and larger vocal ensemble pieces, including a sextet during the onstage birthing scene. In contrast to the previously mentioned pair of operas, Dove composes more traditional vocal characterizations for his singers, including the soaring lyric lines of the Controller's soprano. A conservative musical language also lends the work a more traditional feel. The deftly handled orchestral writing shows the influence of composers like Britten, Adams, and even Stravinsky; nothing to challenge a late twentieth-century listener but plenty to charm.

In a interesting coincidence, *Flight*'s premiere was preceded by a year by *60e Parallèle*, or *The 60th Parallel*, by the French composer Philipe Manoury, another opera in which a group of air passengers are stranded by a storm. Manoury's work, however, explores completely different territory. This is a drama about waiting, and, as in Beckett's *Godot*, the characters are stuck in an unchanging situation. The storm, which has been raging before the opera begins, will continue for an unspecified duration after it ends. Despite the tensions and issues that connect the passengers, little actually happens, and there are no resolutions. Banal conversation fills the time and space, while the wait and the storm continues.

Where the characters in *Flight* are comic caricatures, Manoury and his librettist Michel Deutsch, set about to create more realistic individuals, written with a naturalistic dialogue. The opera is made topical by the inclusion of characters based on possible real people, focusing on five individuals. The primary pair includes a fugitive Balkan war criminal, Wim Kosowitch, and the man hunting him, Rudy. It is suggested that Wim has murdered a fellow passenger offstage during the prelude, and after Rudy accuses him of genocide and the recent murder, Wim strikes him and disappears. It is not clear whether Rudy is sleeping or dead as the opera ends; what is certain is that Wim has not been brought to justice. The secondary pair, Anja and Maria are women in love. The younger of the two, Maria, is still in love with a man she walked out on; her repeated attempts to contact him all fail. Anja is in love with Maria, and can only bring herself to confess it once her friend is asleep. Finally, Dr. Wittkop is on his way to present a lecture on the brain of Einstein, which he is carrying with him in its 200 pieces, having been entrusted with it by the real-life Dr. Thomas Harvey. Action is only implied by the suggested murders, there is no real development of the characters or relationships, instead "drama" happens through a series of reveals.

Once again a creative team presents its audience with an opera scenario wherein the characters have no essential compulsion to sing. Nonetheless there is intrinsic music in *60e Parallèle* which comes not from the characters but the scenario. The starting point for the opera was the Prelude, which for the composer represents the ongoing storm. This music pervades the opera, at times coming to the fore, such as the Prelude and regular musical interludes, at other times it is thinned and almost unnoticeable behind the foregrounded vocal lines. Overlaid on the musical and dramatic structure are apparently unrelated episodes composed of *musique concréte* and unnamed characters. These include heavy metal rock music played through a portable radio, disturbing the surrounding passengers, and later a disembodied child's voice singing nursery rhymes to the sound of bells accompanying an onstage child playing with a ball. Although the episodes provide moments of phenomenal music, they are inconsequential to the drama. They do, however, allow Manoury to include and parody other musical styles, from Ravel's *La Valse* and rock music, to Stockhausen's *Gesang der Jünglinge* and Harvey's *Mortuos Plango, Vivos voco*, both of which feature a child's voice and bells. Apart from these parodies, Manoury's musical language mixes elements of modernism with an expressionist flavor of Strauss and Berg, while the spirit of Debussy haunts some of the vocal lines.

The opera concludes with Maria's line: "Une sensation de vide. Tu sais, là, au creux de l'estomac ... Anja, cette horrible sensation de vide" (A feeling of emptiness. You know, there, in the pit of the stomach ... Anja, that horrible feeling of emptiness).[12] And with that, the music of the storm fades into nothingness.

Despite their obvious differences, these operas, the one comic the other lying between existentialism and nihilism, situate a contemporary human scene into a mythic space from whence humans can fly. The space may be a magical realm or a version of Sartre's afterlife, but it is the place that determines the journey and the drama. In *Airline Icarus* (2003), by the young Canadian composer Brian Current, the situation is markedly different. According to the composer, this compact chamber opera was inspired by the news of a Korean airliner that was mistakenly shot down as a spy plane by the Russian military, and the image of its 12- to 15-minute descent through the air. From this starting point, the librettist Anton Piatigorsky decided "to juxtapose the idea of daily airline travel with this idea of hubris and technology and the myth of Icarus."[13]

Instead of situating the action in an airport, Current and Piatigorsky's opera is set on board a plane belonging to the Icarus airline, bound on a domestic flight to Cleveland. The central section of the work focuses on three characters, an alcoholic "business man" [*sic*], a weight-conscious female advertising executive, and a very nervous academic. The characters make some desultory conversation, and reveal their innermost and yet mundane concerns; nothing interrupts this static journey apart from the flight experiencing a patch of mild turbulence. The opera opens with the musings of the baggage handler and closes with the pilot, providing a more ritualistic frame to the work. There is an effort to mythologize the situation through these figures; the baggage handler sings as he taxis the plane:

> Sometimes
> I think these planes are merely
> Modern demons of the air.
> The million copper capillaries
> Pump to each metallic cell
> The juice to function and to fly.[14]

Where the first two operas placed the mundane inside the mythic, *Airline Icarus* places the elements beside each other, unable to decide whether it's a mythic exploration of Icarus' striving or a comedy of mixed desires and irrational fear. Unfortunately Current's musical language, a somewhat unadventurous modernism, doesn't help to place the story as there is little difference between the two poles. Although this opera is set on board and there is lift-off, it is less of a journey than *Flight* or even *60e Parallèle*.

Media Relations

It is difficult to imagine an aspect of daily life that has changed more over the last generation than our relationship with communication and information technology. The telephone has changed almost beyond recognition, to such an extent that a recent production of *La Voix Humaine* at the Houston Opera included a program note to explain how a party line works. Nevertheless its essential function has remained the same. As "the woman" was able to dissimulate her feelings and, more importantly, conceal the truth down the telephone line in Poulenc's opera, our current technology continues to makes lying easy. Indeed, it enables one to go so much beyond simple deception; presenting ourselves in any way we choose, with endless alternative possibilities or as someone else altogether.

Alternate Visions (2007), by the Canadian composer John Oliver and librettist Genni Gunn, takes a comic look at romantic relationships developed over the Internet. Robert and Valérie are a couple that have connected online, although they each have difficulty relating to others in the real world. Having arranged to meet face-to-face, fear overtakes and they send their respective best friends in their place. When the substitutes actually connect and get physical, all manner of confusions and mix-ups ensue. In the end, Robert and Valérie never manage to get it together outside of cyberspace. As Valérie concludes: "I wish I'd never met you in person. You were a better illusion than you are a man."[15]

This opera immerses the audience in a virtual reality from the beginning. Set in a karaoke bar that doubles as the soundstage for a reality television show in which couples form or break up in front of a live audience, the actual audience forms the nightclub crowd, and the performance takes place around them. With large screens on two walls, the audience is able to enter into Robert and Valérie's online world, while the chorus of three women (including one countertenor) who act as girlfriends and waitresses are not real but only embodied fantasies from Richard's virtual world.

The music, provided by a small ensemble that mixes rock and classical instruments with live electronics, is best described as polystylistic. The electronic elements are the most recognizable as belonging to a contemporary "classical" tradition. There is musical parody, such as an aria influenced by early blues, and quotation from a host of genres that include classical, jazz, rock and pop, opera and musical theatre. National anthems also appear in a not-so-subtle but humorous comment when Richard's nostalgic yearnings for a lost past are underscored by the Canadian anthem, while the TV host, read Satan, offers the important things in life—fame, money, cars—to strains of the American anthem. The music is not exactly challenging or avant-garde, but its polystylistic nature is an interesting reflection on the Internet; realizing both the potential for individuals to slip behind various masks, and the ease with which one can surf between unrelated content.

There is a mix of vocal delivery in *Alternate Visions* that includes both speech and singing; the impetus for song derives both from the setting, a karaoke bar, and from the fact that the characters become someone else, literally taking on a new voice in cyberspace. This idea of becoming someone else, creating a web of alternative personalities, is pushed much further and into a darker direction in the next opera.

Two Boys (2011), by the young American composer, Nico Muhly, places the audience in the middle of an Internet storm. The basis of the story is, like *Nixon*, a real event; the 2003 case of the attempted murder of a teenager from Manchester, United Kingdom. In contrast to the events from the time of Nixon's visit to China however, this news story of ordinary people has a permanent and ongoing record that is easily accessible through the Internet.

The details of the crime, according to the opera libretto, involve a 13-year-old boy, who, through a number of online identities groomed an older boy of 16; eventually inciting the older boy to kill him. The younger boy, Jake, constructs and choreographs a convoluted web involving a cast of online personae based on actual people; a sister who goes missing, her ex-boyfriend, a stalker, and an aunt who works for the secret service, all in an effort to befriend the elder boy, Brian, online. In the real, physical, world Jake forms a friendship with Brian, and over time convinces Brian that he, Jake, has a terminal disease. A crucial fact that will make it easier for Brian to act when Jake's aunt offers him a fee and the opportunity to work with MI5 if he can prove himself courageous enough to knife someone, namely Jake.

The operatic storyline follows the actual story quite faithfully, at least as it appears on news websites. To give the basic story a dramatic shape, Muhly and the librettist, Craig Lucas, frame it in the style of a television police drama. Detective Sergeant Anne Strawson becomes the central focus, her character not dissimilar to the role made famous by Helen Mirren in the U.K. police procedural drama *Prime Suspect*, in which the lead officer has to balance casework with trouble in her personal life. In *Two Boys* this trouble on the home front acts as a trigger to her cracking the case. The boys' story is told in a series of flashbacks that develop out of Brian's police interviews, each time shifting the action and location from the police station to the locales frequented by the boys.

True to the original narrative, which unfolded in online chat rooms, much of the operatic story is told through the medium of recounted texts and instant messages. At the London premier, these online conversations formed part of the video projections that played on the set walls. Texting and electronic messaging however, represent the opposite of the elevation of language that is an inherent component of music theatre. Instead of raising speech to the level of song, texting, with all its abbreviations, corruptions and reductions renders the word fast, easy and disposable. Translating this very contemporary form of silent communication into sound would appear to be a compositional challenge full of exciting possibility. From the very first time a laptop is opened in *Two Boys*, the composer and librettist have taken the disembodied voices of internet chatter, the voices of fingers tapping keyboards, and normalized the resultant text into speech before turning it into choral song. The web of voices, which ranges from three-part harmony to multi-layered semi-improvised plainchant, is, like the rest of the opera, in a recognizably tonal idiom. Muhly's musical language owes much to both Britten (with hints of the pseudo-gamelan from *Death in Venice*) and Adams. If this is how contemporary social media sounds, the drama can't support the Detective's claim that she doesn't understand this new language.

There is an interesting contradiction in this opera. The *Zeitopern* of the early twentieth century engaged fully with its own era, including the popular music—even if imperfectly understood. In *Alternate Visions*, the polystylistic approach gives the performers the opportunity to use their voices in different ways as they engage different aspects of their virtual characters. Drawing a comparison with these approaches to the contemporary, can a group of twenty-first century teenagers from Manchester, in a story that is completely of the moment, be represented onstage by a traditionally operatic tenor and bass, soprano and boy treble? Is it possible that these teenagers, who engage in camsex as well as sing in the church choir, could be completely oblivious to the sonic landscape of popular music, as the opera makes no apparent concession to a contemporary popular sound world?

The overall dramatic intent of *Two Boys* is perhaps a little unclear. A narrative is presented: a murder is attempted and a case solved, but there is little depth of character or motivation to drive the drama on. The ending suggests that Jake's basic motivation was the desire to be loved and wanted, but there was no indication that he wasn't or wouldn't be. The drama achieves neither the tragedy of *La Voix* nor the mythic nature of *Nixon*, and it doesn't appear to challenge the medium in which the crime took place. Considering the opera purely as a mystery, it is unfortunate that the essential key to the case is a visual clue—a recurring spelling mistake common to all of Jake's online personae. For this clue to function at the denouement it has to be a seen, which leaves little necessity for music at the heart of the mystery.

Moving on from an individual's identity and human relationships mediated through technology, the last opera in this section explores the future of relationship once an individual's identity has become one with technology.

Death and the Powers (2010), by the American composer Tod Machover, represents that culmination moment of myth, when mortals gain immortality and are set into the firmament of the stars. But this is also the story of a family: at its head, the powerful and wealthy businessman and inventor, Simon Powers, who is on the cusp of death. In a bid to defeat death he has created The System, a technological environment into which he will be subsumed. Once uploaded his memories, personality and consciousness will continue to live, free of a mortal body. The Powers family, Simon's third wife Evvy, his assistant and adopted son Nicolas and daughter Miranda, come to terms with the transformed Simon, who pulses around them, inhabiting and communicating from the very walls and the light in their home. The central drama revolves around their individual decisions to join him, or not, in The System as the world around them crumbles. Eventually his wife and son follow Simon into The System, but the opera ends with his daughter hesitating, reluctant to abandon the world of suffering humanity.

To an extent this is a futuristic-media-age take on *The Tempest*. Simon, a namesake of the legendary magician, Simon Magus, is Prospero, who having rejected the world for his library is ejected from the world of human society. The island of his banishment is The System. Miranda in turn rejects her father's magic and accepts the world, her humanity and the suffering that it entails as necessary for life.

As the voice symbolizes the essence of the person, the human voice is at the heart of this opera. In Simon's final conversation with Miranda, during the process of his transmogrification he sums it up thus:

> Once, when Miranda was three years old
> She put her hand to her throat
> Just here above the voice-box
> And felt the vibration.
> She said: I can feel it when I talk—
> That must mean Miranda is inside.
> And she was right!
> You were right,
> My intelligent daughter:
> It's the vibration,
> The movement, that matters!
> That's what I love in you—
> The voice, the gesture:
> The ripple, not the water![16]

Once Simon is physically gone, it is only by his voice that he remains recognizable as part of The System. In Machover's hands, Simon's disembodied voice and performance become the *mise en scène*. It should be noted that in addition to his compositional output, Machover is a teacher and academic based at the Massachusetts Institute of Technology, where his work has included the design of new electronic-musical interfaces for use in performance and education. So the singer playing Simon is wired up in the pit and performs there; his voice, gestures and breathing control the set, including the three movable walls towards the back of the stage, and a harp-like chandelier. The remaining living characters then interact and speak with a living set endowed with a musical voice.

In addition to the obvious roles that technology plays in the story and in the transformation of Simon's character into the *mise en scène*, each of the singers and the fifteen orchestral musicians is wired for sound. Not only does this allow for amplification and manipulation of all musical elements of the opera, but the advanced level of technology used enables the composer and sound engineer to project and spatialize the sound with great precision. Despite the electronics available, most of the effects are handled with subtlety; both the electronics and the overall musical language are dominated by the vocal lines which are written in a traditionally lyrical and generally tonal fashion. Indeed, Miranda's final aria and its accompanying orchestration would not seem entirely out of place in a West End musical.

Life on the Small Screen

Although the Internet may be gaining ground as the leading medium of mass popular culture, it tends to reach people individually and is dependent on choice. In contrast, television, which has been a major force in the dissemination of entertainment, culture, news and information over the last sixty years, tends to reach both a mass and communal audience. The following two operas contrast the benefits of the television as an open forum for debate against the tragedy of a life lived in front of camera.

Conversazioni con Chomsky (2010) by the Italian composer Emauele Casale, presents the ideas and work of Professor Noam Chomsky, linguist and major cultural figure across several disciplines, through a series of television-style interviews. This work, described in its subtitle as a "talk-opera," does not fit into easy categorization. The drama, spoken throughout, traces a progression from ideas discussed in a private realm to their more robust treatment in a public arena. For all that the opera is unconventional, the dramatic structure follows the musical form of a baroque *ritornello*. The introduction, in which two students discuss Chomsky's principles of Linguistics and Generative Grammar, is followed by three versions of the Ritornello section; television interviews between the program host and Chomsky. Each interview is in a different key, the first addresses Propaganda, the second, Economic Liberalism and the third, Market Capitalism. Between the Ritornello sections are two Episodes, which feature academics whom Chomsky has helped out of difficult situations. In an extended Coda the interview format is opened out into a talk show, a public forum dealing with Globalization, where the audience is able to question Chomsky directly.

Music is used behind the text to heighten speech, but the text is never sung. There are moments however when the two almost fuse; times when the music sounds like it could be following the melodic and rhythmic contours of the text, and others when the actors' vocal inflections mirror the music. What transforms *Conversazioni* from a spoken theatre with finely wrought incidental music into a form that could be considered opera is the role of an unnamed character, the singer. Between each of the scenes Casale inserts a song, the lyrics either illustrating or commenting on the preceding scene, thus casting the singer into the role of chorus from the ancient Greek theatre.

Conversazioni is a theatre of ideas, ideas that inform the dramatic and musical structures, ideas that move from the internal and invisible to the external and visible—as one of the students explains in the first conversation: "dall'interno all'esterno;... dall'invisibile al visibile."[17] Even though Chomsky, as the progenitor of the ideas, is present as a character there is little attention on him as an individual. Television, on the other hand, as the media through which the internal is made external, plays an increasing role in the drama, holding more people in the camera's eye in each scene and creating the platform on which the concepts and comments become more polemical.

Mark-Anthony Turnage's *Anna Nicole* (2011) also focuses on the power of television to transform, but the transformation the opera charts, of a character fitting into a television-friendly mold and the adaptation of lifestyle required to live in front of a camera is not one that ends well. Like *Louise*, the central character of *Anna Nicole* is a girl drawn from the working poor; her story starts as a Cinderella-like rags-to-riches fairy tale before it descends into tragedy. Turnage's opera takes its inspiration from the true-life story of the eponymous hero, or more accurately, antihero, a surgically enhanced *Playboy* centerfold and model who married a Texas oil billionaire 62 years her senior. On the death of her husband she finds herself cut out of the estate by his earlier family. After a ten-year downward spiral spent fighting in the courts, fighting weight and drug issues, she has a baby daughter. The joy of this potentially positive event is marred when her twenty-year-old son arrives to meet his sister. He is found the next morning in his mother's bed, dead of an accidental drug overdose. Over the next six months the tragic situation deteriorates until Anna Nicole is also dead of an overdose of prescription drugs; drugs taken to relieve the incessant back pain caused by her breast-enhancement surgery.

The opera's tragedy is delivered as a strong moral lesson, commenting on a celebrity-hungry media culture that helped to create *The Anna Nicole Show*. Richard Thomas, who wrote the opera's libretto, is himself a composer of musical theatre, best known for *Jerry Springer, the Opera*. Thomas has given the opera a numbers structure, its episodic nature not dissimilar to the forms of musical theatre. And the libretto's direct-to-camera style of text, often in a self-consciously knowing manner, does well to capture the affected nature of the celebrity reality television format; *The Anna Nicole Show* being one of the forerunners of the genre.

There is a large role for chorus in *Anna Nicole*, a chorus that takes the role of narrator at times, although its predominant function is to act as a Greek chorus, commenting on and questioning the action. In the second act, Anna Nicole's mother, Virgie increasingly takes on the role of chorus. Although this opera is sung throughout, it shares with Casale's work the importance of the chorus in making the opera sing. Musically, Turnage uses stylistic references to pop and jazz to give various scenes a sense of place and atmosphere. Notable examples include the music for the scene in Jim's Krispy Fried Chicken diner in Smith's hometown with Texas blues inspired music scored for banjo and wah-wah-muted brass, and the seedy, burlesque-style jazz in the pole-dancing club. But the composer is capable of more sophisticated musical gestures; creating music to underscore a disconnect between a character's actions and inner feelings. One such moment is the "free ranch" scene, where Anna performs fellatio on her senescent husband in order to secure her and her son's futures. And the pathos of the tragic end is made even more poignant by Turnage's use of silence. Anna's final words are sung unaccompanied as she is encased in a body bag; when she draws her final breath there is no music to relieve the darkness. Is this the way the Icarus myth ends?

> Man I got so close
> I had the dream
> Then lost it before I knew it.
> ...Oh America,
> You dirty whore
> I gave you everything
> But you wanted more.
> You wanted more
> I wanted more.[18]

Persistent Myth

With the notable exception of Casale's *Conversazioni con Chomsky*, the operas based in contemporary life and current events tend toward a more conservative or traditional musical language. In contrast, for many composers who, like Birtwistle, retain a more modernist aesthetic, there is a tendency toward ancient myths as subject matter. As with Birtwistle's *Mask of Orpheus* and the more recent *Minotaur* (2008), there is often a focus on the violence and brutality contained within these early stories.

Medeamaterial (1991) by the French composer Pascal Dusapin takes the central section of the play *Despoiled Shore Medea-material Landscape with Argonauts* by the influential German dramatist, Heiner Müller as its source. The play presents the already brutal story of Jason and Medea in a contemporary manner that doesn't shrink away from the raw and violent elements of the story. Most of the drama is in the form of a monologue, Medea's rant to the exploitive and unfaithful Jason, enumerating all those she's destroyed for and over him—including their two sons. Both Jason and Medea's nurse have small parts; their lines are spoken, disembodied and amplified, then made real as they are repeated and elaborated by the chorus. The opera sings through Medea's state of extreme emotion, though at moments of greatest intensity, which include references to her listening—to the music of the destruction of her people, and to the screams of his new bride—she speaks her text over a silent orchestra. The chorus also acts to extend Medea's words. The opera was composed as a companion piece for Purcell's *Dido and Aeneas*, and so takes its orchestration from the earlier opera, adding only electronics to the strings and continuo. As Medea becomes more impassioned over the duration of the work there is a gradual shift from the sustained sounds of the organ to the more clipped and aggressive sound of the harpsichord, the string writing bridging between the two.

The equally savage myth that explains the origin of the nightingale's mournful song is the basis for James Dillon's chamber opera, *Philomela* (2004). The story tells of Procne, daughter of the Athenian king and wife to Tereus, the king of Thrace. When, after years away from home, Procne desires the company of her sister, Philomela, she sends her husband to fetch her. On the return journey he rapes Philomena, then proceeds to cut out her tongue, thereby preventing her from reporting his crime. She is eventually able to reveal the truth through her weaving, and the sisters get their revenge by killing Itys, Tereus and Procne's son, and feeding him to his father. As the king retaliates, about to murder the women, all three are transformed into birds. The libretto, by the composer, begins by weaving together the three protagonists in a non-narrative way before exploring the story through fragmented flashbacks. The loom is then given voice before the climactic action of the women's sacrifice and the tragedy is brought to a close through the metamorphosis of the three characters.

The role of music is vital to story, giving voice to the voiceless. The dead boy is seen and heard through the use of video and pre-recorded sound, while a sampled chorus and electronics are used to create the voice of the loom. At the close of the opera, the transformation from human to bird is accomplished through the loss of language; the singers are given bird-like vocalizations, words are fragmented, meaning is lost, and the resulting sounds create an awkward, harsh, bird song. The music is uncompromising and at times tough, but then the characters and the drama being enacted are cruel and uncompromising, involving several brutal violations. Overall, the work is not dominated by voices, as there are several lengthy sections of purely instrumental music.

Despite the relatively small sample represented in this essay, myth continues to play a significant part in operatic narrative, albeit with an altered purpose. As illustrated by the works of Birtwistle, Dusapin and Dillon, Gods and Heroes are no longer required to provide legitimacy for a sung drama; instead, composers explore the universal nature of myth through music, eschewing the personal narrative. In relation to these works it may be argued that the operas of Adams and Turnage demonstrate that celebrity, whether earned or bestowed, has successfully replaced the Hero in opera. The central characters in both *Nixon in China* and *Anna Nicole* transcend the individuals on which they were based to become universal figures. Their ordinary human emotions combined with the ritual of music gives them their rightful place on stage irrespective an elevated status as Hero.

Regardless of subject matter or narrative style, the best operas communicate the human emotion of a drama through music. Across the spectrum of possible subjects the best works will also contain some universal truth— either the recognizably god-like in the lowest individual or the individual and personal that we can relate to in the god. To transform these stories into opera it is vital that they sing, that at the heart of the story there is a kernel of music.

Acknowledgments

The author would like to thank the following publishers for their assistance, making scores, libretti and recordings available: Boosey & Hawkes, Chester Music, Durand, Edition Peters, Ricordi, G. Schirmer, and Universal Editions; also the following composers and librettists: Emanuele Casale, Brian Current, John Oliver and Genni Gunn.

Notes

1. Steven Huebner, "Between Anarchism and the Box Office: Gustave Charpentier's 'Louise,'" *19th-Century Music*, Vol. 19, No. 2 (Autumn 1995): pp. 136–160 (p. 144).

2. Gustave Charpentier, *Louise* (Paris, Huegel & Cie., 1900), p. 119–120 (English translation by the author).
3. This has some resonance with Thomas Mann's *Magic Mountain*, which was published just a couple of years before *Jonny*.
4. Ernst Krenek, *Jonny Spielt Auf: Textbuch* (Vienna, Universal Edition, 1926), p.35 (English translation by the author).
5. The term diegetic is most often used in the context of film to describe music that is heard by both characters and audience. In the context of opera, Carolyn Abbate employs the term "phenomenal" to distinguish the music heard as such by the singer and characters on stage from all the other music of opera, which she labels "noumenal." See: Carolyn Abbate, *Unsung Voices: Opera and Musical Narrative in the Nineteenth Century* (Princeton, NJ: Princeton University Press, 1991).
6. Francis Poulenc, *The Human Voice (La voix humaine)* [Libretto] (Paris: Ricordi, 1959), pp. 12–13.
7. Ibid., in Poulenc's Notes on the Musical Interpretation.
8. John Adams, *Nixon in China* [Score] (London: Boosey & Hawkes, 1987), pp. 330–336.
9. In interview, Sellars refers to his planned project as a revolutionary ballet entitled *Shachiapang*. Although this work is one of the eight model plays accepted during the Cultural Revolution, it is actually a Beijing Opera and not a ballet. See: Matthew Daines, "'Nixon in China': An Interview with Peter Sellars," *Tempo*, New Series, No. 197 (July 1996), p. 12.
10. Andrew Porter and John Adams, "'Nixon in China': John Adams in Conversation," *Tempo*, New Series, No. 167 (Dec. 1988), pp. 25–30.
11. Jonathan Dove, from the program note for *Flight*, published online by Peters Editions, www.editionpeters.com/resources/0001/stock/pdf/Dove_Flight.pdf.
12. Phillipe Manoury, *60e Parallèle* (Paris, Editions Durand, 1996) (translation by the author).
13. From an introduction to the opera by Brian Current and Anton Piatigorsky, presented at the New York City Opera Vox Festival 2007. Available through Canadian Music Centre, https://www.musiccentre.ca/node/60772.
14. Anton Piatigorsky and Brian Current, *Airline Icarus*, from the composer's manuscript of the libretto.
15. Genni Gunn, *Alternate Visions*, 2006, from the manuscript.
16. Tod Machover and Robert Pinsky, *Death and the Powers* (London, Boosey and Hawkes, 2010).
17. Emanuele Casale and Roberto Fabbi, *Conversazioni con Chomsky*, from the composer's manuscript of the libretto.
18. Richard Thomas, *Anna Nicole*, 2010, from the manuscript.

Bibliography

Adams, John. *Nixon in China*. The Metropolitan Opera, John Adams (conductor), Nonesuch B009FB3YE4, 2012. DVD/Blu-ray.
Birtwistle, Harrison. *The Mask of Orpheus*. BBC Symphony Orchestra, Andrew Davis and Martyn Brabbins (conductors), NMC D0505, 1997. CD.
_____. *The Minotaur*. The Royal Opera House, Antonio Pappano (conductor), Opus Arte B001F5IO5C, 2010. DVD.
Casale, Emauele. *Conversazioni con Chomsky*. Not commercially available. Video excerpts

can be found on the composer's blog: http://emanuelecasale.wordpress.com/conversazioni-con-chomsky-talk-opera/.

Charpentier, Gustave. *Louise*. New Philharmonia Orchestra, Georges Prêtre (conductor), Sony B002DU7OMW, 2009, CD.

Current, Brian. *Airline Icarus*, Italian premiere available on YouTube: http://youtu.be/Isv4w_iy4iI.

Dillon, James. *Philomela*. Remix Ensemble, Jurgen Hempel (conductor), Aeon AECD 0986, 2009. CD

Dove, Jonathan. *Flight*. Glyndbourne Festival Opera, David Parry (conductor), Chandos CHAN10197(2), 2004. CD.

Dusapin, Pascal. *Medeamaterial*. Orchestre de la Chapelle Royale, Philippe Herreweghe (conductor), Harmonia Mundi HMC 905215, 1993. CD.

Krenek, Ernst. *Jonny Spielt Auf*. Gewandhausorchester, Lothar Zagrosek (conductor), Decca B005G4YEDY, 2011. CD.

Machover, Tod. *Death and the Powers*. Not commercially available, video excerpts can be found on the composer's blog: http://operaofthefuture.com/photos-and-videos/.

Manoury, Philippe. *60th Parallel*. Orchestre de Paris, David Robertson (conductor), Naxos 8.554249–50, 1997. CD.

Muhly, Nico. *Two Boys*. Not commercially available.

Oliver, John. *Alternate Visions*. Augmented Opera, Chants Libres CL2009, 2009. DVD.

Poulenc, Francis. *La Voix Humaine*. Felicity Lott, Orchestre de la Suisse Romande, Armin Jordan (conductor), Harmonia Mundi, HMG 501759, 2012. CD.

Turnage, Mark-Anthony. *Anna Nicole*. The Royal Opera House, Antonio Pappano (conductor), Opus Arte B0054KCVNA, 2011. DVD.

Opera and the Audio Recording Industry

Robert Cannon

The relationship between opera and the recording industry is a complex of aesthetic, technical, commercial and social factors. This essay is designed to introduce these and examine their impact on opera as a live art form.

The Industry

Recordings are a universal aspect of our musical experience, in part an indication of an interest in music, but, as Georgina Born suggests in writing about the music industry's constant innovation in musical hardware: "The industry's drive to proliferate music's mediatized consumption therefore multiplies both the spaces and activities colonized by consumption (the car, pub, mall, underground, queue...; walking, jogging, driving, eating, waiting...) and the forms of aesthetic experience proffered by these media."[1]

At the same time it is all too easy to assume what kind of relationship recordings bear to the original performance, as complementary sides of the same coin. But this is not the case: records have their own aesthetic which can complement, but may also challenge and divert attention from, live or even the original studio performance. This includes the technical, commercial and specific artistic processes that intervene between a performance and its recording. What both actually have in common is a basis in the star system, popular and specialist taste, all susceptible to marketing and other commercial aspects of the music industry, as Andrew Blake indicates:

> Through most of the twentieth century classical recordings were sold as the expected companion of prestige domestic equipment for their reproduction: hi-fi. The target consumer of these expensive goods was affluent, male and middle-aged. Alongside the hardware of conspicuous consumption and precision-

engineered response came the software—the music itself—sold as well-packaged and expensive high-art for the amateur enthusiast.[2]

On the one hand, it is true that music/opera is readily and cheaply available through radio and television broadcasts, downloads and streaming and, for reproduction, can be played on equipment starting at less the £100 ($150). On the other hand it is the case that there is also a direct relationship between music/opera, the desire or need to hear it well reproduced—encouraged by the record review magazines—and the manufacture and advertising of relatively expensive (exclusive?) equipment. One specialist retailer gives the current (August 2012) cost of an entry-level, genuine hi-fi system (CD player, turntable, amplifier and speakers) as about £2,000 (c. $3,420), while CDs range between £5 and £16. With a current average wage in the United Kingdom of £26,000 a basic hi-fi system would therefore represent about eight percent of annual income. By the mid 1920s the number of 78 discs in an opera set ranged from eight or ten for Gilbert and Sullivan to as many as twenty-four for Pathé's 1923 *Manon*. These records cost between 3/6 (18p) (c. $1) and £1 ($4.50) depending on commercial potential or desirability, with an average price of six shillings (30p). An average-length set of fifteen discs would, therefore, have cost something like £4.14 (£4.70) (c. $19) which would have been 11 percent of a nurse's annual wage of £40, making both the gramophones themselves, with a basic model starting at about £2.10 (£2.50) (c. $10) and the records, luxury items, especially with complete opera sets. LPs became standard after 1953 and these cost between 10s (50p) (c. $3) and £2.00 (c. $12). A complete opera on two LPs would have cost between £1 and £4 (or £21 and £42 in current value) (c. between $3.50 and $14, or c. $32 and $65 in current value).

In *The Pursuit of Love*, Nancy Mitford presents her Uncle Matt as a keen record collector—although he is also the man who, having read and enjoyed *White Fang* with such unbounded enthusiasm he could see no reason to read another book. He is, albeit satirically, wealthy, eccentric—and (therefore?) a devotee of the gramophone and the opera:

> Uncle Matthew was no respecter of other people's early morning sleep, and after five o'clock one could not count on any, for he raged round the house, clanking cups of tea, shouting at his dogs, roaring at the housemaids, cracking the stock whips which he had brought back from Canada on the lawn with a noise greater than gunfire, and all to the accompaniment of Galli Curci on his gramophone, an abnormally loud one with an enormous horn, through which would be shrieked "Una voce poco fa"—"The Mad Song" from Lucia-Lo, here the gen-tel lar-ha-hark—and so on, played at top speed, thus rendering them even higher and more screeching than they ought to be.
>
> Nothing reminds me of my childhood days at Alconleigh so much as those

songs. Uncle Matthew played them incessantly for years, until the spell was broken when he went all the way to Liverpool to hear Galli Curci in person. The disillusionment caused by her appearance was so great that the records remained ever after silent, and were replaced by the deepest bass voices that money could buy.[3]

The symbiosis between music as an art and the recording industry is illustrated by three of the books in the table below. A common theme in books designed to give readers the basic information about operas they are likely to see or find being discussed as a topic of conversation at social gatherings, is that any educated person now needed to have a passing knowledge of opera. In his Preface to *Opera Synopses* written in 1913 and still being reprinted in 1956, J. Walker McSpadden advises that "A knowledge of the standard operas is as essential nowadays as a knowledge of the classics of literature.... The general reader, therefore, *whether he frequents the opera or not* [my emphasis], cannot overlook this phase of artistic expression."[4]

This was seized upon by the record companies who had their own vested interest and agenda. In 1920 the British-based Gramophone Co. published *Opera at Home* whose Preface by its chief executive, begins

> The Gramophone Company in offering "Opera at Home" to the public is undoubtedly satisfying a "long-felt want." The number of those who attend operatic performances without even attempting to "understand what it is all about" is amazing.... This book will supply all necessary preliminary information for the prospective opera-goer and, when he has read it, the actual performance will do the rest.[5]

What follows is information about a significant number of operas (by 1928 this had risen to 129 titles) including first performance, first English performance, material about the composer and synopsis. Crucially however, in each case the narrative is interrupted by details of the company's recording/s of individual arias or other passages as they occur in the course of the narration. At the end of each synopsis there are then details of the complete recording, where available (fifteen in 1921 and twenty-three in 1928 with an additional six of extended highlights).

Similarly, the American *The Victrola Book of the Opera*, published by the company in 1921, begins with a Foreword that explains:

Opera in America
The opera has at last come into its own in the United States. In former years merely the pastime of the well-to-do in New York City and vicinity, grand opera is now enjoyed for its own sake by millions of hearers throughout the country.

The Victor Responsible for Much of this Awakened Interest
During the recent season several hundred performances of grand opera, at an estimated cost of millions of dollars, were given in the United States. This great

outlay for dramatic music alone would not have been possible had it not been for the increased interest aroused in opera by the wide-spread distribution by the Victor during the past ten years of hundreds of thousands of grand opera records, at widely varying prices—from the double-faced records by well-known Italian and French artists of Europe, at 37 cents per selection, to the great concerted numbers by famous singers at $6 and $7.[6]

The Victrola volume again gives background material, a synopsis, a pronunciation guide—essential for the social aspect of opera—and recording information for a similar number of titles to *Opera at Home*, although in 1921 there were no complete recordings and only five in 1929. Perhaps surprisingly, this kind of book was still being published as late as 1956 with *The Decca Book of Opera*.

In each case, a commercial catalogue was being offered as an educational benefit. This combination of what appears to be a definitive guide to the opera with a particular company's choices and artists, is potentially subversive, as Georgina Born points out:

> According to Adorno, under the sway of the "culture industry," music and art have been turned into mere commodities, their former autonomy sacrificed to the profit imperative, as so many standardized or "pseudo-individualized" cultural goods are produced and reproduced through the hyper-rationalized process of mass manufacture [Born, 288].

One result of this is a series of strategies by the record companies to define and promote their own product and, in so doing, control their customers' musical preferences and purchasing habits. The most obvious way of doing this is by the control of their lead attractions—conductors, singers and orchestras—through the contract system. This basic function of musical agency becomes more pronounced in the opera recording industry where entire casts are controlled by record labels. In his 1969 address at Montreux, Walter Legge, who established the modern role of the record producer, pleaded that "all the major recording companies ... should pool all the artists they have under exclusive contracts for the purpose of making each year a series of eight or ten major recordings."[7] Ironically, Andrew Blake sees Legge himself as typifying the very tendency that he was criticizing: "What emerged in consequence, in commercial classical music recording, was a star system in which the 'stars' were mostly performers, not composers—stars who operated within a museum-repertoire of a relatively small number of recognized 'masterpieces' from the eighteenth and nineteenth centuries" (Blake, 39).

The result was a vicious circle of promoted stars (conductors as well as singers) who attracted attention through their performances of self-selected, almost entirely nineteenth and early twentieth century standard works, that then became known through those particular performances, attracting convinced devotees. The struggle over the recording of "modern" music epitomizes the censorial and exclusive role of the companies' commercial interests and the conservatism of their chosen stars. Blake again comments that:

> The entire conducting repertoire of the Italian conductor Carlo Maria Giulini comprises an incandescent recording of the Verdi Requiem in 1964—which is still available—and a handful of other relatively successful recordings; he seems to have known very little music, or about music, apart from these few pieces. No producer seems to have tried to persuade him into a more adventurous *modus operandi*, despite the ready audience for his recordings [Blake, 39, 40].

Many producers, few of whom were formally trained or educated musically, had problems with the contemporary repertoire. Walter Legge's assistant Suvi Raj Grubb told the French composer Pierre Boulez while discussing Bartók's piano concertos (!) that "I found very modern music a tough proposition" (Blake, 41). In fact the tone is indicated by another company-produced book, *The Gramophone Shop of Recorded Music* of 1936 introduced by Lawrence Gilman, as Day explains:

> Gilman, the experienced critic of the New York *Herald Tribune*, pointed out that "most of the greatest music in existence" had been recorded, that the whole field of musical art was being covered "with breath-taking swiftness by the gramophone." In addition to the standard works, now virtually all available on record, he pointed out that many of the rarest works of the past, known only by name hitherto to many musicians and music-lovers, could now be studied on record ... right up to "such last words in musical modernity" as the new symphony by William Walton and his "delectable setting" of *Façade*.[8]

This idea of a core, easily identifiable, repertoire is historically bound and exclusive rather than a genuine musicological concept. It underlays—and continues to do so—live concert and opera as well as the recorded repertoire. Writing about Bruckner's Ninth Symphony, Benjamin-Gunnar Cohrs describes it as

> mostly based on the imperatives of the Romantic era. Scholars such as Willem Erauw and Peter Schleuning had already shown that the way music was experienced in Central Europe gradually took on features of a kind of "Ersatz-Religion" in the course of the nineteenth century: As much of the influence of the Church declined, cultural activities adopted its transcendental function in bourgeois life. Since then, the German/Austrian tradition of musical aesthetics has worshipped at a limited canon of selected musical "monuments," as Erauw described cynically, yet accurately: "With Beethoven's symphonies as the new Holy Scripture, the audience would never become bored of listening to the same music, in the same way people in a Church would never tire of listening to the same words at Holy Mass every Sunday." His assertion is confirmed by the dominant position of such "Holy Scriptures" in the world of classical music on the

one hand, and the neglect to which major composers of other countries tend to be subjected to on the other.⁹

In his autobiography, the producer John Culshaw tells how he struggled to get *Peter Grimes* recorded, and touches upon commercial attitudes to modernity as well as the harmful effects of exclusive contracts:

> By the end of 1957, Benjamin Britten had been associated with Decca for about twelve years, and he had been an exclusive artist for the past six. Yet no steps had been taken to record any of his major operatic works. We were paying little more than lip-service to a composer who seemed to be emerging as the most important figure of his generation, and the obvious way to make a start was with *Peter Grimes*.... But the idea was at first greeted with derision. Lewis [Decca's managing Director] said little, but worried about the costs; I don't think Rosengarten [Decca's distributor in Switzerland] had ever heard of the piece, and Farkas [classical manager in New York] said that he might be able to give away six copies in the United States. I had to tread carefully at that point, but I said that if we rejected the idea we should give some thought to abandoning our "exclusive" agreement with Britten and thus give him a chance to try his luck with other companies.... It was at that stage that Rosengarten began to worry, for he could never bear the idea of the competition stealing a lead on Decca. (Beyond that, it seemed to me that a larger issue was at stake, for if we were to abandon so relatively conservative a modern composer we should rule out contemporary music altogether.)¹⁰

The Producer

Culshaw and his contemporary Walter Legge established what was in effect a new role in the recording process that redefined the aesthetics of recording. The role of the record producer is a complex and ambiguous one, mediating between the commercial aims of the company, the actual artists involved in the recording and all aspects of the finished product, becoming thereby the pivotal connection between the technical and aesthetic. He is, therefore, the arbiter and designer of what the listener hears. But unlike the producer of a live—or video—production, it is extremely hard for the listener to know what mediation has taken place. Walter Legge described himself as "the first of what are called 'producers of records'" (Schwarzkopf, 16). In *On and Off the Record*, a series of his own writings edited by his wife, Elizabeth Schwarzkopf, he explains that

> Before I established myself and my ideas, the attitude of the recording managers of all companies was "we are in the studio to record as well as we can wax what the artists habitually do in the opera house...." My predecessor, Fred Gaisberg, told me: "We are out to make sound photographs of as many sides as we can get

during each session." My ideas were different. It was my aim to make records that would set the standards by which public performances and the artists of the future would be judged. [Schwarzkopf, 16].

In the mid–1960s he further described himself to the critic Edward Greenfield as "the Pope of recording" (Schwarzkopf, 107). This emphasizes not only his (and other producers') mastery of the recording process, but also the extent to which his position gave him control over artists and audiences alike. Greenfield acknowledges this when he says that "Legge was known as a king-maker in the recording world—even Karajan's rise owes much to his Philharmonia period, and Klemperer might have remained undeservedly neglected had it not been for Legge" (Schwarzkopf, 108).

Legge's knowledge of music was profound although he had no formal musical education. The artists with whom he worked (or at least those whom his wife, the soprano Elisabeth Schwarzkopf, chose to include in the book) clearly had the greatest respect for him and his judgment. In recording, his "declared principle ... was: 'I want to make records which will sound in the public's home exactly like what they would hear in the best seat in an acoustically perfect hall'" (Schwarzkopf, 73). Greenfield, again, says that "the trademark of his records is that almost invariably they convey musical life and vigor, the fulfillment of an artist's work, and that is a quality unlikely to fade, however sound reproduction develops in the future."[11] And yet, laudable as this is, it masks the other, interventionist side of the producer's (and Legge's) work. John Stean opens *The Grand Tradition* with the deceptively simple idea that "Edison hit on a good word, proud but unpretentious, when he called his new cylinders 'records.' The term has the dignity of simplicity, also that of association with history: we call historical documents records. In spite of which we are still curiously reluctant to regards records as historical documents."[12]

This hides a paradox at the heart of the relationship between any performance and its recording. It is useful to consider three analogues: written reports, photographs and art reproductions. However painstaking an observer may be, it is not possible for a written account of an event to be other than personal and, therefore, subjective. Even a transcript (such as *Hansard*, the official record of parliamentary debate) will only include—and convey—the aspects of the event that the writer selected or was able to observe. On the other hand, the photograph was for a long time taken as an objective, truthful record; but the camera is increasingly understood to be manipulable to the point where photographs and moving images can no longer be used as evidence in court. In some ways closer to the sound recording, art book-plates are recognizably versions of their originals—yet at the same time they are distortions in terms of size, accurate color and all the implications of location. What then of recorded sound, of the apparent contradictions between Gaisberg's "sound photographs," Legge's "records that would set the standards by which public performances and the artists of the future would be judged," and Victrola's claim that:

> many thousands of lovers of the opera in the latter class have discovered what a satisfactory substitute the Victor is [for live opera performance], for it brings the actual voices of the great singers to the home, with the added advantage that the artist will repeat the favorite aria as many times as may be wished, while at the opera one must usually be content with a single hearing; and even though the scenery and costumes may be lacking, the absence of these accessories will be atoned for in some measure by graphic descriptions and numerous illustrations in this catalogue.[13]

This, naive as it sounds, is directly reflected in one of the milestones of opera recording, Decca's *Ring*, produced by John Culshaw. In his book about the making of the recording he says:

> The sound of a good stereo recording played under good conditions in the home will tend to engulf the listener, and may draw him psychologically closer to the characters of the opera than in the theatre. The sense of being inside the drama is heightened by the absence of a visual element: the listener can hear the words and the music, he can hear where the characters are standing and he can follow them when they move; but he has to create his own mental image of what they look like, and in what sort of setting they are moving. Instead of watching someone else's production, he is unconsciously creating his own. (Andrew Porter, reviewing *Rheingold* in *The Gramophone*, wrote: "Listening to these records is not like going to the opera house without looking at the stage. In some mysterious way they seem to catch you up in the work—not in a particular set of performers more intimately than that").[14]

All of this suggests that the aims of the recording are indeed complex—and perhaps contradictory. Leaving aside for the moment the extent to which recording techniques can manipulate the end product, one might assume that the microphone simply hears what is performed and that this is then directly transferred to become a record of the event as it occurred. However, even if this were the case, the record is, in the first instance, at best exactly that: a reproduction of something that, on a particular occasion, was heard. There is a debate over the relative merits of studio and live recordings, each with its own strengths and weaknesses, but in general there is a sense that the live recording is likely to capture an energy, perhaps atmosphere, that a studio session finds it hard to emulate. But this is more to do with performance conditions than the fact of its being recorded, so that whatever the circumstances, at this level the record bears as close a relationship to the original as any sound record can. But it begs the question as to what *was* actually being heard and, therefore, recorded.

At its simplest, the recording schedule itself may help the singer—and help him or her to perform in a way not possible in the opera house:

> One of the reasons why there have always been so few tenors capable of sustaining the part of *Siegfried* in the theatre is that the demands of the role are excessive.... In the first Act ... the principal character is on stage and singing all the time except the first few minutes and during the episode between Mime and the Wanderer.... In Act Two he is on the stage for more than two-thirds of the time, and much of what he has to do after all the shouting in Act One, is quiet and lyrical.... In Act Three he is on the stage throughout except during the opening scene between the Wanderer and Erda.... No wonder that, in the theatre, Windgassen ... has taken trouble to find passages, especially in the first act, where the voice may be conserved without unduly distressing the audience. Under recording conditions, Windgassen did not need or try to conserve the voice [Culshaw, 1967, 145].

Placido Domingo's 2005 recording of *Tristan und Isolde* has been widely acclaimed, although he was too old to have been able to give this "exemplary" performance on the stage. Only a sympathetic recording schedule could have enabled this artificial performance—against which other recordings are now judged:

> [*The Gramophone*] EDITOR'S CHOICE
> In his 60s, Domingo remains a marvel. Indeed, he gives us a performance of Tristan, carefully studied, heroically sung, sympathetically interpreted, that truly crowns his career as a tenor and recording artist.
> I got even more from his reading than I expected, particularly in Act 3, where his tragic utterance and fearless delivery matches that of his many Otellos. In that he, incidentally, follows in the part two other famous Otellos—Vickers for Karajan on EMI and Vinay for the same conductor at Bayreuth—in terms of searing utterance, but neither of those quite matches Domingo in musical accuracy or vocal consistency. Ludwig Suthaus for Furtwngler is more idiomatic and even more shattering in the role, benefiting from long experience of it on stage, but he is another tradition. Domingo's reading is, in its own terms, superb.[15]

Beyond this, technical devices can be used to create effects that the composer may have wanted, but which could never be achieved in actual performance. Culshaw half-admits this when he describes the recording of the scene in Act I scene iii of *Götterdämmerung* where Siegfried (tenor) appears in the person of Gunther (baritone). Brünnhilde believes that it is Gunther—but, of course, it is in fact Siegfried, and the problem is that he cannot sound like Gunther. Culshaw's recordings for Decca, released in the United States on the London label, including *Der Ring*, are emblazoned with the word "Sonicstage." The use of the word "stage" implied that what was being offered was some kind of "performance" (although in reality only a studio recording) at which

"Instead of watching someone else's production [the listener] is unconsciously creating his own."

Sonicstage employed a range of techniques to create a real presence. With the advent of stereo, companies had divided the recording floor into numbered squares so that singers knew where they were to stand and move in order to create the illusion of stage movement. But in the *Ring* this was taken further. In the score at this point, Wagner instructs "Mit verstellter tiefere stimme," literally "With disguised deeper voice." Interestingly William Mann translates this as "He assumes a baritonal voice,"[16] while Stewart Spencer's version is "With a disguised—rougher—voice."[17] The libretto that accompanies the actual recording reads "Then he speaks in an assumed deeper voice."[18] This led Culshaw to use technology to physically change Windgassen's voice:

> There would inevitably be some people ready to object strenuously about our efforts to change a tenor into a baritone by electronic means at the end of Act One. *It does not happen in the theatre* [sic] would doubtless be the phrase thrown at us from certain quarters. There is an answer, however. It does not happen in the theatre because nobody has tried to make it happen, but *the idea is in the score*. When the drugged and deceived Siegfried goes back up the mountain wearing the Tarnhelm, he is required by Wagner to adopt the guise, stance and voice of Gunther.... I would hazard a guess, based on a knowledge of Wagner's enthusiasm for any new and effective way of bringing about the ends he desired, that he would have jumped at the possibility of using a throat microphone if such a thing had existed in his lifetime. The essence of the scene is that the disguised Siegfried must sound frightening to Brünnhilde and anything which darkens or coarsens or, in an ideal world, lowers the tenor's voice is a step in the right direction. We knew that on a record we could do it: we could, in effect, alter the actual structure of Windgassen's voice by rearranging the overtones in such a way as to impart a baritone timbre. No transposition of key would be evident on the record. Whatever the purists might say, we were convinced that Wagner, had he lived to know the possibilities of sound recording, would have demanded the use of every obtainable modern technique when it came to the object of conveying his works in a dramatically effective way on records [Culshaw, 1967. 186, 187].

The idea that if the musical resources or technology had been available, Wagner would have used them, is the same kind of argument that is used to justify a piano instead of harpsichord for Scarlatti or Bach (Glenn Gould's *Forty Eight*), a reinforced choir and orchestra in Bach or Handel (Sir Thomas Beecham's *Messiah*) or Raymond Leppard's Cavalli. However pleasing or disputed the results, they are certainly a departure from whatever is known about the original and its performance conditions. But crucially, in these examples the extent of that intervention is obvious to the listener. In the Siegfried/Gunther case a major shift has taken place that makes the recording into something on its own terms and necessarily standing *apart* even from the singer's performance underlying the recording. The question is, to what extent it complements or begins to challenge, perhaps even supersede, the "real thing" through its perfection and ease of access. Where Legge had wanted to "make records which will sound in the public's home exactly like what they would hear in the best seat in an acoustically perfect hall," Culshaw saw recording as a creative force that sat alongside the live experience in its own right. As Day puts it:

> Culshaw stressed the differences between live and recorded music. He believed that such differences should be creatively exploited, not minimized, that a recording was an interpretation of a musical performance, a musical object in its own right.... What Culshaw and other producers were now asking singers to do was to rethink their own interpretations, to assist the record men to reinterpret the role for the microphone.... A recording is an illusion; much is lost with a recording, the visual element most obviously, but also the sense of occasion, and the intensity of a communal response. But recorded music—especially now with music in stereo—offered the possibility of better clarity, better balance than was ever possible when attending a live performance, and a much greater sense of intimacy [Day, 43, 44].

The problem—the questionability of this—is that most of the time where a producer has interfered with the real performance or recording, the listener does not know, and therefore is likely to hear something—and use it, perhaps as a personal or broader critical benchmark—unaware that it is an artifice. It distracts from what living performers (can) do and therefore distorts the underlying relationship between the listener and the music itself. An example of a producer informing the listener is Keith Hardwick's comment on the Immolation scene in EMI's *Wagner on Record: 1926–1942*:

> I felt that the Ring excerpts must be properly framed by the *Rheingold* Prelude and the *Götterdämmerung* postlude. Incidentally, this last is included thanks to a bit of technical "trickery." Leider's "Immolation" is the finest on record before (and some would say, including,) Flagstad's. But after she has mounted the pyre her record ends with a few truncated orchestral bars. Florence Austral's recording, although less well sung, contains the whole magnificent orchestral finale. I have therefore joined up the two as Brünnhilde's last note ends—I hope that the shades of Leo Blech and Albert Coates will not object!

Here the trickery has indeed created an artifice, but one that is all the more pleasurable—and informative—for being made manifest to the listener.[19]

Techniques

It is therefore at this point that technical considerations become significant. If the recording is of a live performance, has there been interference with it, such as editing and patching to improve the sound or rectify mistakes? A well-known (if minor) example in a studio recording, is the patching-in of Elizabeth Schwarkopf's high Cs to replace (the elderly) Flagstad's in Act II of the Wilhelm Furtwängler recording of *Tristan*. Does this matter, and if so why? Is it important or useful for the listener to know about it? It depends. If one were listening as an admirer of Flagstad, or wanting to research her career, then a number of quite incorrect inferences would be made without this information. Legge recalled how in his Callas/Gobbi *Tosca* "I made [Gobbi] sing the last minute of the first act of *Tosca*—the Te Deum—forty times before I was satisfied" (Schwarzkopf, 240). It echoes Verdi's demands before the first night of *Macbeth*:

> And so there we were, ready, in costume, the orchestra in the pit, the chorus on stage—when Verdi beckoned to Varesi and me, called us into the wings and asked us, as a favor, to follow him to the foyer for another piano rehearsal of that accursed duet.
> "But Maestro," I said, terrified, "we are already in our Scottish costumes: how can we?"
> "'Put a cloak over them."
> "And Varesi, the baritone, exasperated at the unusual request, ventured to raise his voice a little, and said:
> "'But we've rehearsed it 150 times, for goodness' sake!'"
> "In half an hour, it'll be 151."[20]

In fact it sounds as though Legge saw a parity, consciously or not, between Verdi's role as composer and his own (creative) role as record producer. In other recordings it was the stage presence that concerned him. "In those pre-stereo days, effects of distance were more difficult than now. To achieve Tosca's convincing entrance, her three calls of "Mario" were done separately—all from the wings, each one nearer the microphones—and spliced together later" (Schwarzkopf, 197).

In each example, the question arises as to what the recording is *of* and what it is *for*. Was it of a single performance or were several recorded and then melded to create a whole that was better in some way than any single one, and what is the value of that better? The same applies to studio recordings, but enhanced by the ways in which sessions are arranged. Was there a single take, or were the artists at least playing the piece in sequence? In opera the number of performers involved makes a non-secutive schedule economically desirable, but how does this affect the need for dramatic as well as musical development in the main roles? This is especially worrying where some of the (main) singers may never have performed the role on the stage.

However achieved, the recording will always be of benefit as a means of learning about, becoming familiar with and studying opera. So, by 1925 *Opera at Home* was in its third edition, now with a Preface by Sir Hugh Allen, president of the Royal College of Music, whose attitude to recording was emphatically educational. Rather than "The Victor an Excellent Substitute for the Opera" Allen proposes that

> This book opens the door to a reasonable understanding of over 150 operas, out of each of which some definite living performances are used as illustrations. This is at once the most practical and attractive method, and removes at least one of the chief barriers to a complete understanding, and therefore to real enjoyment of the works.
>
> There is undoubtedly a great future for opera in this country, but it will be dependent on:
> 1. Developing the operatic ear by hearing as much as comes in our way with knowledge of the plots and acquaintance with the music.

He then goes on to a passionate appeal for opera in English and English operas before concluding with the required commercial plug:

> We shall never attain our object by listening to operas of which we understand neither the problem nor its solution, sung in a language we are ignorant of, and it is for this reason that The Gramophone Company have taken on themselves to help us all in the right direction, that we are grateful to them, and intend to benefit by their kindly consideration.[21]

The great shift from what was obviously nothing but a recording to something that could be treated as a substitute for live performance was the result of the development of recording technology between the 1890s and the early 1950s.[22] Three elements are central to this:

- the move from acoustic to electrical recording;
- the shift from 78rpm discs to LPs;
- increasingly minimized quality of surface noise.

The very nature of the 78 rpm disc was inimical to the artificial sense of recording as reality made possible with the 33 rpm LP. Complete recordings of large works, and of opera in particular, were originally always going to remain closer to a record rather than a substitute for the real thing. The recorded repertoire was relatively narrow: almost always of operas and performers that were easily available to the record company.[23] This meant that the idea of "mounting" a recording did not arise. Instead, when an entire opera was going to be produced, singers, usually stalwarts of the mainstream repertoire, were normally required to record their own numbers individually in the most convenient sequence. Once everything had been recorded, a complete sequence was created—producing an opera set. Artistically it was assumed that main-role singers knew their roles and needed rehearsals (if any) purely to relate to the conductor. The idea of the recording of a production did not arise. It was this above all that was challenged in the post-war years by Walter Legge and John Culshaw.

A basic problem with early recordings—but which nonetheless helped emphasize their role as distant reflection of live performance—was their limited ability to encompass the full range of sound. Neither cylinders nor discs recorded through the acoustic horn could capture a full acoustic range[24] which meant that it was impossible to record the whole of what singers and instruments, in particular strings and the piano,[25] produced. They were also unable to capture very quiet sound, while loud music tended to make the direct-transfer needle jump and damage the wax. The recording process also made peculiar demands on the singers, interfering with their natural posture, movement and overall mode of delivery. They were required to stand still (which dramatic performers found inhibiting) and direct their voice straight into the center of the horn; in loud or sonorous passages they had to remember to move back several feet, or have an assistant bodily re-position them—and then remember to advance again. In many cases they had to sing in a modified version of their natural voice. As a result, nuance, timbre, volume and range were only approximately recorded.

All of this changed with the invention of the electric microphone and recording process, so that 78s produced from the 1930s onwards were far more sympathetic, with a wide acoustic range that established a full, realistic sound, both vocally and instrumentally. In the 1950s, Decca LPs for example, were marked with the logo of an ear accompanied by the letters FFRR, claiming "Full frequency range recording," while Philips assured its listeners that *"all Philips records are high fidelity records!"* By the 1940s Nancy Mitford's Uncle Matt was already enjoying the improvement:

> Uncle Matthew had most conveniently forgotten all about "Una voce poco fa," and now played, from morning to night, a record called "The Turkish Patrol," which started piano, became forte, and ended up pianissimo. "You see," he would say, "they come out of a wood, and then you can hear them go back into the wood. Don't know why it's called Turkish, you can't imagine Turks playing a tune like that, and of course there aren't any woods in Turkey. It's just the name, that's all" [Mitford, 196, 197].

What recordings of opera (and any large-scale work) still lacked, was continuity. Originally, 78s had to be played one at a time. Lasting about 4½ minutes per side these had to be turned over, making a significant disruption. This was solved in 1927 with the advent of the record changer operating on new electric, as distinct from hand-cranked, players. With an arm that automatically retracted at the end of a side, there was a central spindle that allowed discs to be stacked and then dropped as each side ended. The result was that sides were cut and numbered so that the discs could drop automatically to create an uninterrupted sequence: in a nine disc set disc one would actually be sides 1 and 18, disc two sides 2 and 17 and so on, creating two drop sequences of nine sides each. The advent of the LP with a potential of about twenty-five minutes per side, meant that an entire act of many operas could be played without interruption, making a credible alternative to live performance.[26] It is at this point, in the early 1950s, therefore, that questions of the function of the record beyond that of an historical "record" or study tool come into real focus.

The Development of Complete Opera Recordings 1915–2008

This table shows the development of complete opera recordings (including highlights, abridgements etc.) between 1905 and 1956. The figures in columns 2–4 are based not on general catalogues, but on books, published by recording companies designed to provide opera synopsise but also (in fact as promotion) their own complete recordings as well as single arias etc. (not included here).

Column 1 Complete recordings, 1905–1925
Column 2 *The Victrola Book of Opera*, 8th ed, 1929 (Figure = number of discs)
Column 3 *Opera at Home*, The Gramophone Co., 1921 & 1925 (Figure = number of discs)
Column 4 *The Decca Book of Opera*, 1956 (all LPs)

All discs are 12" unless otherwise noted.

The numbers in column 1 show the number of sides or discs; columns 2–4 show the number of discs.

Hs = Highlights
Ex = Extracts
Ab = Abridged

		1	2	3		4
			1929	1921	1925	1956
Berlioz	*Trojans at Carthage (only)*					3
Bizet	*Carmen*	1908 Grammophon 36 sides	17			
		1911 Pathé 27 sides		Ex	Ex	3
		1920 Columbia 24 sides				
Britten	*Little Sweep*					1
	Turn of the Screw					2
Debussy	*Pelléas et Mélisande*			8 Hs		4
Delibes	*Lakmé*					3
Donizetti	*La favorite*	1912 Pathé 21 sides				
Falla	*Retablo de Maese Pedro*					1
Gay	*Beggar's Opera*			3	5	
	Polly				4	
German	*Merrie England*	1918		11	11	
Giordano	*Andrea Chenier*	1920 Voce del Padrone 17 discs				

104   Opera in the Media Age

		1	2 1929	3 1921	3 1925	4 1956
Glinka	Ivan Susanin					4
Gounod		1908 Grammophon 34 sides		20	20	
	Faust	1912 Pathé 56 sides				
		1918 HMV 40 sides				
	Roméo et Juliette	1912 Pathé 54 sides				3
Handel	Semele					3
	Sosarme					3
Lehar	Graf von Luxemburg					1 Ab
	Lustige Witwe	1907 G&T 15 discs				1 Ab
	Zarewitch					1 Ab
Leoncavallo	Pagliacci	1907 G&T, HMV 11 discs		10	10	
		1909 Odeon (abridged)?				
		1918 HMV?				3
Mascagni	Cavalleria Rusticana	1909 Odeon 22 sides				
		1918 HMV?			10	
Massé	Galathée	1911 Pathé				
	Les noces de Jeanette	1921 Pathé				
Massenet	Manon	1923 Pathé 24 discs				3 Ab
Menotti	Consul					2
Mozart	Cosí fan tutte					3
	Don Giovanni					4
	Entführung aus dem Serail					3
	Nozze di Figaro					4
	Zauberflöte					3
Mussorgsky	Boris Godunov					3 Ab
	Khovanshchina					4
Nogué	Les Frères Danilo	1912 Pathé 8 discs				
Offenbach	Contes d'Hoffmann					3
Pergolesi	Maestro di Musica					1
Puccini	Bohème	1918 HMV	13	15	15	2
	Madama Butterfly	1924 HMV			14	3
	Manon Lescaut					3
	Tosca	1918 Voce del Padrone 12 discs		16	16	2
		1919 Voce del Padrone 12 discs				
	Turandot					3
Ravel	Enfant et les sortilèges					1
	Heure Espagnole					1
Rimsky-Korsakov	Snow Maiden					5
Rossini	Barber of Seville	1919 Voce del Padrone		17	17	
		1918/20 Phonotype				
Strauss, J	Fledermaus	1907 G&T 28 sides				2
	Zigeunerbaron	1909 G&T 30 sides				2

Composer	Work	1	2 1929	3 1921	3 1925	4 1956
Strauss, O	Walzertraum	1907 G&T (excerpts) 20 sides				
	Frau ohne Schatten					5
Strauss, R	Rosenkavalier					4
	Salome					2
Sullivan	Trial by Jury				4	1
	Sorcerer					2
	Pinafore	1907 Odeon 24 × 10": sides				
		1908 G&T 13 × 10" + 4 × 12" sides	"Gems"	8	2	
	Pirates of Penzance	1920 HMV 11 discs		11	11	2
	Patience	1921 HMV 9 discs		9	9	2
	Princess Ida	1924 HMV 10 discs				2
	Iolanthe	1921/22 HMV 10 discs			10	2
	Mikado	1906 G&T 1 × 12" + 16 × 10" sides		11	11	11
		1908 Odeon 24 × 10": sides				2
		1912 Eddison-Ball 6 × 10" discs				
		1917 HMV 11 discs				
	Ruddigore	1922 9 HMV discs			9	2
	Yeomen of the Guard	1907 Pathé 18 × 10": sides				
		1907 G&T 9 × 10" sides		11	11	2
		1920 HMV 11 discs				
	Gondoliers	1919 HMV 11 discs		11	11	2
Stravinsky	Oedipus Rex					1
Tchaikovsky	Eugene Onegin					3
	Queen of Spades	1907 G&T 20 discs				4
Verdi	Aida	1906/7 Zonophone 13 discs	19	20	20	
Verdi		1912 Columbia (excerpts) 17 discs			3	
		1919 Voce del Pad. 26 × 2" + 4 × 10" discs				
	Ernani	1905 ECR: pastiche of several recordings				
	Forza del Destino					4
	Otello					3
	Rigoletto	1912 Pathé		17	17	
		1916 Columbia 17 discs				
		1916/17 Voce del Pad. 9 × 12" + 8 × 10"				3
		1918 Phonotype				
	Traviata	1912 Pathé 32 sides				
		1918 Phonotype 21 discs	15	15	15	3
	Trovatore	1912				

		1	2	3	4
			1929	1921 1925	1956
Wagner	Fliegende Holländer				3
	Lohengrin				5
	Meistersinger			13 Hs	6
	Parsifal				6s
	Der Ring des Nibelungen				
	Walküre	Act I 1913 Anker 6 discs		5 Hs	
	Siegfried			6 Hs	
	Götterdämmerung			7 Hs	6
	Tannhäuser	Act II 1909 Odeon 19 sides			
	Tristan und Isolde			6 Hs	
Weber	Freischütz				3
Weill	Dreigroschenoper				1 Ex

Notes

Complete recording: With few exceptions these are complete recordings (allowing for so-called traditional cuts). A few are extended extracts or abridgements. Unlike the later "highlight" or German Querschnitt these preserve a narrative continuity, as does the 2002 Opera Rara "Essential" *Zaira*, a reduced version of Mercadante's opera where a complete recording was presumably considered unviable. In most cases each opera consisted of a number of double-sided discs. Some, however, consisted of single sided discs (e.g. the 1907 Pathé *Yeomen of the Guard* of 18 discs or the HMV 1918 *Faust* with 40 sides). In the Table, "Disc" indicates a double sided discs and "Side" a single-sided disc. Single sided discs were used to enable easier continuity of playing.

Disc speeds and sizes: These records are described as 78s but in the early period there were variations on the actual playing speed. 78 rpm was widely agreed in late 1927 but many discs were still made at variant speeds after that. Knowing what the precise speed was makes a complete difference, of course, to modern playing and transfers. (The first issue of EMI's *The Record of Singing*, Vol. I, had to be re-recorded with the correct playing speeds used and therefore the correct pitch). While the discs themselves were usually 12 inches, sometimes 10 inches (or rarely in a few Pathé recordings 10 inches) were used, not as alternatives, but in conjunction with the 12-inch discs. This usually applied where the timing of the numbers meant the shorter-playing 10-inch disc was more economical to produce (e.g. the 1906 G&T and 1908 Odeon *Mikados*).

Companies: The following lists the record labels named above. In fact many of them have a complicated commercial history, involving multiple label names, mergers etc. The dates given are those of the general first appearance of the companies referred to.

	The Gramophone Co. Ltd.	1897	UK	
GC	GCR	1902–1912	UK	Gramophone Concert Record
GT	G&T	1907–1912	UK	Gramophone & Typewriter
H	HMV	1902–	UK	His Master's Voice
A	Anker	1910	Russia	
C	Columbia Records	1888	USA	
E	Eddison-Bell	1904	USA	

Gr	Grammophon	1908	Germany	Deutsche Grammophon
O	Odeon	1904	Germany	
P	Pathé Records	1890s	Belgium	
Ph	Phonotype	1901	Italy	
V	Voce del Padrone	1904	Italian distributor of HMV	
Z	Zonophone	1891	USA	

The accompanying table provides a wider context for this in the steady increase in the number of complete opera recordings available. The five numbered columns include:

1. The acoustic period between 1905 and 1925, when thirty-seven operas appeared (in fifty-seven recordings).
2. The 1929 (eighth) edition of *The Victrola Book of Opera* which contains only seven operas (including one Highlights and one Gems).[27]
3. The Gramophone Company's *Opera at Home*. The 1921 edition consists of sixteen operas (one of which is Highlights). But by 1925 there are twenty-eight (six of which are highlights, although five of these are from Wagner, whose length made selection, at this stage, understandable).
4. The 1956 *Decca Book of Opera* which contains sixty-six operas (five of which are abridged and one of which is Highlights).

The rapidity with which items enter and are withdrawn from current listings makes it difficult to assess the number of operas now available. This is increased by the wide range of alternative sources for deleted, pirated and other issues on a plethora of small labels, let alone download and dedicated classical commercial sites, some of which offer their own bespoke re-issues. However two sources for 2008 indicate the enormous expansion of the easily available recorded repertoire. The 2008 edition of *The Penguin Guide to Classical Music* has 466 separate opera titles, while the *Muze Classical Catalogue* for the same year lists about 4,500 recordings, including multiple recordings and issues of many of the titles. Augmented by the additional web-based sources above, this suggests a shift from thirty-seven complete operas before 1925 to well over 1,000 by 2008. This is so great as to create a change in kind more than degree in the impact on listeners and opera-goers.

An Event in Its Own Right

Paradoxically this major gain in availability of recorded opera also entailed dangers. As recording techniques improved, first with the LP with its greatly increased unbroken playing time, greater fidelity and lack of surface noise, and then the invention of stereo, so the role of the recording as Allen's "door to a reasonable understanding of ... opera" changed. In other words the vital but limited task of offering the opportunity for the listener to prepare for seeing the work in the opera house, now potentially created a distorted expectation and perhaps an inevitable disappointment leading seamlessly to the recording as a substitute for attending an actual performance. The contradictions are clear in the Foreword that Erich Kleiber wrote for the *Decca Book of Opera* in 1956:

> There are very obvious advantages in a system by which the finest contemporary performances are made available in every town and village in the world ... and, in the case of certain famous passages, the listener may be assured that he will be unlikely ever to hear themes so well given in the theatre. But there is also a danger implicit in this general raising of standards. No recording can convey the nuances of stage action—and many of our best singers are also distinguished actors. Nor can it convey those intimate vibrations, those gusts and counter-gusts of sympathy and excitement, which color every performance in the theatre and make it significantly different from those given on other occasions by the same performers.[28]

The status, the meaning, of such a record will also be changed by the passage of time. As long as the performers are available, the recording will remain something like an *aide mémoire*, an appendage to the real thing as (though) the recorded event could be repeated. Under these circumstances the recording always remains a second best—except insofar as it is far more widely available than the original performance could be. But as time passes and the possibility of repeating the performance is lost—the performers become too old or perhaps die—the recording is all that exists. It then begins to stand alone. To last—to be retained in catalogues or collections—it must then have some distinctive merit in its own right. But this can be merely sentimental (when or how the recording was acquired) or personal (it remains a favorite), as well as genuinely historically important (a way of performing in that period), collectable (rare/obscure, part of a collection *sui generis* of recordings of that artist or work) or aesthetic (of an acknowledged artistic excellence).

In this way the record becomes something in its own right, the cherished embodiment of something irrecoverable and, in proportion to the value of the original event, itself part of a tradition. There are, of course, reports of, and books about, instrumental and vocal performers going back at least to the Renaissance. But there is an absolute difference between these and books such as John Steane's *The Grand Tradition*, crucially subtitled *Seventy Years of Singing on Record: 1900 to 1970*, or Michael Scott's *The Record of Singing* which accompanied EMI's major historical survey on LP. Both refer to and depend upon recording as the basis of their commentary, analysis and narrative. As Scott says:

> It would be difficult to exaggerate the value of the gramophone in an appraisal of the great singers of the past.... Before the gramophone, the only records [sic] were literary ones—descriptions that would have been beggared by quite primitive recordings. Even the fine prose and vivid word-pictures of writers like Dr. Burney, Stendhal and Hanslick only convey in the most generalized subjective fashion the impression that voices made.[29]

Certainly one benefit of this is that a historical understanding of singing technique and dramatic interpretation can be securely founded through access to recordings. Musicians can listen to earlier performers or, perhaps more significantly, original performances as sanctioned by composers such as Strauss, Britten and increasingly a whole raft of contemporary figures. The stylistically educational value of this is obvious. But it can also block creativity by establishing supposed ideals. There has always been a tendency to hold up the great singers of the past as models, allowing them to cast long shadows over the roles they made famous. But recordings of a singer like Peter Pears in the roles written for him, and above all in recordings conducted by the composer, can easily create not informative references but absolutes that easily become stereotypes, leaving room only for imitation rather than genuine development by new artists. How often does a review hail a young singer as "the new Callas" etc.?

This in turn can easily seduce listeners away from the opera house to performances on CD or DVD, that embody some kind of personal ideal, becoming a substitute for, or alternative to, the live experience. Whatever perfection the singer, conductor or production may be deemed to offer will militate against the effort or desire to support new artists, encouraging the listener to expect imitations or at least performances that embody the virtues of older or some one particular production, thereby undermining the very life of the art form they claim to admire. The record as event in itself can all too often become an exclusive rather than informative one.

Recordings as Tradition

This is enhanced by the way the actual recordings can create a tradition of their own. Working with these recordings allowed, for the first time, a realistic assessment of the past and the construction of a viable history of singing—how its techniques had changed, how taste shifted and what changes there have been in both musical and dramatic interpretation. Volume Two of *The Record of Singing* is therefore able to talk about important shifts with an authority and in an evidential way that would have been impossible before the recording era proper:

> In the later part of the acoustic recording era, the years between 1914 and 1925, the various national styles of singing were at their most characteristic and sharply differentiated.... Out of each national music there evolved a different vocal style, each reflecting at the same time the peculiar characteristics of the language. These gradually came to supersede the time-honored Italian school, the art of which we can still hear exemplified in the recordings of Adelina Patti and Mattia Battestini and, albeit somewhat modified, in those made by many of the leading pupils of Garcia, Sbriglia, the elder Lamperti and Mathilde Marchesi.[30]

Without access to recordings it would not have been possible to write like this—or to do so with any authority.

When Cammarano was putting Macbeth into production in 1848, Verdi wrote:

> Tadolini, I believe, is to sing Lady Macbeth, and I am astonished that she should have undertaken the part. You know how highly I regard Tadolini, and she herself knows it, but for the sake of us all I feel I must say this to you: Tadolini's qualities are far too fine for this role. This may seem to you absurd, but Tadolini has a beautiful and attractive figure, and I want Lady Macbeth to be ugly and evil. Tadolini sings to perfection, and I don't want Lady Macbeth to sing at all. Tadolini has a wonderful voice, clear, flexible, strong, while Lady Macbeth's voice should be hard, stifled and dark Tadolini's voice is angelic; I want Lady Macbeth's to be diabolic.[31]

Singers, conductors, directors, critics all discuss—and disagree—about what this crucial comment really meant, where a recording—let alone a video—would have settled the matter. Without one it is impossible to talk other than generally about this or any aspect of singing before records.

Once recordings are available it is possible to appreciate and comment upon the fine detail of a singer's art, even at a remove. The following is a critique of Callas's 1950 performances in *Il Trovatore*. What the author says is interesting in its own right as a statement about the tradition of singing the role. It is also a vital piece of evidence about Callas's impact on that tradition. The point is, however, that what Kersting says about her, Ponselle and Muzio can be verified:

> By far her most interesting appearance of the 1950 season was that in Verdi's Il Trovatore.... It is far from a polished performance, imprecise in ensemble and not musically complete, and yet not without interest, indeed it is remarkable as a portrayal of Leonora in which Maria Callas is newly discovering Verdi singing.... Maria Callas performed the vocal part with all the finesse of *fioritura* and trills, thereby depicting the character. To take an example: there exist trills at the ends of phrases in "D'amor sull'ali rosee" and "Vanne, sospir dolente" just as in many other parts of the role.

Yet their effect is lost when they are sung as if they were flute like, merely decorative figures.... Even Rosa Ponselle, or even an expressive singer like Claudia Muzio, do not dip the melodic line or the ornamental figures as deeply into the sound of *melancolia tinita* as Maria Callas. Putting it another way: Maria Callas has so much more to offer than notes spun out on a *fil di suono*. She does not make the part comfortable for her voice, but carries through every vocal formula and binds it into the larger shape.[32]

Conclusion

Recordings can enhance or detract from the art form they relate to or serve. There are several major problems or dangers. They can, by their very nature, create artificial standards through studio-conditioned performance and technical interference creating unrealistic expectations which are then used to judge contemporary performances and artists. This can be inhibiting for both artists and composers, especially where audiences are prone to conservative values. (Similarly, broadcast and live transmissions, while beneficial in themselves as a potential widening of experience, can have the same, in reality opposite effect to what might be expected, by enabling audiences to ignore experiment and adventurous programming.) The availability of the (international) best can similarly inhibit audiences' attendance at more local live performances that may well not be able to match the orchestral standards, production and casting values of recorded (in particular video) performances.

On the other hand there are undoubted benefits too. Recordings can make opera available, to people who, for geographical and physical reasons, would never otherwise have access to it. It also allows people to hear and become familiar with rarely performed operas that they would almost certainly never otherwise have the opportunity to hear, often effecting change to the repertoire itself, as with the regular inclusion now of operas by Monteverdi, Vivaldi, Handel or Janáček. This has greatly enhanced the understanding of the history of opera, and, beyond that the history of (late nineteenth and twentieth century) singing and interpretation. It is needless to say that recordings also offer the pleasure of being able to hear great works, learn about and study them in a way and with a frequency that would be otherwise almost impossible.

In their 1956 revue *At the Drop of a Hat*, Flanders and Swann commented on the growing mania for hi-fi in *A Song of Reproduction*. The introduction ran:

> May we ask, could you hear that more or less all right at the top there? ... People make an awful lot of fuss, anyway about the quality of the sound they listen to. Have you noticed; they spend all that time trying to get the exact effect of an orchestra actually playing in their sitting room. Personally, I can't think of anything I should hate more than an orchestra actually playing in my sitting room.[33]

There is, of course, a serious aesthetic point here. Music—opera in particular—is a public art. Even small-scale—chamber—music is written and performed for an audience in a public space. It is an interaction between performer and audience—which is why the live performance is so important even to recordings themselves. Part of this public activity is watching the performers at work making music. In a large, symphonic work, seeing where the sounds come from is itself a guide to the structure. In a chamber piece or in the opera where the focus is on the individual performer, watching the physicality of music being made, is both involving and instructive about the performer's intention. Beyond this, in opera the singer's physicality, scenery and lighting will enhance, complement, emphasize, perhaps deliberately contradict, the score. To remove not simply the visual but the complete physical presence—of both player and listeners—is, therefore, to diminish the activity as a whole. In the case of opera it reduces it to music alone—which is not what any opera was ever meant to be. Even for the most focused listener, to hear the music in the home is to deny its public nature: the way the music creates and engages a whole audience within which the listener is situated as a social as well as an aesthetic being. At a crucial level, the recording denies the relationship, that public commitment in the opera house (or concert hall) between performers and audience. There is a difference in kind between private music consumption and public participation—one that listeners forget at their peril.

The sound record is, therefore, a paradox. In many ways it can "open the door to a reasonable understanding" of an opera or opera in general. But Allen's word "reasonable" is important: any recording is limited precisely because, however fine, it is only a recording and it is vital that this be made clear to those who, for many reasons in this music-suffused world, may (allow themselves to) be lead to think of the recording as a viable alternative to the live experience. The ubiquitous nature of music reproduction makes the recording an increasing presence in its own right, and a potential substitute for the live performer, innovative production and public participation as audience at this most public of art forms. The record is always in danger of being nothing more than the commodification of music itself. But, ironically, without continued live performance the recording industry itself would be starved of its essential material. It is the duty of the conscious, informed musical public to take advantage of the recorded product—and keep it in its proper place.

Notes

1. G. Born, Afterword, in *The Cambridge Companion to Recorded Music*, ed. N. Cook, et al. (Cambridge: Cambridge University Press, 2009), p. 293.
2. A. Blake, "Recording Practice and the Role of the Producer" in *The Cambridge*

Companion to Recorded Music, ed. N. Cook, et al. (Cambridge: Cambridge University Press, 2009), p. 39.
   3. N. Mitford, *The Pursuit of Love* (London: Penguin, 2010), p. 18.
   4. J. W. McSpadden, *Opera Synopses* (London: Harrap, 1913/56), p. 5.
   5. H.V. Higgins, Preface, in *Opera at Home* (London: Gramophone, 1921), p. 7.
   6. Foreword in *The Victrola Book of the Opera* (Camden, NJ: Victor Talking Machine, 1921), p. 7.
   7. E. Schwarzkopf, *On and Off the Record: A Memoir of Walter Legge* (London: Faber and Faber, 1982), p. 240.
   8. T. Day, *A Century of Recorded Music* (New Haven and London: Yale University Press, 2000), p. 63.
   9. N. Samale and Benjamin-Gunnar Cohrs, *Anton Bruckner: Ninth Symphony, Finale (unfinished). Completed Performance Version by Samale-Phillips-Cohrs-Mazzuca (1983–2012). The conclusive revised edition 2012: An Introduction by Benjamin-Gunnar Cohrs* (online), p. 3.
   10. J. Culshaw, *Putting the Record Straight* (London: Secker and Warburg, 1981), p. 176.
   11. Schwarzkopf, p. 116. Perhaps the highlights of Legge's opera legacy are: the De Sabata *Tosca* with Callas and Gobbi; Karajan's *Der Rosenkavalier* with Schwarzkopf, Ludwig, Stich-Randall and Edelmann and *Falstaff* with Gobbi, Schwarzkopf, Zaccaria, Moffo and Panerai; Böhm's *Così fan tutte* with Schwarzkopf and Ludwig; Furtwängler's *Tristan* with Flagstad and Suthaus; Klemperer's *Fidelio* with Jurinac and Vickers and *Die Zauberflöte* (albeit without the dialogue) with Janowitz, Popp and Gedda.
   12. J.B. Steane, *The Grand Tradition* (London: Duckworth, 1974), p. 4.
   13. *The Victrola Book of the Opera*, p. 9
   14. J. Culshaw, *Ring Resounding* (London: Secker and Warburg, 1967), p. 24.
   15. *Gramophone,* 18 September 2012, p. 73.
   16. W. Mann, trans., *Siegfried, Gotterdammerung* (London: Friends of Covent Garden,1970), p. 41.
   17. B. Milington and S. Spencer, *Wagner's Ring of the Nibelungen: A Companion* (London: Thames and Hudson, 2000), p. 306.
   18. L. Salter, trans., *Gotterdammerung* (Decca 455 569), 1997, p. 106.
   19. K. Hardwick, "Producer's note" in *Wagner on Record, 1926–1942* (EMI RLS 7711), 1983.
   20. Marcello Conati, trans. R. Stokes, *Encounters with Verdi* (Ithaca: Cornell University Press, 1986), pp. 26–27.
   21. H. Allen, Preface in *Opera at Home* (London: Gramophone, 1925), p. 8.
   22. The sequence of recording innovation falls into these phases: 1887, acoustic recording (cylinder and discs of various sizes); 1894, commercial acoustic recordings issued; 1925, electric recording; 1927, the record changer; 1948, Columbia introduces the 33⅓ rpm LP (long playing record) and RCA Victor introduces the 45 rpm EP (extended play record); 1953, LP recordings become standard (although 78s continue for some while); 1954, first commercial stereo recordings (following experiments in the 1930s); 1963, cassette tapes introduced; 1983, CDs introduced.
   23. Of particular interest are the complete absence of Mozart operas in the listings until the LP era; the early popularity of Gilbert and Sullivan (with *The Yeomen of the Guard* produced in England, France and the United States) and the (predictable) struggle with the length of Wagner's works.
   24. The ear can respond to frequencies of between 20 and 20,000 cycles per second while the acoustic horn and transfer process was limited to between 168 and 2,000 cycles

so that it could not reproduce the full range between E below middle C and notes higher than three octaves above middle C. While these were audible all these sounds were distorted. Electrical recording started with the ability to capture between 100 and 5,000 cycles, rising to 8,000 by 1934. (See Day, pp. 9–10, 16.)

25. Specially modified instruments were used to try to overcome some of these problems, including the Stroh violin, with a diaphragm and horn instead of a wooden sound box, and pianos with crudely altered hammers and strings.

26. This was continued in the LP era and my own experience of buying Gilbert and Sullivan LPs was the frustration of owning sides 1 and 4 long before I could save up for sides 2 and 3. With the dawning recognition of the damage this did to the LPs themselves, the drop sequence was gradually abandoned. Perhaps its new incarnation is the multiple CD player.

27. "Highlights" and "Gems" can refer either to favorite bits or a more sequential sequence. The following is typical of the early period's offer (in *The Victor Book of the Opera*, pp. 51–52):

Gems from Carmen.
By Victor Light Opera Company (In English) 31843 12 inch. $1
Chorus, "Here. They Are"—Solo and Chorus, • "Habanera" (Loves Like a Bird)—Duet. "Again He Sees His Village Home"—Sextette, "Our Chosen Trade"—Solo and Chorus, "Toreador Song"—Finale.

An amazing number of the most popular bits of Bizet's masterpiece have been crowded into this attractively arranged potpourri, which shows both the skill of Mr. Rogers and the remarkable talent of the Opera Company.

Only such an organization as that of the Victor, which stands absolutely alone among record-making bodies, could successfully cope with the difficulties of Bizet's score. The record is one of the most striking and brilliant of the series, including as it does the rollicking chorus of boys in Act I; the favorite *Habanera*, the lovely *Jose-Micaela* duet, the Sextette from the Smuggler Scene, the popular *Toreador Song* and the brilliant finish to Act II.

28. E. Kleiber, Foreword in *The Decca Book of Opera* (London: Werner Laurie, 1956, pp. 15–16).

29. M. Scott, *The Record of Singing*, Vol. I (London: Duckworth, 1977), p. ix.

30. M. Scott, *The Record of Singing* Vol. II (London: Duckworth, 1979), p. 1.

31. C. Osborne, *Letters of Giuseppe Verdi* (London: Victor Gollanz, 1971), p. 59.

32. Jürgen Kersting, trans. John Hunt, *Maria Callas* (London: Quartet, 2009), pp. 296–297.

33. I am indebted to Christopher Edwards for drawing this to my attention. Text found at Flanders and Swann online.

Bibliography

Allen, H. Preface in *Opera at Home*. London: Gramophone, 1925.
Blake, A. "Recording Practice and the Role of the Producer." In *The Cambridge Companion to Recorded Music*, edited by N. Cook, et al. Cambridge: Cambridge University Press, 2009.
Born, G. Afterword. In *The Cambridge Companion to Recorded Music*, edited by N. Cook, et al. Cambridge: Cambridge University Press, 2009.
Conati, Marcello, trans. R. Stokes. *Encounters with Verdi*. Ithaca: Cornell University Press, 1986.

Cook, N. et al., eds. *The Cambridge Companion to Recorded Music*. Cambridge: Cambridge University Press, 2009.
Culshaw, J. *Ring Resounding*. London: Secker and Warburg, 1967.
Day, T. *A Century of Recorded Music*. New Haven and London: Yale University Press, 2000.
Hardwick, K. "Producer's note." *Wagner on Record, 1926–1942*. EMI (RLS 7711), 1983.
Higgins, H.V. Preface in *Opera at Home*. London: Gramophone, 1921.
Kersting, Jürgen, trans. John Hunt. *Maria Callas*. London: Quartet, 2009.
Kleiber, E. Foreword in *The Decca Book of Opera*. London: Werner Laurie, 1956.
Mann, W., trans. *Siegfried, Götterdämmerung*. London: Friends of Covent Garden,1970.
March, I., E. Greenfield, R. Layton, and P. Czajkowski. *The Penguin Guide to Recorded Classical Music, 2008*. London: Penguin, 2007.
McSpadden, J. W. *Opera Synopses*. London: Harrap, 1913/56.
Millington, B., and S. Spencer. *Wagner's Ring of the Nibelungen: A Companion*. London: Thames and Hudson, 2000.
Mitford, N. *The Pursuit of Love*. London: Penguin, 2010.
Osborne, C. *Letters of Giuseppe Verdi*. London: Victor Gollanz, 1971.
Putting the Record Straight. London: Secker and Warburg, 1981.
Salter, L., trans. *Götterdämmerung*. Decca 455 569, 1997.
Scott, M. *The Record of Singing*, Vol. I. London: Duckworth, 1977.
_____. *The Record of Singing*, Vol. II. London: Duckworth, 1979.
Schwarzkopf, E. *On and Off the Record: A Memoir of Walter Legge*. London: Faber and Faber, 1982.
Steane, J.B. *The Grand Tradition*. London: Duckworth, 1974.
The Victrola Book of the Opera. Camden, NJ: Victor Talking Machine Company, 1921.

Opera Singers as Pop Stars: Opera Within the Popular Music Industry

*Christopher Newell and
George Newell*

Introduction

Since the late nineteenth century—the heyday of opera's universal popularity, when George Makepeace Towle wrote, upon his return to the United States, that "*Lucretia Borgia* and *Faust*, *The Barber of Seville* and *Don Giovanni* are everywhere popular; you may hear their airs in the drawing rooms and concert halls, as well as whistled by the street boys and ground out on the hand organs"[1]—the case for opera being popular music, beloved by all social groups and classes, has become less and less tenable. This decline has coincided with the advent of a popular music industry founded upon the technologies of the phonograph, the radio, and the parent of both, the loudspeaker technologies which changed the ways music could be performed, consumed, and stored, and which, by the start of the Second World War, had become ubiquitous in Western homes. Today, when we listen to songs in the U.K. chart—or almost anything outside of the classical aisle in a record shop or the opera section of iTunes—we hear voices which could almost belong to a different species to that which sang as Violetta and Alfredo, Carmen and Don José, Mimi and Rodolfo.

Yet these are not different species, and nor are opera and the popular music industry mutually exclusive domains. In the last quarter-century, singers like Andrea Bocelli, Charlotte Church, Russell Watson, Katherine Jenkins, Paul Potts, Alfie Boe, and, indeed, the King of the High C's himself, Luciano Pavarotti, have fused the sounds and production techniques of popular music to an operatic voice, and have sold records to a mass audience—sometimes in quantities that compete with any artist, like a Britney Spears or a Christina Aguilera, who conforms to a more conventional understanding of what a pop star is. This essay will examine the place that the opera singer occupies within the modern popular music industry.

Our argument, in brief, is as follows:

1. That, prior to the advent of the recording of and mechanical amplification of music, some opera could reasonably have been described as popular music.
2. That the popular music industry of today, however, is based on music that is recorded and mechanically amplified, and that, partly as a result of this, this music is vocally based.
3. That recording and mechanical amplification favor a particular type of vocal production.
4. That the operatic style of vocal production is not well adapted for recording and mechanical amplification.
5. That, as a result, attempts to cross opera over into the popular music industry are highly challenging—though not impossible.

We will first present a historical overview of opera's popularity up to the dawn of recorded sound, and then discuss how the contemporary popular music industry evolved—demonstrating, along the way, how particular styles of vocal reproduction were favored as suitable for recording, as well as why the operatic style of vocal production fell out of favor in popular music. Finally, we will present an overview of opera's sole foray into the popular music industry today—classical crossover music—and perform a vocal analysis of selected recordings to try to determine how operatic voices are altered when they attempt to cross-over into the popular music industry.

Before we can do any of this, however, it is necessary to clarify the terms popular music and the popular music industry.

What Is "Popular Music"? What Is the "Popular Music Industry"?

The New Grove Dictionary of Music and Musicians defines popular music as "the music that, with the growth of industrialization in the nineteenth century, began to develop distinctive characteristics in line with the tastes and interests of the expanding urban middle classes."[2] This particularly refers to the vaudevillian and music hall traditions in North America and the United Kingdom, as well as to musical theatre.

Prior to industrialization, the urban middle classes were an extremely limited audience. Music could be roughly divided into two categories based on their audiences: art music, which was written by a composer for the entertainment—and to promote the prestige—of a wealthy patron, such as a monarch or a noble; and folk music, which was the regional music played by and for the rural peasantry.

With the Industrial Revolution, however, there was a dramatic expansion in the population of the cities, and with it came an increase in the wealth available to this population, creating a new urban middle class of merchants and professionals. This middle class didn't have the kind of wealth that the aristocracy had, and so weren't able to offer individual patronage to composers and musicians, but, unlike the rural poor, they could afford to pay for concert tickets, and to buy sheet music to reproduce on their home pianos (and possibly their other instruments—the arrangement of complex scores to be played by piano duet or small chamber ensembles was very common). New traditions of music—vaudeville, music hall, musical theatre—developed to take advantage of the new opportunities for profit.

As the nineteenth century became the twentieth, this same urban middle class became the target audience for sales of the newly invented phonograph technology and phonograph records. It is at this point that the process of music-making and distributing became truly industrialized; and it was with the phonograph record, and, later, the radio, cinema, and television, that the audience for a single performance could begin to number in the millions rather than the few thousand who could fit in a concert hall. For this reason, it is the advent of the phonograph record that the authors consider to be the true birth of the popular music industry.

To reiterate, then: popular music, for the purposes of this essay, is music that is not (1) art music, written by a composer under the patronage of an aristocrat outside of the demands of the marketplace, and nor is it (2) folk music, a regional music composed and played by and for the rural poor. It is a music that occupies a middle-ground: that exists for the entertainment of people who (like the urban middle class of the nineteenth century) have some disposable income that can be spent on entertainment, and it depends financially on sales of concert tickets or recordings to these people, rather than upon the patronage system. It is a music that is defined by its relationship with its audience, and that, as such, tends to display certain characteristics that appeal to that audience's tastes and interests—as, of course, successful art and folk musics also do for their intended audiences.

The popular music industry, to us, refers to the industry that aims to profit from popular music. Its origins are to be found in the original industry that sprang up around the end of the nineteenth century/beginning of the twentieth to profit from the newly invented phonograph and the radio.

Now that we've established working definitions of popular music and of the popular music industry, let us evaluate the history of opera—from its origins in sixteenth century Florence to its heyday in nineteenth century Grand Opera. Prior to the twentieth century, was opera ever popular music? Did it interact with the popular music industry at all?

Opera's Populist Past

Opera's invention is usually attributed to the group of sixteenth century Florentine intellectuals known as the *Camerata*, who met between 1570 and 1580 at the palace of Giovanni di' Bardi, Count of Vernio, and who supposedly found modern music lacking in "arousing and guiding strong and specific emotions"[3] compared to the music and drama of the classical Greeks. Early operas tended to be commissioned by royal patrons in the European courts and performed for them and for their courtiers. It thus began completely in keeping with our definition of art music—as an elite genre, created by elites, whose main works were written under the patronage of elites and performed to them. Popular taste, for such operas, was irrelevant.

There were, however, exceptions to this model from the start. Venetian opera houses were open to the public as early as 1637, and the financial success of these early Venetian operas led to many aristocratic families opening theatres in the city, "motivated," as Thomas Walker writes, "by a mixture of patriotism, self-indulgence and hope for profit."[4] This model of financing—part aristocratic patronage; part public support—was to become a feature of Italian opera, but other European courts were slower to cede the opera to the whims of the public.

Nonetheless, opera made the transition from a music of the courts to a music of the urban populace over the course of the next centuries. Bernard Zelechow[5] charts how opera buffa was created "outside of official culture and without magisterial sanction" to counterbalance the more stately opera seria, and how in the Hapsburg lands in the seventeenth century, urbanites were admitted to operas performed at the Court and in the aristocratic houses. By the end of the eighteenth century, the opera house had become "the meeting place of all classes in society" (Zelechow, 92), and entrepreneurs rather than aristocrats ran the great European opera houses, aiming to turn a profit by selling tickets rather than to please a few royal patrons. Zelechow argues that the popularity of opera in the nineteenth century was due to its ability to engage with contemporary, post–Industrial and French Revolutionary social realities and freedoms as a replacement for "dogmatic religion"—the previous ritual that united people of all social classes—where pre–Ibsen and Shaw drama was shackled by the obligations laid down by Greek tragedy. Opera libretti, on the other hand, could depict the struggles of ordinary people with a grandeur befitting monarchs in *Cavalleria Rusticana* and *La Bohème*.

This was the era in which Verdi famously had to enforce the tightest secrecy over the rehearsals of *Rigoletto* in the knowledge that, once it had been heard once, "La Donna è Mobile" would be on the lips of every gondolier in Venice.[6] An audience of businessmen and professionals who at long last (due to the Industrial Revolution) had time for entertainment and could afford it financed opera across Europe through the purchasing of tickets and season passes. Visually, as well as musically, nineteenth century opera could be spectacular: it used huge casts and employed technology to achieve extraordinary effects, and the "vulgar carnival atmosphere" (Zelechow, 93) attracted huge audiences. It was, at this point, a truly populist genre. Henry Raynor writes how, by the nineteenth century, opera "existed first for its audience and then for the singers who drew the public.... [T]he purpose of opera was to give the greatly gifted tenor and soprano a chance to shine and to thrill the audience by doing so." Great tenors and sopranos were huge stars, household names, and aristocrat and bourgeoisie alike "came to hear a great voice doing something brilliant."[7]

Was opera, then, popular music in the nineteenth century, when judged by our definition? We believe the answer to this to be a yes. Yes because it interacted with the marketplace in a similar way to music of the time—like music hall—that is unequivocally described as popular music: it commanded a broad audience that included members of the urban middle classes, and was financed at least in part by ticket sales (and season pass sales) to this non-aristocratic audience; it also sold sheet music of popular arias that members of these middle classes could play for themselves at home, just as vaudeville and music hall artists did. Furthermore, many of its characteristics—the prevalence of arias written as vehicles for star tenors and sopranos; the high-passion plots depicting ordinary people and their struggles—catered directly to the tastes of the middle class audience.

However, as we will see, the nineteenth century was to be the zenith of opera's popularity. There were growing efforts among the upper classes by the beginning of the twentieth century to reclaim opera as high culture. And live, acoustic music's place as popular music was to be eclipsed before long by two inventions: the loudspeaker and the gramophone. These inventions would first bring fame and great profit to its superstars; however, this combination of the efforts of the upper classes to reclaim opera for themselves and the popularity of the new technologies would turn opera from everyone's music—as beloved by the street boys as it was in the drawing rooms and concert halls—to a music and a singing style existing, for much of the latter half of the twentieth century, at the margins of popular culture, listened to by a dwindling social and cultural elite.

Opera and the Popular Music Industry in the Age of the Gramophone

Phonographs were originally sold as a novelty for the wealthy middle class in the 1880s. They were designed to record sounds and then to reproduce them, and as such were marketed as expensive nostalgia-aids: a family could replay "strains sung or prose tit-bits recited in domestic circles"[8] as many times as they liked at their leisure. At this point, they were principally talked about in terms of preserving speech, or, at most, the amateur singing of a daughter.

This changed with the invention by Emile Berliner in the late 1880s to the early 1890s of a way to inexpensively make multiple copies of a recording using shellac discs rather than the phonograph's wax cylinders (though cylinders could be mass-produced, it could not be done as cheaply as Berliner's discs). By the turn of the twentieth century, the profit-model for the industry had been established: it was not the equipment for playing the records that was the principal money-maker; it was the records themselves. This was the model that would define the popular music industry up to today.[9]

The early technology was a long way from the crystal-clear, balanced sound we've come to expect today. The combination of an acoustic needle and a horn had a narrow bandwidth which was extremely "unkind" (Chanan, 30) to instruments, and was progressively more unkind the more instruments were added. Loud, sharp sounds were emphasized: the string bass, for example, was replaced in early twentieth century jazz with a tuba, and later with a guitar section. Singing voices, on the other hand, recorded well—as befits a technology originally devised to reproduce speech—and successful early recordings were invariably of singers, sometimes accompanied by small groups of instruments. This brings us to a vital point about twentieth-century popular music. Though this deficiency was later ironed out, nonetheless, as Simon Frith says, popular music has "increasingly focused on the use of the voice"[10] over the course of the twentieth century.

Opera was ideally suited for success in the early days of the phonograph record and the radio set: it was a medium built around the human voice, and thus recorded well; it already had short popular tunes—in the form of arias—that were suitable for the three-minute single side format used almost exclusively until the 1950s; and, perhaps most importantly, unlike the vaudeville or music hall acts, which were extremely popular in their own countries but virtually unknown outside of them, it had broad *international* appeal.

One other, less tangible, quality of opera gave it an advantage in the early gramophone industry: its cultural prestige. Quotes from the early twentieth century record industry make it clear that those in the business of promoting the gramophone were eager to avoid it acquiring the seedy reputation that the also-new medium of cinema was beginning to have. Opera lent the gramophone a stamp of respectability from a prestigious, high-culture European tradition, and executives were conscious of this, and pursued opera stars to record. As an executive for the new Victor Talking Machine Company said: "There is good advertising in Grand Opera" (Chanan, 30).

This combination of factors led to the initial success of opera recordings on the gramophone. Particularly, tenor Enrico Caruso found success, achieving, in 1904, the world's first million-selling record: the aria "Vesti la Giubba" from *Pagliacci*.

Caruso particularly, observers have noted, recorded very well, both because of the specific aesthetic qualities of his voice, and because he exploited the blindness of the medium, like Louis Armstrong after him, to evoke a distinct, powerful aural "personality."[11] Chanan writes that his "strong tenor voice (with its baritone quality) helped to drown out the surface noise, so that even on the inadequate apparatus of the time, his records sound rich and vibrant" (Chanan, 30), and Evan Eisenberg has written about how Caruso exploited the blindness of the medium to evoke an aurally charismatic personality: "the easy caricature (sometimes self-drawn) of Caruso that the record listener knew was more endearing than his short, fat self in some ridiculous costume.... Caruso had, in Gaisberg's words, 'the one perfect voice for recording,' and his mild hamminess helped make up for the lack of visible gesture" (Eisenberg, 199).

Despite these early triumphs, however, the forces that would lead to opera's decline from the popular sphere were already in motion. John Storey writes how opera was withdrawn over the course of the latter half of the nineteenth century and at the beginning of the twentieth century from the world of popular entertainment. Between 1825 and 1850, New York elites had established specific buildings for the performance of opera in the city, separating it from the performance of theatre; had objectified a code of behavior, including a dress code; and had increasingly insisted that operas only be performed in their original foreign languages. By the turn of the twentieth century, critics were decrying the commonplace practice of staging four acts from four different operas consecutively: "a hotch-potch ... of extracts ... a program of broken candy."[12] In the 1930s, opera adopted a trustee-governed "non-profit educational form," and so was removed from the demands of the popular marketplace—just as it had been when it was financed solely by its aristocratic patrons prior to the nineteenth century. Furthermore, Storey writes about the new requirement that a consumer of opera do his or her "opera homework" (Storey,

37)—that is, prepare to see it aesthetically and to understand it. It began to be presented as an artistic code to be cracked, rather than as a straightforward entertainment.

As opera was gradually reclaimed as high culture by elites, and began being subjected to requirements that differed from popular tastes—that operas be performed in full rather than split into several disconnected arias that would be sung one after the other as part of a recital; that they be in their native European languages rather than translated into English for the ease of a popular audience; and, increasingly, that the true home of opera was in the institution of the opera house rather than on the record—and as it became more insulated from the popular market place, its territory within the popular music industry began to be occupied by new kinds of music—music that slotted comfortably into the new, technology-dominated popular music industry. The popularization of this music—and the marginalization of opera—would lead to a new microphone-and-recording oriented vocal style that would dominate pop music. The authors regard this new vocal style as being *the* most telling distinction between today's popular music—of almost all genres—and opera, and, as such, regard it as worthwhile to briefly explore the evolution of this vocal style.

The Creation of the Popular Music Voice

Opera singing prizes qualities like precision, clarity, and beauty of tone: qualities which are essential for accurately relating music that has been preserved only in the form of notation. Even more than this, operatic singing prizes raw volume: in the world of Grand Opera, pre-loudspeaker, it didn't matter how beautiful one's voice was, how impeccable one's legato nor how pleasing one's timbre, if it couldn't be heard over a Romantic orchestra. Without the loudspeaker, a singer's only amplifier is his or her own body—and the cleverly designed acoustics of the opera house or concert hall. As such, grand operatic voices, first and foremost, are designed with volume in mind; and this striving for volume alters the tone of the voice.

The phonograph changed this. No longer could music only be preserved in the form of notes on a staff, and in memory and anecdote; it could be preserved precisely as it sounded. It is difficult to overstate the importance of this on shaping the way the singing voice was used in the twentieth century. Michael Chanan (p. 47) writes how blues singer Bessie Smith had to go on tour—attend physical performances—in order to observe and learn singing technique from Ma Rainey. But once Bessie Smith had been recorded, the next generation of black women singer could learn from their homes, with ease. What this meant was that they learned "not only songs but also a way of singing, which could not be communicated on paper." This was the revolution brought on by the gramophone: unlike music notation, it could record not only the notes but the way to sing the notes. Rock and popular music scholar Simon Frith, cited in Chanan (p. 20), argues that this is the defining characteristic of twentieth century popular music: the unrepeatable aspects of music could be reproduced exactly. This favored music derived from an Afro-American tradition, which, in the words of Graham Vulliamy, uses features like "varying vocal timbres, [and] the use of improvisation"[13] and which has always used an "oral-aural ... transmission of music," and which, in part, contributed to the early success of the new urban genre of jazz.

Furthermore, the loudspeaker and the microphone allowed a singer to sing quietly and still be heard. That is, it allowed a singer to imbue his or her voice with all the timbral qualities of quiet singing and nonetheless be heard over any instrument. The crooning singing style pioneered by Rudy Vallée was a direct consequence of the advent of the microphone and loudspeaker: a style of singing that gave the impression that the singer was whispering into the ear of audience members rather than bellowing to them all, like an Al Jolson (or a Caruso). Of Sinatra—among the two or three most influential popular vocalists of the twentieth century—it was often said that it felt like he was singing right to you, and only to you. Sinatra in his early days had a vocal trick that was characteristic of this singing style: he would let his voice catch, let it crack, just the tiniest amount, to convey his vulnerability.[14] These kinds of minute, calculated imperfections would have been completely impossible without a loudspeaker to project them over the band: they would have been lost instantly in an opera house, swallowed up by the orchestra. Compare the soprano voice of Maria Callas to that of Eva Cassidy.

One vocal feature that fell away around the time of the crooners was vibrato. Vibrato is rapid pulsations in pitch, volume and timbre and is a natural occurrence in the voice. A long held single note will actually be two closely related notes sung in very rapid succession. Unless the vibrato is very pronounced, the listener will typically be aware of one composite note. Though most singing voices have some degree of vibrato, pronounced vibrato is characteristic of the Grand Opera style of singing; indeed, pronounced vibrato is a natural consequence of loud singing. However, vibrato carried over by opera singers singing pop is often perceived as unacceptable. As the microphone technique used by the crooners eliminated the need to project the voice, vibrato fell out of favor in popular singing. The Broadway voice heard from performers like Liza Minnelli today retains some of the pre-crooner vibrato of early popular music; however, these singers are the exception rather than the rule.

In the 1950s, these two aural worlds—the Afro-American musical world favoring repetitive harmonic structures to allow for improvisation and nuanced varying vocal timbres, and the whiter but still jazz-influenced world of the crooners—collided in the white mainstream in the form of Elvis Presley, who combined in his hysteria-inducing voice the influences of 1940s R&B (which had a vocal style derived from the blues and jazz) and country music (which, by the time of the Nashville sound of the 1950s, had borrowed the string section, the chorus, and the intimate, microphone-friendly singing style of the crooners). By the early 1960s, the enthusiasm for rock and roll had carried over to Britain, and hugely successful groups like the Beatles and the Rolling Stones carried the new singing style to the forefront of British popular music. Since then, almost all British and American popular music—from 1970s rock music, to soul and Motown (which led to the Mod scene in Britain), to disco, punk rock, the New Wave music of the early 1980s, through to today's pop music (hip-hop–influenced contemporary R&B; Britpop- and indie-inspired contemporary rock music; and contemporary dance music, which derives from hip-hop, R&B, and, particularly, disco)—has absorbed more and more influence from African-American sources: the black-gospel style singing pioneered by Sam Cooke and Ray Charles became soul music, to which artists like Stevie Wonder then introduced the melismatic singing style which permeates contemporary R&B—and some pop-rock—singing. Though each of these genres favors its own specific singing styles, they all ultimately derive in part from that initial injection of blues, jazz, and 1950s country (which derived its vocal style from the crooners) influence that rock and roll artists like Elvis brought to mainstream popular music.

Which leaves opera in a challenging position when it comes to staging any kind of an assault on the popular music industry. A century after that first million-selling record by Caruso, the voice—as we have said, the most basic element of almost all contemporary popular music: the creator of its personality and parent of its stars—in popular music has only moved further and further away from the vibrato-laden operatic voice.

Yet nonetheless, in the last two decades, artists like Andrea Bocelli, Katherine Jenkins and others, who use an operatic (or at least pseudo-operatic) voice, who associate themselves to some degree with the world and reputation of opera, and who release albums of popular arias, and, in one particular case (Bocelli), produce recordings and fully staged performances of full-length operas, have proliferated and found popular success on record and in concert. The remainder of this essay will look at these crossover artists—using the insights gleaned from our previous examinations of the histories of opera and popular music—and will attempt to make sense of the strategies these artists and their record labels have used to (somewhat successfully) allow them to cross back over into the popular music industry.

Classical Crossover

The blueprint for many of these classical crossover artists—whether they're aware of him or not—is the 1950s film star Mario Lanza, who achieved stardom in the United States on the screen and on record singing popular arias and Neapolitan folk songs—as well as newly composed songs from his films—in an operatic style. The accompanying album to his film *The Great Caruso* sold millions of copies world-wide. Lanza, however, felt himself to have fallen short of his operatic potential: he felt that, without appearing on the operatic stage, he was no more than a film actor and popular singer. Though even now the potential of his voice is frequently acknowledged, his attempts to acquire some classical training were not fruitful: he was undisciplined and didn't practice. A combination of the crash dieting that the studios required of him to appear onscreen, and the binge-drinking of alcohol "prompted by Lanza's feelings of failure because he had never realized his operatic potential"[15] led to Lanza's death at 38.

Though his career preceded the ascent of what the industry later termed classical crossover music—that term began to be used in the 1980s, and came to fruition with the first Three Tenors concert in Rome on the eve of the 1990 FIFA World Cup final—some of the themes of attempted crossovers by singers using operatic voices can be found here. Lanza's feelings of inadequacy due to his limited performance on the operatic stage parallels with the criticism many crossover artists have received from classical music critics along the lines of: "his/her voice holds up to recording, but it doesn't have the endurance to perform in a full-length opera." The emphasis, in his records, on (1) arias from the time of Grand Opera, (2) Neapolitan songs, (3) Christmas carols, and (4) newly composed songs (sung in an operatic manner but not, in fact, deriving from the operatic tradition) set a model to which crossover artists still conform. The image-conscious way he was marketed, with an eye towards his weight, and the way his limited operatic credentials were stretched and emphasized in contemporary biographies to try to associate him with the cultural prestige of opera can be seen in the way that contemporary crossover singers are marketed on their images (particularly female singers, like Katherine Jenkins, but there are few articles on Andrea Bocelli or Alfie Boe that don't mention their handsomeness, and there are even fewer publicity shots of them that don't have them looking ruggedly unshaven, and somehow extraordinarily slim for tenors) and how they appropriate the cultural prestige of opera in their own record-company-written biographies. Important too is the way Lanza's recording career was promoted through his exposure through other popular mediums—film, television, and the radio. This would become a ubiquitous feature of modern classical-crossover stars' schedules: appearances at sporting events, in TV talent shows: in any mass-entertainment medium that would allow them to promote their brand of music and, in doing so, distance themselves from the perceived snobbery—a perception that we have, indeed, seen being constructed—of the supposedly insular world of the opera house.

The event that triggered the ascent of the operatic voice to (limited) success took place in 1990, when the Three Tenors—Luciano Pavarotti, Placido Domingo, and Jose Carreras, performed on the eve of the 1990 FIFA World Cup in Rome; a performance that was televised internationally, and later released as video and audio recordings. Pavarotti, in particular, has made reference to Lanza being an early inspiration.[16]

Classical crossover is an industry-defined genre encompassing musicians who in some way straddle the ground between popular and classical music. Though the classical crossover genre can encompass everything from an album of Christmas music performed by an internationally renowned classical cellist, accompanied by highly regarded popular music instrumentalists and vocalists (the album *Songs of Joy & Peace* by Yo-Yo Ma & Friends) to a popular rock singer, accompanied by a lutenist, performing the music of Renaissance composer John Dowland (Sting's *Songs from the Labyrinth*), we will only be looking at the facet of the genre that involves singers using an operatic voice.

Table 1 is a snapshot of potential opera pop crossovers artists who have had at least one single in the U.K. Official Singles Chart Top 100. The table is not a full discography and only indicates releases of single records.

Table 1

Artist Name	*Title of Single Record*	*Date of Release*	*Chart Position*
Andrea Bocelli	Canto della Terra	1999	25
Andrea Bocelli and Sarah Brightman	Time to Say Goodbye	1997	2
Andrea Bocelli	Ave Maria	1999	65
Luciano Pavarotti	Nessun Dorma	1990	2
Luciano Pavarotti with Zucchero	Miserere	1992	15
Luciano Pavarotti with Elton John	Live Like Horses	1996	9
Katherine Jenkins	Green Green Grass of Home	2006	62
Katherine Jenkins	Bring Me to Life	2009	74
Russell Watson	Swing Low 99	1999	38
Russell Watson	Nothing Scared—A Song for Kirsty	2002	17
Russell Watson	Can't Help Falling in Love	2006	69
Russell Watson with Shaun Ryder	Barcelona	2000	68
Russell Watson with Faye Tozer	Someone Like You	2002	10

Artist Name	Title of Single Record	Date of Release	Chart Position
Montserrat Caballé with Freddie Mercury	Barcelona	1992	2
Placido Domingo with John Denver	Perhaps Love	1981	46
Placido Domingo with Jennifer Rush	Till I Loved You	1989	24
Placido Domingo with Luis Cobos	Nessun Dorma	1990	59
The Three Tenors	Libiamo	1994	21
The Three Tenors	You'll Never Walk Alone	1998	35
G4	Bohemian Rhapsody	2005	9
Kiri Te Kanawa	World in Union	1991	4
José Carreras with Sarah Brightman	Friends for Life	1992	11
Charlotte Church	Just Wave Hello	1999	34
Charlotte Church	Crazy Chick	2005	2
Charlotte Church	Call My Name	2005	10
Charlotte Church	Even God Can't Change The Past	2005	17
Charlotte Church	Moodswings (To Come at Me Like That)	2006	14

Table shows potential opera pop crossover candidates, the name of single record released, date of release and highest chart position in the U.K. Official Singles Chart. Repeat entries for the same song by the same artist in other years are not included.

Seven of the twenty-seven entries listed are duets with pop singers. This may indicate a lack of confidence on the part of the record producers in the ability of an operatic crossover voice to win an audience without an offsetting pop voice. Though no record has achieved the number one position, three have achieved number two (only one of these—Pavarotti's recording of "Nessun Dorma"—was not a duet with a pop singer), and eight have reached the U.K. Top Ten. As a snapshot of the state of opera-pop crossover activity it indicates a moderately active phenomenon with twenty-seven records in the last thirty-one years placing in the U.K. top 100. Of these twenty-seven records, only two achieved U.K. top 100 positions in the 1980s, demonstrating that—as we have suggested—opera-pop crossovers as a phenomenon truly took off in the 1990s, from the Three Tenors concert onwards.

Significantly, of the above recordings, seventeen feature crossover tenors, and nine feature crossover sopranos, with two records—the Andrea Bocelli with Sarah Brightman recording and the Jose Carreras with Sarah Brightman recording—featuring both a tenor and a soprano (the two Three Tenors records have each been counted as a single-tenor–featuring record for the purpose of this count). Only one record uses another operatic voice type—the G4 recording, which uses two tenors, a baritone and a bass: thus, only one crossover artist who has achieved a single within the U.K. Top 100 has used an alto or a bass voice. This is in keeping with the tendency of the operatic world to confer star status on only tenors and sopranos; the pop music industry, of course, relies on the idea of the "star personality" (Frith, 145) or the "icon of phonography" who uses vocal charisma to weld "a succession of pretty sounds into a compelling whole" (Eisenberg, 199).

From the crossover artists on this list, the authors have chosen four to profile. One, Luciano Pavarotti, was chosen because his '90s and '00s work—as a solo act, in duets with pop singers, and as a member of the Three Tenors—was the first demonstration that there was a place in the popular marketplace for the operatic voice, and, as such, was the precipitating factor for the re-emergence of that voice over the next two decades.

The three other artists profiled—Andrea Bocelli, Alfie Boe and Russell Watson—have all performed the Elvis Presley song "Can't Help Falling In Love," their recordings of which the authors will analyze vocally at the end of this essay. They also represent contrasting—though not entirely dissimilar—visions of the operatic singer in the popular music world.

Profiles of Crossover Stars

LUCIANO PAVAROTTI

When we talk about the opera in popular culture today, we are talking about Luciano Pavarotti. No other single word—not Puccini, not La Scala—means opera to the popular consumer like the name Pavarotti. His two Guinness World Record achievements are testament to his triumphs over the classical music world and the popular music world: on one hand, a world record for the most curtain calls for one performance (165 curtain calls at the Berlin Opera House on February 27, 1988, after performing *L'Elisir d'Amore*); on the other, he is featured on the best-selling classical music album in the world (Carreras-Domingo-Pavarotti: *The Three Tenors in Concert*). That album, released after the first Three Tenors concert, on the eve of the 1990 World Cup final, went Quintuple Platinum in the United Kingdom in 1991.[17]

On television, his annual Pavarotti and Friends charity concerts featured, in various years, popular artists such as Jon Bon Jovi, Bono, Mariah Carey, Sheryl Crow, Celine Dion, Elton John, Meat Loaf, Queen, George Michael, Sting, and the Spice Girls, as well as another of our case studies, Andrea Bocelli. Upon his death, his estate was worth €300 million. Perhaps most strikingly, his name was used as part of a joke in Richard Curtis's deeply populist British film *Love Actually*. (Emma Thompson's character makes a passing remark about her weight: "Nowadays the only clothes I can get into were once owned by

Pavarotti." Alan Rickman, playing her husband, retorts: "I always think Pavarotti dresses very well," and then the conversation moves on—evidently, the reference requires no explanation.)

In addition to his pop culture clout, of course, Pavarotti possessed one of the great tenor voices in opera. His superstardom within the opera world began in the late '60s and early '70s, where his series of high C's as Tonio in *La Fille du Régiment*, sung not in the head voice Donizetti had expected but in a full voice that resounded like trumpet calls (those early performances were recorded, and can be listened to), won instant standing ovations at Covent Garden and at the Met. His '70s recordings for Decca are regarded as some of the definitive recordings of many Italian operas. This was the Pavarotti who Decca successfully sold as "the King of the High C's." His obituaries, which tended to regard his populist efforts post–World Cup with, at best, an admiration for the success of his marketing, nonetheless had little but praise for his voice at its finest. From *The New York Times*: "he possessed a sound remarkable for its ability to penetrate large spaces easily. Yet he was able to encase that powerful sound in elegant, brilliant colors. His recordings of the Donizetti repertory are still models of natural grace and pristine sound. The clear Italian diction and his understanding of the emotional power of words in music were exemplary" (Holland). And from Alan Blyth: "His tenor was notable for a bright incisive tone with penetrating high notes. The sound was typically Italianate, forward and open. He used it with ease and charm to deliver the many love songs that are the property of operatic tenors. He knew how to spin out an effortless legato and to fine away his tone to delicate pianissimo."[18]

The first Three Tenors concert at the Baths of Caracalla, climaxing with a rendition of "Nessun Dorma" from *Turandot* (which was already being used by the BBC as the theme for its television coverage of the World Cup), initiated a practice that will become a recurring theme of our case studies of crossover artists: the linking of the crossover performer's music to a mass-culture event like football. Just as Mario Lanza used film—another mass-culture spectacle—as a showcase for his songs, so Pavarotti, Domingo, and Carreras took their music outside the opera house and away from their records and associated it instead with a deeply populist activity: football. The message, as the authors interpret it, is that the music being performed is not high culture: that it can belong to anyone and everyone.

John Storey writes about the critical ambivalence that accompanied Pavarotti's '90s shift into the popular sphere. His free concert in Hyde Park in 1991 was greeted with class-conscious delight by the tabloids: it "wasn't for the rich," said the *Daily Mirror*, it was "for the thousands ... who could never normally afford a night with an operatic star" (Storey, 42). At the same time, a writer to *Opera* magazine wrote unhappily of the concert: "they talked, joked and laughed and occasionally jumped up and down to see if they could see Pavarotti on the stage, pausing only to produce thunderous applause at the end of each aria.... [H]e has now become so famous that it is imperative to see him when he appears, much as one visits Madame Tussaud's on coming to London, or goes to see the three handed man at the fairground.... The argument that Pavarotti is a man of the people bringing opera to the masses is a load of tosh, since the masses at Hyde Park showed little interest in listening" (Storey, 43). The critical ambivalence with which Pavarotti's pop career was regarded would prove comparatively mild compared to the ire that would meet later crossover singers.

Above all else, Pavarotti was a consummate recording artist. His operatic and pop careers were created by recordings. As a child, he would imitate the image of Mario Lanza in the mirror (Holland). He compared his voice to the voices of the previous generations of recorded tenors: to Caruso; to Gigli. His repertoire was defined by that most-covered by previous star tenors—the lyrical Italian melodies of Donizetti, of Verdi, of Puccini; not Wagner nor other twentieth century opera composers. He never performed onstage in a role written after 1926. And his reputation—and his fortune—was made through loudspeakers as much as it was unamplified in the opera house. Even before he was performing as part of the Three Tenors, he was recording albums of arias, and was performing in stadiums through amplification systems. One obituary notes: "By the normal standard of Italian tenors, Pavarotti's voice was not particularly large; but the tone was ideally focused and easily produced, so that there was hardly ever the sense of strain or excessive vibrato heard in many of the breed. In the bigger venues it needed, of course, to be amplified; but in the opera house his voice carried easily to the furthermost seats without electronic assistance" (*The Daily Telegraph*).

Pavarotti, however, despite his huge popular success, is the exception rather than the rule among the crossover singers we will look at, in that he was first a star in the operatic world who later was able to achieve stardom in the popular music industry. This was reflected in his recorded output: even when singing "My Way," his vibrato was full; his vowels are pure; he sings through his long notes, rather than tailing off—in other words, he did not adulterate his operatic voice for a popular audience. This quality, too, makes him an aberration from the norm, as we will see.

Andrea Bocelli

The Tuscan tenor has one of the more compelling arguments to make for exemplifying an opera star who is also a pop star: at the time of writing, he has sold 80 million CDs internationally, some of them full-length recordings of operas. Unlike Pavarotti, however, Bocelli's reception on the stage has been mixed, and his acceptance within the operatic world—as is commonplace with crossover artists—remains anything but secure.

Eight of his solo albums have achieved chart positions within the Top Ten in the United Kingdom,[19] and his single "Time to Say Goodbye" with Sarah Brightman achieved the Number 2 spot in the U.K. Singles Charts. He has released albums containing both newly written songs sung in an operatic style and albums of popular songs and arias drawn from the classical and operatic repertoire; his albums tend to feature only one of these kinds of song. For example, his album *Sogno* (1999) contains a collaboration with Celine Dion and songs written by Ennio Morricone, but nothing remotely classical; meanwhile his album *Sacred Arias*, released the same year, contains nothing written after 1900 (with the exception of the final bonus track, a song called "I Believe" by Eric Lévi). Furthermore, Decca have released nine full-length opera recordings with Bocelli in the lead tenor role: these recordings are dominated by selections from the era of Grand Opera, like *Carmen*, *Tosca* and *La Bohème*.

The way Bocelli is marketed is telling, however, of his position within the popular-operatic continuum. His biography on his website repeatedly compares him to traditional operatic tenors (Caruso, Corelli, Domingo, Pavarotti) and uses the language of the opera critics to describe his voice—its "tone," its "colour," its "timbre ... with a versatility ranging from the belcanto to the furor of verismo".[20] There is also the occasional sly aside directed at any critics from the opera world who might question Bocelli's credibility based on his popularity—he is described as "a real breath of fresh air in a world—that of the opera—that risks forgetting its own popular origins" (Official Website)—or his position as a predominantly recorded, rather than live, artist—"it is by his recordings that his voice can be guaranteed to be kept constantly up to the minute for generations to come. As Caruso did at the start of the last century, so Bocelli continues to do at the beginning of the millennium" (Official Website). There are near-constant references to his performances in full-length operas—*Pagliacci*, *Cavalleria Rusticana*, *Andrea Chénier*, *Carmen*—and to the staunchly European venues he has performed at. The biography concludes by talking a little about how Bocelli is "constantly extending his repertoire to reach completely new territories of music, such as Baroque and Lieder works" (Official Website). However, the biography also consistently makes reference to Bocelli's extraordinary sales figures.

The way this biography is presented is illustrative of the delicate balancing act involved in marketing a crossover artist, and how the popular music industry constructs narratives of authenticity around their recording artists. The constant stretching to define Bocelli in relation to operatic tradition shows that, far from crossover artists existing independent of traditional opera, their marketing depends on it. These are not artists who are being marketed towards the relatively limited opera market—who are likely to scorn the relative weakness of their voices; their reliance on amplification and post-production enhancements—but to a broader market of people who, judging by the way the artists are being sold to them, are simultaneously impressed by the grandeur of the opera, and are conscious of their being excluded from the world of informed opera-aficionado. What Bocelli's marketing is saying is: here's someone who is an authentic, bona fide opera singer; here are his credentials; here are all the productions he's appeared in; and here are reasons he's outside of that snobbish, exclusionary world.

Bocelli, more than any other artist we will look at here, is marketed with an eye towards religious appeal. Bocelli's website emphasizes his Roman Catholic faith. Pope John Paul II's fondness for Bocelli was well-known, and he performed "Adeste Fideles" in St. Peter's Basilica. His album *Sacred Arias* consists entirely of religious music, and upon the Pope's death, he released a DVD titled *Credo: John Paul II* of him performing music from that album *Sacred Arias*. Bocelli himself talks openly about his faith in conjunction with his singing: "I only know that God has given me a voice which allows me to express what I feel." Much as Pavarotti, as a part of the Three Tenors and on his own, used the environment of the football pitch—and later, concerts in parks and in arenas—to provide his music with a populist context and separate it from the perceived-to-be-insular world of the opera house, so Bocelli appears to attempt to use Christianity to stamp his music with mass-relatability. Two specific mass culture icons have read his voice through the lens of Christianity rather than opera: Celine Dion famously said in 1998 that "If God could sing, He would sound a lot like Andrea Bocelli" (Official Website), and Elizabeth Taylor reportedly said of Bocelli that "God has kissed this man and I thank God for it."[21]

Despite these marketing strategies, it is worth noting that in 2012, Bocelli was forced to cancel his third performance as Romeo in *Roméo et Juliette* in Genoa due to "acute pharyngitis," which critics attributed to his vocal technique. Conductor Fabio Luisi had defended Bocelli's hiring to critics of Bocelli's operatic credentials by writing that Bocelli was "helping the Teatro Carlo Felice ... to come through its difficult situation with this production, which will attract an audience that is probably not used to go to opera performances, but wishes to see Andrea Bocelli doing Opera."[22] This is interesting because it demonstrates that the relationship between crossover music and traditional opera needn't be antagonistic: traditional opera can use crossover artists for self-promotion and to exploit the broader audience crossover stars have at their disposal, just as crossover artists can use the reputation of opera to confer authenticity and perceived class upon themselves. This symbiotic relationship is on display at industry-sanctioned events like the Classic BRIT Awards, where artists like Bocelli and Katherine Jenkins share awards and a stage with more traditional opera performers like Anna Netrebko and Bryn Terfel.

Alfie Boe

Far more than Pavarotti or Andrea Bocelli, the young British tenor Alfie Boe embraces the grey area between classical and popular music. His website biography[23] is wry and class-conscious: it begins by talking about his victory in the 1994 West London Karaoke Championship for "a scorching rendition of Elvis' 'Suspicious Minds'; the locals in the pub that night hadn't seen or heard anything quite like it" (Official Website), and there are later references to how, "[w]hen he was a kid in Fleetwood," he used to try "to catch fish for dinner off the back of the fish lorry," among other consciously homespun references to working-class existence.

His first major role was in Baz Luhrmann's *La Bohème* on Broadway. His website biography's account of this is illustrative of the affected tone of irreverence with which Boe is marketed: "Many—critics, opera managers, singers and directors—said it was a controversial staging and that he was making a wrong move." They were always questioning, 'Why are you doing this La Bohème on Broadway?'" says Alfie. "And I said, 'Why not?' That was always my answer. 'Why not?'" They didn't see Broadway as a legitimate opera stage, and objected to the production's use of microphones for voice enhancement—although more often than not, Alfie's mic would actually fall off, and he'd end up singing acoustically. He never told Luhrmann; nobody could tell the difference anyway. Alfie wasn't concerned about the British opera establishment's misgivings.... [T]his was Luhrmann's mission, and was, he said, exactly what Puccini intended—for the work to be played to whoever wanted to experience it, 'from the street sweeper to the King of Naples'" (Official Website).

Again, we're hearing an ambivalent relationship with the world of opera—an ambivalence far more pronounced here, however, than in Bocelli's marketing. On the one hand, the establishment's misgivings are being dismissed as snooty and stuffy; on the other, the biography earnestly insists that the populism of Boe's style is entirely in keeping with Puccini's original intentions. On the one hand, that establishment's disdain for microphone-assisted singing is mocked; on the other, the biography makes is clear that Boe was perfectly capable of performing without, thus subjecting his voice to the same operatic litmus test that the establishment has been subjecting singers to since that device's invention. The narrative here, then, is one in which Boe is a performer completely capable of—and respectful to—the operatic traditions of the nineteenth century (and so has the stamp of operatic authenticity), but he also rejects the modern operatic establishment, which appears to represent conservatism and snobbishness. Boe's Broadway experience, here, is being used very much as the same kind of populist signifier as Pavarotti's football pitch (indeed, there is the now-customary mention at the end of Boe's biography of his childhood aspiration to be a footballer, which appears to be a shibboleth among young British male tenors attempting crossover to indicate their mass-culture accessibility) and Bocelli's Christianity.

After performing on Broadway, Boe's career has veered into both traditional operatic territory (performances with English National Opera and at the Royal Opera House) and more populist realms (playing Jean Valjean for five months in the West End production of *Les Misérables*).

RUSSELL WATSON

Russell Watson is an English tenor who has been releasing albums of arias and pop songs written and performed in an operatic style since 2000. His first two albums went double platinum in the United Kingdom, his third went platinum, and his subsequent two went gold; he has also been a consistent presence on U.K. television through the decade. His singing career was put on hold for the latter half of the 2000s while he underwent treatment for two pituitary tumors, but, after his recovery, he has continued to record.

In 1999, Watson achieved mainstream exposure singing "God Save the Queen" at Wembley Stadium at the Rugby League Challenge Cup Final, and then singing at Old Trafford before a football match between Manchester United and Tottenham Hotspur. He was subsequently invited to duet with Montserrat Caballé at the UEFA Champion's League Final in Barcelona. By 2001, he had released an album *The Voice* that made it to Number 5 in the U.K. Albums Chart. He thus followed the tradition that we've already seen Pavarotti set down of using the football pitch as an indicator of mass-culture credibility. Like Boe, his biography pays lip service to his working-class background and love of football: "Russell Watson never imagined he'd someday be the world's greatest tenor. Born in Salford, he'd have preferred to make it playing football." Besides this cursory mention of his past, his website biography is dominated by a discussion of his cancer.[24]

Watson's voice has not fared well in classical music criticism. Rupert Christiansen, writing in the *Daily Telegraph* under the headline "Karaoke on a Grand Scale," said of Watson: "He is no more 'like Pavarotti' [quoting Watson's marketing] than I am. His performing ability, as revealed at Wembley, is entirely reliant on massive amplification, and I would very much doubt whether he has the stamina (or the desire) to sing an entire role in an opera house. His technique is negligible—he sings flat and breathily. Stylistically, he is coarse and flat-footed, without grace or subtlety of interpretation. As amateur tenors go, the late Harry Secombe had far superior natural gifts. This is the apotheosis of karaoke, not operatic artistry."[25]

Watson has made several appearances on British reality television since 2006, when he took part in the BBC reality show *Just the Two of Us*. He was a judge on *Last Choir Standing* in 2008, and performed on the *Strictly Come Dancing Christmas Special*, also in 2008. In the last decade, reality television has played a central role in the classical crossover industry. Shows like Simon Cowell's *Britain's Got Talent* have launched the careers of crossover stars like Paul Potts, while other shows like *Popstar to Operastar* provide populist showcases for the operatic voice, while also conferring credibility on crossover artists like Katherine Jenkins who are placed in judging roles. Like football, like Bocelli's Christianity, and like Boe's Broadway, the television talent show is yet another way for a crossover artist to demonstrate their embrace of mass culture, and their relatability to viewers who may feel excluded from the world of the opera house. Just as Elvis Presley's appearance on the *Ed Sullivan Show* assisted in catapulting him to superstardom in 1956, just as the same show would display the Beatles to the United States eight years later, television's role in creating and promoting crossover artists cannot be underestimated.

Key Vocal Features

As we have already discussed, the singing voice has been central to the popular music industry from its beginning, and is ingrained in the very idea of the opera. The final section of this essay will examine the voices of three crossover artists singing the same pop song "Can't Help Falling in Love," originally recorded by Elvis Presley in 1961. From this examination, we hope to extract some insights into the relationships these crossover artists have to opera and to popular music. First, we will discuss selected vocal qualities in the context of their relationship with opera and popular music; then we will conduct the analyses of the records themselves.

Crossover voices elicit a reaction from fans that can be very opinionated. Opera aficionados may accuse the opera singer of selling out or in some way degrading a skill designed for a high and serious art. Categories of appropriate voice types, "Fach,"[26] is a closely guarded territory and even a casual listener from opera or pop will complain about a cross over that doesn't work according to their ears. Complaints of wobbly, vibrato-stuffed voices singing the Beatles and thin colorless voices supplemented by electronic reverb singing Puccini populate pop/classical music reviews. The degree of passion this elicits is itself interesting and points to some of the deeply ingrained historic distinctions that we have already reviewed.

Each candidate for crossover bears the imprint on their voice of the history of their own development as a vocal artist. The voice will be etched with features defined from birth, from training and from usage. Some features will be impossible to change, such as range.[27] Other features will be more modifiable. The authors propose that some features that indicate either an operatic or a popular approach to singing are extremely difficult to modify, and that, as such, these features are telling of a performer's relationship with both worlds. We posit the following table (Table 2) of vocal features. The listing is not intended to be exhaustive, and many additional vocal features may be equally deserving of scrutiny depending on the singer and the song.

Table 2. The Vocal Features That Are Significant Qualifiers of Crossover Compatibility from Opera Singer to Pop Star

Qualifier	Example	Description
Voice type	i.e., soprano, mezzo soprano, alto, countertenor, tenor, baritone, bass—also "Fach," a more precise descriptor used in Germany.	Basic descriptors of vocal range and timbre from high to low.
Singing techniques	Bel Canto Higher/Lower larynx position	Bel Canto is a tradition of singing which emphasizes singing on pure, open vowel sounds with no diphthongs. The consonants need to be clean, crisp and clear. The lower larynx position[28] favors the grander repertoire of the 19th and 20th centuries. It produces less vocal agility than a higher larynx position but more volume and a heavier tone.
Portamento	Slurring between musical notes.	Much favored right up to the advent of recording technology. Now generally discouraged.
Vibrato	A held note that subtly cycles above and below the notated pitch through two closely related pitches.	Natural variation in pitch
Breathiness/intimacy	A song or song section presented in a personal or intimate style—often with a microphone in close proximity to the mouth.	A way of singing that emphasizes paralinguistic vocal sounds such as breath, lip smacks and liquidity.

Qualifier	Example	Description
Approach to lyrics	The lyrics in opera may be sublimated to the music in opera. Examples of the opposite effect such as punk and country music are commonplace in pop music.	Personalizing, coloring and inflecting the words in such a way that it may break up the musical line. Up until the 19th century, singing the words clearly was a priority for an opera singer; subsequently this convention was somewhat eroded.
Virtuosity	Coloratura, melisma. (A florid musical passage with lots of musical notes used decoratively and expressively.)	Ways in which the voice can be used more as a musical instrument than a communicator of words.
Amplification	An opportunity for a voice that does not naturally project to be made louder.	Ways in which the voice is made louder to be heard in large or noisy spaces.
Microphone technique	Withdrawing the microphone from the mouth on louder sections (also see breathiness/intimacy).	Ways in which the voice can be enhanced by physically manipulating the position of the microphone in relation to the mouth.
Post-production/effects	Reverb, echo, thickening, autotune, chorus etc.	Ways in which the vocal sound is manipulated electronically to enhance the sound to make it more phonogenic or effective in a live performance.

Underlying many of the distinctions which separate the opera singing voice from the pop singing voice are the purposes of each of these voices. For an opera singer singing standard repertoire today, the purpose of singing tends to be beauty of tone, and an accurate interpretation of the composer's intention insofar as it can be gleaned from the musical score. This has certainly not always been the case: singers prior to the nineteenth century would be expected to make the vocal line their own by adding ornaments and very often changing or improving the composer's instructions. This ability was not only expected: it was highly prized; and the ability to extemporize was a mark of quality in a singer.[29] Similarly, a modern pop singer's emphasis will usually be on personalizing the lyrics, as well as exercising interpretative freedom on the musical material. Significantly (at least since the Beatles), it is much more likely that a pop music artist will have written or had an active involvement in the writing of the song. In effect, they may own the song's source in a way that an opera singer never does.

Voice type: There are very few examples of even partial crossover from voices other than sopranos or tenors. It is also fair to say that the popular stars of the operatic world are also predominantly practitioners of these higher registers, and arias from the more popular operatic repertoire tend to favor the higher voices. Thus the odds are significantly stacked against lower voices succeeding as crossover artists. These higher voices can be easily heard over heavily amplified instrumentation. A similar phenomenon can be seen in pop music, where commonplace use of the male falsetto register provides both volume and frequencies high enough to carry over the instrumental backing and allow the words to be heard.

Singing techniques: Popular music genres tend to use a singer's personalized approach to the words as an emotional conduit to the audience. Dominant traditions from the evolution of opera run counter to this approach. Opera pedagogy in the nineteenth century made an adjustment from a higher to a lower larynx position to give greater fullness of tone but less clarity to the words, and the Bel Canto style produces a single clear vowel sound with no use of diphthongs and short, well-enunciated consonants.[30]

Portamento: This refers to slurring or gliding between notes. This is a case of a technique once popular in opera that is now largely disdained. It has been adopted by some popular music singers; particularly the 1920s to '50s singers who used the crooning style. Most western classical singing pedagogy now teaches the singer how to avoid doing this except in specific stylistically appropriate cases.

Vibrato: Vibrato elicits passion even among opera aficionados. Debate rages, particularly concerning its appropriateness in the repertoire in the performance of music pre–Mozart. As a natural by-product of some vocal production techniques—particularly techniques which aim to enlarge the voice to project over bigger orchestras into bigger spaces—it cannot be eliminated by many opera singers. Natural vibrato is also present in the voices of some pop singers (notably Elvis in our examples); however, it tends to be less conspicuous, in part because pop singers—as microphone users—are able to sing more quietly than opera singers and still be heard.

Breathiness/intimacy: A breathy voice is a quiet voice; consequently, it is only useful to an opera singer when the accompaniment is at a suitably low level. It can be used as an effect, but the intimate breathiness used by pop singers is only really possible when the voice is amplified.[31]

Approach to lyrics: Arguably, lyrics matter in opera, but the fact that opera audiences are prepared—in some cases insistent—on hearing opera in a language they may not understand is an indication of some degree of flexibility that pop music does not embrace. The lyrics in pop music are vital: they are the relatable bridge between artist and listener. Although the notion of putting across a song is common to both genres, the method of so doing by emphasizing the emotional content of the lyrics (possibly at the expense of the vocal line) is commonplace in pop. It only exists in certain sub-categories of the operatic form, such as recitative.

Virtuosity: Virtuostic singing—singing that deliberately shows off vocal prowess—is a significant feature of some of the operatic repertoire. It has been a feature of the operatic vocal style since the beginning and remains so despite the efforts of composers (particularly some nineteenth century composers) to eliminate unnecessary vocal gymnastics. As with some other vocal features, it can fit into specific genres of pop music (a melismatic style is commonplace in soul music and derived genres), but it tends not to be allowed to obscure the words[32] An example of the use of ornament in pop singing can be found in the analysis of the duet between Andrea Bocelli and Katherine McPhee.

Amplification: Electronic amplification in opera is largely frowned upon. That is not to say that some electronic enhancement is not present in many opera houses, but these enhancements generally do not include singers with microphones. Exceptions, such as outdoor, arena or in-the-round opera (such as those produced by Raymond Gubbay[33] at London's Royal Albert Hall) exist, but, on the whole, these are unusual exceptions.

The dynamic range of an opera is generally very wide with extreme pianissimos and full blooded sfortzandos; balancing this against a large orchestra with perhaps 50 members and a similar number in the chorus would necessitate a rig substantially bigger than the biggest used for an arena rock concert, and the result, without a great deal of intervention, would almost certainly be significantly reduced in quality from an unamplified performance. As a consequence neither the opera voice nor the opera artist is well adapted to amplification. This, as we have already discussed, is not the case with popular music singers.

Microphone technique: Leading on from general principles of amplification, the specifics of microphone technique are unlikely to be known to most opera singers. An opera artist grows up with a conductor in the middle of their field of view; a pop artist looks down the barrel of a microphone for most of their professional life. Transitioning either way—unlearning either approach—is challenging.

Post production/effects: Most performances and recordings of popular music now use electronic systems to modify the voice. Some modifications are made subtly enough that it appears that nothing is being modified, others modify the voice overtly as a vocal color or effect. Repairs can be made using editing techniques and autotuners; voices can be thickened, brightened or compressed; ambience can be added with reverb and echo. In a live opera performance (other than in some contemporary operas) this is very unlikely to occur. Opera recordings are another matter. Further on in this essay, we scrutinize how these techniques have been used in recordings. As a consequence some pop audiences who have expectations of this digital intervention may find it hard to adapt.

Vocal Analyses

In this section, four recordings of "Can't Help Falling in Love" are compared. The first recording is by Elvis Presley, the song's original performer. The other three recordings are by the crossover singers Alfie Boe, Andrea Bocelli (duetting with pop singer Katherine McPhee), and Russell Watson.

"Can't Help Falling in Love" is based on "Plaisir d'Amour" by Jean Paul Egide Martini 1741–1816.[34] It was written by Hugo Peretti, Luigi Creatore, and George David Weiss, and has been recorded and performed by many pop artists.

Version 1: Elvis Presley: "Can't Help Falling in Love."[35] Released in the United Kingdom on October 1, 1961, and featured in the film *Blue Hawaii*. Key: D Major.

Elvis Presley's voice has a distinctive and consistent baritonal quality that contrasts with both the other crossover artists. His technique is surprisingly Bel Canto, replacing diphthongs with pure vowel sounds to give an occasional operatic quality, particularly when singing in the lower register. He sings it in the lower key of D than any of the other artists who all sing in F. There is only a very modest variation in approach from the beginning to the end of the song. Presley is not afraid of repeating the same vocal ideas. He has a low larynx position to provide a full sound, but he lightens his tone at the top to produce a more intimate, tender quality. He uses portamento frequently, slurring up and down to the note. He has a noticeable vibrato towards the lower register of his voice. He uses a breathy tone at the higher register to color the words. The words are presented simply and very clearly, but injected with some sentiment with an occasional subtle choke or sob. He uses the higher and lower registers to play masculinity off against tenderness and passion. There is no great exhibition of virtuosity in the performance. His microphone use is subtle and discreet. The production is lavish with a significant contribution from a male chorus of "oohs" and doubling of some lyrics. The voice is imbued with an unobtrusive reverb which has an enriching effect, especially towards the lower register. The recurring theme of Presley's singing, here, is effortlessness: everything is presented as very plain, very unobtrusive, very unadorned. Everything about the way the voice is presented to us is about persuading us that this is an unlabored, intimate, authentic performance.

Version 2: Alfie Boe: "I Can't Help Falling in Love with You" from the album *Storyteller*,[36] released in November 2012. Key: F Major.

Alfie Boe's voice is initially presented very lightly in contrast to the Presley version. It is sung in a higher key, and the first sung notes are preceded by a longer introduction. Boe has a tenor voice, but initially the performance underplays any tenoral qualities. He appears to adopt a lower larynx position, but is still able to provide the lightness of tone. He has a noticeable slow vibrato on all of the long notes. On the bridge, he suddenly adopts a much more tenoral tone with pure vowels, and takes a more melodramatic approach to the lyric. Very audible breaths are heard at times. Boe deliberately displaces the rhythm of the tune at times, perhaps endeavoring to make the song sound more personal and individual. There is no obvious vocal virtuosity displayed. The intimate and breathy effects are dependent on the technology and the production is more elaborate than the Presley version with some use of doubling strings and electronic sounds and effects but no chorus. Boe's near-rejection of the operatic voice is consistent with a biography that has only a partial relationship with the world of opera.

Version 3: Andrea Bocelli and Katherine McPhee: "Can't Help Falling in Love" from the album *Amore*,[37] released 4 December 2006. Key: F Major.

The Bocelli/McPhee recording provides an opportunity to examine a crossover singer duetting with a pop singer—a common feature of crossover recordings. In this analysis, we will focus on Bocelli, but reference for comparison's sake will be made to McPhee.

Despite his natural tenorial tone, Bocelli is first presented without clearly revealing a Fach. He even seems to adopt a slight American accent. He uses the diphthongs and reduces his natural vibrato (non–Bel Canto). The opening phrase includes only one decorative flourish, on the word "love." He uses the lower larynx position to give a full tone which is less intimate than that attempted by Boe. McPhee enters suitably built up by the accompaniment (bass guitar entry and drums), and deploys a held note and a wave of melismatic effects. Bocelli has a barely noticeable vibrato and approaches the performance straight; this is in contrast to McPhee's virtuoso performance and conspicuous use of vocal fireworks, sobs, chokes, nasal tones and rhythmic improvisation. Neither performer places much emphasis on the lyrics. On the last lyric of the recording, Bocelli shifts into a falsetto. The recording is heavily produced and both voices are given plenty of reverb to add fullness and atmosphere. Bocelli's restrained, "straight" singing, in which his natural vibrato is reduced and he even uses falsetto for a high note, suggests a singer trying to bring his vocal style closer to that of a pop singer.

Version 4: Russell Watson. "Can't Help Falling in Love," from the album *The Ultimate Collection*,[38] released 13 March 2006. Key: F Major.

The Watson version begins with no particular operatic tenorial statement, but clear evidence of a pop vocal style with pronounced use of diphthongs and singing on the consonants rather than the vowels (a non–Bel Canto approach). He is closely mic'd, with audible breaths. He uses minimal expressive devices and rhythmic displacement. In common with version 3, when the orchestral landscape is expanded, Watson becomes a little more demonstrably opera tenor. Watson has a noticeably different timbre between his upper and lower register which, like Presley, he uses to play off masculinity against tenderness. Watson seeks to personalize the lyric but his approach is less directed toward the art song style adopted by Boe. In the latter third of the song Watson plays his operatic (Bel Canto) and pop tenorial voice to the full, abandoning the intimate approach of some of the first part of the song. This development is emphasized by a chorus and full orchestral arrangement. Much of the drama of this version is in the orchestration rather than the production, the basic approach being to start small and get progressively bigger. In this recording, Watson's voice appears to traverse the key features of both the operatic and pop voices, dipping in and out of each voice with relative ease. Again, we're hearing a voice which comes closer to straight pop—or musical—singing than it does to full-scale operatic singing.

Findings

What we learn from close scrutiny is that the distribution and weighting of the vocal factors which constitute crossover are far from predictable or consistent. However, there are a couple of consistencies.

One is that none of the crossover singers sang in a full operatic style: indeed, based on the characteristics we identified and examined, the crossover singers mostly sang in a style much closer to pop—or, particularly, musical theatre singing—than to opera. One reading of this might be that the pop voice is used in yet another attempt by the performers to distance themselves from the world of mainstream opera. The authors, however, would argue that a more straightforward interpretation is that the pop voice—having developed, as we have seen, as a result of recording and of the microphone—is simply better adapted for singing an intimate, low-key pop song like "Can't Help Falling in Love" than the operatic voice.

Another consistency is that the crossover renditions of the song—unlike the Elvis Presley original—all build up to a vocal climax at the end, in which the singer is able to display some degree of vocal virtuosity. The authors speculate that these climaxes are used to confer credibility on the singers—a demonstration of virtuosity at the end is to show the listener that these aren't merely pop singers but are in some way technically more capable, in the way that an opera singer might be. Furthermore, this climax brings the structure of the song closer to the structure of a traditional tenor aria, which typically ends with an impressive high note. The authors see these vocal climaxes at the ends of the songs, then, as attempts to situate what are otherwise fairly conventional renditions of a pop song in line with what the songs' audiences might expect from an operatic-style performer.

What we're seeing, then, is a genre which, vocally, exists on a tightrope between two worlds. On one side is a traditional operatic style, which may not be suitable for the repertoire, which may alienate a casual audience, and which could expose technical defects in less-trained voices. On the other side is a straightforward pop style, which runs counter to the audience's expectations, and which, if it were wholeheartedly adopted, would surely rob the crossover genre of its reason to exist.

Conclusions

If, by traditional operatic vocal standards, the voices of the crossover artists are found a little lacking, the reason they still succeed commercially must have something to do with the way they are able to associate themselves with the credibility and cultural prestige of opera and certain appealing aspects of the operatic style while also deftly transcending the perceived snobbery of the opera house. This reputation for snobbery, as the work of John Storey tells us, was deliberately manufactured between the end of the nineteenth and beginning of the twentieth century.

The things that determine crossover may be predominantly located outside of the vocal phenomenon. They may include how the artist is marketed, how they look, what their backstory is, what they sing and with whom. It is our proposition, however, that within the voices of crossover artists can be found the same themes—a simultaneous associating with and disdaining of the world of opera—that define these artists' careers.

Perhaps, then, the model of crossover music offers a way forward for opera. It is by no means impossible for opera to be popular music—as we have seen, in the nineteenth century, it very much *was* popular music. Despite popular music voices moving away from the operatic style, the fact that crossover records are able to sell tells us that a popular market still exists for voices with some operatic qualities, and for performers who have a relationship with the world of opera.

Notes

1. L.W. Levine, *Highbrow/Lowbrow: The Emergence of Cultural Hierarchy in America* (Cambridge, MA: Harvard University Press, 1988), p. 99–100.
2. G. Grove, S. Sadie and J. Tyrrell J. *The New Grove Dictionary of Music and Musicians*, 2d ed. (London: Grove, 2001).

3. R. Donington, *The Rise of Opera* (London: Faber and Faber, 1981), pp. 79–80.

4. T. Walker, "Baroque Opera: Italy," in *History of Opera*, ed. S. Sadie (London: Macmillan, 1989), p. 21.

5. B. Zelechow, "The Opera: The Meeting of Popular and Elite Culture in the Nineteenth Century," *The Journal of Popular Culture* 25, no. 2 (1991): 91–97.

6. O. Downes, *The Lure of Music: Depicting the Human Side of Great Composers with Stories of Their Inspired Creations* (New York: Harper, 1918), pp. 38–9.

7. H. Raynor, *Music and Society Since 1815* (London: Barrie and Jenkins, 1976), p. 83.

8. M. Chanan, *Repeated Takes: A Short History of Recording and Its Effects on Music* (London: Verso, 1995), p. 41.

9. Berliner's company in the United States was called the United States Gramophone Company, which was to birth the Victor Talking Machine Company. This company was to become RCA Victor following its acquisition in 1929 by General Electric's radio company RCA. Since the 1980s, RCA Records has been one of Sony Music Entertainment's flagship labels. Berliner's United Kingdom company was called the Gramophone Company, and, upon its merger with the Columbia Gramophone Company in 1931, became EMI. EMI was recently sold to Universal Music Group, though some of its labels were sold to Warner Music Group. Between SME, UMG and WMG, Berliner's original two companies are now represented within all the Big Three record companies. This is illustrative, the authors believe, of the extent to which the early days of the gramophone industry have defined the shape of the popular music industry throughout the twentieth century.

10. S. Frith, "Towards an Aesthetic of Popular Music," in *Music and Society: The Politics of Composition, Performance and Reception*, ed. R. Leppert, S. McClary (Cambridge: Cambridge University Press, 1989), p. 145.

11. E. Eisenberg, "On Phonography," in *Music, Culture, and Society: A Reader*, ed. D.B. Scott (Oxford: Oxford University Press, 2000), p. 199.

12. J. Storey, "Expecting Rain: Opera as Popular Culture?" in *High Pop: Making Culture into Popular Entertainment*, ed. J. Collins (Malden, MA: Blackwell, 2002), p. 34.

13. G. Vulliamy G. "On Music and the Idea of Mass Culture," in *Music, Culture, and Society: A Reader*, ed. D.B. Scott (Oxford: Oxford University Press, 2000), p. 155.

14. A particularly ostentatious example of this effect on display can be found in Sinatra's performance of "Moonlight in Vermont" on the album *Sinatra & Sextet: Live in Paris*. At the end of the second rendition of the bridge, Sinatra stretches the lyric "lovely" until his voice audibly cracks, and sings through the next line. It is an unusually showy display of raw craft for the singer, who, with the exception of this moment, tended not to draw attention to his technique in order to maintain the honest, seemingly unaffected sound that the crooning vocal style aspired towards.

15. W. Allbright, Review of *Mario Lanza: An American Tragedy* by Armando Cesari, *The Opera Quarterly* 20, no. 4 (Autumn 2004): 723.

16. B. Holland, "Luciano Pavarotti," obituary, *The New York Times*, 2007, http://www.nytimes.com/2007/09/07/arts/music/07pavarotti.html. Accessed 25 March 2013.

17. This is a certification it shares with albums like Christina Aguilera's *Stripped*, Maroon 5's *Songs About Jane*, Rihanna's *Loud*, Avril Lavigne's *Let Go* and Paul Simon's blockbuster *Graceland*. It sold more copies than Westlife's self-titled debut album (4× platinum), Tom Jones's *Reload* (4× platinum), Britney Spears's ... *Baby One More Time* (3× platinum), Katy Perry's *Teenage Dream* (3× platinum) or Amy Winehouse's *Frank* (3× platinum). Any of these might be held up as an archetypal pop album.

18. *The Daily Telegraph*, Luciano Pavarotti obituary, 2007, http://www.telegraph.co.uk/news/obituaries/1562294/Luciano-Pavarotti-Obituary.html. Accessed 27 March 2013.

19. *Romanza*, 1997, no. 6; *Sogno*, 1999, no. 4; *Cieli di Toscana*, 2001, no. 3; *Sentimento*,

2002, no. 7; *Amore*, 2006, no. 4; *The Best of Andrea Bocelli: Vivere*, 2007, no. 4; *Opera*, 2012, no. 10; and *Passion*, 2013, no. 7.

20. Official Website. Andrea Bocelli Official Website, 2013, http://www.andrea bocelli.com/en/#!/home. Accessed 15 March 2013.

21. A. Duke A, "Elizabeth Taylor Makes First Outing in Months," CNN, 2009, http://edition.cnn.com/2009/SHOWBIZ/Movies/06/09/liz.taylor.outing/. Accessed 25 March 2013.

22. N. Lebrecht, "Norman Lebrecht on shifting sound worlds," 2013, http://www.artsjournal.com/slippeddisc/2012/02/just-in-fabio-luisi-stands-up-for-andrea-bocelli.html#comments. Accessed 25 March 2013.

23. Official Website. Alfie Boe Official Website, 2013, http://alfie-boe.com/. Accessed 27 March 2013.

24. Official Website. Russell Watson Official Website, 2013, http://www.russell watson.com/. Accessed 25 March 2013.

25. R. Christiansen, "Karaoke on a Grand Scale," *The Daily Telegraph*, 2002, http://www.telegraph.co.uk/culture/theatre/4181485/Karaoke-on-a-grand-scale.html. Accessed 25 March 2013.

26. "Fach" is a German method of categorizing opera voices by range, voice quality and in some cases by specific characters from the operatic canon.

27. Exceptions to this rule are rare but not unheard of: Placido Domingo changed from a tenor to a baritone, and many counter-tenors start out as baritones.

28. John Potter (29) discusses the upper and lower larynx position at length in his definitive contribution to the field.

29. J. Potter and N. Sorrell, *A History of Singing* (Cambridge: Cambridge University Press, 2012).

30. This really is a crude generalization. Many of the pedagogical works of the time place great emphasis on appropriate techniques to assimilate the requirement for well enunciated words into the vocal line. It is just that the end result of this pedagogical approach is rarely that successful in the modern opera house with the romantic and modern repertoire.

31. For a very effective example of the use of a breathy tone in pop music listen to "I Vow to Thee My Country" by Beck Goldsmith, http://www.beckgoldsmith.co.uk/.

32. An alternative use of melismas is on the last word of a sentence or at the beginning of a line with a vowel (such as "Oo"). The melismatic device is unrelated to a word so that the main lyric is undisturbed.

33. Raymond Gubbay, http://www.raymondgubbay.co.uk/discover/discover/about-us, has produced classical music events including opera in venues such as the Royal Albert Hall in London. The company will use amplification at times to enable them to produce opera in the round.

34. Andrea Bocelli also made a recording of the original on his album *Sentimento*.

35. Elvis Presley, *Elvis: 30 #1 Hits*, RCA (ASIN: B00006AG5N), 2002.

36. Alfie Boe, *Storyteller*, Decca Records (ASIN: B008DCL9XY), 2012.

37. Andrea Bocelli, *Amore* Decca (ASIN: B000INAWUC), 2006.

38. Russell Watson, *The Ultimate Collection*, Decca (ASIN: B000E97YYC), 2006.

Bibliography

Alfie Boe Official Website. http://alfie-boe.com/. Accessed 27 March 2013.

Allbright, W. Review of *Mario Lanza: An American Tragedy* by Armando Cesari. *The Opera Quarterly* 20, no. 4 (Autumn 2004): 723.

Andrea Bocelli Official Website. http://www.andreabocelli.com/en/#!/home. Accessed 15 March 2013.
Bennett, A., B. Shank and J. Toynbee, eds. *The Popular Music Studies Reader*, 3d rev. ed. London: Routledge; 2005.
Bocelli, Andrea. *Amore*. Decca (ASIN: B000INAWUC), 2006.
_____. *Aria: The Opera Album*. Decca (ASIN: B000B9WD9G), 1997.
_____. *Sacred Arias*. Philips (ASIN: B00002ND9N), 1999.
_____. *Sentimento*. Decca (ASIN: B000061X20), 2002.
_____. *Sogno*. Polydor (ASIN: B0000256R2), 1999.
Boe, Alfie. *Alfie*. Decca (ASIN: B00577WG0S), 2011.
_____. *Bring Him Home*. Decca (ASIN: B004CCS11W), 2010.
_____. *Storyteller*. Decca (ASIN: B008DCL9XY), 2012.
Chanan, M. *Repeated Takes: A Short History of Recording and Its Effects on Music*. London: Verso, 1995.
Christiansen, R. "Karaoke on a Grand Scale," *Daily Telegraph*, 2002. http://www.telegraph.co.uk/culture/theatre/4181485/Karaoke-on-a-grand-scale.html. Accessed 25 March 2013.
Collins, J, ed. *High Pop: Making Culture into Popular Entertainment*. Malden, MA: Blackwell, 2002.
Daily Telegraph. Luciano Pavarotti obituary, 2007. http://www.telegraph.co.uk/news/obituaries/1562294/Luciano-Pavarotti-Obituary.html. Accessed 27 March 2013.
Donington, R. *The Rise of Opera*. London: Faber and Faber, 1981.
Downes, O. *The Lure of Music: Depicting the Human Side of Great Composers with Stories of Their Inspired Creations*. New York: Harper, 1918.
Duke, A. "Elizabeth Taylor Makes First Outing 'in Months.'" CNN.com, 2009. http://edition.cnn.com/2009/SHOWBIZ/Movies/06/09/liz.taylor.outing/. Accessed 25 March 2013.
Frith, S. *Performing Rites: Evaluating Popular Music*. Oxford: Oxford University Press, 1998.
Goldsmith, Beck. "I Vow to Thee My Country." http://beckgoldsmith.bandcamp.com/track/i-vow-to-thee-my-country. Accessed 30 October 2013.
Grove, G., S. Sadie, and J. Tyrrell. *The New Grove Dictionary of Music and Musicians*, 2d ed. London: Grove, 2001.
Holland, B. Luciano Pavarotti, obituary, *The New York Times*, 2007. http://www.nytimes.com/2007/09/07/arts/music/07pavarotti.html. Accessed 03 March 2013.
Jenkins, Katherine. *Believe*. Warner Bros. (ASIN: B002NX0NOU), 2009.
_____. *Sacred Arias*. Warner Bros. (ASIN: B002NX0NOU), 2008.
_____. *The Ultimate Collection*. Decca (ASIN: B002FWYL5G), 2009.
Kaplan, J. Frank. *The Making of a Legend*. London: Sphere, 2010.
Lebrecht, N. "Norman Lebrecht on Shifting Sound Worlds." 2013. http://www.artsjournal.com/slippeddisc/2012/02/just-in-fabio-luisi-stands-up-for-andrea-bocelli.html#comments. Accessed 25 March 2013.
Leppert, R., and S. McClary S., eds. *Music and Society: The Politics of Composition, Performance and Reception*. Cambridge: Cambridge University Press, 1989.
Levine, L.W. *Highbrow/Lowbrow: The Emergence of Cultural Hierarchy in America*. Cambridge, MA: Harvard University Press, 1988.
Potter, J., and N. Sorrell. *A History of Singing*. Cambridge: Cambridge University Press, 2012.
Presley, Elvis. *Elvis: 30 #1 Hits*. RCA (ASIN: B00006AG5N), 2002.
Raynor, H. *Music and Society Since 1815*. London: Barrie and Jenkins, 1976.

Raymond Gubbay Website. 2013. http://www.raymondgubbay.co.uk/. Accessed 30 March 2013.
Russell Watson Official Website. 2013. http://www.russellwatson.com/. Accessed 25 March 2013.
Sadie, S., ed. *History of Opera*. London: Macmillan, 1989.
Scott, D.B., ed. *Music, Culture, and Society: A Reader*. Oxford: Oxford University Press, 2000.
Sinatra, Frank. *Sinatra & Sextet: Live in Paris*. Reprise (ASIN: B000002MO4), 1997.
The Three Tenors. *Carreras Domingo Pavarotti in Concert*. Decca (ASIN: B0000041XX), 1998.
Watson, Russell. *La Voce*. Epic (ASIN: B003Y73FAI), 2010.
_____. *The Ultimate Collection*. Decca (ASIN: B000E97YYC), 2006.
_____. *The Voice*. Decca (ASIN: B00004YVL1), 2000.
Zelechow, B. "The Opera: The Meeting of Popular and Elite Culture in the Nineteenth Century." *The Journal of Popular Culture* 25, no. 2 (1991): 91–97.

Cross-Cuts and Arias: The Language of Film and Its Impact on Opera

Kevin Stephens

Composers and librettists in the twentieth century could hardly avoid seeing films and, in the second half of the century, television. These modern media demand from their audiences a different way of reading from the ways audiences would previously have read theatre performances. Certain elements, sharp cuts between scenes, cross-cutting between different locations, times and plot events, various dissolves and fades between scenes and the cold open or teaser so commonly used, have had an influence on the ways in which some composers and librettists have created their operas. Other important elements of film and television, for example the close-up, cannot be copied exactly on the stage but may be imitated by analogy. This essay explores how the influence of film and television techniques has affected opera as seen through works by Alban Berg, Bernd-Alois Zimmerman, Krzysztof Penderecki, Hans Werner Henze, Michael Tippett, Benjamin Britten, John Adams and Philip Glass.

Speaking about serious filmed musicals at the first International Conference on Opera in Television Salzburg in 1956, Andre Boll, of the International Theatre Institute, Paris said, "We know that even in 'lyrical' performances in the theatre a conflict exists between the dramatic action, which must move on, and the musical composition, which by its nature holds back. How should we reconcile the conflict between the beauty of a formal medium of expression, music, with the speed which is characteristic of every type of film?"[1] Boll's question raises a fundamental issue in the presentation of opera. From the earliest times opera found a way of dividing into recitative, which would move the action on, and aria (or chorus, ensemble etc.) in which the action would pause to allow a musical thought to unfurl, stepping aside from the immediate narration of the plot.

The various reforms of opera have tried to modify this situation, sometimes making recitative take on more of the character of aria (arioso, accompanied recitative, for example in Gluck) and sometimes aiming for unending melody, a continuous flow as in Wagner's music dramas. But even in such a highly focused musical structure as *Tristan und Isolde* the joins are visible—there are chunks of the opera which can be taken out of context and used as separate numbers, as any collector of opera recordings will know.

Contrast this with the fast-moving action of any contemporary television soap opera or drama. Few scenes last more than a minute or two and each scene will be built up from a montage of different shots from varied camera angles. Successive scenes can be in different locations and may be widely spaced in time. Flashbacks or forward premonitions are used, often with little warning. Two or more plot lines will be run in parallel with brief scenes from each shown in turn. In some dramas the action begins immediately and the credits appear only after several minutes of scene-setting action. The audience expects to be able to keep up with this rapidly changing scenario and is expected to be able to do this by the producer/director. All the techniques used derive from those developed in the film industry over the last century or so.

As Dudley Andrew points out, "Every man-made representation derives its power not from its relation to real perception but from its deployment of a system of marks which, through use, has become 'readable as' an image of the real. The viewer works to decipher the marks, using his experience within the system and interpreting the strategy of the artist to interpolate a whole scene."[2] Viewers of film have become adept at reading the system of marks used in film, and composers are included in those audiences. How has the development of these techniques, and the concomitant development of the audience's ability to follow them, affected opera in the twentieth century? At first glance it may seem as if it has not. Most operas continue to unfold at the same leisurely pace, driven by the music. But in many cases composers have been influenced by film techniques and this essay is concerned with the ways in which film technique, and the new ways of seeing and reading films and television programs which audiences have developed, have influenced some twentieth century operas.

Previous studies of opera and film have tended to concentrate on operas which are made into films. Marcia J, Citron's *Opera on Screen*,[3] or her later *When Opera Meets Film*,[4] for example, use narrative theory, gender theory, and media studies to explore what happens when operas become films. Richard Fawkes's *Opera on Film*[5] is a more straightforward discussion of the fascination for opera on the part of some of the great film directors. In Jeremy Tambling's *Opera, Ideology and Film*[6] the author remarks in his introduction that, "film has wanted to be like opera, and opera has not been above learning from film," though there is only a little exploration of this latter aspect in the book. *Opera and Film* by Mervyn Cooke[7] is a self-confessed study of "filmed interpretations of operas written in various epochs," despite the book's title.

The earliest films were single shot films, that is, the camera pointed at the action and filmed it. The effect was akin to the single viewpoint of an audience member sitting in a theatre. What was new, though, was the impact of these striking new images. Mark Cousins describes "a now famous [Lumière brothers, 1895] single shot film called *L'Arrivée d'un train en gare de la Ciotat/ The Arrival of a Train at La Ciotat Station* (France). The camera was placed near the track so the train gradually increased in size as it pulled in, until it seemed that it would crash through the screen into the room itself. Audiences ducked, screamed or got up to leave. They were thrilled, as if on a roller-coaster ride."[8] Audiences quickly realized that the images on the screen were not real and adapted their responses to what they saw. This very adaptability of audiences and their willingness to understand the new ways of viewing scenes as shown in the cinema is vitally important.

Georges Méliès is credited with the first cut, where the picture on the screen is replaced by another (related) shot. In his *La Lune à une metre/The Moon at One Metre* (France, 1896) "we first see an observatory and then cut to a theatrical painting of the moon in close-up, as if we are looking through a telescope" (Cousins 27). By 1898 cuts were frequently used. In 1901 George Albert Smith, "Mr. Smith" of the Brighton School used a cut to a close-up to show detail not immediately apparent to an audience. In *The Sick Kitten* (U.K., 1903, a remake of a lost film of 1901, *The Little Doctor*), "we first see a room, two children and a cat, the master shot. Smith cuts to a close-up of the kitten as it is given a spoonful of medicine. No-one is looking through a telescope, yet Smith simply decided that it would be clearer and more enjoyable for the audience to see this action bigger and in more detail. Filmmakers at the time worried that cutting suddenly into a detail like this would jar an audience accustomed, in the theatre, to being at a constant distance from the action. Smith showed that this was not the case" (Cousins 31).

Cinema developed at a time when the prevailing climate in the theatre was that of realism. Spectacular effects such as those created by Bruce "Sensation" Smith at London's Drury Lane Theatre[9] became an integral part of the drama. As Donahue puts it, "Scenic expression became the protagonist to the dramatic action of the play."[10] Stage sets were usually bulky and complex and scene changes could take some time, often hidden by a so-called "carpenter's scene" taking place before the front door. This affected opera too. A scene change would be signaled by a curtain, the music would stop (a natural break between separate numbers) and the next scene would open when all was ready backstage.

As operas became more continuous in musical texture, a development primarily led by Wagner, there arose the need for music to play throughout the scene changes, to keep the audience's attention and to maintain the dramatic tension. Thus we have the three interludes between the four scenes of *Das Rheingold*, Siegfried's climb up Brünnhilde's mountain in Act 3 of *Siegfried* and the various dawns and interludes (including some of Wagner's most memorable music, Siegfried's journey to the Rhine and Siegfried's funeral procession) in *Götterdämmerung*. In the first Bayreuth production of *Parsifal* (1882) a piece of moving scenery, designed to give the illusion of movement as Gurnemanz and Parsifal journey to Montsalvat between Act 1 scenes 1 and 2 proved to be too long for the music. Wagner's acolyte, Engelbert Humperdinck, composed a few extra bars to fill the gap and, with Wagner's approval, they were used in this first year, though removed later when the scenery was shortened.[11] Though claiming to have cast off Wagner's shadow Claude Debussy composed short interludes for the scene changes in his *Pelléas et Mélisande* (1900).

Such drawn-out procedures have not always been typical of the stage. The Elizabethan and Jacobean theatres in the open air had little in the way of props, scenery and lighting, yet by using the audience's imagination they were able to stage such fast-moving scenes as battles. The technique was inventive. Alan C. Dessen describes the techniques used. "Rather than avoiding battle scenes, Elizabethan theatrical professionals found practical solutions, with particular emphasis upon the part standing for the whole. Thus, in place of the sweep of battle possible in the cinema, the Elizabethan playwright provided small groups of combatants (in twos and fours) in 'excursions' on- and off-stage, with all this activity accompanied by elaborate sound effects ('alarums') that included trumpet calls, the clash of steel, and the firing of weapons."[12]

A perfect example is found in *Macbeth* Act 5 Scenes 6 & 7. Scene 6 has Malcolm, Young Siward and MacDuff standing for their whole army and throwing down the boughs of Birnam Wood as they close in battle. The scene is eleven lines long. Scene 7 is 40 lines but it divides easily into three sections and if the usual convention, of ending a scene when everyone has left the stage, were applied here then it would be three short scenes. First Macbeth fights and kills Young Siward and exits, then Macduff enters searching for Macbeth, finally Malcolm and Siward are entering the castle. The pace seems to quicken as these tiny fragments of battle are played out and they culminate in Scene 8 which is the final fight between Macbeth and MacDuff who was "from his mother's womb/untimely ripp'd."[13] The rapid switching between scenes (implying different parts of the battlefield), and the increasing pace leading up to the climactic scene are reminiscent of the cinema techniques of cutting and cross-cutting. Something that was later invented as part of the language of cinema had previously existed in the theatre and had relied on the audience's use of its imagination. It is interesting to note that in Verdi's operatic version of *Macbeth* this cross-cutting approach to the battle and Macbeth's demise is abandoned in favor of a single continuous scene (Act 4, Scene 3b), though Verdi's Act 4 does include four separate locations.

Shakespeare's *King John* sets out its stall perfectly in the very first stage direction, added by Nicholas Rowe in his 1709 edition: "The scene: sometimes in England, sometimes in France." The play moves freely between these locations and the audience uses its imagination, recognition of characters and other clues to keep up with the action. The pattern is clear, a simpler stage picture and mode of presentation means that action, scene changes, and fast-moving drama can be presented much more effectively. Fortuitously the development of the cinema came at the same time as simpler staging and modern electric lighting techniques were being introduced into theatre. These made it possible for staged theatre to mimic (at least to a certain extent) some of the new devices introduced in the new cinematic art form.

Harley Granville-Barker "restored the full texts of Shakespeare's plays to performance by abolishing pictorial scenery and slow declamation, substituting instead nonrealistic decoration and rapid natural speech."[14] In the field of opera Adolphe Appia introduced abstract stage settings and atmospheric lighting to Wagner production. "He believed that the primary force in opera was music, and that whatever the prescription of the stage instructions it alone held the clues to the staging, whose business it was to be the "opened eyes of the score"—an idea wholly consonant with Wagner's "deeds of music made visible." Scenery painted on flats had to be abolished. The settings needed to be vaguely suggestive, or even coldly abstract, in order that they should be capable of changing with time even as the music does. The principal agent of change was to be the recently invented electric lighting console with its ability to orchestrate a play of light on the stage in exact sympathy with the music."[15]

Frank Gray[16] gives a detailed background to the first cuts and film edits and relates this innovation to the previous practice of lantern-slide shows in which "each slide was designed to serve a particular function within the delivery of a linear, spoken narrative." Gray shows both that G. A. Smith had previous experience with lantern-slide shows and that the technology of the time allowed that "dissolving views (shifting from lens to lens) and special effects (such a superimposition) could be created. Each time a change of slide occurred, this edit/cut would introduce a new slide that could depict a new event or character within a new space or time or perspective" (Gray 52). In other words some of the potential audiences for cinema had previous experience of rapidly changing viewpoints.

The next step after the cut was the development of the technique of cross-cutting. Audiences of film and television are now completely familiar with this technique which allows, for example, the parallel running of separate plot lines in soap operas, or the portrayal of simultaneous events in separate locations (which may be related, or whose relation may be made clear by the cross-cutting). In the beginning such audience familiarity could not be assumed. "Until [Edwin Stanton] Porter's apparent innovations in 1903, directors assumed that such spatial jumps would confuse audiences" (Cousins 37).

Porter's supposed innovation was to show in one sequence of *Life of an American Fireman* (U.S., 1903) "the arrival of a fireman outside a blazing house. The image cuts to a room inside the house where the fireman rescues a mother, then cuts to an exterior shot of the mother on the street. The camera then returns inside the house to show the rescue of the mother's child by the fireman and then re-establishes itself outside again" (Cousins 37). In fact there are two versions of this film in existence, one with the cross-cutting as described, the other with the outside scenes in a continuous flow followed by the inside scenes. There is some controversy over which version is the original[17] but it does not matter who was the first to claim credit for the technique as its development hinges on "the genesis of filmic expression, on the convergence of narrativity and cinema, and on the evolution of narrative constructions at which first Griffith and then other filmmakers would excel a few years later" (Gaudreault 39).

On the opera stage the idea of cutting from one scene immediately into another can cause problems for directors. Nevertheless this did not prevent composers from attempting the feat. A notable cut is in Berg's *Wozzeck*. In Act III Wozzeck has killed Marie by the pool. He sings the word "Tod" and the orchestra plays two successive long-held B's with drum beats between, each on an overwhelming crescendo. At the end of the second B wild piano music starts up and we are plunged straight into the scene in the inn. It is a tremendous shock and contrast and there is a minimal amount of time to allow the scene change. In performance the two B notes usually last about 30 seconds and this gives the director an opportunity to darken the stage to prepare the next scene. The director must find a way of achieving this swift cut, and heavy realistic settings will certainly not help. This way of writing virtually forces the director's hand and rules out detailed realistic settings. In *Wozzeck* the whole opera consists of short fast-moving scenes with fairly short or non-existent transitions. In part Berg found this in Büchner's play, *Woyzeck*, but the fast cut to the inn scene is so sharp edged it implies a cinematic influence.

Film editing is the art, technique, and practice of assembling shots into a coherent sequence which help to tell the story of the film in a logical way that can be easily followed by the audience. Montage is a term used by the Russian director Sergei Eisenstein to describe the film technique in which a series of brief shots are edited into a sequence which suggests a series of events unfolding more quickly that they would in real time. These techniques have been compared to the way atonal and twelve-note music operates.

Jeremy Tambling examines the use of film in the atonal and twelve-note works of Schoenberg and Berg, picking up remarks made by the composers Ernst Krenek and Hanns Eisler and Berg's biographer, Willi Reich. "The atonal operas of Schoenberg, and the works of Berg are cinematic in this insistence on the continuous, with the disruption of what Krenek called 'the concept of self-contained static systems': a breaking up he saw as analogous to the method where 'film sequences are cut and combined'" (Tambling 75–76).[18] In other words, rather than having separate self-contained musical numbers which hold up the action, as in much nineteenth century opera, Schoenberg and Berg are seeking a more fluid and filmic approach. Tambling does acknowledge that Wagner's *Das Rheingold* and *Parsifal* may be exceptions, but neither unfolds at any kind of speed.

"Hans [*sic*] Eisler comments that it was as if Berg composed with a stopwatch in his hand, and added that 'complex stage directions are often accompanied by complex musical forms, such as fugues, in order to make them articulate,' which methods 'strove towards a type of technical procedure that might almost be called a musical close-up'" (Tambling 76). This is something of an aside in Eisler's book,[19] commenting on the precision timing of the scenes in Berg's operas and how this procedure aligns itself with the editing procedure of a film, though the relationship with a close-up is difficult to see, being something unique to film and difficult to replicate on the opera stage, even if only by analogy.

"Reich reminisces about Berg's speaking of his 'pet idea of having *Wozzeck* filmed ... he pointed out how the formal arrangement of his first opera corresponded almost exactly to the technique of film, and that a film would be able to realize certain details to perfection by means of close-ups and long shots ... details that never emerged with the desired clarity in the theatre'" (Tambling 76–77).[20] Berg's idea is that the procedure corresponds to film technique, but the effect on the audience is rarely that of a film, with limited exceptions, the sudden cut to the inn scene being one such.

Berg was writing *Wozzeck* between 1914 and 1922. Levi shows that the influence of film was becoming more pronounced in Germany at this time. "In the restless artistic climate of the 1920s, musicians responded positively to technological developments in film, radio and recording. The enormous growth in popularity of the silent film during the Weimar Republic exercised an especially profound influence. Not only were young composers inspired to write scores specially designed to accompany such films, but more significantly, cinematic techniques affected structural approaches to composition to the extent that notions of musical continuity were frequently abandoned in favor of more abrupt juxtapositions of ideas. The possibility of adapting film techniques to the operatic stage proved irresistible to composers committed to divesting modern German opera of its pre-war associations with Wagner."[21]

Levi refers to operas by Krenek and Hindemith but sees the strongest absorption of cinema techniques in the work of Brecht and Weill. "In the collaborative music-theatre work *Mahagonny Songspiel* (1927), elements of silent film guide the entire dramatic conception. The work contains no dialogue and no real plot, but a sense of narrative flow is achieved through the use of montage techniques, projections, titles announced by the actors which serve an explanatory purpose similar to silent film captions, and production instructions or gestures."[22]

Later Brecht and Weill collaborated on the full scale opera *Aufstieg und Fall der Stadt Mahagonny* (*Rise and fall of the city of Mahagonny*, 1931) which was ultimately to be the cause of their disagreement. "Brecht's theory of epic theatre, essential to the piece and unmistakably expressed in it, conflicted with Weill's notion of reformed opera. Weill saw the work's structure based on purely musical laws, with every musical number being a complete musical scene and projected inscriptions creating the possibility for the entry of new music in every case. In contrast, Brecht considered the intervening texts—comparable to those used in silent movies—as an important vehicle for his principle of Verfremdung (defamiliarization)."[23]

In Brecht's later work he acknowledged the influence of silent cinema, especially the work of Charlie Chaplin. It was less the use of captions than the style of acting which impressed. In 1936 he wrote, "The epic mode of acting owes much to the silent film. Chaplin, the former clown, didn't have the tradition of the theatre and approached the presentation of human behaviour in a new way."[24]

Berg included a film sequence at the end of Act 2 scene 1 of his second opera, *Lulu*. It shows the events between the two plays Berg was adapting, Wedekind's *Erdgeist* and *Die Büchse der Pandora* and shows Lulu's arrest for the murder of her husband, Dr. Schön, in the previous scene, her trial and escape. The music accompanying the film sequence is in the form of a palindrome, it reverses in the middle and plays backwards. Film can be played backwards, most usually for comic effect, though here the reversal is symbolic. It marks the high point of Lulu's ascent in the world and the beginning of her decline, during which characters from the first part of the opera return in different guises culminating in the return of Dr. Schön as Jack the Ripper who murders Lulu and her faithful companion, Countess Geschwitz.

The work of Bernd Alois Zimmermann provides an ideal example of the twentieth century opera composer responding to the dynamic of film and television techniques. Zimmermann (1918–1970) found his way as a composer only in the post-war period when 12 note music came to be widely influential. His only opera, *Die Soldaten* (Soldiers) was composed from 1958 to 1964 and based on a play by Jakob Michael Rheinhold Lenz. His original conception of it was regarded as unperformable by the Cologne Opera which had commissioned it, so its first production in Cologne in 1965 (and every other subsequent one) has been given in a modified "performing edition" which has now come to be accepted as practical.[25]

Act 2 scene 2 is a complex one. Like Berg in *Wozzeck* Zimmermann gives each scene the name of a musical form or forms, and this scene is labeled Capriccio, Chorale, Ciacona II. It commences with a duet between Marie and her lover Desportes at Marie's father's house in Lille. She has received a letter from Stolzius, her former fiancée. Desportes is furious at this impudence and tries to dictate her reply. As he tries to grab the pen their interaction changes so that they are chasing each other in a form of foreplay, the accompanying Capriccio music is brittle, playful and rhythmic. The character of the scene changes. "During the screaming and squealing from next door, Wesener's old mother [this is Marie's grandmother] creeps through the room, her glasses perched on her nose; she sits down in a corner of the window and sings, her voice rough with age" (Stage directions, Zimmermann, 1975, 274). The music sung by the old woman as she grieves while watching her granddaughter's downfall, "is set to a folk tune quoted from Lenz while the orchestra borrows the chorale 'Ich bin's, ich sollte büssen' from Bach's *St Matthew Passion*" (Clements 442).

Stolzius and his mother in appear in a third part of the stage, at their home in Armentières but at a later time than the other activities. Stolzius is reading the letter from Marie (which is still being written across the stage). He is furious that Desportes has "turned her head" and is convinced that Marie is an innocent, while his mother denounces the "trollop." Stolzius determines to get his revenge on Desportes. This conversation is set to the Ciacona (Chaconne) music.

By having the three separate events occurring simultaneously on the stage Zimmermann has paralleled the cinematic and television technique of cross-cutting between different scenes. It is a technique that can be seen every day in any TV soap opera. We have a short section of the old lady singing her lament, cutting to Stolzius and his mother frantically arguing, cutting back to the lovers' playfulness, each section lasting only a short while, exactly as in the parallel plot lines of a TV soap. At times the three kinds of music are simultaneous, echoing the less frequently used cinema technique of the split screen, or perhaps Eisenstein's concept of montage. Zimmermann has not only compressed space, he has compressed time too, with the angry receipt of the letter taking place as it is being written.

We Come to the River by Hans Werner Henze and Edward Bond, commissioned by the Royal Opera and first performed at the Royal Opera House, Covent Garden, in July 1976, formalizes this simultaneity of events by having the stage divided into three areas, each with its own "orchestra" and thus each with its own distinctive sound. "Stage I is in the foreground, and is primarily used for monologues and to depict the world of the oppressed. On this stage the Deserter awaits his execution, the wife of Soldier 2 frets for her husband, and the General, chained to a block, meets his end."[26] The orchestra here comprises flute, oboe and clarinet, guitar, harp, piano, viola d'amore and viola da gamba, each player doubling on multiple other instruments, mostly small percussion.

"On stage II the central scenes take place. There the general learns of his approaching blindness, there he comes face to face with his victims, there also is the courtyard of the madhouse. It is where the governor is assassinated and where the Emperor takes his formal picnic on the riverbank" (Blackford). The instrumental ensemble comprises string quintet and a small woodwind and brass group, again with multiple doublings, largely bells. "Stage III, deep in the background, is the scene of the terrible atrocities—the execution of the Deserter, the murder of the two women and child. Here the officers amuse themselves with prostitutes, singing the *Eton Boating Song*—and from this stage the two assassins, who are to blind the General, appear" (Blackford). The opera, conceived on a lavish scale, also features a virtuoso percussionist with a huge range of instruments and a military band.

We Come to the River is in two parts and, especially in Part 1, action can take place on each of the three stages simultaneously. "Henze's music in *We Come to the River* ranges from atonal to neoclassically tonal styles. Among the latter one finds both pastiche (straightforward imitation of a style or genre) and parody (more subtle play upon a style, genre, or a given work—thereby providing a commentary upon the source, or its semiotic significance). The opera also features the timbral and rhythmic organization of two percussion cadenzas, (2) controlled aleatory passages for instruments (where the visible musicians actually enact a brief dramatic role in standing and reacting to violence on stage), and most strikingly, the complex stratification of musics when two or three stages are simultaneously pursuing different actions and pacings, each involving its own characteristic instruments, textures, and even styles."[27] For example, in Part 1 Scene 3 the stages represent the guard room, the assembly rooms in the town and the general's tent. This allows contrasting scenes to play out together, each with its own characteristic music. The effect is that attention is constantly switched between the stages and the musics and something akin to Eisenstein's concept of montage is achieved. On the other hand, "with three stages simultaneously active, and with three competing musics,

Henze's opera can generate irony, and even sustain a dialectic among ideologies, but it also degenerates at times into a mere echo of life's multiplicities" (Hatten 308).

Krzysztof Penderecki's *The Devils of Loudon* is an operatic version of a play by John Whiting, in turn based on a story by Aldous Huxley which studied demonic possession in a French witchcraft trial of 1634. It was commissioned by the Hamburg State Opera and first produced there in 1969. In the '60s Penderecki was regarded as a leading figure of the avant-garde. He had pioneered a musical style based on huge clusters of notes, an unforgettable sound with large groups of instruments playing many adjacent notes at the same time, often only quarter tones apart. Sometimes the resulting clouds of sound would expand and contract, or slide about, and these long-held sounds would be contrasted with sharp spiky passages in which instruments were pushed to their limits and played in unorthodox ways.

Act 1 Scene 1 shows Jeanne in her cell. She is suffering from the kind of delusions which form the main subject of the opera. It lasts six minutes and 51 seconds.[28] Scene ii takes places in the street outside the church in daylight and shows a short conversation between Mannoury and Adam, the town's pharmacist and surgeon, in which they discuss the supposed relationship between Father Grandier and the young widow Ninon. It lasts two minutes and 40 seconds. The third scene is a different interior and shows Grandier and Ninon together sharing a bath tub. It is over in two minutes 20 seconds. Each scene has a different location and although there is music linking them it is very short. Between Jeanne's last words in Scene 1 and Mannoury's first words in Scene 2 there is about 35 seconds of music. Between Mannoury's last words in Scene 2 and Ninon's first words in Scene 3 there is about 30 seconds. And after Scene 3 there is only 15 seconds of music before we are in the street again for a more extended Scene 4. "Most of the opera's 30 scenes are short, some occupying no more than a page or two of score, each making its succinct dramatic point and then giving way to the next."[29]

The musical links are the equivalent of cross-fades in the cinema with the music moving from one type of sound to another to create the different settings and moods. Jeanne's visions are accompanied mainly by long held clusters on instruments and voices with whispers and shrieks at times. Mannoury and Adam are accompanied by isolated fragmentary wisps of notes on a variety of solo instruments while Ninon and Grandier's bath scene is accompanied by a duet between solo alto flute and a solo double bass.

Jeanne's opening scene begins with about 30 seconds of quiet clusters setting the scene. She has a vision of Grandier which is a premonition and is staged—Grandier actually appears onstage as he will appear in the final scene of the opera, carried to his burning on a litter with his legs smashed and dangling uselessly after the torture he has undergone. The cluster sounds rise to a frenzied climax in this passage.

Just before Claire arrives the clusters suddenly stop as if Jeanne has woken from her dream suddenly. This is the aural equivalent of a sudden cut in a film, say from a flash forward back to reality. After Claire has left the visions begin again, only this time she sees Grandier in the bathtub with Ninon as he will be in scene iii. Again the clusters build up and at the height of this vision the choir is singing a complex multi-layered and highly dissonant contrapuntal passage which gives the effect of a constantly shifting, almost boiling cloud of sound. Again Jeanne wakes suddenly from her dream as the choir stops. After her last words—"Is that it?"—the clusters grow again but very quietly and the sound of church bells is heard. The clusters die away and the fragmentary notes of scene ii begin. The effect of these 35 seconds of music is that of a slow dissolve in a film from one scene to another—aspects of scene 1 are still audible while aspects of scene 2 are beginning to be heard.

At the end of Mannoury and Adam's dialogue the orchestra starts playing longer groups of notes very fast which shoot upwards. These upward shooting groups become shorter and shorter until there is only a single note. Finally a long held double bass note leads into the bathtub scene and the double-bass and flute duet. The effect of this is that the music of scene 2 is breaking up into fragments and dissipating—the aural equivalent of a flickering fade-out.

Michael Tippett's *The Knot Garden*[30] is consciously modeled on film and television techniques. In a preface to the score the composer wrote, "The dramatic action is discontinuous, more like the cutting of a film. The term used for these cuts is Dissolve, implying some deliberate break-up and re-formation of the stage picture." In other writings Tippett points out that "the dramaturgy of both *The Knot Garden* and *The Ice Break* derive a lot from the methods of cinema and television. The scenes dissolve into each other at greats speed (and, incidentally, both operas are therefore uncuttable)."[31] Ian Kemp describes the opera[32] as "small in scale [and] ... correspondingly swift-moving.... Its impression of speed is due, paradoxically, to its rapid sequence of stops and starts—abrupt switches from one short, self-contained scene to another, and strident punctuations by means of Tippett's musical equivalent of the television technique of dissolve. This is not the gradual disintegration of a picture and the formulation of another from a void, but a crisscross of lines which blots out what has just happened and clears the air for something new." Meiron Bowen describes the fast-moving music as "a perfect vehicle for the cinematic mode of presentation which eliminates normal operatic transitions and substitutes so-called 'dissolves' (marked by repeated appearances of purely schematic music—or 'non-music'), as the composer was tempted to call it."[33]

Tippett had three examples from the history of theatre in mind when writing this opera. One is Shaw's *Heartbreak House,* and another is Mozart's and Da Ponte's *Così fan tutte.* In the case of these two it is the way the characters are brought together in different combinations as the psychology of the situation is explored. In *Così,* there is the added attraction of a central character, Don Alfonso, who manipulates and controls the situation. This is also a key factor in Shakespeare's *The Tempest,* which not only influences the opera but actually is a model. Charades from it are played out in Act 3, a scene from it is quoted, and the opening storm which is a device for bringing the characters together in the knot garden is replicated in the opera. But Tippett is searching for a modern way to approach this situation.

Tippett is trying to express through his music and theatrical situation the deepest inner feelings and changes of psychological state which happen to his characters. As Ian Kemp points out, Mangus loosens up his charges in "a nightmare of painful and unpalatable encounters," in Act 2 (Bowen 404). Expressing all this led Tippett to the techniques of expressionism. He uses short, almost aphoristic scenes. The many details of plot and logical development needed to sustain naturalistic theatre are abandoned. Tippett could have done this in the manner of Berg, but he lived in a different age and he consciously rejected a naturalistic type of theatre and replaced it with the fast moving dissolves and (in Act 2) cuts of film and television.

Benjamin Britten was very much involved with film in the early part of his creative career, working as a composer for the Post Office Film Unit from May 1935 as well as devoting "most of his time to writing music for cinema, theatre and radio, nearly fifty scores in all,"[34] up to 1938. "He was already an avid film-goer" (Oliver 46), and these experiences undoubtedly left a mark on the future opera composer. Jeremy Tambling makes a case for *Billy Budd* as an opera "constructed ... most cinematically" (Tambling 85). His argument relies heavily on "the use of the flashback technique, beloved of the cinema in the 1930s" (Tambling 85). In fact flashback or analepsis is much older than 1930s cinema and the technique used in *Billy Budd* is more of a framing device (also older than cinema) with Captain Vere as an old man introducing the story from his past in a prologue, then the main plot of the opera being enacted, and ending with the old Vere regretting that he could have saved Billy Budd in a final postlude.

In 1967, while Tippett was busy writing *The Knot Garden,* Benjamin Britten received a commission for an opera to be written specially for television. *Owen Wingrave,* a strongly pacifist opera based on a Henry James story, was the outcome. It was filmed in the Snape Maltings in November 1970, just a few months after the building had reopened, rebuilt very quickly following a disastrous fire in 1969. "While not particularly interested in television, he accepted the challenge posed by the medium, though there is no doubt that he always intended that *Owen Wingrave* should ultimately be a stage work."[35] The composer's approach to television was not comfortable. "He chose Wingrave for television because it was a 'very intimate, reasonable story. At first I thought I would write it in a very conversational Pelléas-like way, but then I felt I must give the singers something really to sing.' The medium presented him with a new set of problems. 'You have to persuade viewers to take the occasion seriously. On the other hand you can't really calculate for those who are bored, arrive late, or are interrupted by the telephone. You can't keep repeating the plot, like a cricket score or something. Then there's the whole problem of making singers seem credible on television.' Britten always had the stage in mind as the opera's ultimate home; he would never have wasted all the labour involved in writing an opera on a medium which offered only one or two showings."[36]

This paragraph nibbles at the problems posed for a composer who is asked to write a television opera. Most composers imagine opera as a primarily a theatrical medium. In composing for television they do not generally approach the commission in the way that a regular television writer of, say, dramas, soap operas or situation comedies would—exploiting the potential of the medium and not worrying about translation to another medium. A television writer would not worry about the fact that his work might be shown only once or twice—in fact twice would be a bonus because of the repeat fees. As the medium of television has developed it has grown its own history, so that classic series and productions from many years ago are now repeated to find new audiences. A television writer would be delighted if his work were to attain that status, and would not worry unduly whether it would work onstage or not. Stage productions would be a further bonus, and the problems involved in translating from television style to stage could be tackled later. It is now more usually the other way round, the novelist or playwright hoping for their work to be turned into a film or TV adaptation where the real money lies.

The television producer behind the *Owen Wingrave* project was John Culshaw, a close friend of Britten's from his days at Decca where he had produced the pioneering Solti Ring cycle and masterminded the historic series of Britten conducting his own works, and who was now head of BBC TV music programs. The whole experience seems to have been a rather unhappy one. Michael Kennedy describes it. "Britten himself ... left no doubt that he had been scarred by the 'difficulties he had experienced in preparing *Owen Wingrave*.... Television was a very complicated and powerful medium and recording for it involved a tremendous amount of intensity. He would not be producing another opera for television for a long time.' He had been irritated by the long delays, by the demarcations between which of the technical staff could do what, and by the feeling that money was being wasted. Ill health kept him from many important camera rehearsals and he was often presented with results he did not like but could not alter" (Kennedy 1981, 103).[37] The opera was broadcast on 16 May 1971 and within a week was seen in the Unites States and in Europe from Iceland to Yugoslavia. Sean Day-Lewis warned *Daily Telegraph* readers before the broadcast that "the work is very much opera first and television second ... it often looks like a studio production of a stage work ... it is not calculated to convert those who find the broad and melodramatic strokes of an opera a ludicrous convention."[38] So it proved. After stage productions in 1973 at Covent Garden and Santa Fe the opera has proved to be one of Britten's less enduring successes. But within months of the first broadcast the composer was at work on the opera which was to show all the flair, flexibility and virtuosity that television and film are capable of, even though designed entirely for the stage.

Britten's *Death in Venice* is one of the most filmic of post-war operas. Colin Graham[39] points out that "*Owen Wingrave* had been conceived for a television performance but paradoxically the libretto of *Death in Venice* reads even more like a film script than its predecessor and makes greater 'cinematic' demands on the staging."[40] Its first scene shows Aschenbach, the famous writer, pacing the streets of Munich. "He stops before the entrance to a cemetery,"[41] and within a few bars, "he notices the texts on the façade of the mortuary chapel." A few seconds later "he is suddenly aware of the Traveller standing on the steps of the chapel" (Vocal score, 8). Now all of this is feasible in a "realistic" nineteenth century setting providing that the entrance to the cemetery and the mortuary chapel are both onstage at the start of the scene, so that Aschenbach's musings as he paces the streets actually occupy only a few steps on the stage. In fact it is much more profitable to think of the scene as cinematic. The fourth wall of the proscenium arch is the lens of the camera following the writer as he strolls through the streets. The gate of the cemetery comes into view as the camera follows him, and later the chapel appears. The whole scene is conceived as a follow-shot or tracking shot in which the camera follows a character, using various techniques, a tracking device or trolley, a crane, panning or zoom lenses.

After encountering the Traveller, who advises him to go south, Aschenbach decides to take the advice. "So be it," he sings, "I will pursue this freedom and offer up my days to the sun and the south. My ordered soul shall be refreshed at last" (Vocal score, 17–18), and within two bars he is "on the boat to Venice with a group of youths shouting to their girlfriends on shore" (Vocal score, 18). Such a rapid transition is exactly like a sudden cinema cut moving from one scene to the next in an instant, with a corresponding sudden change in the music. Following Aschenbach's encounter with an elderly fop on the boat, the vessel docks and "the youths and elderly fop rush on shore, followed slowly by Aschenbach" (Vocal score, 33).

It is only now that Britten introduces the overture, entitled *Venice* (Vocal score, 35–7). This is the equivalent of another film technique, the cold open, or teaser, which became widespread in television and film in the 1960s. The cold open is explained by David Morley thus[42]: "In the opening scenes of certain films or TV drama, the viewer is plunged straight into some action. It hooks them in, but it also gives them some idea of the pace and context; introduces key characters; establishes the mood of what follows and the expectations that the viewer might possess." The credits and opening music follow after several minutes. In some cases, for example many of the James Bond films, the cold open is detached from the main story consisting mainly of a violent escapade or action sequence by the hero. But in most cases the cold open gives clues about the drama to follow. Britten has done the same, grabbing the audience's attention with his sharp focus on the interior thoughts of Aschenbach and the scene on the boat taking the audience right to the heart of Venice.

As the overture ends Aschenbach is taking a gondola from Venice to the Lido. The Gondolier is played by the same singer who took the part of the Traveller in scene 1 and the elderly fop in scene 2. The same singer, a bass-baritone (John Shirley-Quirk in the first production) is later to sing the hotel manager, the hotel barber, the leader of the players and the voice of Dionysus. Such multiple part-playing is rare in opera—characters are sometimes "doubled" but only if they have the same voice type and do not appear onstage together at any point, for example the Commendatore and Masetto in Mozart's *Don Giovanni* were played by the same singer in both the Prague and Vienna premieres and have often been doubled since. Playing seven parts, as here, is most unusual for opera, but there are precursors in film, most famously Alec Guinness as Duke Etherel, the Banker, the Rev. Lord Henry d'Ascoyne, General Lord Rufus d'Ascoyne, Admiral Horatio d'Ascoyne, Young Henry d'Ascoyne, Lady Agatha d'Ascoyne and Lord Ascoyne d'Ascoyne in *Kind Hearts and Coronets* (1949).

Scene 4 (Vocal score, 55–76) is typical of many in the opera. It begins on "the first evening at the hotel" but the stage directions do not specify where in the hotel. The Hotel Manager greets Aschenbach and asks if he has had a pleasant journey—he was wise to come by gondola, more pleasant than the boat. By the end of page 56 he is showing Aschenbach his room and demonstrating the wonderful view of the beach which is indicated in the music by a broad arpeggio figure on woodwinds on a bed of string sound (Vocal score, 57, figure 59 et seq.) At figure 60, a few bars later, he shows the private balcony where the writer "may sit and see the world go by." There follows one of Aschenbach's piano-accompanied, freely notated soliloquies in which he ponders what has happened so far and how "odd, unreal," it was. At its end the "view" theme returns (Vocal score, 63, figure 65) and he contemplates the view—"But there is the sea and nearby Serenissima."

The opening of the scene seems to take place perhaps in a corridor, on the way to the room. Then we are inside the room with its view and balcony. Aschenbach's soliloquy must take place on the balcony as he can see and hear the sea ("How I love the sound of the long low waves, rhythmic upon the sand") (Vocal score, 64). Next he watches as "the hotel guests with their children begin to process before dinner" (Vocal score, 65, stage direction at figure 66). There follows a complex ensemble scene (Vocal score, 65–73, figures 66–75) as the various nationalities of guests pass by, culminating with the Polish boy Tadzio and his mother. We have to assume that this is taking place outdoors, perhaps on a terrace below Aschenbach's balcony. So the stage must be arranged in a way that allows Aschenbach to enter the room, admire the view, sit on the balcony and observe the guests—easy in a film but more difficult to achieve onstage with its single audience perspective. The scene has been composed as if part of a film with little regard for the practicalities of staging, yet this has stimulated directors to undertake the task, and indeed the whole opera, in a variety of ways with considerable success.[43]

The Third act of John Adams's *Nixon in China* provides an excellent example of how cinematic values have pervaded an opera score. Six characters, Richard Nixon, Pat Nixon, Henry Kissinger, Mao Tse Tung, Chiang Ch'ing (Madame Mao) and Chou En Lai, occupy the stage. The Nixons reflect on their past history, his time in the war, Chairman and Madame Mao recall events from their past lives, poverty, struggle, his affair with a starlet, and at one point they dance together. Kissinger leaves early for the toilet and does not return. Chou En Lai reflects on how far China has come with its perpetual revolution: "How much of what we did was good? Everything seems to move beyond our remedy. Come, heal this wound." Sometimes these thoughts are separated as if the scene cuts from one conversation to another, and sometimes they go on simultaneously in an ensemble akin to a split screen technique. Originally this act was supposed to be a banquet scene, but Peter Sellars, who had brought poet Alice Goodman and composer John Adams together specifically to create this opera, changed that. "I was so moved by that third act I said 'this can't be a stupid party scene.' I changed the set and changed the entire conception just after we sang through the piece."[44]

Sellars replaced the party scene with six beds that looked like coffins.[45] "That act is such a nocturnal scene, the music is so nocturnal, the sense of the sex of going to bed and at the same time of being laid to rest—those images. The night that that happened John was shocked, Alice was shocked. John was resistant for years, really—he was nice about it though" (Daines and Sellars,

16). The result is that the audience gained the impression that both couples and Chou En Lai were in their own spaces, their own rooms, and the focus of attention kept switching between them. There was little sense of any communication between them, which was, of course, the point of the whole opera, that Nixon's visit was "planned as a domestic political television bonanza for the elections," (Daines and Sellars, 16), there was little understanding between the two sides and the final Shanghai communiqué "has no substance, which is what Act 3 begins with. The leaders have stayed up all night, and they still haven't agreed on a wording that makes sense" (Daines and Sellars, 16). Sellars subsequently revised the setting of this act for a Los Angeles production which followed the deaths of Chou En Lai and Mao and the Tiananmen Square massacre, inserting more action and more layers of referential detail (Daines and Sellars, 17–18).

Einstein on the Beach, created by composer Philip Glass and director Robert Wilson in 1976, is qualitatively different from the other operas described here. Instead of being built through the conjunction of music with a coherent dramatic plot it is built largely through a series of visual images which are accompanied by music. The opera began with a series of lunchtime meetings between Wilson and Glass at which they initially agreed to collaborate, then decided that Einstein would be their subject. "One Thursday, Bob brought with him the title page of what became the first of many storyboards, or visual workbooks, records in the form of drawings of our discussion and ultimately the basis of Bob's designs."[46]

One initial decision was that the work would run for about four hours (it turned out to be about 40 minutes longer). "We also arrived at the visual themes: the Train, the Trial, the Field-with-Spaceship" (Glass, 30). Other important early decisions included the four-act structure, the acts separated by interludes called Knee Plays (referring to knees' joining function in anatomy), the lack of any intervals and the idea that the audience could drift in and out of the performance at will. "So, by the end of this initial period of meetings, which had stretched into the late fall of 1974, we knew quite a lot about the piece we were making.... Our 'libretto' had already begun to take shape in the form of the previously mentioned sketchbook of visual themes. That became the basis for the music I was soon to begin writing. As for the text, both sung and spoken, that would be developed during our rehearsal period, still almost a year away" (Glass, 31–32).

Thus the whole work is visually conceived, and analysis of it makes most sense from a visual angle, as described by Craig Owens.[47] "Each of three motifs (train, trial, and field) is broken up into a set of images which, since homologous, may be reintegrated. The locus of this process of reintegration is the consciousness of the individual spectator. Structure is thus inborn, that is, emerges while the work is performed as the spectator spontaneously apprehends the relations obtaining among images. Thus, coherence is not a result of any logical sequence of images (the series train-trial-field repeated three times) as program notes suggest, but resides in intuitively grasped similarities among images derived from a common motif. This is clearly demonstrated in Wilson's text. The train, as it appears in Act 2, its observation deck receding into the night, reappears as a building in Act 4. This relationship, rather than the individual images in isolation, is the subject of these two scenes and makes them a unit. Similarly, the sharply delineated triangle of light projected by the locomotive's headlight in the opening scene is congruent with that which streams from an elevator shaft in the final scene—a visual linking of end with beginning. And the fluorescent bed in the center of the courtroom during the trial scenes in Acts 1 and 3 becomes, in Act 4, a column of light which slowly ascends into the flies and which, in turn, is reminiscent of the strip of light which painted itself down the backdrop in the first scene. These images do not function as isolated signs; instead their conjunction reveals patterns of interrelationship which make Einstein a complex, resonant experiential unit, or gestalt" (Owens, 27). The music follows these visual links by using related themes and ideas, as described by the composer.[48]

How does this relate to film? After all, most films begin with a script and the visual imagery of the director follows from that, with the music coming in last. But there were films which began with visual imagery, the disturbing films of the surrealist movement for example. Speaking of Buñuel's first film Peter Harcourt points out that, "The images in *Un Chien Andalou* have all been preselected for us according to an idea about the workings of the subconscious."[49] And of the director's second film, L'Age d'Or, he says, "As with all of Buñuel, it is less a complexity of effect than a potential complexity of response—an elusive, subjective matter. Images many of which are unavoidably real are thrust before our eyes in a way that may disturb or arrest us but which eludes easy interpretation." John Russell Taylor refers, in connection with Buñuel, to "a sort of imagist poetry which comes from an intense heightening of individual sense impressions, so that certain selected objects take on the quality of a fetish, an instrument of ritual significance in the re-enactment of some private myth."[50] There could not be a better description of the effect of *Einstein on the Beach*.

Cinema and its successor television have changed the way we perceive and understand visual images. As Dudley Andrew puts it, "Now the first elements of cinematic representation are perceptual. Earlier we discussed the tension of belief and unbelief in cinema as equivalent to the oscillation between looking and seeing or seeing and recognizing which is the integral structure of perception in general. It is this equivalence that permits the casual, though philosophically naïve, claim that 'reality' is rendered in cinematic perception. More accurately we should say that the structure of cinematic perception is readily translated into that of natural perception, so much so that we can rely on information we construct in viewing films to supplement our common perceptual knowledge (which is also, as we have often noted, constructed knowledge)" (Andrew, 41). Elements of the structure of cinematic perception have been successfully transplanted to the operatic stage.

Some composers have found ways to imitate the rapid-moving scenes and cuts of film and television by using musical devices to link scenes, as sharp cuts, or as slower dissolves. They have found ways to present multiple events onstage, thus allowing the audience to switch its attention from one to another as in the cross-cutting technique of film. Britten discovered late in life the fluidity of movement that could be captured onstage, in the manner of follow-shots in a film. Philip Glass and Robert Wilson explored the idea of creating opera primarily from visual impulses rather than musical ones and in so doing re-imagined some of the effect of surrealist film imagery. These ideas have demanded a different, more flexible manner of scenic presentation which happens to chime with one direction opera production was already taking. New demands are also made of audiences, but since the audiences, like the composers and librettists, have almost all experienced films and television, they have little difficulty in reading the situations.

Notes

1. Andre Boll's words are reported in Kenneth A. Wright, *Television and Opera*, Tempo, New Series, No. 45 (Cambridge: Cambridge University Press, Autumn 1957), p. 8.
2. Dudley Andrew. *Concepts in Film Theory* (Oxford: Oxford University Press, 1984), p. 30.
3. Marcia J. Citron, *Opera on Screen* (New Haven and London: Yale University Press, 2000).
4. Marcia J. Citron, *When Opera Meets Film* (Cambridge: Cambridge University Press, 2010).
5. Richard Fawkes, *Opera on Film* (London: Duckworth, 2000).
6. Jeremy Tambling, *Opera, Ideology and Film* (Manchester: Manchester University Press, 1987), p. 8.
7. Mervyn Cooke, *Opera and Film*, in *The Cambridge Companion to Twentieth Century Opera*, ed. Mervyn Cooke, 267–290 (Cambridge: Cambridge University Press, 2005).
8. Mark Cousins, *The Story of Film* (London: Pavilion, 2004), p. 23.
9. For example the ascent of a balloon in *The Great Ruby*, the running of the 2000 Guineas in *The Whip*, the sinking of a troop ship in *The Sins of Society*. See the Victoria and Albert Museum website, http://www.vam.ac.uk/users/node/8606, accessed 14 March 2013.

10. Joseph Donahue. *The Cambridge History of British Theatre*, Vol. 2 (Cambridge: Cambridge University Press, 2004), p. 325.

11. Stewart Spencer, *Wagner Remembered* (London: Faber and Faber, 2000), p. 269.

12. Alan C. Dessen, "Shakespeare and Theatrical Conventions," in *The Cambridge Companion to Shakespeare Studies*, ed. Stanley Wells, p. 90 (Cambridge: Cambridge University Press, 1986).

13. *Macbeth,* Act 5 Scene 8, lines 2493–4.

14. Christine Dymkowski, *Harley Granville-Barker: A Preface to Modern Shakespeare* (Cranbury, NJ, and London: Associated University Presses, 1986), p. 11.

15. Patrick Carnegy, "Designing Wagner," in *Wagner in Performance*, ed. Barry Millington and Stewart Spencer, p. 55 (New Haven and London: Yale University Press, 1992).

16. Frank Gray. "*The Kiss in the Tunnel* (1899): G. A. Smith and the Emergence of the Edited Film in England," in *The Silent Cinema Reader*, eds. Lee Grieveson and Peter Kramer, pp. 51–62. (Routledge: London, 2004).

17. Explored in detail by André Gaudreault in "Detours in Film Narrative: The Development of Cross-Cutting," *Cinema Journal* 19, no. 1 (Autumn 1979): pp. 39–59.

18. The Krenek quotation is from Ernst Krenek, *Exploring Music* (London: Calder, 1966), p. 108.

19. The Eisler quotation is from Hanns Eisler and Theodor Adorno, *Composing for the Films* (Oxford: Oxford University Press, 1947), p. 122.

20. The Reich quotation is from Willi Reich, *The Life and Work of Alban Berg*, trans. Cornelius Cardew (London: Thames and Hudson, 1965).

21. Erik Levi, "Music in Modern German Culture," in *The Cambridge Companion to Modern German Culture*, ed. Eva Kolinsky and Wilfried van der Will, p. 243 (Cambridge: Cambridge University Press, 1999).

22. Elmar Juchem, "Kurt Weill," in *Music of the Twentieth-Century Avant-Garde: A Biocritical Sourcebook*, ed. Larry Sitsky, p. 558 (Westport, CT: Greenwood, 2002).

23. Quoted in Eric Bentley, "Are Stanislavsky and Brecht Commensurate?" in *Brecht Sourcebook: A Critical Anthology*, ed. Carol Martin and Henny Bial, p. 5 (Abingdon: Routledge, 2000).

24. Andrew Clements, "*Die Soldaten*" in *The New Grove Dictionary of Opera*, vol. 4, p. 442 (London: Macmillan, 1992).

25. Bernd Alois Zimmermann, *Die Soldaten*, full score pp. 252–306 (Mainz: Schott, 1975).

26. Richard Blackford, *Music Note*, program book for the world premiere performance, Royal Opera House, 1976. Pages not numbered.

27. Robert S. Hatten, "Pluralism of Theatrical Genre and Musical Style in Henze's 'We Come to the River,'" *Perspectives of New Music* 28, no. 2 (Summer 1990): p. 293.

28. The timings relate to the recording sung in German, *Die Teufel von Loudon*, by the Hamburg State Opera, conducted by Marek Janowski (Philips 446 328-2, 1970). There have been some slight changes to the opening scenes in a subsequent revision but the changes do not affect the argument here.

29. Bernard Jacobson, *Dramatic Work with Religious Theme*, CD booklet (Philips 446 328-2, 1970), p. 2.

30. First performed 2 December 1970 at the Royal Opera House, Covent Garden. All references are to the vocal score (London: Schott, 1970).

31. Michael Tippett. *Tippett on Music*, ed. Meiron Bowen, p. 272 (Oxford: Oxford University Press, 1998).

32. Ian Kemp, *Tippett, the Composer and His Music*, pp. 402–3 (London: Eulenberg, 1984).

33. Meiron Bowen, "A Tempest for Our Time," in *The Operas of Michael Tippett* (ENO Opera Guide 29), p. 94 (London: John Calder, 1985).
34. Michael Oliver, *Benjamin Britten* (London: Phaidon, 1996), p. 52.
35. Michael Kennedy, "*Owen Wingrave*" in *The Viking Opera Guide*, ed. Amanda Holden, Nicholas Kenyon and Stephen Walsh, p. 160 (London: Viking, 1993).
36. Michael Kennedy, *Britten* (Master Musicians series), p. 100 (London: J.M. Dent, 1981).
37. The interview quoted is from the *Daily Telegraph* of 2 June 1971.
38. Sean Day-Lewis, *Daily Telegraph*, 10 May 1971.
39. Graham directed the first production at the Aldeburgh Festival in 1973, given by the English Opera Group and the English Chamber Orchestra conducted by Steuart Bedford.
40. Colin Graham, "The First Production" in *Death in Venice* (Cambridge Opera Handbooks), p. 67 (Cambridge: Cambridge University Press, 1987).
41. Benjamin Britten (music), Myfanwy Piper (libretto). *Death in Venice* vocal score, p. 6 (London: Faber Music, 1975).
42. David Morley, *The Cambridge Introduction to Creative Writing*, p. 222 (Cambridge: Cambridge University Press, 2007).
43. There is a wide variety of video recordings of sections of many productions online at sites such as YouTube.
44. Matthew Daines and Peter Sellars, "'Nixon in China': An Interview with Peter Sellars," *Tempo*, New Series, no. 197 (July 1996): p. 16.
45. This was for the original production by the Houston Grand Opera, first performed 22 October 1987.
46. Philip Glass. *Opera on the Beach*, p. 29 (London and Boston: Faber and Faber, 1988).
47. Craig Owens, "'Einstein on the Beach': The Primacy of Metaphor," *October* 4 (Autumn 1977): pp. 21–32
48. Philip Glass, "Notes: Einstein on the Beach.," *Performing Arts Journal* 2, no. 3 (Winter 1978): pp. 63–70.
49. Peter Harcourt, "Luis Bunuel: Spaniard and Surrealist," *Film Quarterly* 20, no. 3 (Spring 1967): p. 8.
50. John Russell Taylor. *Cinema Eye, Cinema Ear: Some Key Film-Makers of the Sixties* (London: Methuen, 1964).

Bibliography

Andrew, Dudley. *Concepts in Film Theory*. Oxford: Oxford University Press, 1984.
Bentley, Eric. "Are Stanislavsky and Brecht Commensurable?" In *Brecht Sourcebook: A Critical Anthology*, edited by Carol Martin and Henny Bial. Abingdon: Routledge, 2000.
Blackford, Richard. "Music Note." In the program for the world premiere performance of *We Come to the River* by Hans Werner Henze and Edward Bond. Royal Opera House, London. 1976.
Bowen, Meiron. "A Tempest for Our Time." In *The Operas of Michael Tippett* (ENO Opera Guide 29). London: John Calder, 1985.
Britten, Benjamin (music), Myfanwy Piper (libretto). *Death in Venice* (vocal score). London: Faber Music, 1975.
Carnegy, Patrick. "Designing Wagner" in *Wagner in Performance*, edited by Barry Millington and Stewart Spencer. New Haven and London: Yale University Press, 1992.
Citron, Marcia J. *Opera on Screen*. New Haven and London: Yale University Press, 2000.

_____. *When Opera Meets Film*. Cambridge: Cambridge University Press, 2010.
Clements, Andrew. "*Die Soldaten*" in *The New Grove Dictionary of Opera*, vol. 4. London: Macmillan, 1992.
Cooke, Mervyn. "Opera and Film" in *The Cambridge Companion to Twentieth Century Opera*, edited by Mervyn Cooke, pp. 267–290. Cambridge: Cambridge University Press, 2005.
Cousins, Mark. *The Story of Film*. London: Pavilion, 2004.
Daines, Matthew, and Peter Sellars. "'Nixon in China': An Interview with Peter Sellars." *Tempo* New Series 197 (July 1996).
Dessenn Alan C. "Shakespeare and Theatrical Conventions." In *The Cambridge Companion to Shakespeare Studies*, edited by Stanley Wells. Cambridge: Cambridge University Press, 1986.
Donahue, Joseph. *The Cambridge History of British Theatre*, vol. 2. Cambridge: Cambridge University Press, 2004.
Dymkowski, Christine. *Harley Granville-Barker: A Preface to Modern Shakespeare*. Cranbury, NJ, and London: Associated University Presses, 1986.
Fawkes, Richard. *Opera on Film*. London: Duckworth, 2000.
Gaudreault, André. "Detours in Film Narrative: The Development of Cross-Cutting." *Cinema Journal* 19, no. 1 (Autumn 1979): 39–59.
Glass, Philip. *Opera on the Beach*. London and Boston: Faber and Faber, 1988.
_____. "Notes: Einstein on the Beach." *Performing Arts Journal* 2, no. 3 (Winter 1978): 63–70.
Graham, Colin. "The First Production." In *Death in Venice* (Cambridge Opera Handbooks). Cambridge: Cambridge University Press, 1987.
Gray, Frank. "*The Kiss in the Tunnel* (1899): G. A. Smith and the Emergence of the Edited Film in England." In *The Silent Cinema Reader*, edited by Lee Grieveson and Peter Kramer. London: Routledge, 2004.
Harcourt, Peter. "Luis Bunuel: Spaniard and Surrealist." *Film Quarterly* 20, no. 3 (Spring 1966).
Hatten, Robert S. "Pluralism of Theatrical Genre and Musical Style in Henze's *We Come to the River*." *Perspectives of New Music* 28, no. 2 (Summer 1990).
Jacobson, Bernard. "Dramatic Work with Religious Theme." CD booklet of the recording of *The Devils of Loudon* by Krzysztof Penderecki sung in German as *Die Teufel von Loudon*, by the Hamburg State Opera, conducted by Marek Janowski. Philips 446 328-2, 1970.
Juchem, Elmar. "Kurt Weill." In *Music of the Twentieth-Century Avant-Garde: A Biocritical Sourcebook*, edited by Larry Sitsky. Westport, CT: Greenwood, 2002.
Kem, Ian. *Tippett, the Composer and His Music*. London: Eulenberg, 1984.
Kennedy, Michael. *Britten* (Master Musicians series). London: J.M. Dent, 1981.
_____. "Owen Wingrave." In *The Viking Opera Guide*, edited by Amanda Holden, Nicholas Kenyon and Stephen Walsh. London: Viking, 1993.
Krenek, Ernst. *Exploring Music*. London: Calder, 1966.
Levi, Erik. "Music in Modern German Culture." In *The Cambridge Companion to Modern German Culture*, edited by Eva Kolinsky and Wilfred van der Will. Cambridge: Cambridge University Press, 1999.
Morley, David. *The Cambridge Introduction to Creative Writing*. Cambridge: Cambridge University Press, 2007.
Oliver, Michael. *Benjamin Britten*. London: Phaidon, 1996.
Owens, Craig. "'Einstein on the Beach': The Primacy of Metaphor." *October* 4 (Autumn 1977): 21–32

Reich, Willi. *The Life and Work of Alban Berg*. Trans Cornelius Cardew. London: Thames and Hudson, 1965.
Spencer, Stewart. *Wagner Remembered*. London: Faber and Faber, 2000.
Tambling, Jeremy. *Opera, Ideology and Film*. Manchester: Manchester University Press, 1987.
Taylor, John Russell. *Cinema Eye, Cinema Ear: Some Key Film-Makers of the Sixties*. London: Methuen, 1964.
Tippett, Michael. *Tippett on Music*, edited by Meiron Bowen. Oxford: Oxford University Press, 1998.
Wright, Kenneth A. "Television and Opera." *Tempo*, New Series, no. 45. Cambridge: Cambridge University Press (Autumn 1957).
Zimmermann, Bernd Alois. *Die Soldaten*. Full score. Mainz: Schott, 1975.

Opera on Optical Video Disc, or the Latest (and Final?) Avatar of the Gesamtkunstwerk

Pierre Bellemare

This essay explores the potential of optical disc technology when put in the service of opera, an art form that, ever since Grétry, prides itself in the fanciful notion that it is some sort of a "total" art work, a potentially harmonious combination of music and singing, with poetry and literature, combined with choreography and the display of all of the scenic arts. First with the DVD-ROM and now the Blu-Ray era, these new digital video media have become the gold standard when it comes to the enjoyment of operatic spectacles in a domestic setting. This is not to say that these products always or even generally measure up to the ideal. On the contrary, the catalogue of available titles is full of duds, and, in this essay, attention will be paid to the causes of their various shortcomings, some of which are inherent in the new technology or the medium (to say nothing of opera itself), while others are more simply a reflection of cheese-paring, commercial miscalculations or downright ineptitude. The essay concludes with some consideration of the impact of these new technologies on the future state of the operatic repertory both on the stage and in the digital world.

The Coming of the DVD

The DVD, or Digital Versatile Disc, introduced in 1995, is the last in a series of five technologies aimed at adding the video to the audio in recordings of operatic performances. It was preceded, in chronological order, by the "opera film" meant for theatrical release, introduced in the late 1920s, the TV broadcast (or telecast) of operatic performances, introduced after the Second World War, the VHS videocassette, introduced in 1976, and, finally, the Laserdisc (LD), introduced in 1978.

(The Blu-ray technology, introduced in 2006, does not count as a distinct step in the successive evolution of the "opera on video" line of products, given that a Blu-ray disc is nothing but an enhanced DVD, with better sound and better picture.) We thus have an historical development in five clearly delineated stages.

The first stage was the introduction of the opera film as an alternative to the traditional operatic performance in the theatre. The idea was to offer to the public spectacles more lavish and grandiose than anything ever seen on the operatic stage. The result was to democratize a musical genre traditionally reserved for royalty, the aristocracy, and the bourgeoisie. Millions of people who would never have had the opportunity of seeing an opera in live performance, or could not afford a seat anyway were now given a chance to taste "the best of opera" for a fraction of the cost of a "real opera" ticket.

The second stage, and a crucial one for the subsequent rise of something like the DVD, came with the transition from the film opera to the telecast. For the first time in history, opera lovers could "attend" an operatic performance in their own home. All that was required of them was access to a television set on the day and time of the broadcast. The public's potential exposure to the operatic genre itself grew immeasurably. Thus, it has been claimed that, on February 16, 1980, when the Met decided to telecast its production of Richard Strauss' *Elektra*, starring Birgit Nilsson, Leonie Rysanek, and Mignon Dunn, more viewers saw the work on that occasion than the sum total of the audiences of all of its stage productions since the world premiere, in Dresden on January 25, 1909.

By 1980, the third and fourth stages of the development of the opera on video had already occurred. The third stage was the advent of the videocassette, and, notably, the VHS videocassette, destined to supplant its Betamax rival, whereas the fourth stage was the coming of the luckless Laserdisc. The feud between VHS and Beta needs not detain us here, for lack of relevance to our topic. The fact is that Betamax never took much of an interest in opera, which is a pity as the Sony Betamax system offered noticeably better sound and image quality and might have made a more satisfactory medium for recording op[era.. But both VHS and LD were to build substantial catalogues of operatic titles, in a marked effort to gain control over that small, but potentially lucrative, segment of the video market. That turf war between Beta and VHS is one of those territorial conflicts in which the two belligerents bleed each other to death, to the eventual benefit of a third party, in this instance, the DVD.

Future generations may find it difficult to understand how two systems as different in quality as VHS and LD could ever be seriously in competition with one another. Should it not have been obvious from the start that the LD technology was vastly superior to VHS? Maybe. It was clear, at any rate, that the coming of the LD represented a giant leap forward into the digital era, the age of the optical disc. In essence, the LD already was all that the DVD would later be. The only important difference between the two products was one of size, the DVD being of that of a compact disc (CD), while the LD was of that of a LP. The VHS technology had little, or anything, to commend itself, with the LD being incomparably superior to the VHS in every respect, especially what matters the most: the quality of sound and picture. What, in the end, decided the outcome of the issue on a global scale, were financial considerations: videocassettes were cheap, whereas LDs and the machines used to play them were considered prohibitively expensive. As a result, videocassettes proliferated, while LDs remained comparatively uncommon luxury items.

As for opera enthusiasts they did what was expected of them in this age of consumerism, and they began to make collections of recorded material, sometimes in both formats, given that a number of titles were available in only one format to the exclusion of the other. All things being equal, LDs were more popular than VHS with discriminating collectors.

As already mentioned, the list of titles of operas available on VHS and LD was considerable, as testified by Alan Blyth's book *Opera on Video. The Essential Guide*.[1] That guide was published in 1995, the year when the DVD entered the market. The list of the recordings that are reviewed in it reflects the state of opera on video in the twilight years of the LD/VHS period. Not surprisingly, that list covers all of the core repertory—*Carmen, Traviata, Bohème*, and the like—usually in two or three different versions, with all of the key bases covered by both LD and VHS, plus a substantial chunk of the wider repertory—works such as *La Cenerentola, Pelléas et Mélisande, Peter Grimes*—that are also regularly performed in the opera houses of the world, although less often, certainly than the war-horses. And here and there, a rarity. Thus, it is interesting to note that John Corigliano's *The Ghosts of Versailles*, which was to take so much time to resurface on DVD, and then only as part of a very thick and very expensive box set (*James Levine: Celebrating 40 Years at the Met*), had been widely available on both LD and VHS.

It is generally assumed that the tug-of-war between the two formats was a draw, but that is not quite the case. For one could argue that the LD won, considering that the DVD, which was destined to carry the prize, appears to be nothing more than a modified version of the LD.

The transition from both VHS and LD to the DVD was perceived negatively by many collectors of opera on video. They saw that the coming of the new format would signal the death knell of the old ones. While videocassettes would continue to self-destruct and the industry would stop producing LDs, cherished collections, amassed to great expense were doomed to obsolescence.

Admittedly, recorded opera combining audio and video has long been with us, first in the form of filmed opera, and then in that of the telecast. But, unless you had the run of a home theater or access to a film collection or the vaults of some TV network, you could not acquire, own or even possess copies of filmed operas, let alone telecasts. Such items came to you as occasional treats, such as when a certain filmed opera was being released in a local movie theater at a certain specific date and time, or a made-for-TV operatic show would be broadcast on this or that channel, at this or that precise moment. Now, all of that has changed and you can buy your own copies of the very same shows and filmed operas, even make a complete collection of them.

This situation has existed for a long time, from even before the DVD, when VHS and LD, still reigned supreme. As already mentioned, each format had its own catalogue of operatic titles, but neither was a major success with opera buffs. The LD almost made it because of the high quality of both sound and picture inherent in the digital technology, of which it was one of the early commercial forms. But the product was comparatively expensive and its format—similar to that of the vinyl LP—somewhat unwieldy. As for the VHS, it was cheap in every respect, inexpensive, but not of much value either, due to its reliance on magnetic tape, a medium that is not very durable, especially under repeated use, in addition to being prone to distortions. As a result the sound was often of poor quality and the cassettes themselves too plain-looking to become collector's items. Add to this that the cassettes in question were bulky, occupied much shelf-space, and it will be understood why opera lovers were never that enthusiastic about the VHS. It proved to be short-lived, lasting only nineteen years, from 1976 to 1995.

The DVD, on the other hand, was an instant success, for obvious reasons. It combined the sonic perfection of the CD, which, since the early eighties, had become the gold standard of the digital reproduction of sound and music, with the visual perfection of the digital picture, another gold standard in its own right. The resulting product was incomparably superior to the VHS cassette and destined to become an instant success with opera buffs, the optical disc format for which they had been waiting for many years.

Now what about the Blu-ray technology officially introduced in 2006, and which was supposed to supersede the DVD? The sales of both Blu-ray discs and players are consistently growing and it clearly appears that, *over time*, Blu-ray could indeed elbow the DVD out of the market. But that will take time. Older opera buffs specializing in classical music (including opera), still remember the transition from the LP to the CD, when the newest technological advance would not only force them to buy new equipment, but update part of their music collection, while in many cases retaining the earlier media as well. The same thing happened at the time of the transition from the VHS to the DVD. But that was less of a problem for collectors of opera on video than for film collectors in general, given the comparative unpopularity of the VHS format in that highly specialized market. People who had begun building a collection of opera recordings on LD, on the other hand, had no choice but to abandon a technology doomed to obsolescence.

Mindful of those precedents, consumers have been naturally reluctant to invest in yet another new technology when they are reasonably satisfied with the previous one. For there lies the dilemma: while Blu-ray clearly represents an advance over the DVD in terms of the higher definition of sound and picture, the difference is not sufficient as to force the DVD out of the market. The industry has always been aware of that aspect of the issue and, to avoid shooting itself in the foot, it has ensured that the transition would be as smooth as possible by seeing to it that Blu-Ray players are DVD-compatible. As a result, seven years after the introduction of the Blu-Ray, sales of DVDs and DVD players are still going strong. At the same time, the Blu-Ray's share in the market in general continues to increase. Whatever the case, in the operatic submarket, at any rate, the release of a new title in one format is almost inevitably matched by a simultaneous or near simultaneous issue of the same recording in the other format. Add to this that certain European labels persist in marketing their products on DVD only, and one gains the impression of a market still in flux.

In a way, that flies in the face of common wisdom. One might have thought that, confronted by a new recording technology that offers better sound, consumers and collectors of opera on DVD would have deserted *en masse* to the Blu-Ray camp. Some did convert, no doubt, but many, evidently, have remained faithful to the DVD.

The DVD Regions

To protect its proprietary interests, the entertainment industry has divided the DVD world into six zones or regions, as follows:

Zone 1: United States, Canada, Bermuda, U.S. territories
Zone 2: all of Europe (to the exclusion of Russia, Ukraine, and Belarus), plus the Middle East, Egypt, Japan, South Africa, Swaziland and Lesotho, Greenland, and the French Overseas departments and territories
Zone 3: Southeast Asia, South Korea, Taiwan, Hong Kong, Macau, with the exclusion of mainland China
Zone 4: South America, Central America, the Caribbean, Mexico, New Zealand, Australia, Papua New Guinea and much of Oceania

Zone 5: India and most surrounding countries, Russia, Ukraine, Belarus, the parts of Africa (except for Egypt, South Africa, Swaziland, and Lesotho), Central and South Asia, Mongolia, North Korea
Zone 6: Mainland China

In the early years of the DVD some operatic titles were issued in Region 2 but not in Region 1, many of the latter still awaiting a North American release. The list of those recordings constitutes a small catalogue of between two or three dozen titles, including rarities, like Auber's *Les Diamants de la Couronne*.

Eventually, the industry was to come to the realization that, even on a world scale, the potential market for such products was so small that it simply made no sense to fragment it. As a consequence, the majority of operatic DVDs are now issued "region free" or are said to belong to some a semi-fictional entity unofficially known as Region 9 or Region 0, even "Region ALL." These are DVDs playable on machines from all of the different regions.

Subtitles

Subtitles were introduced at about the same time as talking pictures, as a replacement for the intertitles of the silent cinema. This is a pity, for, over some fifteen years, intertitles had grown into a delicate art form, whereas subtitles were never more than a poor substitute for them. The charm of the intertitles is that they would never interrupt the flow of the action, being used only if they were required, when they were required, and in the measure in which they were required. Subtitles, on the contrary, generate a constant tension between the need to read them and that of watching what is happening on the screen at the same time. When little is said, there is no problem. But when the actors (singers) have a lot to say (sing) in a very short period of time, the subtitles cannot keep up with the text or, at any rate, the videographer has to rush them, and the viewer can easily get confused. Interestingly, this tends to be less of a problem with opera than in feature films. The reason for this is that it usually takes less time—and often much less time—to sing a text than to recite it, which makes the videographer's job all the easier.

This holds especially true in baroque opera, where an individual aria can last for a considerable time, and there is plenty of time to follow the short subtitled text. In the complex ensembles of classical and romantic opera, on the other hand, there is no way that subtitles could ever follow as many as seven or eight different tracks of competing sung text.

People who complain about those things need to acquire a better understanding of the conventions of the operatic genre. Thus, in baroque opera, a precise understanding of the wording of an aria is barely required. Some idea of the intent of the piece, as an aria of revenge or anger, of jubilant or unrequited love, of hope or despair, usually suffices. The sections of the score that need to be elucidated by means of subtitles are not the lyric parts but the recitatives. The people for whom those operas were composed were perfectly aware of the fact. Nor is the audience expected to understand and be able to follow in detail the various strata of sung text in a classical or romantic ensemble, not even in the quartet from the third act of *Meistersinger*, or the concluding fugue in *Falstaff*, for that matter.

Film opera has made use of subtitles ever since the 1930s. At the time, and still for a long time, subtitles were embedded, which, in practical terms, meant that the subtitled text would be literally burned into the celluloid. This had three major negative consequences, namely:

1. that the subtitled text, once embedded, could not be removed;
2. that only one set of subtitles could appear on any given copy of the film; in other words, there was never enough room for subtitles in more than one language;
3. and finally, that the subtitles would sometimes be nearly impossible to see, especially in black and white films, when the subtitles in white were superimposed on a blindingly bright background, making them utterly illegible. The old Soviet English language version of Eisenstein's *Ivan the Terrible* is particularly notorious in that regard.

Certain reissues of historical material on DVD bear the mark, quite literally, of the bygone days when subtitles were embedded. That is notably the case with a series of stellar performances of Italian war-horses by an Italian company touring Japan that have been issued by the small company Hardy Classics. The only known source copies of those performances known to exist have embedded subtitles in large Japanese script. For the convenience of its clientele, Hardy has added English subtitles of its own, superimposing them over the Japanese text, which makes for a stage awash with literacy!

Similarly, pirated copies of telecast operatic performances often come with embedded subtitles in the language of the intended audience, because that is how they were broadcast in their country of origin.

Except for the issue of matching the pace of the dialogue, which is inherent in subtitles and will never go away, the designers of the DVD have succeeded in solving all of the three problems outlined above. Thanks to the advances in digital technology, their subtitles are optional, removable, and clearly legible. As a result, various courses of action are now open to the industry, and, for every one of those choices, examples can be found of companies specializing in opera on DVD that, as a matter of policy, have opted for this or that facility to the exclusion of the others.

One choice is to dispense with subtitles altogether. But this is less and less of an option, given that, by now, consumers have come to expect the presence of that feature on such costly products—just as opera-goers who pay good money for premium seats in the house naturally expect subtitles to come with them.

Another solution consists in providing subtitles in English only. The rationale for this is obvious. English is the universal language, the number one vehicle of trade and commerce, and all manners of cultural exchanges. If, for financial reasons, there is to be only one set of subtitles, it better be in English. At this point in time, English remains the preferred linguistic option when it comes to marketing your product to as wide an audience as possible. More and more, however, and because the technology allows it, the various labels prefer to come up with a wide array of different linguistic options between which the consumer is invited to select the ones that he prefers. That linguistic menu tends to vary from label to label and sometimes there will be a special menu for an individual release or a particular line of products. Thus, and thanks to the current ascendancy of the Liceu on the Spanish operatic scene, DVDs of productions hailing from Barcelona and released on the TDK label will feature Catalan as one language option. Generally speaking, though, the languages encountered the most often are four of the five main West European languages, namely French, English, Italian and German. The fifth one, Spanish (Castilian), remains under-represented, but that could change in the future, with the growth of the trade in luxury products in the larger South American markets.

So much for European languages. But one must also account for the large, and rapidly expanding, Asian markets. Evidently opera sells well in the Far East. Western consumers are reminded of that whenever they notice that the DVD that they just bought includes subtitles in Japanese, Korean, Mandarin Chinese, and/or Thai—an increasingly common occurrence, and expect Vietnamese and perhaps Farsi (and what about Hindi?) to join the club in the years to come.

Two more choices need to be mentioned. One is the "no subtitles" selection, which is there for the convenience of those opera buffs who could not care less about the lyrics, may already be sufficiently familiar with the work not to need subtitles, or even regard subtitles as a nuisance. It is perhaps telling that this particular option is one that rarely, if ever, fails to be offered to the consumer. One option that is often missing, on the other hand, is that of watching an opera with subtitles in the language of the performance. Not all labels include subtitles in that language, and some seem to exclude them as a matter of policy. That apparently used to be the case with Decca products, but no longer.

The reason for not including such subtitles are not altogether clear, but they seem to have something to do with the mistaken notion that people whose mother tongue is the language of the performance do not need subtitles in that language because, presumably, they can understand everything that is sung. This is not at always the case. For one thing, there is a significant gap between operatic Italian, *Tragédie Lyrique* French, and Wagnerian German, and modern colloquial Italian, French, or German. Eighteenth and nineteenth century librettos are written in quaint poetic idioms that modern native speakers of the "same" language will never be able to fully understand until they embark on a special study of it. Their situation is the same as that of a modern student of English when confronted with Shakespeare or the language of the King James Bible. In both cases, footnoted texts and subtitles can be helpful.

Many an opera buff will want to grasp the sung words because they think, rightly, that the lyrics are as much part of the singing as the melody itself. They will ask for subtitles in the language of the performance, and now more than ever, in an age of declining standards in idiomatic singing and clear diction. Sad to say, but, in today's world, there is no better test to expose the shortcomings of a singer in those respects than to subtitle his singing in the language of the performance. Phonetic singers, especially, who delude themselves into thinking that they have learned a role when all they can do is to mouth something that sounds like the words, thus become immediately detectable.

Not to include subtitles in the language of the performance is to ignore the interests of those opera fans, admittedly only a minority, who, to maximize the pleasure that they draw from an opera performance, are willing to invest some time and energy in the study of the language of the performance, at least to a certain extent. For such people, subtitles in that language constitute an invaluable asset.

Subtitles are costly, requiring a variety of skills from different specialists, translators and technicians, with little financial return on the investment. The first costs that need to be absorbed relate to the translation of the sung texts. Next the various sets of text in different languages must be formatted to serve as subtitles. And finally the resulting titles must be integrated into the DVD. Multiple translations of the sung texts from opera librettos exist, dating back to the LP era and before, but they are only of limited use, because they were never meant to serve as a source for subtitles. Therefore new translations need to be produced. Subtitling is a difficult craft that can easily go unappreciated. Thus people who can understand both the source language and the translation will sometime point at minor discrepancies between the two versions. What they fail to understand is that the art of subtitling lies not so much in providing a perfectly accurate reflection of the original, as in matching the pace of the dialogue, which inevitably requires some summarizing, and small cuts, for example. The nearly universal inclusion of subtitles as part and parcel of operatic DVDs constitutes an extraordinarily positive development: discriminating opera lovers are now in possession of an instrument that can make their appreciation of opera as a fusion of music and poetry progress by leaps and bounds.

Accompanying Documentation and Extra Features

In the vinyl era, audio recordings usually came with some accompanying documentation. The documentation could be a summary, or quite elaborate, the equivalent of a short lecture on the music featured on the LP. Some of those notes or essays were neatly written and packed with information. They could be found printed on the back cover of the record sleeve, or take the form of "inserts," sheets inserted in of the cardboard sleeve containing the LP.

Among all recordings, the ones that qualified the most for a deluxe treatment were naturally the box-sets containing more than one LP. These usually included a large booklet featuring the usual essays, and often much more information. But *la crème de la crème* were the boxsets containing complete recordings of operas, "*les intégrales d'opéra*," as the French call them. In their case, the booklet would normally contain, not only the usual essays, artists' biographies, and the like, but the featured work's full libretto or, failing that, a detailed synopsis. In some cases, one would get only a plain English translation of the libretto, but, in others, the libretto in the original language, plus complete translations in as many as three other languages would be provided. With the coming of the CD the discs themselves, and their containers (the "jewel box"), got smaller. The notes and the essays remained, but they disappeared from the back-covers to take refuge in the accompanying booklets, crammed inside the jewel box. At the same time, those booklets caused serious difficulties. For example, it often took some effort to accommodate any booklet of any size within the exiguous space of a jewel box. The music industry having become increasingly international, meant that the editorial content of those booklets was getting standardized, which meant fewer and shorter essays but translated into a host of different languages. Evidently, the two trends were at loggerheads, one favoring slimmer booklets and the other resulting in the production of thicker ones.

The music industry is still struggling with that contradiction, at least as far as audio CDs are concerned. But with regards to operatic DVDs, the contradiction, on the whole, has been resolved on three fronts. First: the accompanying booklets. The vast majority of operatic DVDs will include one of those, and, as a rule, it will be a booklet of the multilingual type. DVD cases being more capacious than jewel boxes, that booklet will be easier to accommodate. Consumers expect a recording, any Classical music recording, to come with some sort of documentation. With such booklets, those expectations are minimally satisfied. Too often, the contents of the booklet in question will be limited to the cast, a list of tracks, and a synopsis of the work.

Second: the librettos. With rare exceptions, printed librettos have practically disappeared from opera DVDs. The reason for that is obvious: with multilingual subtitles available a printed libretto is superfluous. Except for a few nostalgic souls, no one will argue that the transition from paper to digitalized titles did not represent real progress, indeed, a major leap forward.

Third: the special features, or extras. In common with feature films, operatic DVDs often include additional materials. In feature films, these will usually include deleted scenes, commentaries by the director, or others, extending through the film, interviews with the star of the film and other actors, and a "featurette" on the making of the film. With operatic DVDs one gets the operatic equivalent, with a behind-the-scenes look at the production at the core, enriched and supplemented by interviews with the usual people: the conductor, the stage director, the singers, and sundry other parties involved in the venture. Sometimes the accompanying documentation is so voluminous that special arrangements need to be made to house it. So, when, in 2008, Arthaus decided to release their Walther Felsenstein edition, they planned the event on a grandiose scale. They released a large LP-sized box deep enough to contain not only the 12 DVDs corresponding to the seven operas produced and directed by Walter Felsenstein,[2] but a bunch of other goodies, including facsimiles of sketches and drawings of sets and costumes, photographs, production notes, and, as a *pièce de résistance*, a 103-page book.

The Felsenstein edition constitutes an example of a DVD release bursting at the seams with extra material of the traditional kind. But the excess ballast could just as well take the form of footage, and increasingly one finds on the market DVD sets containing two, or even as many as three DVDs, one of which is entirely devoted to extra features. Sometimes that supplementary disc will assume a life of its own as a promotional tool available separately. This is what happened with *Wagner's Dream*, a companion piece to the Robert Lepage *Ring* cycle at the New York Metropolitan Opera, which was designed not only to document the behind-the-scenes story, but also to give prospective buyers of the whole *Ring* an opportunity to sample the merchandise.

Listening to Opera on DVD with One's Eyes Shut

Certain opera lovers are absolutely allergic to filmed operas, which they regard as a poor relation to live performances. For them, opera in the theatre is the "real thing" and they will not settle for anything less. Others will forever prefer audio to video recordings, lest the stage director's vision might interfere negatively with their enjoyment of the work or clash with their own personal conception. They are thus left to the theater of their imagination.

One must always bear in mind that it took a number of years for recorded opera to acquire a visual dimension. Between the invention of the phonograph, in the last decades of the nineteenth century, and the introduction of the talkies, in 1926, with radio arriving in between, recorded opera was essentially a matter of sound, and remains so to a large extent, insofar as, even now, when fans of the art-form listen to opera, it is, more often than not, through audio recordings on LPs or compact discs. And that continues to hold true even for those who, in more recent years, have built extensive collections of video (DVD) recordings. Chances are that they spend less time watching these than listening to the CDs, LPs, and tapes that they have cherished often for decades.

And, as a matter of fact, there certainly are problems with the visual aspect of opera that tend to stand out on a TV screen, big or small. To begin with, there is the obvious point to make about the suspension of disbelief inherent in all opera, a form of theater in which people converse with each other not in speech, as they do in real life, but in song (and with instrumental accompaniment to boot!) In the same vein, opera is notorious, traditionally, for casting performers not for their looks, but for their voice. As a result, the operatic stage is often full of performers who can sing the part, but do not look the part. And of course we all know of operatic stars of both sexes who have to count on the costume department to conceal the fact that they are seriously over-weight. There is also the issue of age, a very thorny issue, especially with divas and other *Kammersängerinen*, but also with male performers. Finally, it is undeniable that staged opera can be ridiculous. This is a widely known fact, certainly since the Three Stooges and the Marx Brothers.

Two points nonetheless need to be raised. A minor one relates to anomalies, details that do not quite fit and for that reason attract much more attention to themselves than they would normally deserve. An example is the issue of the headset wireless microphones (HWM) that singers are now required to carry when performing at the Mörbisch Summer Festival, the Seefestspiele Mörbisch. This festival, which specializes in Viennese operettas, is held annually in the lake district of the Austrian Burgenland and its productions are filmed, and marketed worldwide under the Videoland label. Those productions, which are glitzy, deliciously campy, and fun to watch, are presented on a gigantic stage set up on the shores of Lake Neusiedl. But here is the rub. In such a cavernous venue no one in the audience could hear the soloists if one had to rely exclusively on the natural acoustics. Electronic amplification is required, and provided in the form of HWMs.

The microphones in question are stylish and very discreet, and thus barely noticeable from the audience, which sits at some distance from the stage. But on screen, they cannot be missed in close-ups, and on video there is no question that they distract the viewers from the performance. One gets used to them, though, and, at times, they can even be incorporated as a joke to hilarious effect. If you want to see the venerable Kaiser Franz Joseph equipped with a HWM, then watch the Videoland DVD of Ralf Benatzky's *Im weißen Rößl*!

My second point relates to a much more important issue, which is that of overall consumer satisfaction, the caveat emptor element. In other words, when you buy a DVD of an opera production for yourself, you must realize that, once you get this in your collection, and for as long as you keep it there, you will be stuck with the director's "vision" of the featured work. The descriptive buzzword here is "Eurotrash." While no one seems able to provide a precise definition of the term, which surfaced in recent years on the Internet, it appears to designate opera productions that are as intellectually worthless as they are intellectually pretentious. The word is often associated with the German operatic stage, in part because some would claim that the objectionable fad finds its source and origin in the Regietheater movement that flourished in post–World War II Germany, later to spread elsewhere and exert a powerful influence on directors like Peter Sellars and Patrice Chéreau. Typically the term "Eurotrash," evidently meant to be used derogatively, refers to productions that are characterized by, among other things, strong political overtones, attempts at using the opera as an opportunity for Agit-Prop and a denunciation of capitalism and its institutions (including opera itself), as well as a certain morbid fascination for Europe's Nazi past.

As an example of "Eurotrash," some may be tempted to cite the first, and so far, only DVD of Wagner's *Rienzi*, released early in 2013, on Arthaus. *Rienzi* was an opera of which Hitler was particularly fond, and the director, Philipp Stölzl, makes some considerable mileage out of this. But this is no reason to trash what, overall, proves to be an excellent production. Eurotrash, then? No, but *Regietheater*. No matter how one decides to label them, operatic productions that propose to reshape harmless operatic masterpieces into something utterly new and "different," easily lend themselves to ridicule.

An egregious example of such ridiculousness is what one might call "the entomological Butterfly," a Torre del Lago production from Puccini's hometown that was released in 2004 under the Italian Dynamic label. That production stars Daniela Dessi, Fabio Armillato, and Juan Pons, with Placido Domingo conducting. The whole affair is based on the bizarre notion that, Cio Cio San being a butterfly, all of the other characters should appear as insects too. And thus Goro becomes a cockroach, Suzuki a moth, and Kate Pinkerton a wasp! That exercise in absurdity was the brainchild, so to speak, of the director, Tiziano Mancini, aided and abetted by Guillermo Mariotto (the costume designer) and Arnaldo Pomodoro (the set designer).

Yet another example is the 2011, Arthaus released DVD of a recent Opéra de Paris production of Tchaikovsky's *Pique Dame*, starring Vladimir Galouzine as Herman, with Gennadi Rozhdestvensky conducting and Lev Dodin directing. The peculiarity of that production is that, in the best *Regietheater* tradition, it moves most of the action to an asylum for the insane, complete with padded cells, straightjackets and orderlies in white scrubs. The effect can be one of unrelieved boredom and claustrophobia.

Which raises the issue of consumer satisfaction. Opera on DVD can be pricey. How likely it is that opera enthusiasts who buy that kind of product will be satisfied with their purchase? To which, I respond, rather boldly, perhaps, that chances are that they will be less satisfied with a DVD than they would had they bought an audio recording, even one originating from the same performance.

The reason for this is manifest. The crux of the matter is that, when one buys an opera on DVD, one gets not only an interpretation of the text, both musical and poetical, but also someone's visual realization of the musical and poetical concept. And that conception, forever enshrined on the disc, can easily clash with that of the viewer, especially in this age of "modern" productions that oftentimes do not look at all like the traditional *Carmen* or *Bohème* that your average opera goer naturally expects to see.

Musical interpretation, at any rate as we understand it now, is something else altogether: it has clear limits set by the score itself. The visual realization, on the other hand, is unpredictable. It may be something that one will like, or something that one will hate. How can we know in advance? In the days of the VHS and the LD, a couple of useful guides to opera on video were published, one by Alan Blyth and one edited under the auspices of the Metropolitan Opera Guild. So far, no such guide has been issued specifically for opera on DVD although Ken Wlaschin coves much of that ground in his *Encyclopedia of Opera on Screen* (Yale, 2004).

Instead people go to the Internet to search for reviews of the DVDs that they consider buying. Websites such as Amazon are very useful in that respect: they usually feature comments by consumers who have bought the product and now wish to share their opinions. Some individual titles are extensively reviewed, while others are largely ignored. Thus I could find as many as half a dozen reviews of the entomological *Butterfly* on Amazon, as compared to only one of the "madhouse" *Pique Dame*.

Now, since the launch of YouTube, in February 2005, consumers have an immense emporium where they can sample all manner of new video products, including operas on DVD. This development is highly significant with regard to the theme of this current collection of essays, as it is one of the first universal examples of the contemporary online media supporting the marketing and popularity of opera. There they will find an extensive variety of audio and/or video files, from individual arias illustrated with vintage photographs to complete recordings of live operatic performances that may, or may not be, otherwise be available through commercial channels. In most cases, those files have been posted by opera buffs with access to the material in question without any claim to ownership. (When the owners find out about the alleged infringement, they may contact YouTube and have the file removed.)

Of late, however, the industry has also taken to using YouTube as a preferred vehicle through which they can keep consumers abreast of their new titles and forthcoming releases by means of previews and other forms of advertisement (for example, by posting material, such as excerpts from interviews, culled from the "extra features" section of the DVD.) Consumers and collectors can thus gain a more precise idea of what to expect from the products that they contemplate buying, notably in terms of visual realization. In this respect, classical music has adopted a platform for dissemination that popular music had already adopted, almost as soon as it became available. This is one important example of one sector of the recording industry following the success achieved by another.

The "director's vision" is not the only issue that consumers need to take into account while planning a purchase. Another—as one would expect—is the quality of the singing, and of the musical performance in general. DVDs are also judged by the normal standards of quality of sound and picture. That was always a key issue in the classical CD industry, with regard, especially, to so-called "historic performances" often only preserved in poor sound. But that kind of source material, very common in audio, is fairly rare on video. A famous example is that of a 1973 telecast of Wagner's *Tristan und Isolde*, hailing from the *Théâtre Antique d'Orange*, with Jon Vickers and Birgit Nilsson in the title roles, with Walter Berry as Kurwenal, and Karl Böhm conducting. This is a dream cast and both the singing and the orchestral playing are absolutely outstanding. The difficulty here is that the video is practically unwatchable—and unlistenable. Whoever was in charge of capturing the performance on videotape for a French television transmission on that hot summer evening of 1973 evidently fell asleep at the wheel. Over the years, attempts have been made to clean up the sonics, and improve the quality of the picture, with mixed results. In North America, the Orange Tristan is available on DVD under the Kultur label. Kultur is a small U.S. firm that specializes in reissues, under license, of previously released material. Their products are sturdy and dependable, but they also have a reputation to cut corners with subtitles and documentation.

Reviewers have generally expressed dissatisfaction with their version of the Orange production.

The quality of the camera work can also be a problem. Sometime people may be allowed to tape a performance without the necessary material or technical expertise to do so. In the early days of opera on television, static shots abounded. Of course, in those days, everything was filmed in black and white. Today's audiences tend to reject anything and everything in black and white, and firms specializing in opera on DVD naturally hesitate in reissuing that kind of material, unless the exceptional quality of the singing warrants it. That appears to be the line of policy followed by the courageous Italian firm Hardy Classics, among a few others. Their Japanese series, noted above, notorious for its large embedded subtitles that take up a third of the screen, includes some productions in black and white. These include a 1973 performance of Gounod's *Faust* with Alfredo Kraus, Nicolai Ghiaurov, and Renata Scotto, which is part of the same series, is in color, but the sets are minimal and the use of close-ups excessive. The singing, however, is heavenly. That DVD has been reissued by the American-based company VAI (aka Video Classics International), yet another small firm specializing in, among other things, classical music programs on DVD.

New Releases

The existing catalogue of opera on DVD is large and growing, with new titles being added all the time, while others are deleted. Note, however, that deleted titles regularly make comebacks, often released by another label. So much so that the unsuspecting consumer must be careful not to buy the same recording again in a new package. That is all the more of a risk that the websites specializing in classical music CDs and DVDs do not always provide the data required to avoid falling into that trap. To keep abreast of new releases (and reissues), the consumer has a choice of on-site sources. Conceivably, the most popular of those sources is the wide, and widening, Amazon network. On the various Amazon websites, new releases can be announced months in advance, or only a few weeks earlier and the estimated dates of release are subject to change. On Amazon.com, for example new titles usually become available on a Tuesday, notably the last Tuesday of the month.

As already mentioned, the catalogue of existing DVDs that are available or have been available at some point, is large and growing. Every month, except perhaps in the dead of winter or in the summer doldrums, a number of new titles are added to it, from half a dozen to ten, or more. As a rule, most of these new releases feature works that are already available on DVD. Indeed, every month at least one third and sometimes as much as half of the "new" offerings is certain to be made up of video recordings of operas already existing in multiple versions—the sempiternal warhorses, like *Don Giovanni, Le Nozze di Figaro, Die Zauberflöte, Lucia di Lammermoor, Rigoletto, Traviata, Carmen, Aida, Tosca, Madama Butterfly, La Bohème, Salome, Der Rosenkavalier*, and a few others—in a word, the core repertory of the world's opera houses, great and small.

The material issued on DVD comes from a variety of sources: film operas, TV broadcasts rescued from oblivion in the vaults of the great national networks, lots of material previously issued on either VHS or LD, or both, but, more and more often, live performances taped especially for the purpose of DVD release. Many of the major opera houses, such as the Met or the Liceu, have signed contracts with record companies, with an aim at marketing their productions in that fashion. Everybody, it seems, would like to have their *Butterfly* or their *Traviata* on DVD, and, as a result, we have a glut of those. And yet, in spite of this abundance of riches, a number of gaping holes remain in the filmography, mainly lesser works by important composers, and important works by lesser composers.

Wagner can serve as an example of the former. Generally speaking, his works are very well represented on DVD. That is especially true of his trilogy with prologue, *Der Ring des Nibelungen*, of which there are no fewer than thirteen different versions currently available, most of which are associated with specific productions or individuals, stage directors and/or conductors. Here is the list:

1. The Boulez/Chéreau Ring, named after the conductor, Pierre Boulez, and the stage director, Patrice Chéreau. A production from the Bayreuth Festival, 1980–1981. [Deutsche Grammophone]
2. The James Levine Ring, named after James Levine, the conductor, a production from the New York Met, 1990. [Deutsche Grammophone]
3. The Kupfer/Barenboim Ring, named after Harry Kupfer, the stage director, and Daniel Barenboim, the conductor, a production from the Bayreuth Festival 1991–1992 [Warner Classics]
4. The Stuttgart Ring, named after Lothar Zagrosek conducting the Stuttgart Staatsoper in 2004 [TDK/Euroarts]
5. The Amsterdam Ring, with Pierre Audi, director, and Hartmut Haenchen conducting the Netherlands Philharmonic Orchestra in Amsterdam, 2006 [Opus Arte]
6. The Liceu Ring, with Bertrand de Billy conducting the Orchestra of the Gran Teatre del Liceu, Barcelona, 2006 [BBC Opus Arte]

7. The Copenhagen Ring, with Michael Schønwandt conducting the Royal Danish Orchestra in 2006 [Decca]
8. The Valencia Ring, named after Zubin Mehta, conducting the Orquestra de la Comunitat Valenciana, 2007–2009 [C Major]
9. The Weimar Ring, with Michael Schulz and Carl St. Clair conducting the Staatskapelle Weimar, 2010 [Arthaus]
10. The Lübeck Ring, with Anthony Pilavachi, stage director, and Roman Brogli-Sacher conducting the Philharmonisches Orchester der Hansestadt Lübeck, 2011 [Musicaphon].
11. The Lepage Ring, named after the stage director, Robert Lepage, the latest production of Wagner's Ring at the Met, with James Levine and Fabio Luisi conducting, 2011–2012 [Deutsche Grammophone]

At the time of writing, two more have been added to the releases list, to mark the bicentennial of the composer's birth. They are:

The Frankfurter Ring, 2013 [Oehms]
The Teatro Colon Ring, 2013 [C Major][3]

And there will be more to come, no doubt.

By contrast, there is, as yet, only one DVD recording of a fine, but heavily cut production of the composer's first success, *Rienzi*, and none of his earlier efforts, *Das Liebesverbot* and *Die Feen*. Maybe someone will take advantage of the bicentennial to make up for that.

Verdi, whose bicentennial also falls in the year 2013, has been luckier. Unitel Classic, in collaboration with the Teatro Regio di Parma, has launched the TUTTO VERDI collection, a complete traversal of Verdi's operas, plus the *Requiem*. Alternative versions of other works, like *Aroldo*, *Jérusalem* or the French version of *Vespri* or *Don Carlo*, are ignored, but video recordings of all of those had already been issued on DVD by other labels. By contrast, Richard Strauss has been shabbily treated by the music industry. In his case, at the time of writing, nearly half of an important composer's operatic *œuvre* is missing from the DVD catalogues. *Guntram*, *Feuersnot*, *Die Ägyptische Helena*, *Die Schweigsame Frau*, *Friedenstag*, and *Daphne*, all still await their first release on DVD. *Intermezzo* is available but in an English language version only—a superb Glyndebourne production, starring Felicity Lott and John Pringle, that was one of the gems of the VHS era.

Some important composers are completely or almost completely absent from the line-up: minor but key figures of nineteenth century opera, such as the Germans Marschner, Spohr, Von Flotow, and Lortzing, the Frenchmen Grétry, Méhul and Auber, the Italians Pacini and Mercadante, and other composers of valuable operas that opera buffs specializing in the late Classical and early Romantic periods have become acquainted with through CD recordings, such as the Opera Rara series. Franz Joseph Haydn tends to fall into the same category. The release on CD, by Philips, of a collection of eight of his Esterhazy operas conducted by Antal Dorati and released in the 1970s had been a revelation: previously, only a few specialists had any inkling of how fine an operatic composer Papa Haydn had been. To this day, recordings of only two of those eight operas, *Il Mondo della Luna* and *Orlando Paladino*, have come out on DVD. A DVD recording of a shortened version of a third work, not included in the Dorati series, the drama giocoso *Lo Speziale*, was available in the early years of the medium, but it has long gone out of print.

While the twentieth century is relatively well covered, there are holes there as well, even with important composers, whose major works have been issued on DVD, and sometimes more than once, such as Leos Janacek and Benjamin Britten. This is particularly obvious in the case of Janacek, whose minor works for the musical stage—*Sarka, The Beginning of a Romance, Osud, The Excursions of Mr. Broucek*—are nowhere to be found on DVD. The same holds true of Britten. His main operas, much admired and often staged, are all available in at least two DVD versions. But some of his lesser-known scores are yet to receive their premier recording on DVD. They include *Paul Bunyan*, his first venture on the lyric stage, as well as *The Church Parables, The Rape of Lucretia* and *Noye's Fludde*. Even *The Little Sweep*, either on its own or as part and parcel of *Let's Make an Opera!*

Other composers, including Handel, Rossini, and Donizetti, were so prolific that one would have believed that it would take years for all of their many operas to appear on DVD. As a matter of fact, however, much of Rossini is now available, with but a few gaps left (*Ciro in Babilonia, Otello, Adina, Matilde di Shabran*). Not so with Donizetti: in his case, it will indeed take years to sort out the wheat from the chaff in his colossal output. But new titles are trickling in all the time as additions to the catalogue, more recently a first ever DVD of *Poliuto* (on Bongiovanni), and a second DVD of *L'ajo nell'imbarazzo* (on Hardy).

As for Handel, most of his principal works for the lyric stage (*Rinaldo, Serse, Giulio Cesare in Egitto, Tamerlano. Agrippina, Semele, Rodelinda*), and quite a few of the lesser ones, are now available on DVD. Those that are not (as yet) account for about a third of the some forty-two scenic works composed by the master. Some of those are among his most obscure operatic scores, and perhaps negligible, like *Muzio Scevola, Ezio, Siroe, Tolomeo*. But other very fine Handelian operas still await their entry into the catalogue, works such as *Floridante, Flavio*, and *Giustino*, critically acclaimed when they were first released on compact disc. DVD technology has also facilitated the advent of a new form of musical spectacle, the staged oratorio. Handel's filmography already contains two of those, a *Belshazzar* (Bel Air) and a thought provoking *Messiah* (C Major).

At the current time, hardly a month goes by without the release of a world premiere of an opera on DVD. Those releases usually fall into one of two categories: baroque and classical operas by a composer other than by one of the major ones, Handel, Rameau and Gluck; contemporary works. About one new release a month is of a baroque or classical opera. Some of those operas will already be familiar to aficionados, having previously been issued on CD. The others enjoy their world premiere recording in any medium. As a sampler, consider the list of the six DVDs of such baroque and classical operas released in Region 1 in the first six months of 2013. Three of them belong to a series devoted to Pergolesi's operatic production. One work, *L'Olimpiade*, has long been available on CD, but for the two others, *Il Prigionier Superbo* and *La Salustia*, this is a world premiere recording in any medium. Of the three other titles, Marc Antoine Charpentier's "Jesuit opera" *David et Jonathas*, was already familiar to fans of baroque music, thanks mainly to a CD recording conducted by William Christie. But the two others are video recordings of works heard and seen for the first time on DVD. They are: Leonardo Vinci's *Partenope*, an early eighteenth century Neapolitan opera on the Dynamic label, and, on BBC Opus Arte, *Dove è Amore è Gelosia*, an *intermezzo giocoso* by Giuseppe Scarlatti, said to have been a member of the Scarlatti clan, but so obscure that the exact nature of his relation to Alessandro and Domenico remains a matter for speculation.

DVD technology can also be used to promote contemporary opera. By way of a sampler, here is a short list of fifteen important contemporary operas issued on DVD in recent years:

1. Mark Adamo's *Little Women* (Naxos)
2. John Adams' *Nixon in China* (Warner)
3. John Adams' *The Death of Klinghoffer* (Decca)
4. John Adams' *Doctor Atomic* (Sony)
5. Thomas Ades' *Powder Her Face* (Koch International)
6. Harrison Birtwistle's *The Minotaur* (Opus Arte)
7. John Corigliano's *The Ghosts of Versailles* (Deutsche Grammophone)
8. Philip Glass' *Satyagraha* (Paradox)
9. Einojuhani Rautavaara's *Rasputin* (Ondine)
10. Kaija Saariaho's *L'Amour de loin* (Deutsche Grammophone)
11. Aulis Sallinen's *The Palace* (Arthaus)
12. Aulis Sallinen's *The Red Line* (Ondine)
13. Tan Dun's *The First Emperor* (EMI)

14. Tan Dun's *Marco Polo* (BBC/Opus arte)
15. Karl Tikka: *Luther* (Ondine)

With the passing of generations, what used to be considered contemporary may become "classic" or "a modern classic." Benjamin Britten and Francis Poulenc were the first two opera composers whose works were to achieve that status in the second half of the twentieth century. Now other prominent composers from the same period are following in their footsteps, generating interest, numerous productions and new recordings both on CD and DVD.

DVDs of Bernd Aloïs Zimmermann's *Die Soldaten* and Olivier Messiaen's *Saint François d'Assise* have been available for some time. In the years to come expect to hear more titles appearing on DVD, operas like Ginastera's *Bomarzo*, and *Don Rodrigo*, Blomdahl's *Aniara*, Samuel Barber's *Vanessa*, and his *Antony and Cleopatra*, the operas of Aribert Reimann, of Menotti and Hans Werner Henze, and those of Philip Glass and of Harrison Birtwistle, among others.

There are also gaps resulting from major important operas from the eighteenth and nineteenth century having fallen through the cracks, so to speak, and thus remaining absent from the DVD catalogue. Meyerbeer's grand guignolesque *Robert le Diable* used to be one of these but now it is slated for rescue through release on DVD (on Euroarts) in the early summer of 2013. However this is but one of a number of very fine scores, including quite a few masterpieces that used to be very much admired and frequently performed. Most of those are from the French repertory and date back to the time when Paris was the center of the operatic world. One may thus think of, among others, Grétry's best opéras comiques, notably *Zémire et Azor*, *Richard Cœur de Lion*, and *Les Pélerins de la Mecque*, Gluck's *Écho et Narcisse*, and *La Rencontre Imprévue*, Monsigny's *Le Déserteur*, Philidor's *Tom Jones*, Jean-Jacques Rousseau's *Le Devin du Village*, Méhul's *Joseph*, Spontini's *La Vestale*, Chérubini's *Lodoiska* and *Les Abencérages*, Auber's *La Muette de Portici*, and *Fra Diavolo*, Hérold's *Le Pré aux Clercs*, Boieldieu's *La Dame Blanche*, Adolphe Adam's *Le Postillon de Longjumeau*, Halévy's *La Reine de Chypre* (so much lauded by the young Wagner!), Berlioz' *Béatrice and Bénédict*, Félicien David's *Le Désert*, Gounod's *Mireille*, Reyer's *Sigurd* (pourquoi pas?), Meyerbeer's *Le Prophète*, Ambroise Thomas' *Mignon*, Chabrier's *Gwendoline* and *Le Roi malgré lui*, Gustave Charpentier's *Louise*, Ernest Chausson's *Le Roi Artus*, Gabriel Fauré's *Pénélope*, Rabaud's *Marouf*, even Vincent d'Indy's controversial *Fervaal* and *La Légende de Saint-Christophe*—virtually none of which have, so far, appeared on DVD.

Finally there are a couple of gaping holes that will never be filled. Arguably the two people who, in the 1950s, did more than anyone else to bolster and argue anew the case for opera considered as a legitimate form of theater, Maria Callas and Wieland Wagner. Now these two influential figures have this in common—their filmed legacies are small, almost insignificant. As far as we know, none of the epoch-breaking productions that Wieland Wagner designed for the Bayreuth Festival between 1951 and 1966 has been preserved on film or video. What we have are still photograph, a few interviews, and some clips of newsreels and rehearsals. As for Maria Callas, whose audio legacy is otherwise considerable, all of the footage that we have of her acting out a role in sets and costume is limited to two recordings of Act II of *Tosca* made for special occasions: (1) a gala in honor of French president René Coty, at the Paris Opera, on December 19, 1958; and (2) a concert telecast from Royal Opera House, Covent Garden, London, on February 9, 1964. Both of those films have been issued on EMI.

DVDs and the Future of Opera

Finally, to conclude, a few thoughts on DVD technology and the future of opera.

It is safe to assume that, from now on, people will come to opera mainly through the internet, DVDs or something like DVDs. In the perspective of the media, we do, as it were, live in the third age of opera. The first age was that of live opera, and it lasted from the late sixteenth to the end of the nineteenth century. Next came the age of recorded music, from the Mapleson cylinders[4] to the advent of the Compact disc, in the 1980s. Now we live in the age of multi-media, which began in the late 1920s, with early attempts at combining sound, voice, voice and picture into one multifaceted medium, eventually resulting in the invention and universal triumph—so far—of the DVD.

So what could be the impact of DVD technology on the future of opera? To begin with, the multiplication of widely available videos of opera performances cannot help but stimulate an interest in the art form and bring it to new audiences, as has already happened with the Japanese market, in which, although they do not produce very much of that material themselves, have long been avid consumers of opera on video. Another important aspect to consider is that of the documentary value of opera on video. Here one must remember that, to a large extent, the life of a work in the repertory depends on its dramatic potential, or "stageability." There are operas packed with excellent, even superlative music, and yet they do not hold the stage very effectively. One example is Rossini's *Guillaume Tell* (*Guglielmo Tell*), a musical masterpiece, no doubt, but also a very long opera that suffers from grave defects in terms of timing and pacing—as clearly revealed by the video. It is certainly telling that, even as we are experiencing a major Rossinian Renaissance, we still have but one DVD of the composer's late *chef-d'œuvre* (a 1989 production from La Scala, on Opus Arte). Even more telling, in my opinion, is the fact that, after the immensely successful premiere of this, his most "modern" score, the composer quietly decided to retire.

Conversely, much of the music in Leoncavallo's *Pagliacci* is facile and of questionable quality, but in the end, it all works very well, thanks to the opera's tight dramatic structure. Vulgar? Yes, perhaps, but very effective—as demonstrated by numerous video recordings.

Opera companies that do not already have one, need to set up reference libraries of operas on DVD. When working on a new production, they would find it worth their while to check on past documented scenic realizations of the same opera to look for insights as to how to resolve certain issues inherent in the staging of the work.

As we know, opera is rife with such issues. Let us suppose, for instance, that you have been hired to stage and direct *Götterdämmerung*. How are you going to deal with the final scene—very brief but so demanding? Will you need to rent a horse? Will you have to build a funeral pyre and set it on fire, and then ask your soprano to ride into it on horseback? And what about the collapse of Valhalla, and the ensuing universal conflagration, to say nothing of the Rhine overflowing its banks and Love redeeming us all with a humongous hug at the end. It always pays to see how others have dealt with the apparently impossible!

A third and final point. It will be interesting to compare the future course of the evolution of opera on DVD with that of the progress of the DVD in general. Until now, the two have developed in parallel, not unexpectedly, given that opera on DVD is nothing but a subset of DVD in general. This could change, though, as cinema, the main provider of source material for DVDs, continues to veer away from realism and shows signs of turning into a highly artificial medium dominated by optical illusions, CGI, and special effects. One can hardly imagine opera DVDs following suit. Gone are the golden days of the film opera, and its heavy reliance on studio work. The new opera DVDs that keep coming out are, almost invariably, video recordings of live performances, with or without the benefit of an audience. Admittedly, there is room for technical gimmicks in such venues, including some that might look great on video. But one can only go so far with such gimmicks on a live stage, and all in all, chances are that the opera DVD of the future will remain anchored to the traditional operatic stage, and will look very much like the opera DVD of the present.

There are, however, a few truly exceptional operatic spectacles immortalized on DVD that seem to designate some ways of transcending the limitations of conventional opera. Here are four examples: Kenneth Branagh's film of *The Magic Flute* (2006), which is a delight to see for its skillful uses of all of the technical resources of today's cinema. But if that is indeed the future of opera on video, or DVD, where does that lead us? Are we not back to square one, in equally traditional film opera? Yes, we are, but film opera is great, or at least can be, can it not? Hans-Jürgen Syberberg's unique *Parsifal* (1983), which was entirely shot in a studio (or warehouse), thirty years later, one is still amazed to see how, with very limited means at his disposal—not much more than the resources of the theater—the director was able to create a "place of the imagination" that is not of this world. For, if opera is a highly artificial art form, why not locate it in some space that is just as strange and artificial? And Syberberg ended up creating a peculiar symbolic realm that is neither of the cinema nor of the theater, but partakes of both, and which he could use to situate both Klingsor's flower maidens, and Grail knights—the servants of illusion and truth, respectively. The end result is a film, and could never have been anything else, Syberberg's vision of *Parsifal* being unstageable (a common enough problem in *Regietheater*.)

Faced with the same need to create new spaces for the mind, using technological means and old-fashioned set dressing, Ingmar Bergman reached comparable solutions in his celebrated film of *The Magic Flute* made for Swedish TV in 1975. In Bergman's vision, we follow Mozart's *Singspiel* as it is being performed in an actual theater (Drottningholm) but made up to function as a film set. As with Syberberg, we find ourselves in an interstice between two worlds—the world of truth and that of the performance, which itself is but an illusion, with the video track acting as the common ground where the various elements of the film and the visual and musical performance can come together and coalesce into one *Gesamtkunstwerk*. The result, once again, has to be a film.

And, finally, a word about an extraordinary DVD (on the Naïve label) of a production of Rossini's early farce *La Pietra del Paragone* taped live at the Théâtre du Châtelet in Paris in 2007. That unique spectacle, featuring one of the composer's lesser known works, is the brainchild of Pierrick Sorin, an award-winning French video artist who here takes advantage of the operatic occasion both to demonstrate, to hilarious effects, the state-of-the-art techniques of optical illusion currently used in film and TV (for example, blue screen effects), and to gently "deconstruct" them. There is not at any moment any doubt about where we are—in a theater, in front of a live audience—and what we are doing there—experiencing the arts of illusion. Thanks, in no small measure, to the power of the young Rossini's music at its madcap best, and the high tech tricks conjured up by Mr. Sorin, in fusion with the music, the available space—nothing but an empty stage—is metamorphosed into a magic ground, a place of enchantment, a fairy ring.

There perhaps resides the future of opera on DVD—in magic, music and illusion!

Notes

1. Alan Blyth, *Opera on Video: The Essential Guide* (London: Kyle Cathie, 1995).
2. Walter Felsenstein (30 May 1901—8 October 1975) was an Austrian-born, German theater and opera director renowned for his meticulously staged operatic productions, some of which are preserved on film, including, among others, his *Don Giovanni*, *Tales of Hoffmann* and *Cunning Little Vixen*. Preaching by the example, and theoretical writings, in which he argued against routine and expounded on the principles behind his work, Felsenstein, himself influenced by Konstantin Stanislavsky, is widely considered one of the founding fathers of the Regietheater school of operatic stage direction. After the Second World War, he chose to reside and work in East Berlin, where he founded the Komische Oper in 1947. Under his directorship, foreign works were invariably performed in the vernacular, more often than not in new German translations by Felsenstein himself.
3. This is a recording of an abridged version of the Ring—compressed to a mere seven hours, on four DVDs plus one disc of supplements. This version, allegedly, has the blessing of the Wagner family.
4. From January 16, 1901, to sometime in 1903, the then librarian of the Metropolitan Opera House in New York City, Lionel Mapleson, having acquired a Bettini cylinder recorder and reproducer, used it to capture the voices of most of the singers then on the roster of the Met, including some whose recorded legacy is either very meager or practically inexistent, such as tenor Jean de Reszke and soprano Milka Ternina, two major opera stars of the time. Those recordings, more than a hundred of which have come down to us, were made in the theater during performances. The collection is unique for the time, in this that it includes the orchestral accompaniment, which was almost never the case at the time. The quality of the sound ranges from passable to barely listenable.

Bibliography

Blyth, Alan. *Opera on Video: The Essential Guide*. London: Kyle Cathie, 1995.
Citron, Marcia J. *Opera on Screen*. New Haven and London: Yale University Press, 2000.
_____. *When Opera Meets Film*. Cambridge: Cambridge University Press. 2010.
Fawkes, Richard. *Opera on Film*. London: Duckworth, 2000.
Gruber, Paul, ed. *The Metropolitan Opera Guide to Opera on Video*. London and New York City: Metropolitan Opera Guild and W.W. Norton, 1997.
Wlaschin, Ken. *Encyclopedia of Opera on Screen: A Guide to More Than 100 Years of Opera Films, Videos, and DVDs*. New Haven and London: Yale University Press, 2004.

Wunderkammer: Light as a Scenographic and Dramaturgical Tool in Opera

Hansjörg Schmidt

Light is an extraordinary medium. It is deeply woven into our lives and cultures. Any performance, and any space that contains a performance, uses light or indeed the absence of light, in a dramatic and meaningful way. The medium of opera has always been very aware of what light can bring to a performance, and this essay will look more closely at how the operatic form has been shaped by its relationship with light: Wagner and Appia of course made some key advances in this regard, but so have Max Reinhardt, Patrick Woodroffe and Heiner Goebbels. This essay will look at works by all of them, and how the light has been designed and incorporated into a musical score, a production context, and a narrative. We will also find that the styles of lighting in opera are becoming much less defined, and that a range of other media is being used to shape an audience's experience of music theatre: architecture is used to mediate character and mood in Goebbel's work, and the language of rock and roll is used to emotionally connect with the audience in Patrick Woodroffe's lighting for opera. Some of these works are very much driven by the music, such as *Stifter's Dinge*[1] or *Roméo et Juliette*.[2] Others use music (and light) in a much more indirect and subtle way, as we will see in Max Reinhardt's *Jedermann*. The essay will also look at another practice that actively and creatively uses technology as a medium for constant change and development: Surgery. As keyhole surgery has brought with it an ever increasing dependence on technology and a move away from the human medium, so has the arrival of automated lighting systems revolutionized the way we can light, and see, opera.

To understand the relationship opera has with light it is important to look at the qualities of light within a performative context more closely: The use of daylight in a church service, a hospital ward or on the stage of London's Globe theatre is much more informed and structured than we may at first glance think. The use of artificial (man-made) light such as candle or electrical light can of course create moments of considerable drama and can become a complex and eloquent dramatic language. And light does share many of its qualities with music: both languages[3] are driven by the need to communicate a deeper meaning. Storytellers will deploy the register and tonal quality of their voices to support and communicate the meaning of their tale—more so if the storyteller is a professional raconteur, and less so if the storyteller is part of a larger institution (for example, a priest or a doctor). And all these musicians employ light: the raconteur may chose the flicker of a camp fire to support his tale, or the glow of the footlights. A doctor may choose to either allow the light in or to block it out. So the two languages have always been closely aligned, both technically and artistically: the first lighting control desk was based on an organ.[4] Richard Wagner's use of light to support the productions of his operas is well documented and will be explored in more detail later on. But there are other, more discreet but equally powerful expressions of this duality: Max Reinhardt's use of light and voice in his production of *Jedermann*,[5] for example. And the relationship of light and music in the work by Heiner Goebbels and the clod ensemble. Max Reinhardt's (1873–1943) work as a director for theatre and film had a considerable impact on the shape of visual theatre in Germany at the beginning of the twentieth century. His influence on German artistic life at that time can hardly be overestimated, and many film directors (Fritz Lang in particular) were influenced by Reinhardt's productions. An Austrian Jew, he emigrated first to Britain and then the United States in 1938. Heiner Goebbels (born 1952) is a German composer and theatre maker. The clod ensemble is a London based performance company who produce innovative work that links music, movement and light.

So this essay will look at opera and the medium of light, introducing the concept of light as a medium for communication, governed by the wish to generate meaning—a meaning that can be very pure and emotive, such as sadness or joy. Or highly complex and abstract, such as corruption or jealousy. The essay will examine the historical closeness of light and music, and how the two have continuously pushed each other's formal and functional qualities forward. And finally it will look at examples of *mise-en-scène* from a range of productions that use light and music in order to tell stories.

The British theatre director Simon McBurney has increasingly used technical media (particularly video projection) to frame his productions. McBurney is the co-founder and Artistic Director of Théâtre de Complcité (now called Complicite), a ground-breaking English theatre company. He uses the following model to illustrate his interest in visual communication and time: McBurney argues that photography deals with the past, film with the Future, and theatre with the present.[6] This model is governed by the role of the audience: the relationship between a photograph and the person studying it is governed by the fact that the photo presents a frozen moment that may have occurred some time ago. We may include a cave painting or a Caravaggio into this category, as well as a holiday snap. Mainstream film maintains audience interest by inviting the spectator to second guess what may be about to happen, at some point in the future. And theatre wants to share a series of moments with its audience, to create a collective presence. The theatre director Peter Brook, in his book *The Empty Space*,[7] looks more closely at the creation of theatrical moments in his chapter on what he calls *Holy Theatre*. Brook's career as a director started with the Royal Shakespeare Company in 1947. He moved to Paris in 1970, running the Bouffes du Nord theatre until his retirement in 2008. In his book, Brook tells this story of an incident he witnessed on a ruined *Reeperbahn* in Hamburg, in 1947: As he walks down the street he hears a surprising sound, children's laughter, coming from the shell of a house. Inside he finds two ragged looking clowns performing to a group of children. Improbably, the clowns start to call out names of food: *Schinkenwurst, Bratkartoffeln*. The children are rapt, and what Brook calls a true theatrical silence descends. So this is a good example of theatre living in the presence, creating a moment of *complicité* that transcends everything else. No other artform can achieve this sharing of a present moment quite so effectively—except for sculpture, maybe, and architecture to some degree. But theatre, and I include opera in this category, is better at this than most. This is one principal reason why the creative arts require subsidy, as the nature particularly of the work described above is hard to package and to sell as a commodity. It is the opposite of commercial goods, in fact, as live performance aims to fulfill a need in a way that is hard or even impossible to market.

How, then, does light fit into this? There is both an easy and a rather complex answer: We all have a close relationship with light, and know much more about it than we think. In Peter Brook's example, we all can imagine the scene—a ruined house, the clowns, the children sitting on the floor. Is it evening or daylight? Is there a candle or a fire burning inside the house? Maybe there still is electricity, a bare light bulb dangling from the ceiling. So to some degree we all are lighting designers. The same applies to our daily lives: we know that the light from the new energy saving bulb for the standing lamp somehow doesn't feel right. We may ask for a reading light for our desk at work, to offset the harsh light from the ceiling fluorescent. Or we feel the urge for daylight when working in a room with no windows. So our relationship to light is quite complex: we often instinctively know what is good and appropriate lighting for a given scenario. And we also often shy away from doing anything about it as we feel we do not understand the underlying technology. So here is a concise guide to how light works:

Technically speaking, light is a flow of electromagnetic energy (the same energy that is used to transmit radio signals, for example). This flow becomes visible within a set band of the electromagnetic spectrum, what we perceive as light. This spectrum doesn't transmit as white light, but along a range of spectral colors: ultraviolet into (visible) blue at the low bandwidth, green and yellow in the center, and red towards (invisible) infrared at the higher end. Our brain puts these colors together to perceive white[8]—light fracturing in drops of water to make a rainbow makes this process visible.

Several important things to note here: yellow and green colors *appear* brighter than reds and greens. Therefore a steward in a yellow safety jacket stands out from a crowd. It isn't because he somehow radiates light, but because our brain perceives this color to be brighter. We don't really know why that is (scientific understanding of vision stops at the point when the signals coming from the eye reach the brain), but think it is because we have developed color vision under the forest canopy, where those were the dominant colors. The ideal white light source is the one that is composed equally across the spectral colors. Hence the disadvantage of discharge (fluorescent) and LED sources compared to Tungsten, as both have irregular spikes across the visible spectrum.

These qualities all impact on the lighting designer's work: yellow/green costumes or scenery will appear brighter on stage then blue or red ones. So the lighting designer will have to adjust composition accordingly, which sometimes is an impossible task—the chorus dressed in yellow robes will appear much brighter than the tenor in front of them in his red cloak. There is very little the lighting designer can do about that. Once a lighting designer has chosen her palette (the lights she would like to use), and considered the impact of lamp types and materials used on set, she needs to start the process of designing. The lighting design will often grow out of a collaborative process and therefore generates slowly and is subject to constant change. But there are some aspects of a design that remain constant, most importantly the relationship of the light to the performance space.

The light source may be an electric light or natural light, a direct or an indirect source. In nature, the sun provides a direct source (casting a shadow and profiling an object) while the reflected light from an overcast sky provides a diffuse, more general light. Arguably this is why, in Europe, sculpture has developed so strongly as an artistic mode of expression in countries along the Mediterranean Sea, while Northern Europe developed the flat art of painting. Church architecture has also been driven by a culture's relationship to natural light: Churches in Rome are created to celebrate the drama of a shaft of sunlight piercing a dark (and cool) interior, while the Churches of England celebrate the sky by offering panoramic views through large windows. The same spatial relationships can be attributed to light for the opera stage. One great advantage is that 99 percent of opera productions will take place in a proscenium arch theatre. So the observer's position is fixed. Other than in a church, the light source is broken into a multiple array of lights. The designer's task is to identify what lights (out of the many hundreds that are available) should be used to create the visual structure and sculpting that is necessary to provide the right visual composition for each scene. So the process of designing in opera, in stark contrast to the design of light in architecture, becomes about carefully selecting the right tool out of the many available, rather than considering how to best shape the light coming from the only tool at hand (the sun). So in this respect lighting for opera is much more closely related to painting then it is to photography, for example.

Stage lighting, like surgery or the financial markets, is often seen as something of a dark art: apart from the people practicing it, no one feels they understand it and therefore it is either encountered very nervously (by directors, designers, conductors) or very cautiously (audiences and critics). So it feels important to challenge this perception: the craft of stage lighting is in fact quite straightforward. As mentioned earlier, we all are lighting designers when we consider light in our home or our workplace. And the myth that we don't really understand light prevents us from being more actively involved in demanding good lighting design for our everyday life. Stage lighting operates in the same categories as domestic lighting: we use spot lights fitted with lenses for directional light, and wash lights with reflectors for diffuse, general light. The hundreds of lanterns above an opera stage will, by and large, be made up of a combination of those two types. These lights are usually painted black, which is an important hint to the main difference between theatre lighting and light for the built environment: what is interesting in live performance is what the light does when it hits a surface, much more so than in other applications of light where the appearance of the light source is of equal importance to what the light does once it hits its intended surface. In that regard, and as mentioned above, light in performance is very close to painting.

As a painter will frame his canvas, so light can appear from an infinite (and often impossible) range of sources, so in the case of an average opera staging no light fixtures are visible. What is offered to the audience's gaze is a very carefully framed picture of light reflecting from surfaces: scenery, props, faces. Different from a church, for example, most if not all of these surfaces have their own light source, and each light source is very closely controlled with regard to its intensity, color and focus. So while a church interior might be lit by one lantern (the sun), and the light focused by one window, a scene from an opera production will be lit by 100 light sources, with each one carefully focused on a specific detail, forming a total picture that may (or may not) suggest to the audience a single source. So this is where the use of light moves from the application of craft to a notion of design: a designer is required to make a multitude of choices: what fixtures to use, from what angle and in what color and at what intensity each fixture should be applied, and so on. In many ways there is a striking similarity between a lighting designer facing the task of lighting an opera production and a surgeon about to commence an operation: both are master craftsmen, both have a fixed set of tools at their disposal. Both are interfering with a highly complex organism. The similarities between the two practices, and indeed the wider parallels between the opera stage and the anatomical operating theatre have been elegantly demonstrated in the clod ensemble's production *An Anatomy in Four Quarters*,[9] where the program notes compare images of the theatre's technical infrastructure with an anatomical drawing. The similarities are indeed striking, as both drawings aim to reduce a complex mechanism to an easy to use and carefully crafted map. This analogy is helpful in terms of our understanding of the design and use of the medium light in an operatic context: the lighting designer uses a medium that is highly complex and has been developed and fine-tuned over hundreds of years. He applies this medium to an equally complex organism that is made out of a range of materials, all of which require distinct and careful attention, never forgetting however that all these parts are only successful if they can work as a whole. It is a very difficult but, if undertaken correctly, hugely rewarding task that allows an operatic production to move from an essentially aural concert performance to a sensory experience.

Theatrical lighting design and surgery have seen fundamental and wide ranging changes driven by the wish to continuously improve and develop practice and outcomes: the arrival of automated lighting systems revolutionized the lighting industry in a way similar to the introduction of keyhole surgery in the operating theatres. The arrival of keyhole surgery brought with it an ever increasing reliance on technology: in today's operating theatres the surgeon might not know who he will be working with until the day of the operation, as the human network is of lesser importance than the technical one. At pre-keyhole procedures the surgeon would expect to be operating with a dedicated team that had been working together for many years.

Automated lighting systems in theatre and opera houses allow for a very direct connection between light and music, as these intelligent lanterns can be made to move the light beam across the stage in a prerecorded sequence—this is why this technology was initially developed for stage shows by rock bands such as Genesis and Pink Floyd, who were interested in the spectacle and the emotional impact of a series of light beams moving in sync with the music, thereby visualizing that music's energy. Lighting designers now have to acquire a considerable and wide ranging set of technical skills and knowledge so they can use ever more complex technologies. And these technologies have acquired an independence from preliminary thought and planning that is starting to challenge the traditional role of the lighting designer—the fact that a lighting designer or technician can remotely access and change attributes of an automated light fixture (position, color, texture, and so on) allows for a greater independence in responding to a stimulus such as music, to be more intuitive. To respond with light as a musician can respond to a change in mood or direction. It is interesting to study what happens when an intuitive lighting designer works on an Opera project, where traditionally careful pre-planning is essential.[10] A good example for this culture clash is the production of *Roméo et Juliette* at the Wiener Staatsoper, with lighting designed by Patrick Woodroffe.

This was a controversial production, bringing the aesthetics of Rock and Roll to the Opera House.[11] It is also one of the most successful productions in the Staatsoper's current repertoire, bringing in new, and predominantly younger, audiences. The production is driven by spectacle—the director, Jürgen Flimm, set out to create a scenography that was purely driven by light and as he was very aware of the technological advances in lighting for Rock concerts, he hired the most successful lighting designer from that sector, Patrick Woodroffe. Woodroffe created a large on stage metal structure that consists of several steel towers packed with automated lighting units. The towers themselves can track across the stage and rotate 360 degrees, as can all the lights. Everything moves, or has the potential to do so as and when required—Woodroffe has created a kinetic work of art, and indeed the Staatsoper refers to his contribution as *Lichtkunst* (light art), rather than lighting design. The production is clearly not the purist's idea of an opera. What is unusual is that Woodroffe has put the lights onstage, so the sources are visible and are part of the visual picture. Conventionally in theatre and opera we hide the light sources so they are out of view—they are usually painted black and a great deal of effort is spend on carefully masking and framing the visual picture. As we have seen in the lighting triangle, light itself only becomes visible when it hits a surface, so if we want the light beams themselves to become visible we need to put something in the air that provides a surface for the light to catch: smoke, or in its more subtle version Haze. These small water particles allow for the light beams to become visible, and equally for the moving light beam to become a scenographic tool, underscoring and supporting the energy of the music as well as adding to the sense of spectacle by creating a rich variety of seemingly physical structures that can appear and disappear at will. Bread and butter stuff for rock and roll, but still highly controversial in opera. Nevertheless, there is a rich history of light used as a form of purer scenography, which goes back to works by Louie Fuller[12] and Gordon Craig.

Both artists recognized the ability of light to fundamentally transform a scenographic space, and to do so more quickly and elegantly than any piece of built scenery might do. Both also were great show people, and used a darkened auditorium and carefully controlled light to mask the mechanics of the stage machinery, to create an illusion rather than to recreate reality.

For *Roméo et Juliette,* Woodroffe is breaking two conventions: placing the lights on stage and making them visible is a statement of intent which will be different from any opera you have seen before. Making the beams themselves visible tells us that this will be a sensory spectacle, and asks us to trust the light and the music to carry us through the narrative. This is smarter and more complex than may at first glance appear: the one scenographic obstacle that Flimm and Woodroffe struggled with for a long time was how to create Juliette's balcony. Flimm particularly felt that this would be the one moment in the Opera where they might have to introduce "conventional" scenographic language, offering a sense of height and condensing their vocabulary to a strictly denotative language. However, to everyone's surprise, they found that preview audiences very happily accepted a luminous disc in the floor as the balcony. Arguably, this is the moment in the production that proves that Flimm's gamble had paid off: the audience trusts the light to carry them through the story, and in the process the notion of spectatorship had moved from a linear, passive role to a dynamic and complex partnership that enabled audiences to respond to a quite complex and abstract sign system. And thereby this connects to a line that runs back to Reinhardt's Salzburg *Jedermann*, Gordon Craig's *Hamlet* and indeed Richard Wagner's Bayreuth productions. All of those are connected by a wish to disembody the spectator, to allow for their imaginations to soar and to create an emotive connection between audience and narrative. I think it is useful to offer a small detour here from opera, and to have a closer look at Max Reinhardt's production of *Jedermann* at the Salzburg Festival.

The Salzburg *Jedermann*, adapted by Hugo von Hofmannsthal from the medieval Everyman story, is performed annually, for a period of six weeks over the summer, in front of the Salzburg Dome, starting in the early evening and concluding at sunset. It is the centerpiece of the Festival. Reinhardt's original staging—a simple wooden trestle and a striking use of daylight and the Dome facade—continues to be used today, although there are regular tweaks and adjustments to keep the productions in touch with a changing cultural and social context. The audience (all 2000 of them for each performance) is seated on a simple raked auditorium, filled with wooden benches. The production is deeply anachronistic. Tickets for the performances are hard to come by and not cheap, and the audiences tend to consist of Austrian and Central European Bourgeoisie displaying their evening wear and quiet satisfaction with where life has taken them. So when this audience settles down to watch the story of a wealthy man being taken to Hell by another man in a skeleton outfit, the response should really be one between disinterest and polite boredom. The opposite takes place: a hush falls over the crowd, and a very powerful sense of Peter Brook's *Holy Theatre* develops: the production responds to a need in the audience, as the Hamburg clowns in Brook's example at the beginning of this essay recognize and play with the children's need for spiritual food. The need in Salzburg is a need for morality and purpose, but at the very least a need to slow down and to reflect on life and death. It is quite an extraordinary thing to witness, and it is put into context by two external elements: if the weather is poor the performances are moved into the *Schauspielhaus*, and recently there have been attempts to present performances at night time, under theatrical lighting. In both scenarios the production suffers considerably, and changes from approaching Holy Theatre to being a good example of what Brook calls *Dead Theatre*. The reason why *Jedermann* is so powerful is because of its use of sound and light: The sound is that of the human voice within an architecture of stillness. And the light is that of the receding daylight. Both are carefully orchestrated: the positioning of the wooden trestle stage and the character of the square facing it allows for voices to travel and soar, and at the same time muffles the noises of the outside world to a degree that makes them otherworldly and eternal. Death banging his fists against the inside of the Dome's metal doors and thereby announcing his entrance to this day makes audiences jump. The performance length and time is carefully aligned to the daylight receding over first the mountain tops and then the Salzburg rooflines, creating a range of effects both bold—such as the shadow of a spire falling over the Dome facade as *Jedermann* approaches redemption, and subtle—the increasing monochromacity of the scene as the full spectrum sunlight is replaced by reflected light of ever decreasing intensity, thereby triggering our eyes' rods to take over from the cones, and color vision to reduce. So one can argue, I think, that the reason why these productions have proven so successful, and so resistant to change, is because of their pure and powerful aural and visual scenography. It is not impossible to imagine this approach to be successful for an opera production, and it reminds us of something we may have lost in our European Opera tradition. The person to both blame and celebrate for this is Richard Wagner.

Wagner and his scenographer, Adolphe Appia, shaped the way we produce opera today. The *Gesamtkunstwerk*, the notion of a complete piece of work that combines staging, scenography, text/music, and audience experience into a coherent whole started with their productions at the Bayreuth *Festspielhaus*. There are many aspects of this work that demand careful analysis and contextualizing, but for the purpose of this essay we will look at the application of light, and equally the controlled absence of it. Wagner and Appia's simplest and probably most far reaching decision was to take control of the auditorium lighting. A great Romantic and an admirer of the sublime, Wagner wanted his music to come from somewhere else, from a place that could not be seen and therefore was removed from the physical reality of the *Festspielhaus*.

Appia and Wagner also wanted to closely control the audience's sensory responsiveness. This utilizes a staging model where we start with nothing, and after that everything we see is very carefully controlled, framed, and carved out of darkness. Compare this to *Jedermann*, where we see everything, and where there is no control of the attributes of light apart from time. So this provides a useful frame of reference: Wagner's work is about space. A space for the music, a space for the audience, and a space for the *mise-en-scène*. All of this presented, managed and connected by the light. Reinhardt, on the other hand, is about time. The time of day, the time of the narrative, and the time of the telling. So here is the crossroads that sends European opera on its way towards a theatre of composition and space, towards a directors theatre that connects the immaterial music with a very material world. And as a consequence light becomes increasingly dramaturgical, telling us where to look, how to interpret an action or indeed a piece of music. To this day this is how we apply light to an opera production, very similarly to its application in theatre and musicals. Compare this linear and dramaturgical approach to light used in dance or architecture: here we can find a lighting language that has developed along a different route, away from the *Gesamtkunstwerk*. Light is often highly abstract and based on time rather than space. A good example is the light used in the built environment of Daniel Libeskind's extension to the Jüdisches Museum in Berlin.

The building is defined by the careful orchestration of windows to manage daylight, and the most poignant example of this is the Holocaust tower, a cathedral like room where only daylight is used to illuminate the space, entering through a single opening at the top of the tower. It is a very expressive space, so much so that the museum decided for it to remain empty—the building itself becoming an exhibit, a memory, a testimony to the Holocaust and the suffering of the Jewish people. The light plays a very important part in this: the placing of the light source (the window) is simple and bold. The change of light as triggered by the change in weather and time outside makes this a living space and not a dead one, combining the past with the presence in a very powerful way. A similar visual language can be found in contemporary dance, for example in the aforementioned clod ensemble production *An Anatomy in Four Quarters*. The piece invited the audience of 200 (in an auditorium seating up to 1500 people) to observe the stage from a multitude of viewing points, starting in the upper circle and then moving to the dress circle and the stalls before ending up on stage!

For the first quarter (seen from the upper circle), the stage was cross lit so no light hit the floor and therefore the dancers appeared to float in midair. The light was not selective, or focusing on a particular detail. The dancers' movements created shapes and patterns, and the audience chose where they wanted to look. The scenography is made of the relationship between the audience watching from far away (the second circle) and the bodies on stage.

There are opera productions that use this more abstract compositional language and a predominantly temporal structure as *mise-en-scène*. Heiner Goebbel's work is a good example of this: *Stifter's Dinge* is hard to classify, but I think it can with some justification be labeled as an opera, performed by five automated pianos and an array of odd instruments and industrial wreckage. The piece uses music and scenography to present the life of Adalbert Stifter, an Austrian Romantic poet and painter. There are no human performers or singers—Goebbel's music is performed by the pianos, and the scenography is created by stage automation and light that includes some very sophisticated video projection. So the audience witnesses a *Wunderkammer* of animated objects and imagery, creating some quite extraordinary pictures that surface out of some very beautiful music. They are watching an Opera. What is very unusual is the role the light plays—the light has a very material quality: we can see not only the light hitting surfaces, but also where the light comes from. The light is in perpetual motion, constantly moving and shifting. Sometimes very slow, and sometimes very fast.

The set for *Stifter's Dinge* has a vertical stack of pianos upstage and some water tanks stage left and downstage. The light is integrated into all of this, with both the surfaces and the light sources visible. Rather than objects appearing out of darkness (there are no blackouts in this piece), the audience is invited to explore this world as they might explore a building, allowing their gaze to wander as Adalbert Stifter might explore his native country's mountain landscapes. What this points towards is that the way we mediate narratives in differing contexts (an opera stage, a museum) is becoming much less defined and has started to mesh. Goebbels is using an architectural language to light his opera, as Woodroffe is using the language of rock and roll to develop light for *Roméo et Juliette*. What distinguishes these works is a desire to define a space and a narrative through action. Gerard Genette's Narrative Discourse[13] discusses Robert Siodmak's film *The Killers* as an example of what the author calls Focalization, the process of focusing a narrative through a specific mode of telling. Genette argues that there are two types of focalization: internal and external. In internal focalization, the narrative is focused through the consciousness of a character. In external focalization, the narrative is focused on a character, not through him (such as onto Burt Lancaster's character in The Killers). So we can argue that light in *Satyagraha*, for example, is internally focused: it helps the reader or audience to understand a character from within. In this type of narrative the light is used more conventionally, and is allowed to travel away from the light source in a carefully controlled way, lighting elsewhere. And *Stifter's Dinge* is an example of light supporting external focalization: the constant movement of the light and the multitude of fixtures focus the narrative onto the (absent) character of Adalbert Stifter. The *mise-en-scène* is alive with the specs and dots of the lighting objects.

Looking back at *Stifter's Dinge* in performance, there are moments of transformation such as when chemicals are released into the water pools and smoke rises from them to create a sublime landscape as in a Romantic painting. It is then when the piece acknowledges the *Gesamtkunstwerk* and all aspects of the production become synchronized, creating powerful interludes reminiscent of the Sea Interludes in Britten's *Peter Grimes*.

So Goebbels does not set out to challenge the convention of the *Gesamtkunstwerk*, but offers up a post-modern Opera that incorporates and acknowledges a wide range of styles and conventions to create something that is utterly original. And maybe *Stifter's Dinge* also hints at a use of light in opera that can both challenge and develop our often conservative use of light in music theatre.

In summary, there might be an opportunity here to explore a new way of lighting opera. What is so exceptional about the medium of light is that it can adapt and respond to surrounding factors very quickly and efficiently. As we have seen, light responds to shifts both in technology and in culture: the arrival of the automated lighting rig in rock and roll has translated swiftly and seamlessly into other lighting applications, and as Patrick Woodroffe has shown can have a fundamental impact on how an opera is read and understood by an audience. Alongside these technical advances, light has been equally proficient at crossing cultural or stylistic divides, and is a powerful narrative tool, as Daniel Libeskind has shown in his architecture for the Jüdisches Museum. Heiner Goebbels is a very good example of this modern approach, allowing the light to mesh with the other scenographic elements in a way that still is very unusual. The lighting for *Satyagraha* is beautiful and richly textured, but it also operates in a rather conventional fashion which is to paint surfaces with light, and to act as a dramaturge by guiding the audience through the narrative. There is nothing wrong with this approach, and indeed often there is no choice due to the very limited amount of time available to create the lighting for an opera production. But there is another way: Goebbels has shown it in *Stifter's Dinge*, and Robert Wilson's work follows a similar path. Both of these practitioners of course work in the Central European system, where much more time is given for the creation of a work as opera houses can afford to close their doors for much longer due to higher subsidies. But nevertheless, light for Goebbels and Wilson is something that needs to be created as carefully as the interpretation of the musical score, and to be constructed organically as part of the whole, rather than added on at a very late stage. And therefore the lighting designer should be considered an artist rather than a designer, particularly so in opera. So every time we settle down in our seats to watch an opera, we ideally have no idea how what we are about to see will look. We as an audience take the same journey as Wagner's audiences did when he for the first time took the houselights out. Therefore, rather than moving back towards the stillness and serenity of *Jedermann*, lighting in opera could embrace the openness and external focalization of *Stifter's Dinge*, providing a visual scenography that can be as challenging, immaterial and complex as the music we listen to. So we can truly start to listen with our eyes as much as with our ears.

Notes

1. Heiner Goebbels, *Stifter's Dinge*, co-produced by Theatre Vidy Lausanne with T&M Nanterre Paris, Schauspielfrankfurt, Berliner Festspiele, Grend Theatre Luxembourg, Teatro Stabile Turinao.
2. Charles Gounod, *Roméo et Juliette*, Wiener Staatsoper, director, Jürgen Flimm.
3. As will become evident later on, I propose to consider light and music as languages equal to the spoken word.
4. Designed by Fred Bentham in 1935, the Strand Light Console became the first remotely operated lighting control system. This was revolutionary in two aspects: lights could be controlled from a single platform (rather than from multiple points across the stage and fly floors), and this platform could be moved away from the stage. A specially made church organ console remotely controlled banks of resistance dimmers.
5. Hugo von Hofmannsthal, *Jedermann*, Zirkus Schumann Berlin (1911), Salzburger Festspiele (1920), director, Max Reinhardt.
6. Simon McBurney, keynote speech, Projection in Performance conference, Guildhall School of Music and Drama, London, 2009.
7. Peter Brook, *The Empty Space* (London: Penguin), p. 46.
8. This hints at the very important role perception plays. We see with our brain rather than with our eyes.
9. Clod Ensemble, *An Anatomy in Four Quarters*, Saddlers Wells Theatre, London, 2011.
10. The role and restrictions of the lighting designer are further discussed in Nick Hunt's essay.
11. And indeed the aesthetics of the Bregenz Festival at the other end of the country.
12. Fuller's work in this context is fully explored by Sebastian Trainor in *Women in the Arts in the Belle Epoque* (Jefferson, NC: McFarland, 2012).
13. Gerard Genette, *Narrative Discourse: An Essay in Method* (Ithaca: Cornell University Press, 1983).

Bibliography

Banham, Reyner. *Theory and Design in the First Machine Age*. Oxford: Architectural Press, 1960 (2001).

Brook, Peter. *The Empty Space*. London: Penguin, 1968 (2008).
Eco, Umberto. *The Role of the Reader*. Bloomington: Indiana University Press, 1984.
Fryer, Paul, ed. *Women in the Arts in the Belle Epoque*. Jefferson, NC: McFarland, 2012.
Genette, Gerard. *Narrative Discourse: An Essay in Method*. Ithaca: Cornell University Press, 1983.
McKinney, Jocelyn, and Philip Butterworth. *The Cambridge Introduction to Scenography*. Cambridge: Cambridge University Press, 2009.
Ranciere, Jacque. *The Emancipated Spectator*. London: Verso, 2009.

Opera, Art and Industrial Production: Lighting at the Royal Opera House, London

Nick Hunt

The lighting designer sits at a *production* desk. The lighting operator and the stage manager giving cues to both performers and technicians, once located in a lighting box and at a prompt desk, now occupy a *control room*. Opera, we might infer from this terminology, has become industrialized.

To describe an activity as industrialized suggests certain characteristics, such as being capital-intensive, making use of technology to automate and standardize processes, and making use of organized, managed labor. The relevant statistics for the Royal Opera House in London are certainly suggestive in this regard: its rebuild in the 1990s cost £178m (approximately $267 million); the Opera House has automated systems for handling scenery including the ability to drive a complete set from a rehearsal room onto the stage; it has standardized lighting layouts that allow any production in the repertoire to be lit in two hours; it employs 900 staff, including a lighting department of 50, of whom 28 work in a day-on, day-off shift pattern; the lighting department staff work under the direction of a senior lighting manager, two lighting managers, a lighting control manager, and a lighting systems manager.

In this essay I want to examine how what we might see as industrial production processes fit with the idea of performance-making as an artistic endeavor, and I want to focus on lighting for large scale opera, with particular reference to the Royal Opera House in London. While we might not immediately think of stage lighting in terms of media, many of the technologies that have enabled and underpinned the twentieth and early twenty-first century media revolution first made their impact on theatre and opera production in the field of lighting. The first lighting systems to use electronics appeared in the 1930s in the United States and the 1940s in the United Kingdom, and today lighting control relies on complex digital, networking and communications technologies. Further, the manufacturing and support companies that provide performance lighting equipment and services are part of a sophisticated and substantial international industry—all shaped by the same technological, commercial, social and cultural forces that are charted in other essays under the heading "media."

There are grounds, then, for thinking about opera production—and specifically lighting—as an industrial process at both the global scale of the entertainment lighting industry and at the local scale of a single opera house. However, the development of the role of the lighting designer since the mid twentieth century, emerging from technical and management roles, points to a different, more artistically focused account of lighting practices. Early lighting designers such as Michael Northen[1] were at pains to establish their role as equal to that of the set and costume designer, and more recently the conception of "scenography"[2] has proposed that designers of all kinds form a collaborative team with directors, musical directors, choreographers and others, suggesting that all these figures might come under the heading of theatre makers, and even theatre artists. This professional evolution of the lighting designer's role from technical implementation to artistic collaboration has been championed not only by individuals but also by professional bodies such as the Association of Lighting Designers. The ever-increasing emphasis on the artistic aspect of the lighting designer's role since its inception has been a reflection of the growing importance given to the contribution of light to theatre and opera performance, and has taken place over the same period as the introduction of public subsidy of the arts in the United Kingdom. I would suggest this is no mere coincidence, and that the definition of performance forms such as opera as art—and so by implication something made by artists—has gone hand-in-hand with a shift away from a purely commercial business model. To justify public funding, theatres and opera houses must proclaim themselves cultural institutions and arts organizations, to distinguish themselves from producers of commercial entertainment as product. The United Kingdom's Royal Opera House is a registered charity, and receives public subsidy through the British Arts Council of £25 million per year. Its stated object is unashamedly focused on the artistic education of the public:

> To promote and assist in the advancement of education so far as promotion and assistance shall be of a charitable nature and in particular, so far as of a charitable nature, to raise the artistic taste of the country, and to procure and increase the appreciation and understanding of the musical art in all its forms.[3]

Such a mission, and such a substantial level of public funding, creates a pressure to produce a diverse repertoire and a full performance schedule with minimal down-time, to meet not only box office requirements but also the expectations of funding bodies, government and tax-payers. The result is the repertoire system in which a different production from the repertoire is performed each evening. Paradoxically, the Royal Opera House must somehow allow creative and artistic practices to flourish within a rigidly constrained schedule and stage delivery system. In specifically lighting terms, then, I want to ask: to what extent do systems of reliable *re*-production dominate those of inventive first creation?

The Repertoire Lighting Rig

Opera houses operate one of two systems: *stagione* (literally, season) in which one production will be mounted and performed for a short, intensive run, or *repertoire*, in which performances of productions from the repertoire will alternate, and each production will have its performances spread over a period of several months or even longer. For the major roles in grand opera, singers cannot perform every evening for an extended period; in the *stagione* system therefore a production will remain on stage but there will not be performances every night, or the production will have several casts which can alternate. The repertoire system enables there to be a performance of one production or another from the repertoire, while avoiding consecutive performances of the same production.

In the repertoire or rep system, productions have to be repeatedly brought on and off stage, and the technical systems and processes need to accommodate this pattern of operation. As a repertoire house, the Royal Opera House always performs a different production on consecutive evenings, so there is a constant pattern of evening performance, overnight turnaround ready for a morning rehearsal of an incoming production, and an afternoon turnaround ready for the evening's performance of another production. The Royal Opera House also has the added complication of housing both an opera company and a ballet company. In lighting terms, this repertoire production pattern has historically led to the development of rep rigs—lighting systems that cover the stage with systematic area lighting from a variety of directions and colors, arrived at through custom and practice, institutionalizing and normalizing (we might suspect) the lighting of performances within the aesthetic potential that the largely fixed rep rig made available.

The lighting installations in repertoire opera houses are designed around one principle requirement: the need to be able to change the lighting over from one production to another in a defined time, which may be as little as two hours. To meet this requirement, rep rigs are largely fixed, so that lights are neither moved nor refocused from one production to the next. Some changing of gels[4] may be permitted, and a limited amount of refocusing, and lighting designers are permitted to add specials to the rig for their particular production, provided there is space in the rig in the required place. In recent years, automated lights have become an important part of repertoire rigs, allowing refocusing and recoloring by remote control, but again these lights cannot generally be moved to a different position in the rig during the change-over, and so the lighting designer is still presented with a palette of equipment, and so of possible lighting qualities and effects, that is designed to meet a general expectation of what will be wanted, rather than the needs for a particular production. As the lighting designer Rick Fisher[5] puts it,

> Because [rep theatres] are play or opera factories they are set up to produce plays or operas, and as long as you are sticking to putting your play or opera onto *the stage*—which increasingly is happening less and less, as everyone wants to reinvent those spaces—but *if* you are sticking to having them on the stage ... you usually inherit a pretty good system of lights that you have to work within.[6]

Fisher goes on to describe what are, for him, the benefits of starting with a rep rig:

> I like working in rep—it frees me from the thing I hate the most which is drawing the lighting plan. Still I find starting with the blank piece of paper is terrifying, because I think there's nothing. In the beginning there was not light. In the beginning there was darkness—and an empty piece of paper. In a rep situation in the beginning there's a lot of light, and I'm much happier turning off the lights I don't like and don't need than I am trying to figure out how to rig the lights that I do need [Fisher, 2012].

Lighting designer Paule Constable[7] concurs: "while you can argue that [repertoire rigs] narrow your options, what they do is give you a backbone to your design."[8] However, the rep rig is also subtly determining of nuanced artistic choices. Fisher points out that the colors and lighting angles of the rep rig are often not exactly what he would have chosen—instead they are chosen by the lighting department of the theatre, based on an understanding of lighting designers' most common requirements or expectations. This understanding is of course historically determined, acquired over time from past productions, and so inherently conservative of existing and past practices and aesthetic judgments and tastes.

For some designers, choosing to create the design primarily from the rep rig is perhaps less a matter of preference and more a sense that adding to the rep rig brings its own difficulties. Lighting designer John B. Read[9] has lit ballets at the Royal Opera House for over thirty years, and states,

> I'm very wary about adding extra kit. One of the reasons for that is that when you are gone and out of the way you don't know whether it's going to be there or

not, with due respect to them. There may be a situation where if you are lighting one act of a triple bill for example, and it comes in with something else, what you wanted isn't possible because there is some scenery hanging up on those pipes where you wanted to put some kit. What are you going to do? They're going to move your kit down—it may not do the same job that you wanted—you've got to be very careful about all of that. The skill is to use the permanent rig and make it look better than anyone else can do it.[10]

Nick Ware, senior lighting manager at the Royal Opera House notes that while some lighting designers will choose to work mainly with the rep rig, others try to ignore it and work around it. The particular requirements of ballet—symmetrical area lighting covering a large proportion of the stage—mean that the rep rig is set up primarily for ballet. While there is a rep rig for opera, the lighting may often be rather more bespoke, with the lighting department allowing designers to install more equipment that is specific to the particular production. As Ware puts it,

> The standard rig for the opera quite often depends on the lighting designer. Some will come and embrace the standard rig and be willing work with it, and others will just want to ignore it totally, not to fight with it but to imagine it's not there and try and work round it, which can be hugely frustrating for us but is very difficult to argue with. They've got a certain style, the director has picked them because they've got a certain style, and there is certain equipment that isn't in the standard rig.[11]

For Constable (unlike Read), the rep rig is a trap for designers, encouraging formulaic and uninteresting work: "If you just went in there and said 'I am going to let the rep rig do this for me' you'd produce very, very, very dull work. You have to commit to ideas. That's the way to make it risky and interesting" (Constable, 2012).

If lighting designers who want to ignore the rep rig induce frustration in lighting managers such as Ware, it is because of the difficulties in meeting the requirements to turn round between productions in a limited time when the designer has specified a largely bespoke rig. Again, the requirement to install a production on the stage in as little as two hours, and to remove it in as little as one hour, is critical here. Lighting designers, lighting managers and other production staff all speak about the importance of making the production "rep-able," so that it can be successfully re-installed on stage in the required time. As Will Harding, production manager at the Royal Opera House, puts it, "the rep informs everything we do; everything we make is really about the rep."[12] Lighting designers are acutely aware of the limitations imposed by the available turnaround time. While the lighting cues can be loaded into the lighting control system in a matter of moments, being stored in electronic memory, the non-automated lights in the rig need to be manually focused, and therefore need to be physically accessible, constraining what equipment can be put where in the rep rig, and so further constraining lighting designers' technical choices. As Harding puts it, "the light has either got to be [an automated light], or a fixed focus, or you've got to be able to walk up behind it and point it" (Harding, 2012). The focusing process not only has to take place within the two-hour set-up time, but also will happen at the same time as the set is being brought onto stage. If a light has to be focused tightly to a particular piece of scenery, that piece of scenery may never be brought onto stage during the turnaround, only at the relevant point during the show. According to Fisher:

> You do have to keep in mind that there is a certain changeover time [so] if you're doing something that you want to be focused to a particular piece of scenery, and it's a piece of scenery that you know doesn't exist at the pre-set of the show, it may not get built ever in the changeover for the show. If it comes on in act two nobody's going to put it up to have it focused to in the changeover because there isn't physically the time. So you have to start to think about those things [Fisher, 2012].

Read concurs: "if you are too arty with it, you can say goodbye to it after the first changeover—you won't see it again." Fisher will simply not entertain some options in a repertoire context: "Sometimes I don't even allow myself to go there because I know that it's not really rep-able" (Fisher, 2012).

Constable also acknowledges the challenges of the turnaround time and the demands that this places on the staff responsible, and points to the responsibility she feels as a lighting designer towards the lighting team: "the guys who focus your show in every day in the rep—you have to really invest in them, because they've got a nightmare job. You really want them to believe in what you're doing, so it is much more collegiate" (Constable, 2012).

The rep rig and its associated systems and processes have been created in response to the perceived needs of the Royal Opera House as a publicly funded and accountable institution, as well as being a continuation of the established traditions and practices of international large-scale opera production within which the house of necessity operates. The rep rig exerts a powerful influence on the creative processes and possibilities available to lighting designers, limiting or proscribing certain approaches while encouraging or mandating others. As we have seen, different lighting designers respond differently, establishing their own strategies to undertake creative work that meets their own expectations of quality. Similarly, the managers responsible both for the initial delivery of the production and also for maintaining it in the repertoire system attempt to balance the often conflicting demands of supporting lighting designers' creative process while achieving the subsequent repeatability required for what I have termed "industrial production."

The Repertoire Rehearsal Process

The need to work within a limited turnaround period is not the only time constraint on lighting in the repertoire system. There is a pressure to minimize the number of evenings when the theatre is dark, with no public performance, so as to maximize box office revenue and meet service expectations placed on publicly funded arts organizations. At the Royal Opera House the pressure on the production process for a new opera is particularly intense. Some U.K. opera houses such as the English National Opera at the London Coliseum, and Glyndebourne, schedule three or four days when a new opera can be on stage uninterrupted by performances. Other houses, particularly in continental Europe and the Metropolitan in New York, have *bauprobe* rehearsals with mock-ups of the set and time to work on lighting ideas and other technical elements as part of the earlier development process of the production. However, at the Royal Opera House there is a performance of an existing work from the repertoire each evening, while lighting, technical and dress rehearsals take place only in the mornings, followed by an afternoon turnaround to the evening's show. Because stage rehearsal time is limited and comes in short, three-hour sessions, as much work as possible must be done away from the stage itself. Harding says,

> We try and draw as much away from the stage as we can, so scenery is built in the build area, we fit as much set as we possibly can into the rehearsal room so the actors get as much acting [as possible] on the set and not on a markout ... we do everything we can to do anything technical off stage prior to us getting on stage ... if you go into anything thinking that you'll sort it out in the technical [rehearsal] the chances are it'll get cut because you won't have time to deal with it [Harding, 2012].

Stage time dedicated specifically to lighting is very limited—for the most part lighting takes place during rehearsals with the singers and either a piano or the full orchestra. Thus the time spent in stage rehearsals cannot be about discovering the role of light in the production, it must be a process of delivering ideas that have already been decided on and pre-agreed as far as possible. Constable contrasts this with her approach to drama, which can be more exploratory:

> The thing about opera is that when you get into the space, particularly these repertoire spaces, you have got *no* time. You are not going into a space and a rehearsal process to explore a piece—you are going in to realize it. So your responsibility is that you have to get to know it. I think it is true for everybody in opera—with a play the director can go "this is the world I want, this is how I'm going to do it" but you can explore the play with the actors—you can't do that with grand opera, you have to have made those decisions way beforehand.

So, it tends to be production driven, as opposed to nurturing individual relationships [Constable, 2012].

Just as Harding's production team is working to draw as many technical activities away from the stage as possible, the lighting department supports designers in developing their ideas in advance. Nevertheless, the pressure of limited rehearsal time is still acute, as Ware points out:

> We do quite a lot of pre-research if a designer has got a specific concept but it needs to be developed and expanded, and we'll run with that. The problem is there's no time when we get to stage to do that conceptual work. You need to be ready to go when you hit the stage because there is no experiment time. It scares the living daylights out of me—I sit and look at designers and think, how do you do it? I take my hat off to a lot of them, because it's absolutely raw out there from a designer's point of view. I don't think there's a designer who'll tell you it isn't [Ware, 2012].

Constable, as a very experienced lighting designer for opera, has a series of strategies to maximize the value to her of the limited rehearsal time on stage: "my big obsession with lighting is that anything you can do so that during a tech you are freed up to look at the stage and not be looking for [information] is good" (Constable, 2012). Preparation is the key for Constable, not to fully predetermine the lighting before the stage rehearsals but to provide a structure within which to work, or perhaps to counter and resist: "even if it's wrong it is something to rage against—something actual in front of you to respond to, and that's the point where I know I can start running with something" (Constable, 2012).

Constable prefers to spend at least two weeks attending rehearsals before the first on-stage rehearsal; one reason for this is to ensure she is fully familiar with the blocking (the performers' positions and moves on stage) so that when in lighting rehearsals she does not have to consult notes or other members of the team for that information. Constable will also pre-plan all of the cue-points where there will be a change in the lighting, and mark these in her score. She will also give these cues to the stage manager who will be cuing the performance, so that even if during the first stage rehearsals the lighting states have not all been created, the stage manager can still call the cues:

> They are calling cues and you're not asking them to do things, so the machine of it is keeping running, and the cues are always in front of you and you are always in the right place, so you can see a cue and change it. It sounds incredibly, kind of methodical, but the irony is that by being methodical you get your freedom to be very free with it [Constable, 2012].

For some styles of opera, Constable will number the cues according to the page numbers in the score, so that she can check which cue is on stage and know which page in the score has been reached—another in a series of detailed techniques that help her be in control of the process. As Constable explains, "it's little things that make it easier—not letting the machine run you. The first time I did an opera, the machine ran me, I didn't run the machine, and I thought 'there's got to be a way this can be creative' and then you find there is" (Constable, 2012). Indeed, for Constable the apparent limitation of a rigid rehearsal schedule with only short, intense morning sessions does have a beneficial aspect:

> Doing one rehearsal a day and then leaving it gives you brilliant time to think, and you're not trying to answer every question in the moment. You do three hours of intensive work, and it is exhausting because you are talking about running big rigs at the speed of musical theatre, and you can never say "stop," So, it's incredibly intensive, but you've got the whole afternoon and evening to go through your notes and sort out what you want to do [Constable, 2012].

Lighting in Virtual Space

In addition to the strategies adopted by individual lighting designers such as Constable to take control of the machine of opera production, the Royal Opera House itself has developed a system to remove elements of the production process away from the intensity of the stage rehearsals. Increasingly the lighting—and sometimes other performance elements—is modeled in a 3D computer simulation. Originally intended to model just the lighting so as to prepare an initial lighting plot prior to the first on-stage rehearsal, the system is now used to model automated scenic elements such as flown set pieces and revolves, as well as video projection in what James Simpson, the Opera House's Lighting Visualizer, calls a "virtual opera house."[13]

Simpson typically becomes involved in a production around four to five weeks before the first stage rehearsals, relatively late in the overall planning process. However, he may be involved earlier if there is a need to test out scenic elements in the virtual environment, such as a stage revolve where the speed of movement needs to be visualized in order that the correct motor and gearing can be provided to meet the artistic requirements of the director and set designer. Simpson's first task is to construct a virtual model of the set, to sit within the standard model of the opera house's stage and auditorium. Once this is complete, a virtual lighting rig is created, at which point it is possible to program the lighting in the virtual environment using the same lighting control system that is used in the theatre itself. It is therefore theoretically possible to light an entire production in the computer model, since the color, intensity and beam distribution of every light source that will be used can be visualized and programmed as a series of lighting cues into the control console that will operate the lighting for the actual performance. However, Simpson warns against trying to do too much in the virtual environment, saying that some lighting designers "build up a show that's so messy they can't break it apart again when they get back on stage" (Simpson, 2012). With as many as several hundred lights available from which to construct each lighting state, it is possible to use a large number in the virtual plot, and then for the lighting designer to be unable to work out once on stage how the lighting they see is made up from the many sources, in order to make any required modifications. Because many lighting designers have not used computer visualization before working at the Opera House for the first time (visualization is only just becoming established in theatre lighting, and the Opera House is in many ways leading this development in the United Kingdom) Simpson's role is to help designers make the most of its potential while avoiding the pitfalls: "we have to do a lot of guiding to make sure [designers] are using the visualization system effectively" (Simpson, 2012).

A particular benefit of working in a virtual environment is being able to focus automated lights before the first stage rehearsals. With the increasing numbers of automated lights in the Opera House, each of which can have many variable parameters to set (including position, beam size and edge quality, beam shape, color, and texture) setting these once on stage takes up a great deal of limited lighting time. Similarly, lighting designers will often determine which lights they will use for each lighting state, without setting their intensity (brightness) in the pre-programmed lighting plot, preferring to do this once they are on stage where they can balance intensities between light sources and in relation to the set, costumes and performers.

While visualization brings considerable benefits, it also has limitations; useful preparation can be done, but creating a complete lighting plot for a production within the computer model is not practicable. Although some lighting designers tend to shy away from the visualization process adopted by the Opera House through unfamiliarity and an awareness of the potential traps, others embrace it. For Constable, it offers an important opportunity to further the preparation that is all-important to her:

> You have to find your time [to light the show]. At the Royal Opera House ... they work in a virtual theatre with virtual rendering of your show, and I use that time to put a cuing structure in. I do my moving light focus groups. I do the stuff that I'm adding to the show—the HMIs in the stage left wing that are doing the key lights, all of that, I put it in so I know it's there and done. [Once I get on stage] I can alter the levels, I can do anything I want to, I can change it, but it's there and ready for me to look at [Constable, 2012].

Once again, we see that Constable's strategy is to pre-plan as much as possible not so that everything is determined prior to the production's arrival on stage, but to give her the time—within the strict parameters of the repertoire system—to look, to think, and to respond to the emerging performance. She is, perhaps, seeking to retain the kind of relationship with the production that lighting designers early in their careers develop working in small, informal theatres with minimal equipment, where the need to be a lighting *manager* is less and opportunities to be an *artist* may be greater:

> That's the real key about working under that kind of pressure—it's anything you can do to take the pressure off yourself and allow yourself to be back in the Old Red Lion [pub theatre], and going "what am I looking at?" It's the same rules, it's anything to get that pressure of time away from you [Constable, 2012].

Opera's longue durée

As well as the time constraints imposed by the demands of the turnaround between rehearsals and performances, and of the stage rehearsal schedule, there is a third timescale that I want to consider: the life of a production.

Large-scale opera is created by directors, conductors, designers and singers who work internationally and who are in many cases in high demand. Co-productions between opera houses in different countries are common, to share the high cost of staging the largest works. As a result, productions are planned many years in advance, in order to secure the desired singers and creative teams, as Constable recounts:

> Because of the nature of the singers [opera houses] are employing, the lead time is immense. Generally the delivery time for a white card model [of the set] is going to be at two years before the show is on stage. So I always think of doing a production as like being in a holding pattern—you know, waiting to land at Heathrow. If you are doing an opera you are waiting for a long time, there is a slow build towards that point.... It is three or four years generally [Constable, 2012].

Just as a production may be several years in the planning, it will often have a life in the repertoire that extends into years and sometimes decades. While initially a production will typically have between half a dozen and a dozen performances during its first season, some productions will be stored and revived in later seasons, perhaps years afterwards. This extended lifetime, often with long intervals between performances, has a variety of implications for designers and—especially—for the staff responsible for managing and operating the repertoire system. With an expected life running into decades, cast changes are inevitable and this has an impact on how directors and designers think about the production. Unlike the typical theatre situation, where a production may be conceived around a particular leading actor or core cast, an opera production will typically need to be artistically and conceptually robust enough to accommodate several changes of singers, sometimes even within the same run of performances. As Constable puts it, "If you are doing a piece of popular repertoire—Mozart, Verdi—they are hoping it will stay in the repertoire for twenty years, so it has got to be strong enough to support huge numbers of different people being thrown into it, so it tends to be production driven" (Constable, 2012). High concept opera, then, may be a matter of pragmatics as much as the artistic desires of directors.

Typically, the lighting designer is not present when a production is revived after a period of time, or when it transfers to another opera house. This is in part a financial matter—the lighting designer would have to be paid to supervise the revival—but largely it is a question of the availability and desire of lighting designers to be involved. Experienced designers could spend a substantial proportion of their time simply relighting operas they originally lit which are being revived or transferred, and most designers don't have the time or, often, the willingness to do this. Instead, one of the Opera House's lighting managers will oversee the process. While the lighting manager will often have been closely involved in the original production, changes of staff and the long time between first performance and revival can mean they are to a greater or lesser extent reliant on the production documentation—a process Simpson describes as "lighting archaeology" (Simpson, 2012).

For recent productions, the computer files from the lighting control system and the visualization system, together with plans, written descriptions, photographs and video recordings, will provide reasonably comprehensive information to recreate the lighting in the context of the Opera House's repertoire lighting rig. However, operas are sometimes revived that predate the visualization system or the current lighting control system, and earlier video recordings may be of relatively poor quality (the Opera House's earliest archive videos are in Betamax format from the nineteen-eighties) and even current cameras see things too differently to the human eye to balance on-stage lighting colors and intensity contrasts accurately from video recordings.

Furthermore, the repertoire rig has changed over the years, and even when equipment is replaced on a like-for-like basis, modern luminaires are generally brighter, and may have a slightly different color output than the older models they replace, so even if dimmer intensities and color filter choices have been recorded, there is no guarantee that these will give the original look. To complicate matters further, costumes may fade and are sometimes remade if they have become worn, while the paint finishes on the set may have been repeatedly retouched to cover up minor damage from handling and storage. Touch-up painters tend to paint down, so the touch-up doesn't stand out compared with the older paint, thus sets get darker and darker. According to Harding, the set of the Opera House's long-standing production of *Turandot* "has gone from being a mid-brown to almost an ebony black" (Harding, 2012).

While the Opera House's current systems, in particular the computer visualization and lighting control console, capture and archive more information than previously, new issues emerge: technology develops on a far more rapid timescale than the lifetime of a production in the repertoire, so there are difficulties with software versions, file formats and the digital archiving of documents. Besides these technical challenges, the original director is likely not to be present for a revival, so it will be overseen by an assistant or staff director from the opera company whose memory of the first performances may be unreliable or based solely on video recordings. Then there is also the matter of the changing expectations and tastes of audiences, directors and designers. Furthermore, lighting designers may change their mind, as Read points out when describing repeatedly relighting the Kenneth MacMillan ballet of *Romeo and Juliet*, first staged at the Royal Opera House in 1965 and revived regularly ever since:

> I can look at it again and maybe say ... I've used gobos [to create dappled light] there and maybe I shouldn't use gobos there. I go through stages of using gobos in her bedroom in the third act ... sometimes they work and other times they don't work. That sort of level and detail you can change your mind [Read, 2012].

The need to retain productions in the repertoire and to be able to revive them many years after their first performance in the context of a technical and organizational system that must also meet the needs of present and future productions presents as we have seen diverse practical challenges as well as raising questions of changing taste and judgment. The underlying issue however is the tension between opera as a live art form—an event made in the here-and-now for an audience that is physically present in the moment of performance—and an established and institutionalized pattern that I have termed industrial production, designed to be able to reproduce any performance from the repertoire on demand, to meet the requirements of schedule, box office, artistic policy and funding regimes. I am not arguing that institutional structures are inherently destructive of the immediacy of live performance and the ways in which it is made—rather, I am pointing out there are tensions that inherently arise. Institutional culture, then, is critical to artistic success, or at least to creating an environment in which creative artistic work can take place despite the significant pressures that militate against it. Constable is positive about the opportunities to take artistic risks in opera:

> You could argue [opera] is less risk-taking, but I think my work in opera is much more risky, because there is a bigger trust of image, and of image worlds. There is

more pressure to tell a story—the story-telling has to be complete with opera. The thing I think about opera is when it's good nothing can touch it, but it is the most elusive form out there. It is so hard to get close to being any good, because there are so many different elements at play. So I think weirdly it's more risk taking [though] I think it would be hard to go to [some opera houses] with something *very* experimental [Constable, 2012].

However, Constable also points to a specific aspect of institutional culture that we might read as a marker of the importance given to the design aspects of opera. In some opera houses, including the Royal Opera House, singers are only paid to perform, not to rehearse, so the perceived value and importance of on-stage rehearsal time as a part of the creative process is arguably diminished:

> That's a huge separation in culture because it means the part that we do is not valued, so there is at the worst end of it a sense of it being a backdrop to those divas. The best of it, when you work in a house that wants to try and do both, is extraordinary [Constable, 2012].

While productions may have a lifetime in the repertoire that in some cases stretches to decades, institutions evolve over similar periods of time, determining the organizational formations and production processes that structure the making, performance and revival of any one production. It is by these institutional frameworks that the role of the lighting designer is constituted, and it is these institutional frameworks that designers operate within, accommodate to, and—to some extent at least—resist.

Conclusion

The repertoire system is found in many large-scale theatres and opera houses, and in terms of U.K. theatres is perhaps seen in its most extreme form at the Royal Opera House. This pattern of operation has developed over historical time and is now institutionally entrenched. The rep system is highly determining of lighting practices because it imposes the need to make the production "rep-able" (able to alternate with other shows in the rep), because it limits the on-stage rehearsal process, and because of the need to plan far in advance productions that may remain in the repertoire for many years. The result as we have seen is a series of tensions between the needs of the creative process of making a performance and the needs of a production process to reproduce it. At the beginning of this essay I noted the management structure in the lighting department at the Royal Opera House, and I have drawn extensively on interviews with managers as well as lighting designers. While in professional terms these roles are distinct, and designers may in some cases have aspirations to be artists, lighting designer Rick Fisher is cautious, saying that "there is compromise—it's not a fine art" and,

> I think you could arguably say modern lighting design has grown out of the role of a technician and moved to more of a collaborative artist—I don't think we are a fine artist in any way, shape or form, and sometimes I don't even know if we are really a designer. We are maybe a lighting chooser.... When you are working in a rep system you are sometimes even more of a chooser than a designer. Yes you do ultimately mix the look, and it's amazing how different people using the exact same lighting system can make completely different looking shows [but] I think that there's a whole other layer of things the lighting designer has to be worried about, maybe more so than any of the other designers, which is a management side—the management of equipment, the management of time and resources, in order to allow your shows to be replicated in the way that they need to be [Fisher, 2012].

As a lighting manager, Nick Ware is bullish about what the Opera House achieves:

> Some designers are incredulous about the standard rig [but] for the scale and size of what we do we are pretty much as flexible as we can be.... As far as creating great art, I think we do that, and I think we do that very reliably. It's great when you get designers who get it—and most do—we're not being negative because we don't want to do something. We want to protect it as we revive it on a day on, day off basis. We want them to create things that we can achieve [in the turn-around time] [Ware, 2012].

Where opera *performance* is measured out in the rhythms and temporal structures of the music, opera *production* is determined by the meter of the repertoire system: the daily rhythm of the turnarounds between performance and rehearsals, the rhythm of the stage rehearsals for a new production or revival, the planning and development process for a new opera over months and years, the lifetime of a production over years and decades, and a slowly but constantly evolving institutional culture. As we have seen, individual practitioners and entire institutions have adapted their processes and techniques to accommodate and work within these temporal patterns. The lighting of opera within a repertoire system of the intensity found at the Royal Opera House takes place under acute conflicting pressures: on the one hand, lighting has come to be seen as an essential part of opera, with far greater expectations and demands made of it than previously, while on the other hand the needs of the repertoire schedule—itself designed to support the most intensive performance schedule possible—dictate almost every aspect of the lighting process. The result is what Will Harding describes as the "drawing away" from the stage of as much design and technical preparation as possible, so that artistic work has become in part virtualized, not just in the most obvious sense of the use of virtual computer models to develop the lighting plot but in a more subtle sense: the abstraction of creative decision-making processes away from the live stage. The results of these creative decisions are then captured and stored as lighting plots, plans, cue lists, annotated scores, focus notes, photographs, videos and other assorted (often digital) documentation, all for reproduction at a later date days, months and years hence and, sometimes, in another theatre. The pressures of the rep system thus perform an *ontological* shift, moving the various practitioners' understanding away from the here-and-now of the *performance as an event*, and emphasizing its properties as a *product*—something designed in advance and reproduced on demand. Such an ontology is one of industrial production.

In the field of performance scholarship, we have come to understand that artistic works are not simply a matter of the artist's free imagination as an autonomous subject, but arise out of a complex pattern of cultural influences and constraints that are historically inflected. My aim in this essay has been to point out that, while performance scholarship has given extensive consideration to the operation of these influences at the level of cultural policy and the interaction between signature artists such as directors, writers and performers, there is also a less well accounted for level of influence that operates through channels that we might broadly see as industrial production. Greater consideration of this aspect of performance-making may lead to a richer understanding of what we see on the opera stage and how it gets there.

Acknowledgments

I am most grateful to all those who have given so generously of their time and knowledge during my research, and whose passion for and dedication to the art of opera is genuinely inspirational: Paule Constable (freelance lighting designer), Rick Fisher (freelance lighting designer), Will Harding (production manager, Royal Opera House), John B Read, (freelance lighting designer), James Simpson (lighting visualization, Royal Opera House) and Nick Ware (senior lighting manager, Royal Opera House).

Some of the material in this essay was presented under the title "Light Industry: Creative Lighting Practices in Large-Scale Repertoire Opera and Theatre Production" at the Performance Studies International (PSi) conference, University of Leeds, U.K., June 2012, and at the Theatre and Performance Research Association (TaPRA) conference, University of Kent, U.K., September 2012.

Notes

1. Michael Northen (1921–2001) was one of the first U.K. lighting designers to be credited as such. Starting as a stage manager, from the 1950s he began designing lighting

for the leading theatre designers and directors in the United Kingdom, including Peter Brook, Sophie Fedorovitch, John Gielgud, Tyrone Guthrie, Robert Helpmann, Tanya Moiseiwitsch and John Piper. Northen helped to establish and shape the role of the lighting designer as it is found in the United Kingdom today.

2. I use the term scenography here in the sense proposed by Pamela Howard, to refer to a holistic approach to *mise en scène* with equal status to the dramatic text and the performers. (Pamela Howard, *What Is Scenography?*, 2d ed. [London: Routledge, 2009]).

3. Royal Opera House, Covent Garden Limited, public benefit assessment report by the Charity Commission (July 2010) http://www.charitycommission.gov.uk/Charity_requirements_guidance/Charity_essentials/Public_benefit/assessroh.aspx#e.

4. The colored, transparent filters that are used to color the light from a theatre lighting fixture. "Gel" refers to gelatin from which such filters were once made.

5. Rick Fisher is a leading international lighting designer originally from the United States, but now resident in the United Kingdom. He lights for theatre, dance and opera, with notable credits including *An Inspector Calls* and *Billy Elliot, the Musical*. Fisher has won both the Olivier and Tony awards for best lighting design, and was chairman of the Association of Lighting Designers in the United Kingdom.

6. Interview with the author, 9 March 2012, London.

7. Paule Constable is a leading theatre, dance and opera lighting designer in the United Kingdom and internationally. She has lit for all the major opera companies in the United Kingdom including the Royal Opera House, for the Metropolitan Opera in New York, and for major opera houses across Europe, North America, Australia and New Zealand. She is a multiple Olivier Best Lighting Design award winner and was the first recipient of the Opera Award for Lighting in 2013.

8. Interview with the author, 18 October 2012, at the National Theatre, London.

9. John B. Read is a leading United Kingdom and international theatre, dance and opera lighting designer. He was for over two decades Lighting Consultant to the Royal Ballet (based at the Royal Opera House), and established many of the principles and techniques for ballet lighting that are widely used today. He has also lit operas for the Royal Opera House and at many other opera houses internationally.

10. Interview with the author, 23 May 2012, at Rose Bruford College, London.
11. Interview with the author, 10 February 2012, at Royal Opera House, London.
12. Interview with the author, 10 February 2012, at Royal Opera House, London.
13. Interview with the author, 10 February 2012, at Royal Opera House, London.

Bibliography

Constable, Paule. Interview with the author, 18 October 2012, at the National Theatre, London.
Fisher, Rick. Interview with the author, 9 March 2012, London.
Harding, Will. Interview with the author, 10 February 2012, at Royal Opera House, London.
Howard, Pamela. *What Is Scenography?*, 2d ed. London: Routledge, 2009.
Read, John B. Interview with the author, 23 May 2012, at Rose Bruford College, London.
Simpson, James. Interview with the author, 10 February 2012, at Royal Opera House, London.
Ware, Nick. Interview with the author, 10 February 2012, at Royal Opera House, London.

After *The Twilight of the Gods*: Opera Experiments, New Media and the Opera of the Future

Michael Earley

As many critics and scholars regularly note[1] discussions surrounding lyric opera or lyric theatre today still reference an art form that, in its development in the western cultural tradition of the last 400 years, is still based on the following triad:

1. A music-composer-based narrative theatre form that is performed by instruments and predominantly singing voices, which has always been encircled by and mingled with multiple arts and technologies in their respective shape and formation;
2. Institutional structures that reflected a. the necessary production conditions defined by the specific historical representation forms (e.g. instrumental and orchestral, soloists and choirs, dancers) and b. the different historic hierarchies of a social and artistic character;
3. Architectural containers or buildings (equipped with historically established technologies), defined by stage, proscenium, pit and audience spaces, which reflect relational hierarchies and define a profoundly bidirectional form of performing, seeing and hearing.[2]

The grip of the traditional and historic operatic canon (primarily the eighteenth- and nineteenth-century repertoire but even the twentieth- and twenty-first-century repertoire) has preserved and enforced the above triad, even when it has been under stress from modern and contemporary influences.[3] Opera studies, as an academic discipline as opposed to a performance discipline, tends to approach its subject with this triad in mind and as a firm anchoring point from which to explore the genre and its history. The triad should be borne in mind when considering just how far experiments in opera change or reposition these terms.

The introduction of new and enabling technologies (most of which are discussed in more details elsewhere in this volume) has been to optimize the effect, albeit modernized, of the traditional performance technologies (e.g., design, set construction, light, sound, supplemented by video projections, subtitles, broadcasting, recording, etc.) but not change the very shape and function of the operatic triad. In such instances technology does not seek to dominate the traditional, but, in many cases, is tamed or made discrete (for the most part) in order to service and support traditions. So while the operatic productions of those representative of the "new directors' theatre" (the notorious works of the Catalan theatre and opera director Calixto Bieito, the American Peter Sellers or the British Katie Mitchell, for instance) postmodernize the terms of stage production, politics, context, setting and narrative, the music of the great tradition that is a central support to the triad is rarely sacrificed or radicalized.

The changes in opera, as an art form and a staging practice, shifted radically from before to after Richard Wagner. *Götterdämmerung* ("The Twilight of the Gods"), the last of the four operas that comprise "The Ring of the Nibelung," is a crucial watershed and tipping point in opera's changing fortune and in opera's new status as an intellectual and artistic enterprise. And while we could just concentrate on Wagner as a subject and his final opera as a trope for change in an art form (especially as his recent 200th anniversary has concentrated new critical interests in his achievements), his final works do act as a prelude of sorts for things to come as well as a summary for a more refined totality of gestures that marked opera at the end of the nineteenth century. In his long essay "The Artwork of the Future," with its articulation of the *Gesamtkunstwerk*, a total work of art incorporating music, drama, dance, scenography and (critically for Wagner) political and socio-cultural engagement, Wagner consolidates all the different aesthetic hierarchies that will be tested and contested across the twentieth century and down to our own time. *The Twilight of the Gods* (1876) as a cultural pivot and a testimony of where opera had arrived since its inception is a good vantage point from which to view opera's experiments on different levels, not least of which in its adoption of radical new staging models and eventually new media and practices.

When we think of opera experiments we normally think first of the steady and sometimes abrupt and profound changes in the music shaping, from tonality to atonality, for instance.[4] The modernist music battleground was where most twentieth century operatic skirmishes were fought. Or it might be the radical ways that opera has been produced onstage and, more commonly nowadays, deconstructed in performance by a host of new directors in dispute with tradition (though not, I would hasten to add, without much change musically). A rich critical literature has been building to make the case for what is frequently called "director's opera" or *Regieoper* over the last hundred years, hastened by post-war developments at Bayreuth and modern productions of Wagner, always the most celebrated and high-profile instances of new directions in opera staging. In fact, the *Regieoper* movement can be traced through productions of Wagner's "Ring" alone. The added new emphasis on post-dramatic theatre and staging[5] has hastened suspicion of opera's inherited traditions. Wagner's own stagecraft and his staging of his own work, fixed in the known stagecraft of its time, sadly undermined the promise of his forward looking visions.[6] Not until the post–World War II era, and the new direction of Bayreuth undertaken by his grandson Wieland Wagner, did the promise implied in "The Artwork of the Future" and the so-called "basic features" mentioned in the later part of the manifesto,[7] emerge and take exciting hold as a vision for a new theatricalization of opera. And the changes, especially more recently, are largely directorial and, by extension, scenographic (helped by changes in stage technology and the embracing of new media). As Herbert Lindenberger observes:

> The last thirty years or more have also, above all in Europe, constituted the age of the so-called *Regieoper*, in which directors such as Patrice Chéreau, Hans Neuenfels, and Peter Sellars have radically rethought (some would say dismembered) a good bit of the traditional canon. Through unexpected visual effects they project—for example, a medieval potentate in black tie, or TV monitors displaying multiple images of a character singing her aria downstage—or through the changes in decor that they have instituted, most notoriously, perhaps, introducing the Rhine Maidens as prostitutes tending a dam during Wagner's own time or Don Giovanni operating among gangs in the South Bronx, they have, in effect destabilized and retheatricalized works whose unselfconscious theatricality had never before been in doubt. And Sellars, one might note, in 1992 directed a production of Messiaen's opera [*Saint François d'Assise*] for the Salzburg Festival with a full panoply of TV monitors.[8]

The new post-war Bayreuth, like the new opera beginning to emerge in cultural centers across Europe and the United States, took its cue first from Wieland Wagner's experiments (influenced at first by the visionary designs of the Swiss theoretician and designer Adolph Appia, who himself was in thrall to Wagnerian music drama) and set the trend for re-visioning opera in experimental directorial ways without touching the music or disrupting the triad. And so to this day the controversy that surrounds each new production of the *Ring Cycle* at Bayreuth is, in the main, cosmetic so to speak, involving staging, scenography, and interpretation. The music, however, the genuine core of the operatic experience, remains sacrosanct.[9] The triad, at least as far as the music is concerned, remains firmly fixed.

This distinction and the way most old technology has been used or harnessed to serve the triad need to be made clear at the outset. Because while opera adopts and adapts increasingly to new media interventions that cover a wide range of stage crafts and technologies, and even seeks to deconstruct narrative through dramaturgical interventions that adopt new cultural theories, in many instances the traditions of opera are merely re-costumed, re-painted or then re-gilded and amplified in a different way. So as Intermediality (the crossing of boundaries between art forms and technologies) has been a growing phenomenon in cross-performance contexts,[10] authentic Intermediality in opera is still best served and progressed under experimental conditions if breaks with the traditional triad and works of a new kind are to be forged. It is through the history of opera experiments, which have taken many forms, that we see the all too familiar triad both challenged and transgressed by novel and still emerging forms that test the boundaries by means of newly expressive works.[11]

Increasingly, productions like those of the prolific Dutch composer, writer, director, video artist and filmmaker Michel van der Aa, such as his 2013 production of *Sunken Garden*, "an occult–mystery film-opera" with a script/libretto by *Cloud Atlas*–author David Mitchell, have moved into the mainstream by way of creative co-productions with sympathetic producing organizations (it was co-commissioned by English National Opera, the Toronto Luminato Festival, Opera de Lyon, the Holland Festival and the Barbican Centre, London). The willingness, indeed, for new opera experiments to flourish is a result of a growing recognition that a new tradition is being formed and is supportable. The technological hybridity of an opera like *The Sunken Garden* (its use of 2D and 3D film, computer-generated graphics, music and sound with a contemporary, non-linear, anti-narrative text) is both a curiosity to some but also demonstrates vital signs of a new kind of energetic mastery wrought through a coherent and confident use of technologies that have all been convincingly manipulated by younger artists like van der Aa. Also in evidence at his productions is a much younger and switched-on audience open to and fully embracing new directions in opera as a result of their association with distinctive new music.[12]

Significant of a new generation of composers, producers and stagers of their own work, van der Aa was first trained as a sound engineer at the Royal Conservatory in The Hague before going on to study first musical composition, then filmmaking and eventually stage direction. Like many of the multi-disciplinary artists who make New Opera/Music Theatre (a tradition much more firmly rooted in continental Europe than in the United Kingdom or the United States), he adopts an auteurist approach to the making of performance compositions and his wide-ranging concerns and attachment to new media becomes the subject, in part, of the artist's work. In that he is not unlike Wagner who called for much the same single-minded totality of artistic expression and control but with technologies that were far too pre-modern to turn an overarching aesthetic philosophy into a reality. In van der Aa's case the reworking or re-engineering of operatic form is happening from within the operatic establishment that controls the triad; an establishment that is increasingly embracing the experimental and the new with greater frequency and security, if only by relegating it to more experimental spaces that are away from or outposts from main houses and the economic pressures that weigh heavily on the costs of producing opera. But van der Aa's development is also significant because his work moves away from the periphery (where most new music theatre and new opera takes place) and seeks to be more at the center of operatic action.

Van der Aa is in a new tradition of contemporary visual and performance artists whose ambitions take the instincts and materials of opera into new areas where it merges and sits comfortably with other forms of art making. Artist and performer Matthew Barney's *River of Fundament*, being made with composer Jonathan Bepler, is an epic five-hour operatic film that Barney has been working on since 2007 and is expected to finally finish and release in 2014.[13] Barney and Bepler have been developing the work through a diverse series of multi-disciplinary, site-specific projects loosely based on realizing sections of Norman Mailer's 1983 novel *Ancient Evenings*. For *River of Fundament*, Barney and Bepler have been collaborating to produce a seven-part film project that will continue to draw upon the thematic undercurrents of Mailer's novel. Set in pre–Christian Egypt, *Ancient Evenings* elaborately chronicles the seven stages of the soul's departure from the deceased body as it passes from death to rebirth in accordance with Egyptian mythology. *River of Fundament* combines the traditions of narrative cinema with elements of live performance, sculpture and opera. The long durational scale of the project and its mythical conjuring are, of course, very reminiscent of Wagner's *Ring* cycle and is a further development of Barney's epic urges as seen in his *Cremaster Cycle* (1994–2002) of films and his other associated art/performance events.

It is not until we get to the broadly technological twentieth century and the digitalized twenty-first century (or can we call this the post-technological century?) that the experimental features of new opera and shifts in the triadic balance are best seen in full light. But going back to the beginning of the twentieth century we can find greater historical context for the current wave of new experiments in opera to come.

Opera experiments since Richard Wagner and the turn of the nineteenth into the twentieth century and then into our own times provide us not only with a reflection on changes in musical styles and musicology but also with the art form's ever changing relationship with staging, technologies and, more recently, new media. The very word experimental in relation to such a tradition-bound musical and dramatic genre as opera is problematic, and does not sit easily with the even more tradition-bound audiences, the very fixed repertoire and the opera houses themselves; the classic triad, again. The term experimental usually sparks controversy, conjuring up such oppositions as traditions vs. novelty, the mighty canon of the romantic repertoire under attack from avant-garde revisionism, nineteenth-century colorful and Baroque excess vs. grey contemporary minimalism. Certainly the practices of some twentieth- and twenty-first–century opera productions and the plethora of new composers re-visioning opera musically for new audiences, new media and new times are undeniable. Even the word opera has become seriously problematized as current and sometimes even more problematic and contentious replacement and qualifying terms like "music drama," "new music theatre," "new opera" and even more now "digital opera" and also "postopera"[14] invoke shifts in where we place critical emphasis to demarcate some distinction from the monoculture and hegemony that represents the lyrical, romantic bedrock traditions of opera. At the root of this change are shifts to aesthetic attachments and to newer media.

The history of opera experiments is as old as the form itself, which evolved, one might say, as a form of ongoing experiments from its beginning. The Elizabethan Masques, the initial collisions of Renaissance polyphony and Baroque *basso continuo* of Monteverdi, the French experiments of Rameau as he elbowed Lully out of the scene, and more to come during a turbulent eighteenth century all helped to define and to establish a genre as it reached maturity. But once the form did settle down into its classical mode (despite occasional fits of dissonance) in the nineteenth century opera turned its back on its experimental past, except where musical modernity ushered in a host of changes, principally with Strauss, Schoenberg, Berg, Stravinsky, Busoni, Weill and others. But musicological change, which has been well documented by many, is really not the kind of experimentation under discussion here. As the nineteenth gave way to the twentieth century the well-entrenched triad began to feel pressure.

The legendary Futurist Opera *Victory Over the Sun*, first staged on 3 December 1913 at the Luna Park Theatre in St. Petersburg—a populist theatre but a short distance from the more imposing Imperial Mariinsky Theatre—was probably the key event by both the Russian and international avant-garde to view opera differently and construct new terms for it.[15] It remains to this day one of the great transitional theatre pieces—post–Wagner—that helped to define and shape modern experimental approaches to anti-narrative performance art through its mixture of music, movement, nonsensical sound text (a made-up language called *ZAUM*), extraordinary proto–Supremacist sets and abstract costumes by Kasimir Malevich, which still survive in many drawings (really the only extended and extant evidence we have of this important production). It was also a conscious piece of Futurist propaganda and something of an early Happening.[16] This was a theatre piece at the opposite end of the spectrum from the Russian theatrical realism of Stanislavski, Chekhov and Gorki or the traditions of Western and Russian classical opera. It was a radical collage of music and text that was unlike anything we know of as opera. Its impact and notoriety, following its brief performance, was profound. It challenged the settled status quo through its deliberate celebration of disorder, chaos and liberation through destruction. In brief the piece tells of the sun being captured by strong men of the future. It is a punchy, potent modernist allegory set against the backdrop of approaching revolution and massive political change. It only received two performances and was revived briefly in 1920 during the new Soviet era it seemed to predict. Artistically, *Victory Over the Sun* was something of a suicide mission for the young Russian Futurists who invented and staged it. Association with a belligerent new art form marked them.

Victory Over the Sun was the work of four young artists: Mikhail Matiushin (the modernist composer), Viktor Khlebnikov and Aleksei Kruchenykh (librettists of the nonsensical text that featured the machine-like language *zaum*) and Kazimir Malevich (designer and Suprematist artist). The score is now lost, except for a brief excerpt of 24 bars. The text was written in an absurdist language called *zaum* and still exists, foretelling what would happen to avantgarde dramaturgy during the era of 1920s and 1930s with Dadaism and Surrealism. There were reports at the time that the chief librettist Kruchenykh had been carted off to an asylum following the opening performance. Only Malevich, a Suprematist painter of vision and substance, survives as a significant figure a century later.

Victory Over the Sun is one of those unclassifiable works of art performance that has assumed cult and renegade status. Its brevity and the commotion it caused (Futurists were always out to cause commotion) is part of its mythology. Even in its own time *Victory Over the Sun* must have been conceived as a gesture of youthful revolt; "a slap in the face of public taste," as the Futurists were to label their work, a call to arms for international Futurists everywhere to revolt against the conventional and trite traditions. It is little wonder that *Victory Over the Sun* was performed on the same bill as Vladimir Mayakovsky's poetic drama *Vladimir Mayakovsky: A Tragedy*. The whole enterprise surrounding *Victory Over the Sun* made use of musical, literary and performance languages that sought to divest words, sounds and gestures of their conventional meanings; to de-romanticize opera of all previous associations. This is art seeking a new medium through performance. The threat that *Victory Over the Sun* posed to traditional opera was profound.

At the same time as their Russian counterparts the contribution of Italian Futurists, under the artistic leadership of Filiipo Tommaso Marinetti, would equally find notoriety in undermining classical music and its assumptions just as Futurism, invoking an age of mechanized industrialization and mechanical reproduction, sought to undermine the entire western humanist tradition. While producing no great opera experiments to rival the Russian Futurist's *Victory Over the Sun*, in the Italian Futurist's arsenal of provocation was the political/artistic manifesto that articulated (though not always delivering) gestures to dismantle the traditions of art.[17] Their great musical experiments were in creating an "art of noise." Luigi Russolo, who wrote the manifesto "The Art of Noise" in 1913, found in modern factory and industrial sounds an overwhelming music that became liberated music in its own right. Noise was Futurism's contribution to moving the boundaries that might subsequently have influences on opera itself. The recognition of the potential of brute noise as a source of art still informs the work of new performance sound a century later.[18] Russolo's patented creation of the *Intonarumori* or Noise Intoner set new precedents for percussive, and later electronic, instruments that would reshape orchestral sound and become, in their own way, objects of performances themselves; alien presences in the orchestra pit. With the experimental *Intonarumori* we begin to get an ongoing parade of instruments, machines and inventions across the century, increasingly electronic and less hand-driven, that would shape the change of sound away from the purely traditional acoustic orchestral to technological apparatuses that would sometimes inform opera to come, especially the move towards synthesized sound.[19] An opera/liturgical oratorio like Olivier Messiaen's *Saint François d'Assise*, for instance, composed between 1975 and 1983, makes use of the ethereal *ondes martenot*, the electronic instrument that features prominently in the composer's *Turangalila Symphonie*. Synthesized sound refocuses aural patterns, adding new depth and dimensions to a musical landscape. A multiaurality decenters the listener and shifts what is heard to multiple channels.

Alongside the Futurist experiments were those of the Bauhaus in Germany, which, like the Futurists, saw art mixing and making a compact with industry to create a new technology of invention. Although theatre and performance, rather than opera, were a central element of Bauhaus aesthetics, László Moholy-Nagy's essay "Theatre, Circus, Variety" probes the idea of a "Theatre of Totality with its multifarious complexities of light, space, plane, form, motion, sound, man—and with all the possibilities for varying and combining these elements—must be an ORGANISM."[20] Further along in this seminal writing that sets out to define new working principles for performances, Moholy-Nagy speaks of his concept of the Mechanized Eccentric that would infuse performance with the qualities of machinery and technology. And then as part of the unfolding futuristic predictions for new art forms we find the prediction:

In the future, SOUND EFFECTS will make use of various acoustical equipment driven electrically or by some other mechanical means. Sound waves issuing from unexpected sources—for example, a speaking or singing arc lamp, loudspeakers under seats or beneath the floor of the auditorium, the use of new amplifying systems—will raise the audience's acoustic surprise-threshold so much that unequal effects in other areas will be disappointing.[21]

The essay ends with a vision of a stage that is truly transformed into a weightless mass of planes and standing "in a very free relationship with one another, without the need for any direct contact."[22] The very programmatic disruption of the triad offered by movements like Futurism and arts schools like the Bauhaus paved the way for new ways of looking at art where sound and the totality of effects become an increasingly desired outcome.

Over the course of the twentieth century opera has taken a turn partly generated by recognition of new art forms in sympathy with technology and greater interface with the digital word. The very premises of the operatic triad are increasingly contested to such a point that oppositions, like "New Music Theatre," break the link with an operatic tradition and set in place a new tradition:

> As the centre of musical culture has moved away from live, acoustic sound towards loudspeaker sound, there has been an inevitable effect on the way music is written, performed, produced, and received. In a very general way, we can note the tendency for live music to sound like recorded music, an esthetic preference that can be found in concert performances of classical music and in the opera house just as much as in rock concerts or popular musicals. In new music and music theater—once the old prohibitions against amplification have been superseded —all this offers a wide range of choices in the creation of the performance of new work.[23]

Since the twentieth century the speed of change and the adaptation and take-up of new technologies and artificial intelligences, and the turning of these into art forms and practice, is radically in steady process and can change within weeks, much like the technology of micro processing where contemporary art forms have made many compacts, becoming even more compact and portable. So what is said here may even be partially anachronistic by the time it is published. The laptop is the new keyboard, sound maker, orchestra, canvas and film studio—often in the hands of and under the direct musical-authorial-directorial control of a single artist (as in the work of van der Aa). In a contemporary world of artistic transgression, where science and technology devastate previous definitions, former categories—be they history, fiction, memory, language, image or illusion and even drama and music—lose validity and can, in fact, become too restrictive. Art forms cross over and borrow properties from one another, and younger, newer artists are easy about this annexation. And so the very term "opera" is steadily under continued assault or reappropriation by artists for other means.

Perhaps one of the most celebrated experiments and appropriations of operatic form and content reconstituted into something new and daring was Philip Glass's and Robert Wilson's *Einstein on the Beach*, composed in 1975 and first performed in 1976. Opera, in the cases of Glass and Wilson, meant only "a work"[24] and, indeed, Robert Wilson had been calling even his non-musical, epic theatre works "operas" for some time (even ones that were silent) before their famous collaboration took place. Although *Einstein on the Beach*, which was revived in 2012 in Europe and the United States, owes its celebrity to the fusion of Glass's musically repetitive minimalism and Wilson's theatre of images and extraordinary scenography, it is a major milestone in late twentieth century operatic experimentation that lasts, on average, over four-and-a-half hours. The processed features of Glass's musical minimalism are like something generated by a computer. And once mixed with the robotic gestures that Wilson required of his performers and Andy DeGroat and Lucinda Childs required of dancers, *Einstein on the Beach* can be seen as a highly constructed piece of music theatre (not unlike the 1913 *Victory Over the Sun* or a work envisioned by Bauhaus thinking filtered through Moholy-Nagy). The arithmetic, additive processes in Glass's score and the mimed writing by performers within the scenography are reminders that we are watching an opera about a scientist, Albert Einstein. But we are also dreaming an opera with a future tense, as dream is one of the liberating factors that will propel so much of Robert Wilson's work. Curiously, however, the work calls for little in the way of electronic intervention (only electronic piano/organ, miked voices and the all-important lights (designed by Beverley Emmons) and scenography (by Robert Wilson).

The history of such a well-known new music theatre work like *Einstein on the Beach*, which sets the worlds of traditional opera and new opera on a collision course and unbalances the triad, also demonstrates that work like this in a whole new key are formed as works in conscious opposition to the artistic status quo.[25] For *Einstein on the Beach* set the downtown New York experimental world of new artists against the uptown classical world of old artists. But its history, as recounted by Glass and others, also charts how a new market and appetite for new opera in new forms was also being appreciated, finding productions and attracting audiences that might just become a new generation of opera goers.

Almost as a means of distancing itself from opera and all that its traditions imply, experiments in operatic work (more often than not some combination of music, singing, narrative, scenography and technological enhancements) have widely adopted the term "music theatre"[26] In Salzman's and Desi's *The New Music Theater*, which is part history of a new movement and part polemic, the development of music theatre falls into three distinct phases: 1900–1930, reflecting the experimental, abstract and revolutionary character of modernism; 1940–1970, linking the concentration of musical serialism to forms of political engagement that are both world political and active alternatives to the established musical and operatic institutions; and 1970 to the present day, finding in the "technological (r)evolutions" the theatricalization of concert performances along with extensive use of new and old media that has been increasingly digital.[27] In the third phase the multiplicity of musical and theatrical forms together with hybrid electronic platforms has produced a bewildering array of new music theatre intentions to such an extent that the argument with traditional opera has ceased as a whole new genre has taken root. This is an important step, as far as upending the triad is concerned by replacing it with a new post-digital triad. There are now new music/operatic forms that inhabit their own space and time, attracting their own new audience. Music theatre has established itself as a new genre(s) in its own right, with its own variety and variations that sometimes draw on new music, new performance and new visual arts. What joins it all together are its synthetic properties: the use of computers and platforms, artificial light, performance techniques that embrace heterodoxy, a blending of visual arts that are part painterly, part sculptural and manifoldly digital. The space of performance no longer even needs to be an opera house or a traditional theatre; it can be in a warehouse (increasingly so). In reviewing and remarking on performances of the radical operas *Light* (*Licht*) by Stockhausen and *Europeans 1 and 2* by John Cage, Alex Ross remarks that "the vogue for repurposing industrial-age spaces towards cultural end ... has been a boon for avant-garde works that are still ill-suited for traditional venues."[28] In fact, since the Millennium new opera/music theatre has found a more harmonious and sympathetic home in the detritus of the post-industrial age (e.g. abandoned mines, derelict warehouses, deconsecrated churches, abandoned office buildings, galleries rather than theatre spaces. The concert halls and operatic theatres that may have once shown an overt hostility to new forms have become, within the last decade, more receptive to experimentation.[29] Operatic works nowadays are just as likely to take place in a gallery where none of the three categories of the triad are operative or, increasingly, just on one or more video screens, the focus more and more becoming as much about the technology as the music. The music might even become a parody of the classical tradition.

Opera in a Small Room (2005) was an installation conceived by Canadian (sound) artist Janet Cardiff and her collaborator/partner George Bures Miller. In their own description of the piece:

> There are twenty-four antique loudspeakers out of which come sounds, arias, and occasional pop tunes. There are almost two thousand records stacked

around the room and eight record players, which turn on and off robotically synching with the soundtrack. The sound of someone moving and sorting albums is heard. The audience cannot enter the room. To see and hear this world, they have to look through the window, holes in the wall, the cracks in the doorway and watch his shadow move around the room.[30]

Art this is, as an installation, but is it opera? Well, yes and no. It is certainly theatrical and operatic. It draws on the pure nostalgia of opera: a man (it is almost always a man) listening alone in his room to opera, a fatal attraction to song and aria, to *liebestod*, the vinyl tradition of ghostly great performances, a shadowy world, a world that almost feels funereal and otherworldly. But the textures of the piece draw on sophisticated technology and media to support a kind of illusion. It references the phonograph record (our first hint that technology would enter the world of opera and recorded sound); but it also uses more sophisticated digital technology to create a simulacrum of the opera experience. And it is art, visual art, using sound to define new parameters and new properties. In miniature we have a *mise en scène* of emotions, solitude, private contemplation. A cabinet of curiosities and memories that take us back to the Renaissance and the birth of opera. An uncomfortable and transient experience that says this is a history that has ended and indeed become dated through the renaissance of better technology. A simulacra within a greater simulacrum using synchronous effect without the presence of any human form except the ghostly and partial ... and the enhanced and unrelenting robotic technology that drives the installation. But it is also playful and thoroughly absorbing, much like being overwhelmed by opera in a darkened theatre but contradictory because we know that opera happens more often in grander bigger theatres and not in cabin-like room isolated in the Canadian wilderness or in the corner of an art gallery.

Opera in a Small Room, although conceived for a gallery and not a theatre, is, in miniature, the apotheosis of what opera has made of technology: it has cooperated with and appropriated opera, in some ways being respectful of its music, but frustrated with its traditions and trappings, seeking to make something new through the intervention of other arts and media. And the history of experimental opera is encapsulated in *Opèra in a Small Room*: embracing but also casting suspicion on a tradition, dressing the outmoded in new modes of presentation and representation.

Take another, somewhat similar example, a portable opera like John Cage's *Europera 5* (1991), written for piano, soprano, tenor, 78-rpm Victrola and tape recorder. The work is a collage scored for two singers, each singer performing five arias *of their own choosing* from the standard opera repertoire (signs of Cage's chance variations). A pianist accompanies (if that is what he does) them by playing six different opera transcriptions. They are joined (accompanied?)

by a single 78-rpm Victrola-player, playing six historical opera recordings and a performer playing a pre-recorded tape, plus the use of a radio and a mute television set. Here you have all the makings of contemporary experimental opera: singers, instrumentalists and the invasive and pervasive old vs. new media. As a description of the piece notes "the separation of the various elements in *Europera 5* produces a spaciousness and awareness of distances that is so characteristic of Cage's music. Cage also offers us a unique sense of historical distance—the singers performing the older operatic music in our presence; the pianist performing 'romanticized' interruptions of romantic music and the Victrola presenting old music in old performances, coming through to us by means of an old nostalgic technology. It is only in the silences and the use of the radio that our present time intrudes."[31]

The problematics of new opera in relation to the triad are here emphasized: post-modern disassociation from but clinging to relics of the past; playfulness and parody pitted again deadpan seriousness; the open declaration that for most of us who cannot afford the high prices of opera the experience of opera comes to us via the radio and recordings. *Europera 5* instantly declares its minimalism (because it is something by John Cage), its playfulness (always part of a Cage performance), an openness to chance (a patented trademark of Cage's) but exposes something that is also essential in opera—a love and potent nostalgia for favorite arias sung by soprano and tenor, singing of love and death. In this Cage's mixture of affections and wariness is much like that of Cardiff's and Bures' *Opera in a Small Room*. While Cage's work undercuts all that is essential in lyrical opera and its suspension of absurdity he also celebrates, upholds and reinforces it. The classical and the modern and the very contemporary are held in perfect balance but also in perfect tension. Cage wanted his piece to be a bricolage of diverse and tangible references and what he described as a collage of sorts, of a pulverized sort, of European opera. It's "Europera," which are the words Europe and opera put together but it also sounds like "Your Opera," pejoratively directed at a European tradition. As always with Cage, and any composer working in new opera, there is the simultaneity of homage and burlesque critique sitting side by side. Self-consciousness and self-referencing are the stock in trade of new music. Surprises are found inside the familiar alongside startling and knowing effects. To experiment is to take the old and re-fashion (or "re-function" as Brecht said) it into something surprising. "You see," Cage said at the premiere of his first *Europera*, "I've come to the desire to free each person in the performance from anyone like a conductor—or, for that matter, from a lighting director or costume designer or scene painter or any the traditional opera craft expert."[32] As Richard Kostelanetz, a long-time Cage expert, writes: "What Cage did for *Europera*, essentially, was to ransack the archive of traditional operas that were no longer protected by copyright; from them he selected fragments, each no more than 16 measures long, that could, by the workings of chance, be reassembled differently for each performance."[33]

And so what might the future be for experiments in opera? One can look to the Massachusetts Institute of Technology (MIT) for an indication and to its "Opera of the Future" research group:

> The Opera of the Future group (also known as Hyperinstruments) explores concepts and techniques to help advance the future of musical composition, performance, learning, and expression. Through the design of new interfaces for both professional virtuosi and amateur music-lovers, the development of new techniques for interpreting and mapping expressive gesture, and the application of these technologies to innovative compositions and experiences, we seek to enhance music as a performance art, and to develop its transformative power as counterpoint to our everyday lives. The scope of our research includes musical instrument design, concepts for new performance spaces, interactive touring and permanent installations, and "music toys." It ranges from extensions of traditional forms to radical departures, such as the Brain Opera, Toy Symphony and Death and the Powers.[34]

Death and the Powers, a new opera composed by project leader Tod Machova with a libretto by Robert Pinsky that premiered in 2010 and has been steadily refined since, is the work of a team of faculty, staff, and graduate and undergraduate students at the MIT Media Lab in Cambridge, Massachusetts, that brought a host of innovative technologies to the stage, anchoring them to a Faustian narrative of a wealthy businessman and inventor, Simon Powers, out to harness technology and achieve endless life. From robots to visuals to sound-producing Hyperinstruments like a giant Chandelier, more than 40 computers are required to run the production, all backed by extensive wired and wireless networks. These computers run a broad range of distributed control systems that were developed expressly for the production, in which each component can share information with any other in order to create a synchronized and unified presence for the central character in his hyper-technological environment called "The System."

A mixture of human and robotic performance, the production makes much use of animation and animatronics and of robotic movement and lighting. If need be, puppeteers above the stage can assume manual control of any parameters of a robot using a typical video game controller. An absolute position tracking system monitors the location of robots and actors onstage to help the robots navigate, as well as affect sound and visuals.

After the character Simon Powers enters The System, the singer portraying him exits the stage, though he continues to sing and act as if he were onstage. In a new technique called Disembodied Performance, gestural and physiological sensors, as well as voice analysis, capture the singer's offstage performance, which is then used to generate in real time the visual representation of Simon Powers in the bookshelf displays and other aspects of the production. Mapping software was created that can connect sound, robots, and visuals to the singer's performance. A custom graphics environment allows these live performance parameters to generate expressive graphic representations of Simon in The System.

Another method of representing The System's omnipresence is through sound. Over 140 speakers are used to create a unique sonic environment. Two formats of surround sound are used in the production. Wave Field Synthesis uses an array of tiny speakers across the front of the stage to create the impression of a sound emanating from any point on the stage. Ambisonics technology is used to move sound all around the theater. Software and plug-ins for common audio packages were engineered to allow the hundreds of streams of audio to be processed in real time.

All of this technology—although complex—is designed to work invisibly behind the scenes, helping to draw audiences into the unusual, mysterious, and "animate" world of Simon and The System. The Chorus of Operabots and three large bookshelf periaktoi are controlled centrally using software developed specifically for choreographic robots onstage. This software includes a 3D visualization for monitoring.[35]

Curiously, *Death and the Powers* resembles something from Wagner in its ambitions: a new kind of *The Twilight of the Gods* set in a high tech world of robotics and capitalism. The music for the production, though obviously integral to the experience of *Death and the Powers*, might be subordinate to the elaborate technical means used to carry out this experiment in opera that has been created largely in a laboratory rather than a rehearsal room. But we might also think that a hundred year after the first experimental opera, *Victory Over the Sun*, *Death and the Powers* continues a tradition set in motion by the Russian Futurists. And what has refined over that time is a greater use and reliance on technology to mediate the experience of opera and bring some kind of oppositional force to the enduring triad that forms the experience of opera.

Notes

    1. See, for instance, *The Cambridge Companion to Opera Studies* (2012), edited by Nicholas Till, for a good summary of the issues.
    2. I am indebted here to an unpublished address given by Andreas Breitscheid, German composer and former artistic director of Forum Neues Musiktheater, Stuttgart Staatsoper, who made his remarks at Astonished and Terrified: Opera and the Transformation of the World by Technology, a conference organized by the Centre for Opera and Music Theatre, University of Sussex, June 22–23, 2012.

3. As contemporary an operatic masterpiece as George Benjamin's *Written on the Skin* (2012; with a libretto by Martin Crimp and first directed by Katie Mitchell), fusing the legacy of twentieth-century modernism and twenty-first–century tonality, still preserves the triadic distinctions and balances.

4. Shifts in musical styles and their effect on opera composition are noted coherently in Richard Taruskin's *Oxford History of Western Music* (2005), particularly the volumes *The Early Twentieth Century* and *The Late Twentieth Century*.

5. "Postdramatic theatre" is a phrase coined by Hans-Thies Lehmann to chart the new forms of theatre and theatre making, in uneasy relationship with tradition and text, that emerged throughout the latter stages of the twentieth century. See Hans-Thies Lehmann, *Postdramatic Theatre* (New York: Routledge, 2006), especially his views on musicalization, pp. 91–93.

6. See Patrick Carnegy, *Wagner and the Art of the Theatre,* for a good overview and incisive survey and also an analysis on approaches to Wagnerian productions.

7. For the most recent translation of Wagner's seminal work see Richard Wagner, "The Artwork of the Future," translated by Emma Warner, in a special issue of *The Wagner Journal*, 2012.

8. Herbert Lindenberger, *Situating Opera: Period, Genre, Reception* (Cambridge: Cambridge University Press, 2010), pp. 217–18.

9. The 2013 200th anniversary of Wagner saw extreme controversy when the new version of the *Ring*, directed by the provocative German director Frank Castrof, had opening night audiences booing for 20 minutes. Yet it was written into Castrof's contract by the Bayreuth management that not a note of Wagner's score was to be changed. And, indeed, the production was accorded a music triumph even if the staging was heavily criticized by Alec Ross in *The New Yorker*. The music, however, as conducted by Kirill Petrenko, was thought superb by Ross and other critics.

10. See Freda Chapple and Chiel Kattenbelt, eds., *Intermediality in Theatre and Performance* (Amsterdam: Rodopi, 2006) for a larger applicability of the term across new forms of performing arts.

11. An example of such change would be the way the *International Journal of Performance Arts and Digital Media* devoted an issue (vol. 8, no. 1, 2012, edited by Áine Sheil and Craig Vear) to surveying a series of digital experiments in opera that posit new means and new meanings that take us away from the triad under discussion. Ongoing digital experiments also take place in pockets around the world, not easily detected and often secreted within closed experimental worlds.

12. In the month prior to *The Sunken Garden*'s first performance at London's Barbican Centre the sound artist Ryoji Ikeda's *superimposition* appeared, employing a spectacular combination of synchronized video screens, real-time content feeds, digital sound sculptures and—for the first time in Ikeda's work—human performers; *superposition* explores the thrilling conceptual world opened up by quantum theory. The totality of the work certainly resembled the kind of new operas being written and performed more often in the second decade of the twenty-first century.

13. The work's premiere at the Brooklyn Academy of Music in New York continues the then-new tradition established by that institution in the 1970s to present contemporary work by that performing arts institution that has always sought to define new traditions in theatre, music and dance.

14. For the use of the term "postopera" and its relation to "postdramatic" see Jelena Novak, "From Minimalist Music to Postopera," in *The Ashgate Research Companion to Minimalist and Postminimalist Music* (Burlington, VT: Ashgate, 2013), pp. 129–140.

15. For a full history and understanding of the work see *Victory Over the Sun: The*

World's First Futurist Opera, edited by Rosamund Bartlett and Sarah Dadswell (Exeter: University of Exeter Press, 2012).

16. Happenings, from the 1950s and 1960s, in which the influential American composer John Cage would play a role, would provide the re-shapings and appropriations that would influence new kinds of music theatre experiments like Nam June Paik's multi-screen *TV Cello* (1964) and *Opera Sextronique* (1967). The sensation seeking of Happenings and the associated Fluxus moment from the 1960s and after often saw traditional opera as one of its primary targets.

17. However, the Futurist spectacles or Futurist evening produced from January 1910 onwards were precursors of the Happening and would sometimes feature operatic gestures, especially in the recitation of sound or tone poems and cabaret acts.

18. See Paul Hegarty, *Noise/Music: A History* (New York: Continuum, 2010), for a useful survey of the growth of sound art and its associations with performance.

19. For a very graphic and useful history of electronic devices that would help shape these changes see Simon Crab's online "120 Years of Electronic Music" (http://120years.net/wordpress/). "This site charts the development of electronic musical instruments from 1870 to 1990. For the purposes of this project electronic musical instruments are defined as instruments that synthesize sounds from an electronic source. This definition leaves out a whole section of hybrid electronic instruments developed at the end of the last century that used electronics to manipulate or amplify sounds and tape recorders, wax recording devices, Musique Concrete and so on. It has been decided to leave in some non-electronic instruments such as the Futurists 'Intonarumori' due to their importance in the history of and influence on modern music. The main focus of the site is on instruments developed from the beginning of the century until the 1960s. The more modern and current Synthesizer companies have been included for the sake of historical completeness but are already well documented elsewhere on the Internet."

20. Lásló Moholy-Nagy, "Theater, Circus, Variety," translated by Arthur S. Wensinger in Randall Packer and Ken Jordan, eds., *Multimedia: From Wagner to Virtual Reality* (New York: W.W. Norton, 2001), p. 22.

21. Packer and Jordan, p. 24.

22. Packer and Jordan, p. 26.

23. Eric Salzman and Thomas Desi, *The New Music Theatre*, (Oxford: Oxford University Press, 2008), p. 27. Salzman and Desi is one the primary means of defining the breakaway movements that contest the operatic tradition in the late twentieth century.

24. When interviewed in 2012 about the revival of *Einstein on the Beach* Philip Glass told an interviewer: "the work came to be called an opera because it needed to be produced in a hall with a proscenium stage and an orchestra pit, as well as ample flies and wing space, plus singers and dancers.... So, we did *Einstein on the Beach*, and people would ask, why are you calling that an opera? We would answer that we never called it an opera. But, of course, that's a very provocative thing to say," Glass remembers. "We had these ludicrous conversations with audiences, and, finally, I said, 'Look I call an opera things that you see in an opera house. What's a stable? A stable is where horses live.'" https://www.musicworks.ca/featured-article/featured-article/philip-glass.

25. See Philip Glass's heavily anecdotal account of the genesis and progress of *Einstein on the Beach* in Philip Glass, *Music* (New York: DaCapo, 1995), pp. 27–62.

26. Salzman and Desi attempt a fuller understanding of the term "music theatre" and the different forms it now takes. The term music theatre, however, has been adopted by different experimental camps to mean different things and, indeed, the way the genre functions and is practiced in Europe, for instance, may differ remarkably from America.

27. Salzman and Desi, p. 376.

28. Alex Ross, "Opera in the Clouds," *The New Yorker*, September 10, 2012, p. 105.
29. More than just the occasional new opera/new music theatre work features on the schedule of major opera houses around the world and quite specifically in the smaller experimental spaces like the Linbury Studio Theatre at London's Royal Opera House.
30. See the artists' website: http://www.cardiffmiller.com/artworks/inst/opera.html. Materials: Mixed media with sound, record players, records and synchronized lighting. Duration: 20 min. loop. Dimension: 2,6 × 3 × 4,5m." See also the interview with Miller: http://www.youtube.com/watch?=vXeGVGEBNYks.
31. See http://www.moderecords.com/catalog/036cage.html.
32. http://www.nytimes.com/1988/07/10/arts/music-john-cage-s-first-opera-written-by-the-numbers.html?pagewanted=all&src=pm.
33. http://www.nytimes.com/1988/07/10/arts/music-john-cage-s-first-opera-written-by-the-numbers.html?pagewanted=all&src=pm.
34. http://www.media.mit.edu/research/groups/opera-future.
35. The description for this work is freely taken from http://opera.media.mit.edu/projects/deathandthepowers/technology.php.

Selected Bibliography

Bartlett, Rosamund, and Sarah Dadswell, eds. *Victory Over the Sun: The World's First Futurist Opera*. Exeter: Exeter University Press, 2012.
Carnegy, Patrick. *Wagner and the Art of the Theatre*. New Haven: Yale University Press, 2006.
Causey, Matthew. *Theatre and Performance in Digital Culture*. New York: Routledge, 2006.
Chapple, Freda, and Chiel Kattenbelt, eds. *Intermediality in Theatre and Performance*. Amsterdam: Rodopi, 2006.
Glass, Philip. *Music by Philip Glass*. Edited by Robert T. Jones. New York: Da Capo, 1995.
Hegarty, Paul. *Noise/Music: A History*. New York: Continuum, 2010.
Kittler, Friedrich. "World-Breath: On Wagner's Media Technology." In *Opera Through Other Eyes*, edited by David J. Levin. Stanford: Stanford University Press, 1994.
Lehmann, Hans-Thies. *Postdramatic Theatre*. Translated by Karen Jürs-Munby. New York: Routledge, 2006.
Machon, Josephine. *Immersive Theatre: Intimacy and Immediacy in Contemporary Performance*. New York: Palgrave Macmillan, 2013.
Nyman, Michael. *Experimental Music: Cage and Beyond*, 2d ed. New York: Cambridge University Press, 1999.
Packer, Randall, and Ken Jordan, eds. *Multimedia: From Wagner to Virtual Reality*. New York: W.W. Norton, 2001.
Potter, Keith, Kyle Gann and Pwyll ap Siôn, eds. *The Ashgate Research Companion to Minimalist and Postminimalist Music*. Farnham: Ashgate, 2013.
Reich, Steve. *Writings on Music, 1965–2000*. Edited by Paul Hillier. New York: Oxford University Press, 2002.
Ross, Alex. *The Rest Is Noise: Listening to the Twentieth Century*. London: Fourth Estate, 2008.
_____. "Stockhausen and Cage." *The New Yorker*, September 12, 2012, 104–106.
_____. "Wagner Summer: A New 'Ring' in Bayreuth; 'Die Meistersinger' in Salzburg." *The New Yorker*, August 26, 2013, 107–109.
Salzman, Eric, and Thomas Desi. *The New Music Theater: Seeing the Voice, Hearing the Body*. New York: Oxford University Press, 2008.

Taruskin, Richard. *Music in the Early Twentieth Century*. Vol. 4 of *The Oxford History of Western Music*. New York: Oxford University Press, 2005.
_____. *Music in the Late Twentieth Century*. Vol. 5 of *The Oxford History of Western Music*. New York: Oxford University Press, 2005.
Till, Nicholas, ed. *The Cambridge Companion to Opera Studies*. New York: Cambridge University Press, 2012.
Wagner, Richard. "The Artwork of the Future," translated by Emma Warner. *A Special Issue of The Wagner Journal* (2013): 13–86.
Žižek, Slavoj, and Mladen Dolar. *Opera's Second Death*. New York: Routledge, 2002.

About the Contributors

Pierre **Bellemare** teaches canonical Latin at Saint-Paul University in Ottawa. He has written essays and articles on Richard Strauss' poetic imagination, the Montreal leg of Mascagni's North American tour of 1902, the Internet forum Opera-L, as well as introductions to individual works by Puccini, Lortzing, Donizetti, Hadley, and Meyerbeer.

Robert **Cannon** was vice principal of Rose Bruford College of Theatre and Performance, U.K., where he started what is still the only degree in opera studies in the world. He has written for *Opera Magazine, Opera Now* and the *BBC Music Magazine* and is the author of the *Cambridge Introduction to Opera*.

Michael **Earley** is a professor of drama and principal and chief executive officer of Rose Bruford College of Theatre and Performance in London. He has worked as editorial and publishing director of Methuen Drama and as chief producer of plays for BBC Radio Drama, where he directed over 50 productions for broadcast over Radio 3 and Radio 4. His publications have included books on acting.

Paul **Fryer** is associate director of research and director of the Stanislavski Centre at Rose Bruford College of Theatre and Performance. His research is opera, the opera singer and the early (pre-sound) film industry, and has published three books on opera and on women in the performing arts. He is co-editor of the e-journal *Stanislavski Studies*.

Nick **Hunt** is head of the School of Design, Management and Technical Arts at Rose Bruford College of Theatre and Performance. His interests include the performative potential of light and the lighting artist, digital scenography, and the roles and status of the various personnel involved in theatre-making. He is an associate editor of the *International Journal of Performance Arts and Digital Media*.

Daniel **Meyer-Dinkgräfe** is a professor of drama at the Lincoln School of Performing Arts, University of Lincoln. He has numerous writings on theatre and consciousness and is founding editor of the web journal *Consciousness, Literature and the Arts*.

Christopher **Newell** is a consultant for the Toshiba Speech Lab in Cambridge and is research theme leader for the Creative Economy at the University of Hull. He has 25 years' experience of directing opera including at the Glyndebourne Opera House, the Royal Opera House Covent Garden, the National Theatre and in the West End, where he taught Dustin Hoffman Shakespearean verse speaking.

George **Newell** is a freelance writer based in Norwich. He co-authored the libretto to a melodrama for singer and artificial voice, *My Voice and Me*, which premiered at the Tête-à-Tête opera festival in 2013, and has written with his father and Paul Barker for *Logopedics Phoniatrics Vocology*.

Sam **O'Connell** is an assistant professor of theatre and interdisciplinary arts and the theme semester director at Worcester State University in Worcester, Massachusetts. His research and publications address music as performance, intersections of media technology of live performance, and musical theatre history.

Hansjörg **Schmidt** is a lighting designer and the program director of lighting design at Rose Bruford College of Theatre and Performance. His research interests lie in lighting, site-specificity and narrative, and he has presented papers on his lighting for two innovative performance projects at design symposia in Zurich, Riga and Cardiff.

Trevor **Siemens** is a freelance composer and tutor in opera studies at Rose Bruford College of Theatre and Performance. He has composed two chamber operas, and his works for various ensembles and individuals have been performed in the United Kingdom, Europe, Canada and Brazil.

Kevin **Stephens** has been a music editor, arts administrator, community musician, researcher, music journalist, festival director, music lecturer, arts consultant and module author and tutor for Rose Bruford College of Theatre and Performance's distance learning opera degree. He wrote the BBC Music Course and was artistic director of the Hexham Abbey Festival.

Index

Aa, Michel van der 232, 233, 237
Adams, John 66, 69, 87, 149, 165, 192
advertising 1, 2, 3, 4, 5, 6, 7, 9, 12, 13, 14, 15, 16, 17, 20, 21, 22, 23, 24, 25, 26, 27, 28, 29, 31, 77, 89, 122
Aguilera, Christina 116, 145
Airline Icarus 77
Allen, Hugh 101
Alternate Visions 78, 79, 80
An Anatomy in Four Quarters 203, 207
Anna Nicole 7, 66, 83, 84, 86, 87, 88
Appia, Adolphe 153, 198, 206, 207, 231
At the Drop of a Hat 111

Bach, J.S. 1, 3, 11, 98, 157
Le Bal 46
Il Barbiere di Siviglia 13
Barkley, Charles 2, 16
Barley, Matthew 233
Baroque opera 14, 16, 17, 44, 82, 132, 145, 178, 179, 192, 234
Bayreuth Festival 50, 54, 60, 62, 97, 152, 189, 194, 205, 206, 231, 244, 246
BBC (British Broadcasting Corporation) 14, 21, 22, 29, 87, 136, 192, 249, 250
BBC Music Magazine 22
Beineix, Jean Jacques 11, 15, 16
Bepler, Jonathan 233
Berg, Alban 76, 149, 154, 155, 156, 157, 161, 234
Bergman, Ingmar 11, 196
Berliner, Emile 121, 145
Betamax 174, 223
Billy Budd 161
Birtwistle, H 70, 71, 72, 74, 85, 86, 193
Bizet, C. 2, 3, 26, 28, 42, 103, 114
Blu-Ray 38, 45, 173, 174, 176, 177
Blyth, Alan 130, 175 186
Bocelli, Andrea 25, 26, 30, 116, 125, 126, 127, 128, 129, 132, 133, 134, 135, 136, 140, 141, 142, 146, 147
Boe, Alfie 116, 134, 135, 136, 141, 142, 143

Boll, Andre 149
Born Georgina 89, 92
Botha, Johan 56
Boulez, Pierre 93, 189
Brecht, B. 156, 241
Brightman, Sarah 127, 128, 132
British Airways 2, 3, 15, 16, 28
British Television 1, 13
Britten, Benjamin 75, 80, 94, 109, 149, 161, 162, 163, 164, 168, 191, 193, 209
Brook, Peter 200, 206
Bruckner, A. 93
Bubka, Sergei 2
Buñuel, L 167

Cabranes-Grant, Leo 32
Cage, John 239, 240, 241, 245
Callas, Maria 19, 20, 100, 109, 110, 111, 113, 114, 124, 193, 194
Camel (opera singers advertising) 3
Camerata 65, 119
"Can't Help Falling in Love" 141, 142, 143
Capurro, G. 1
Cardiff, Janet 239, 241
Carlson, Marvin 38, 39, 40
Carreras, Jose 17, 127, 128, 129, 130, 148
Caruso, Enrico 3, 10, 19, 26, 27, 122, 124, 125, 126, 132
Casale, Emanuele 82, 83, 84
Catalani, A. 11, 15
Cavalieri, Lina 3
Chanan, Michael 121, 122, 123, 124
Charpentier, G 66, 67, 68, 86, 87, 88
Chéreau, Patrice 185, 189, 231
Christiansen, Rupert 44, 60, 62, 135, 146, 147
Church, Charlotte 116, 128
cinema 11, 24, 33, 34, 35, 36, 37, 38, 39, 41, 59, 118, 122, 151, 152, 153, 154, 155, 156, 157, 159, 160, 161, 163, 167, 168, 178, 195, 196, 233
Classic FM 19, 21, 22, 30

251

clod ensemble 199, 203, 207
Cocteau, Jean 70
Comencini, Luigi 11
commercials 1, 9, 12, 13, 15, 16, 20, 31
Constable, Paule 215, 217, 219, 220, 221, 222, 223, 224, 225, 227, 228
Conversazioni con Chomsky 82, 83, 84
Craig, Edward Gordon 204, 205
Cremaster Cycle 233
crooners/crooning 124, 125, 139, 145
crossover performance/performers 115, 125, 126, 127, 128, 129, 130, 131, 132, 133, 135, 136, 137, 138, 139, 141, 142, 143, 144, 237
Culshaw, John 94, 96, 97, 98, 99, 102, 162
Current, Brian 77, 78

Davidson, Randall 2
Davies, Peter Maxwell 11
Death and the Powers 81, 82, 242, 243
Death in Venice 19, 80, 163, 164, 165, 170
Debussy, C. 1, 76, 152
Decca 2, 94, 96, 97, 102, 130, 132, 162, 181, 190, 192
The Decca Book of Opera 92, 103, 107, 108
Decker, Richard 56
Delibes, Leo 2, 3, 5, 16, 29
Dessay, Natalie 2
The Devils of Loudon 159, 160
Di Capua, E. 1
Dillon, James 85
Dion, Celine 132, 133
Dog Days 47
Domingo, Placido 3, 17, 20, 56, 97, 127, 128, 129, 130, 132, 146, 148, 185
Donizetti, G 130, 131, 191
Dove, Jonathan 74, 75, 76, 77
Dusapin, Pascal 85, 86
DVD (Digital Versatile Disc) 173, 174, 175, 176. 177, 178, 179, 180, 183, 187, 188, 189, 191, 192, 193, 194, 195; and CD, features and documentation 182, 183, 184, 185, 186; opera and new technology 194, 195, 196; regions 177, 178; repertoire and releases 188, 189, 190, 191, 192, 193, 194; sound/picture quality 187, 188
Dvořák, A. 3, 12, 43

Edison, T.A. 95
Einstein on the Beach 166, 167, 238
Eisenstein, Serge 154, 157, 158
Eisler, H. 155
Elizabethan theatre 152, 234
The Empty Space 200
English National Opera 10, 20, 21, 22, 27, 44, 135, 218

Europera 5 240, 241
"eurotrash" 185, 186, 187
Evans, Wynne 3, 27
Expressionism 69, 161

fach 56, 57, 59, 136, 137, 142, 146
Farrar, Geraldine 3, 19
Felsenstein, Walter 183, 197
Fiat 1, 13, 14, 15
La Fille du Régiment 130
film 149, 150, 151, 154, 156, 168, 169, 170, 171, 179
Fisher, Rick 215, 217, 226, 227, 228
Fleming, Renée 3, 27, 33
Der Fliegende Holländer 46
Flight 74, 75
Flower Duet (*Sous le dôme épais*) 2, 15
Fuller, Louie 204
Futurist Opera 234, 235, 236, 243

Gaisberg, Fred 94, 95, 122
Gambill, Robert 57
Garden, Mary 3
Garrett, Lesley 2, 20, 21, 30
Gelb, Peter 8, 34, 35, 36, 38
Gentile, Louis 57
Gesamtkunstwerk 51, 196, 206–207, 209, 230
Gilman, Lawrence 93
Giulini, Carlo Maria 93
Glass, Philip 73, 149, 166, 168, 170, 193, 238, 245, 246
Go Compare 3, 27, 30
Goebbels, Heiner 198, 199, 208, 209, 210
Gorecki, Henryk 18
Graham, Colin 163
gramophone 3, 90, 109, 120, 122, 124, 145
The Gramophone Co. 91, 101, 103, 106, 107, 145
The Gramophone Shop of Recorded Music 93
The Grand Tradition 95, 108
Granville-Barker, Harvey 153
The Great Caruso 126
Greenfield, Edward 95

Hansel and Gretel 33, 39
Harding, Will 216, 217, 218, 224, 226, 227
Henze, H.W. 149, 158, 159, 193
high art 1, 4, 21, 35
high definition (HD) 4, 32, 33, 34, 35, 36, 37, 38, 39, 40, 41, 42, 59
Hofmannsthal, Hugo von 205
Humperdinck, Engelbert 33
Hvorostovsky, Dmitri 26

industrialisation of opera 212, 213, 214

jazz 1, 11, 14, 15, 47, 68, 69, 70, 78, 84, 121, 124, 125
Jedermann 198, 205, 206, 207, 210
Jenkins, Katherine 2, 115, 116, 126, 127, 134, 136, 145, 147
Jerry Springer, the Opera 84
Jolson, Al 124
Jonny Spielt Auf 68, 69, 87, 88
Jüdisches Museum Berlin 207, 209

Kaufmann, Jonas 57
Kennedy, Michael 18, 162
Khlebnikov, Viktor 235
King John 153
Kleiber, Erich 108
Klemperer, Otto 95, 111
The Knot Garden 160, 161
Kopernikus 47
Krenek, E 68, 69, 87, 88, 155, 156, 169
Kruchenykh, Aleksei 235

Lakme 2, 5, 15, 28, 29
Lanza, Mario 26, 126, 127, 130, 131, 145, 146
Largo al Factotum 1
Laserdisc (LD) 173, 174, 175
Legge, Walter 92. 93, 94, 102
Leoncavallo, R. 10, 104, 195
LePage, Robert 8, 183, 190
Libeskind, Daniel 207, 209
lighting: design 200, 201, 202, 203, 204, 210, 212, 213, 215, 216, 217, 219, 220, 221, 222, 223, 224, 225, 226, 227; rig/installation 214, 215 216, 217; rock and roll 203, 204; and surgery 198, 202, 203; in virtual space 220, 221, 222
Lind, Jenny 3
Lindenberger, Herbert 231
Little, David T. 47
Lohengrin 50, 54, 56, 61, 62, 63, 64
Losey, Joseph 11
Louise 66, 67, 68
Loussier, Jacques 1

Macbeth 100, 110, 152, 153
Machover, Tod 81, 82, 242
Mahler, G. 11, 19, 47
Malevich, Kasimir 234, 235
Manoury, Philipe 75, 76
Manovich, Lev 37, 38, 42
Marinetti, Filiipo Tommaso 235
marketing 3, 6, 8, 9, 11, 12, 13, 15, 17, 18, 19, 20, 21, 22, 23, 24, 25, 26, 29, 31, 89, 130, 133, 135, 177, 180, 187, 189
The Mask of Orpheus 70, 71, 72, 73, 87
Matiushin, Mikhail 235

Mayakovsky, Vladimir 235
McBurney, Simon 199
McLaren, Malcolm 15
McLuhan, Marshall 5, 6
Medeamaterial 85
Méliès, Georges 151
Messiaen, Olivier 231, 236
The Met: Live in HD 33, 34, 35, 36, 37, 38, 39, 40
Metropolitan Opera (New York) 3, 4, 10, 20, 32, 33, 34, 38, 40, 41, 42, 48, 87, 183, 197
microphone (use/technique) 96, 98, 100, 102, 123, 124, 125, 134, 138, 140, 141, 185
Miller, George Burns 239
Milnes, Sherrill 7
Minotaur 85, 87, 192
Mitford, Nancy 90, 102
Moholy-Nagy, László 236, 238
montage 150, 154, 156, 157, 158
Monteverdi, C 66, 111, 234
Mörbisch Summer Festival 184, 185
Muhly, Nico 66, 79, 80
Müller, Heiner 85
music theatre 47, 65, 68, 73, 80, 198, 209, 232, 234, 237, 238, 239

Nessun Dorma 14, 28, 130
New York City Opera 7, 29, 87
Nike 2, 5, 16
Nixon in China 66, 69, 72, 86, 87, 165, 166, 170, 171, 192
Norman, Jessye 17

Offenbach, J 3
Oliver, John 78, 86
On and Off the Record 94
O'Neill, Simon 58
Opera 23
Opera at Home 91, 92, 103, 107
Opera of the Future (research group) 242
Opera in a Small Room 239, 240, 241
Opera Now 23, 24, 28
opera seria 66, 119
Opera reviews in Germany and UK 44, 45, 46
Owen Wingrave 161, 162, 163

Palmer, Tony 18
Parsifal 152, 155, 196
Pavarotti, Luciano 14, 17, 18, 19, 20, 29, 30, 116, 127, 128, 129, 130, 131, 132, 133, 134, 135, 145, 147, 148
Pears, Peter 109

Index

Penderecki, K. 149, 159
Peri, J 66
Peter Grimes 94, 175, 209
Philomela 85, 86
phonograph 116, 118, 121, 123, 129, 184
PolyGram 17, 18
Ponchielli, A. 3
pop (music/singers) 80, 116, 117, 120, 121, 123, 124, 125, 127, 128, 129, 131, 135, 136, 138, 139, 140, 141, 142, 143, 144
popular culture 4, 5, 8, 10, 28, 32, 82, 121, 129, 145, 148
popular music 5, 80, 116, 117, 118, 119, 120, 121, 123, 124, 125, 129, 131, 132, 136, 139, 140, 144, 187, 237
popularization of opera 7, 8, 15, 16, 18, 24
Porter, Edwin S. 154
Potts, Paul 116, 136
Poulenc, F 69, 70, 78, 87, 193
Presley, Elvis 125, 129, 136, 141, 143
The Pursuit of Love 90

Rachmaninov, S. 1
radio broadcasts 4, 9, 19, 21, 22, 24, 32, 34, 35, 40, 42, 90, 116, 118, 126, 145, 161, 184, 201, 241
Read, John B. 215, 216, 228
The Record of Singing 106, 108, 109
Regieoper 47, 48, 49, 53, 59, 231
Reinhardt, Max 198, 199, 205, 207
repertoire lighting 213, 214, 25, 216, 217, 218, 219, 220
reviews and reviewing 17, 43, 44, 45, 46, 53, 55, 58, 59, 186, 239
Rigoletto 11, 40, 42, 120, 189
Ring cycle 8, 50, 162, 183, 231, 233
Roméo et Juliette 133, 198, 204, 205, 208
Rosi, Francesco 11
Royal Opera House, Covent Garden 4, 10, 27, 44, 87, 88, 135, 158, 169, 170, 194, 212, 213, 214, 215, 216, 217, 218, 220, 221, 225, 226, 227, 228, 246, 250
Rusalka 43
Russolo, Luigi 236
Ryan, Lance 58

Saatchi and Saatchi 2, 15
Saint François d'Assise 193, 231, 236
Satyagraha 209
Schneider, Peter 54, 55, 61, 64
Schoenberg, A. 155
Schwarzkopf, Elizabeth 94, 95, 100, 113
Scott, Michael 108
Scottish Opera 10, 44, 60, 62
Sellars, Peter 73, 165, 166, 185, 230, 231

Siegfried 54, 97, 98, 113, 152
Simpson, James 220, 221, 223, 227
Sinatra, Frank 124, 145
60e Parallèle 75, 76, 77
Smith, Bessie 123
Die Soldaten 157
Sonicstage 97, 98
Sontag, Susan 36, 41, 42
Spears, Britney 117
Steane, John 95, 108
Steel, George 7
Stifter's Dinge 198, 208, 209, 210
Stone, Oliver 11
Strasnoy, Oscar 46
subtitles (film, video) 178, 179, 180, 181, 182
Sunken Garden 232, 244
Sutherland, Joan 2

Tambling, Jeremy 150, 155, 161
Tchaikovsky, P.I. 1, 2, 12, 186
Te Kanawa, Kiri 19, 23, 128
Tear, Robert 10, 24
television 1, 3, 21, 27, 78, 82, 83, 84, 90, 118, 129, 130, 135, 136, 149, 150, 153, 160, 161, 162, 163, 164, 166, 167, 168, 174, 187, 188; advertising 1, 2, 3, 4, 5, 12, 13, 26
Thomas, Richard 84
Three Tenors 4, 17, 126, 127, 128, 129, 130, 131, 133, 148
The Three Tenors in Concert 129
Tippett, M. 160, 161
Tommasini, Anthony 33, 34, 40, 42
Tosca 100, 111, 132, 194
Tristan und Isolde 49, 50, 53, 57, 60, 61, 62, 63, 64, 97, 150, 187
Il Trovatore 110, 111
Turandot 28, 130, 224
Turnage, Mark-Anthony 7, 66, 83, 84, 86, 87
Two Boys 66, 79, 80

Upshaw, Dawn 18

Vallée, Rudy 124
Der Vampyr 46
Verdi, G. 3, 11, 29, 56, 93, 100, 105, 110, 113, 114, 115, 120, 131, 153, 190, 223
VHS 173, 174, 175, 176
Victory Over the Sun 234, 235, 236, 238, 243
The Victrola Book of the Opera 91, 92, 96, 107
Vivier, Claude 47
vocal features 137, 138, 139, 140
La Voix Humaine 69, 70
Volpe, Joe 34, 35
von Stegmann, Matthias 50, 53

Wagner, R. 8, 19, 46, 49, 50, 53, 54, 55, 56, 60, 61, 62, 63 64, 66, 98, 99, 106, 107, 113, 115, 131, 150, 152, 153, 155, 156, 169, 170, 172, 181, 183, 185, 187, 189, 190, 193, 194, 197, 198, 199, 205, 206, 207, 210, 230, 231, 233, 234, 243, 244, 245, 246, 247
Wagner, Wolfgang 50
Wagner on Record 1926–1942 99
Wall St. 11
La Wally 11
Ware, Nick 216, 219, 226, 227
Watson, Russell 110, 127, 129, 135, 141, 142
Watts, Quincy 2
We Come to the River 158, 159
Weber, C.M. 46, 106
Weill, K. 156, 234

Welsh National Opera 10, 27
Werktreue 47, 48, 49, 50, 53, 59
Werther 26, 44, 60, 62
Wiener Staatsoper, 204
Wilson, Robert 73, 166, 168, 209, 238
Woodroffe, Patrick 198, 204, 205, 208, 209
Wozzeck 154, 155, 157

YouTube 186, 187

ZAUM 234, 235
Zeffirelli, Franco 11
Zeitopern 66, 68, 69, 74, 80
Zelechow, Bernard 119, 120
Zimmermann, B.A. 156, 157
Zinovieff, Peter 71

www.ingramcontent.com/pod-product-compliance
Lightning Source LLC
Chambersburg PA
CBHW051216300426
44116CB00006B/592